LEADERSHIP

Theory and Practice • Seventh Edition

PETER G.NORTHOUSE

Western Michigan University

Los Angeles | London | New Delhi
Singapore | Washington DC | Boston

SAGE

Los Angeles | London | New Delhi
Singapore | Washington DC | Boston

FOR INFORMATION:

SAGE Publications, Inc.
2455 Teller Road
Thousand Oaks, California 91320
E-mail: order@sagepub.com

SAGE Publications Ltd.
1 Oliver's Yard
55 City Road
London EC1Y 1SP
United Kingdom

SAGE Publications India Pvt. Ltd.
B 1/I 1 Mohan Cooperative Industrial Area
Mathura Road, New Delhi 110 044
India

SAGE Publications Asia-Pacific Pte. Ltd.
3 Church Street
#10-04 Samsung Hub
Singapore 049483

ISE ISBN 9781506311166

Library of Congress Cataloging-in-Publication Data

Northouse, Peter Guy.

Leadership : theory and practice/Peter Northouse, Western Michigan University.—Seventh Edition.

pages cm
Includes bibliographical references and index.

ISBN 978-1-4833-1753-3 (pbk. : alk. paper)

1. Leadership. 2. Leadership—Case studies. I. Title.

HM1261.N67 2015
303.3'4—dc23   2014044695

Acquisitions Editor: Maggie Stanley
Associate Editor: Abbie Rickard
Editorial Assistant: Nicole Mangona
Production Editor: Libby Larson
Copy Editor: Melinda Masson
Typesetter: C&M Digitals (P) Ltd.
Proofreader: Sally Jaskold
Indexer: Sheila Bodell
Cover Designer: Gail Buschman
Marketing Manager: Liz Thornton
Digital Content Editor: Katie Bierach

Printed and bound in Great Britain by
Ashford Colour Press Ltd

MIX
Paper from
responsible sources
FSC® C011748

15 16 17 18 19 10 9 8 7 6 5 4 3 2 1

Brief Contents

Detailed Contents

Preface

This seventh edition of *Leadership: Theory and Practice* is written with the objective of bridging the gap between the often-simplistic popular approaches to leadership and the more abstract theoretical approaches. Like the previous editions, this edition reviews and analyzes a selected number of leadership theories, giving special attention to how each theoretical approach can be applied in real-world organizations. In essence, my purpose is to explore how leadership theory can inform and direct the way leadership is practiced.

NEW TO THIS EDITION

New to this volume is a chapter on *adaptive leadership*, which examines the nature of adaptive leadership, its underpinnings, and how it works. The chapter presents a definition, a model, and the latest research and applications of this emerging approach to leadership. In addition, the strengths and weaknesses of the adaptive leadership approach are examined, and a questionnaire to help readers assess their own levels of adaptive leadership is provided. Three case studies illustrating adaptive leadership are presented at the end of the chapter.

This volume also presents an entirely new chapter on psychodynamic leadership written by a leading expert in the field, Manfred F. R. Kets De Vries, and Alicia Cheak. Like the other chapters, this chapter provides a theoretical explanation of psychodynamic leadership, applications, cases studies, and an assessment instrument.

This edition also includes an expanded discussion of the dark side of leadership and psuedotransformational leadership and the negative uses and abuses of leadership. New research has been added throughout the book as well as many new case studies and examples that help students apply leadership concepts to contemporary settings.

This edition retains many special features from previous editions but has been updated to include new research findings, figures and tables, and everyday applications for many leadership topics including leader–member exchange theory, transformational and authentic leadership, team leadership, the labyrinth of women's leadership, and historical definitions of leadership. The format of this edition parallels the format used in earlier editions. As with previous editions, the overall goal of *Leadership: Theory and Practice* is to advance our understanding of the many different approaches to leadership and ways to practice it more effectively.

SPECIAL FEATURES

Although this text presents and analyzes a wide range of leadership research, every attempt has been made to present the material in a clear, concise, and interesting manner. Reviewers of the book have consistently commented that clarity is one of its major strengths. In addition to the writing style, several other features of the book help make it user-friendly.

- Each chapter follows the same format: It is structured to include first theory and then practice.
- Every chapter contains a discussion of the strengths and criticisms of the approach under consideration, and assists the reader in determining the relative merits of each approach.
- Each chapter includes an application section that discusses the practical aspects of the approach and how it could be used in today's organizational settings.
- Three case studies are provided in each chapter to illustrate common leadership issues and dilemmas. Thought-provoking questions follow each case study, helping readers to interpret the case.
- A questionnaire is provided in each of the chapters to help the reader apply the approach to his or her own leadership style or setting.
- Figures and tables illustrate the content of the theory and make the ideas more meaningful.

Through these special features, every effort has been made to make this text substantive, understandable, and practical.

AUDIENCE

This book provides both an in-depth presentation of leadership theory and a discussion of how it applies to real-life situations. Thus, it is intended for undergraduate and graduate classes in management, leadership studies, business, educational leadership, public administration, nursing and allied health, social work, criminal justice, industrial and organizational psychology, communication, religion, agricultural education, political and military science, and training and development. It is particularly well suited as a supplementary text for core organizational behavior courses or as an overview text within MBA curricula. This book would also be useful as a text in student activities, continuing education, in-service training, and other leadership-development programs.

Instructor Teaching Site

SAGE edge for Instructors, a password-protected instructor resource site, supports teaching by making it easy to integrate quality content and create a rich learning environment for students. The test banks, which have been expanded for this edition, include multiple-choice and true/false questions to test comprehension, as well as essay questions that ask students to apply the material. An electronic test bank, compatible with PCs and Macs through Diploma software, is also available. Chapter-specific resources include PowerPoint slides, study and discussion questions, suggested exercises, full-text journal articles, and video and audio links. General resources include course-long projects, sample syllabi, film resources, and case notes. Printable PDF versions of the questionnaires from the text are included for instructors to print and distribute for classroom use. A course cartridge includes assets found on the Instructor Teaching Site and the Student Study Site, as well as a bonus quiz for each chapter in the book—all in an easy-to-upload package. Go to **edge.sagepub.com/northouse7e** to access the companion site.

Student Study Site

SAGE edge for Students provides a personalized approach to help students accomplish their coursework goals in an easy-to-use learning environment. Mobile-friendly eFlashcards and practice quizzes strengthen understanding of key terms and concepts and allow for independent assessment by students of their mastery of course material. A customized online action plan includes tips and feedback on progress through the course and materials, which allows students to individualize their learning experience. Learning objectives, multimedia links, discussion questions, and SAGE journal articles help students study and reinforce the most important material. Students can go to **edge.sagepub.com/northouse7e** to access the site.

Media Icons

Icons appearing at the bottom of the page will direct you to online media such as videos, audio links, journal articles, and reference articles that correspond with key chapter concepts. Visit the Student Study Site at **edge. sagepub.com/northouse7e** to access this media.

ICONS

Ⓝ Northouse on Leadership

📚 SAGE Journal Article

🎙 Audio

📕 Reference Article

▶ Video

Acknowledgments

Many people directly or indirectly contributed to the development of the seventh edition of *Leadership: Theory and Practice*. First, I would like to acknowledge my editor, Maggie Stanley, and her talented team at SAGE Publications (Nicole, Abbie, MaryAnn, Liz, Katie, and Lauren) who have contributed significantly to the quality of this edition and ensured its success. For their very capable work during the production phase, I would like to thank copy editor Melinda Masson, and senior project editor Libby Larson. In her own unique way, each of these people made valuable contributions to the seventh edition.

For comprehensive reviews of the seventh edition, I would like to thank the following reviewers:

Meera Alagaraja, *University of Louisville*

Mel Albin, *Excelsior College*

Thomas Batsching, *Reutlingen University*

Cheryl Beeler, *Angelo State University*

Mark D. Bowman, *Methodist University*

Dianne Burns, *University of Manchester*

Eric Buschlen, *Central Michigan University*

Steven Bryant, *Drury University*

Daniel Calhoun, *Georgia Southern University*

David Conrad, *Augsburg College*

Joyce Cousins, *Royal College of Surgeons in Ireland*

Denise Danna, *LSUHSC School of Nursing*

S. Todd Deal, *Georgia Southern University*

Caroline S. Fulmer, *University of Alabama*

Greig A. Gjerdalen, *Capilano University*

Andrew Gonzales, *University of California, Irvine*

Carl Holschen, *Missouri Baptist University*

Kiran Ismail, *St. John's University*

Irma Jones, *University of Texas at Brownsville*

Michele D. Kegley, *University of Cincinnati, Blue Ash College*

David Lees, *University of Derby*

David S. McClain, *University of Hawaii at Manoa*

Carol McMillan, *New School University*

Richard Milter, *Johns Hopkins University*

Christopher Neck, *Arizona State University–Tempe*

Keeok Park, *University of La Verne*

Richard Parkman, *University of Plymouth*

Chaminda S. Prelis, *University of Dubuque*

Casey Rae, *George Fox University*

Noel Ronan, *Waterford Institute of Technology*

Louis Rubino, *California State University, Northridge*

Shadia Sachedina, *Baruch College (School of Public Affairs)*

Harriet L. Schwartz, *Carlow University*

Kelli K. Smith, *University of Nebraska-Lincoln*

David Swenson, *The College of St. Scholastica*

Danny L. Talbot, *Washington State University*

Robert L. Taylor, *University of Louisville*

Precious Taylor-Clifton, *Cambridge College*

John Tummons, *University of Missouri*

Kristi Tyran, *Western Washington University*

Tamara Von George, *Granite State College*

Natalie Walker, *Seminole State College*

William Welch, *Bowie State University*

David E. Williams, *Texas Tech University*

Tony Wohlers, *Cameron University*

Sharon A. Wulf, *Worcester Polytechnic Institute School of Business*

Alec Zama, *Grand View University*

Xia Zhao, *California State University, Dominguez Hills*

I would like to thank, for their exceptional work on the leadership profile tool and the ancillaries, Isolde Anderson (Hope College), John Baker (Western Kentucky University), Renee Kosiarek (North Central College) and Lisa Burgoon (University of Illinois), and for his feedback in the construction and scoring of the adaptive leadership questionnaire, Paul Yelsma (Western Michigan University).

A special acknowledgment goes to Laurel Northouse for her insightful critiques and ongoing support. In addition, I am grateful to Marie Lee, for her exceptional editing and guidance throughout this project. For their reviews of and comments on the adaptive leadership chapter, I am indebted to Sarah Chace (Marian University), Carl Larson (University of Denver), and Chip Bailey (Duke University).

Finally, I would like to thank the many undergraduate and graduate students whom I have taught through the years. Their ongoing feedback has helped clarify my thinking about leadership and encouraged me to make plain the practical implications of leadership theories.

To Laurel, Lisa, Madison, Scott, and Kallie

SAGE was founded in 1965 by Sara Miller McCune to support the dissemination of usable knowledge by publishing innovative and high-quality research and teaching content. Today, we publish more than 750 journals, including those of more than 300 learned societies, more than 800 new books per year, and a growing range of library products including archives, data, case studies, reports, conference highlights, and video. SAGE remains majority-owned by our founder, and after Sara's lifetime will become owned by a charitable trust that secures our continued independence.

Los Angeles | London | Washington DC | New Delhi | Singapore | Boston

1

Introduction

Leadership is a highly sought-after and highly valued commodity. In the 20 years since the first edition of this book was published, the public has become increasingly captivated by the idea of leadership. People continue to ask themselves and others what makes good leaders. As individuals, they seek more information on how to become effective leaders. As a result, bookstore shelves are filled with popular books about leaders and advice on how to be a leader. Many people believe that leadership is a way to improve their personal, social, and professional lives. Corporations seek those with leadership ability because they believe they bring special assets to their organizations and, ultimately, improve the bottom line. Academic institutions throughout the country have responded by providing programs in leadership studies.

In addition, leadership has gained the attention of researchers worldwide. A review of the scholarly studies on leadership shows that there is a wide variety of different theoretical approaches to explain the complexities of the leadership process (e.g., Bass, 1990; Bryman, 1992; Bryman, Collinson, Grint, Jackson, & Uhl-Bien, 2011; Day & Antonakis, 2012; Gardner, 1990; Hickman, 2009; Mumford, 2006; Rost, 1991). Some researchers conceptualize leadership as a trait or as a behavior, whereas others view leadership from an information-processing perspective or relational standpoint. Leadership has been studied using both qualitative and quantitative methods in many contexts, including small groups, therapeutic groups, and large organizations. Collectively, the research findings on leadership from all of these areas provide a picture of a process that is far more sophisticated and complex than the often-simplistic view presented in some of the popular books on leadership.

This book treats leadership as a complex process having multiple dimensions. Based on the research literature, this text provides an in-depth description

 Leadership Defined   Role of Leadership

and application of many different approaches to leadership. Our emphasis is on how theory can inform the practice of leadership. In this book, we describe each theory and then explain how the theory can be used in real situations.

LEADERSHIP DEFINED

There are many ways to finish the sentence "Leadership is . . ." In fact, as Stogdill (1974, p. 7) pointed out in a review of leadership research, there are almost as many different definitions of *leadership* as there are people who have tried to define it. It is much like the words *democracy*, *love*, and *peace*. Although each of us intuitively knows what we mean by such words, the words can have different meanings for different people. As Box 1.1 shows, scholars and practitioners have attempted to define leadership for more than a century without universal consensus.

Box 1.1 **The Evolution of Leadership Definitions**

While many have a gut-level grasp of what leadership is, putting a definition to the term has proved to be a challenging endeavor for scholars and practitioners alike. More than a century has lapsed since leadership became a topic of academic introspection, and definitions have evolved continuously during that period. These definitions have been influenced by many factors from world affairs and politics to the perspectives of the discipline in which the topic is being studied. In a seminal work, Rost (1991) analyzed materials written from 1900 to 1990, finding more than 200 different definitions for leadership. His analysis provides a succinct history of how leadership has been defined through the last century:

1900–1929

Definitions of leadership appearing in the first three decades of the 20th century emphasized control and centralization of power with a common theme of domination. For example, at a conference on leadership in 1927, leadership was defined as "the ability to impress the will of the leader on those led and induce obedience, respect, loyalty, and cooperation" (Moore, 1927, p. 124).

 Defining Leadership

1930s

Traits became the focus of defining leadership, with an emerging view of leadership as influence rather than domination. Leadership was also identified as the interaction of an individual's specific personality traits with those of a group; it was noted that while the attitudes and activities of the many may be changed by the one, the many may also influence a leader.

1940s

The group approach came into the forefront with leadership being defined as the behavior of an individual while involved in directing group activities (Hemphill, 1949). At the same time, leadership by persuasion was distinguished from "drivership" or leadership by coercion (Copeland, 1942).

1950s

Three themes dominated leadership definitions during this decade:

- **continuance of group theory,** which framed leadership as what leaders do in groups;
- **leadership as a relationship that develops shared goals,** which defined leadership based on behavior of the leader; and
- **effectiveness,** in which leadership was defined by the ability to influence overall group effectiveness.

1960s

Although a tumultuous time for world affairs, the 1960s saw harmony amongst leadership scholars. The prevailing definition of leadership as *behavior* that influences people toward shared goals was underscored by Seeman (1960) who described leadership as "acts by persons which influence other persons in a shared direction" (p. 53).

1970s

The group focus gave way to the organizational behavior approach, where leadership became viewed as "initiating and maintaining groups or organizations to accomplish group or organizational goals" (Rost, 1991, p. 59). Burns's (1978) definition, however, was the most important concept of leadership to emerge: "Leadership is the reciprocal process

(Continued)

 Leadership in Nursing

(Continued)

of mobilizing by persons with certain motives and values, various economic, political, and other resources, in a context of competition and
conflict, in order to realize goals independently or mutually held by
both leaders and followers" (p. 425).

1980s

This decade exploded with scholarly and popular works on the nature
of leadership, bringing the topic to the apex of the academic and
public consciousnesses. As a result, the number of definitions for leadership became a prolific stew with several persevering themes:

- **Do as the leader wishes.** Leadership definitions still predominantly delivered the message that leadership is getting followers
  to do what the leader wants done.
- **Influence.** Probably the most often used word in leadership
  definitions of the 1980s, *influence* was examined from every
  angle. In an effort to distinguish leadership from management, however, scholars insisted that leadership is *noncoercive*
  influence.
- **Traits.** Spurred by the national best seller *In Search of Excellence*
  (Peters & Waterman, 1982), the leadership-as-excellence movement brought leader traits back to the spotlight. As a result,
  many people's understanding of leadership is based on a trait
  orientation.
- **Transformation**. Burns (1978) is credited for initiating a movement defining leadership as a transformational process, stating
  that leadership occurs "when one or more persons engage with
  others in such a way that leaders and followers raise one another
  to higher levels of motivation and morality" (p. 83).

Into the 21st Century

Debate continues as to whether leadership and management are
separate processes, but emerging research emphasizes the *process* of
leadership, whereby an individual influences a group of individuals to
achieve a common goal, rather than developing new ways of defining
leadership. Among these emerging leadership approaches are

- **authentic leadership,** in which the authenticity of leaders and
  their leadership is emphasized;
- **spiritual leadership,** which focuses on leadership that utilizes
  values and sense of calling and membership to motivate
  followers;

▶ The Future of Leadership   Working Across Generations

- **servant leadership,** which puts the leader in the role of servant, who utilizes "caring principles" to focus on followers' needs to help these followers become more autonomous, knowledgeable, and like servants themselves; and
- **adaptive leadership,** in which leaders encourage followers to adapt by confronting and solving problems, challenges, and changes.

After decades of dissonance, leadership scholars agree on one thing: They can't come up with a common definition for leadership. Because of such factors as growing global influences and generational differences, leadership will continue to have different meanings for different people. The bottom line is that leadership is a complex concept for which a determined definition may long be in flux.

SOURCE: Adapted from *Leadership for the Twenty-First Century,* by J. C. Rost, 1991, New York: Praeger.

Ways of Conceptualizing Leadership

In the past 60 years, as many as 65 different classification systems have been developed to define the dimensions of leadership (Fleishman et al., 1991). One such classification system, directly related to our discussion, is the scheme proposed by Bass (1990, pp. 11–20). He suggested that some definitions view leadership as the *focus of group processes.* From this perspective, the leader is at the center of group change and activity and embodies the will of the group. Another set of definitions conceptualizes leadership from a *personality perspective,* which suggests that leadership is a combination of special traits or characteristics that some individuals possess. These traits enable those individuals to induce others to accomplish tasks. Other approaches to leadership define it as an *act* or a *behavior*—the things leaders do to bring about change in a group.

In addition, some define leadership in terms of the *power relationship* that exists between leaders and followers. From this viewpoint, leaders have power that they wield to effect change in others. Others view leadership as a *transformational process* that moves followers to accomplish more than is usually expected of them. Finally, some scholars address leadership from a *skills perspective.* This viewpoint stresses the capabilities (knowledge and skills) that make effective leadership possible.

 Perspectives of Leadership

Definition and Components

Despite the multitude of ways in which leadership has been conceptualized, the following components can be identified as central to the phenomenon: (a) Leadership is a process, (b) leadership involves influence, (c) leadership occurs in groups, and (d) leadership involves common goals. Based on these components, the following definition of leadership is used in this text:

> **Leadership** is a process whereby an individual influences a group of individuals to achieve a common goal.

Defining leadership as a *process* means that it is not a trait or characteristic that resides in the leader, but rather a transactional event that occurs between the leader and the followers. *Process* implies that a leader affects and is affected by followers. It emphasizes that leadership is not a linear, one-way event, but rather an interactive event. When leadership is defined in this manner, it becomes available to everyone. It is not restricted to the formally designated leader in a group.

Leadership involves *influence*. It is concerned with how the leader affects followers. Influence is the sine qua non of leadership. Without influence, leadership does not exist.

Leadership occurs in *groups*. Groups are the context in which leadership takes place. Leadership involves influencing a group of individuals who have a common purpose. This can be a small task group, a community group, or a large group encompassing an entire organization. Leadership is about one individual influencing a group of others to accomplish common goals. Others (a group) are required for leadership to occur. Leadership training programs that teach people to lead themselves are not considered a part of leadership within the definition that is set forth in this discussion.

Leadership includes attention to *common goals*. Leaders direct their energies toward individuals who are trying to achieve something together. By *common*, we mean that the leaders and followers have a mutual purpose. Attention to common goals gives leadership an ethical overtone because it stresses the need for leaders to work with followers to achieve selected goals. Stressing mutuality lessens the possibility that leaders might act toward followers in ways that are forced or unethical. It also increases the possibility that leaders and followers will work together toward a common good (Rost, 1991).

 N The Ethical Dimension of Leadership   Effective Leadership

Throughout this text, the people who engage in leadership will be called *leaders,* and those toward whom leadership is directed will be called *followers.* Both leaders and followers are involved together in the leadership process. Leaders need followers, and followers need leaders (Burns, 1978; Heller & Van Til, 1983; Hollander, 1992; Jago, 1982). Although leaders and followers are closely linked, it is the leader who often initiates the relationship, creates the communication linkages, and carries the burden for maintaining the relationship.

In our discussion of leaders and followers, attention will be directed toward follower issues as well as leader issues. Leaders have an ethical responsibility to attend to the needs and concerns of followers. As Burns (1978) pointed out, discussions of leadership sometimes are viewed as elitist because of the implied power and importance often ascribed to leaders in the leader-follower relationship. Leaders are not above or better than followers. Leaders and followers must be understood in relation to each other (Hollander, 1992) and collectively (Burns, 1978). They are in the leadership relationship together—and are two sides of the same coin (Rost, 1991).

LEADERSHIP DESCRIBED

In addition to definitional issues, it is important to discuss several other questions pertaining to the nature of leadership. In the following section, we will address questions such as how leadership as a trait differs from leadership as a process; how appointed leadership differs from emergent leadership; and how the concepts of power, coercion, and management differ from leadership.

Trait Versus Process Leadership

We have all heard statements such as "He is born to be a leader" or "She is a natural leader." These statements are commonly expressed by people who take a trait perspective toward leadership. The trait perspective suggests that certain individuals have special innate or inborn characteristics or qualities that make them leaders, and that it is these qualities that differentiate them from nonleaders. Some of the personal qualities used to identify leaders include unique physical factors (e.g., height), personality features (e.g., extraversion), and other characteristics (e.g., intelligence and fluency; Bryman, 1992). In Chapter 2, we will discuss a large body of research that has examined these personal qualities.

 Development of Leadership   Followership

To describe leadership as a trait is quite different from describing it as a process (Figure 1.1). The trait viewpoint conceptualizes leadership as a property or set of properties possessed in varying degrees by different people (Jago, 1982). This suggests that it resides *in* select people and restricts leadership to those who are believed to have special, usually inborn, talents.

The process viewpoint suggests that leadership is a phenomenon that resides in the context of the interactions between leaders and followers and makes leadership available to everyone. As a process, leadership can be observed in leader behaviors (Jago, 1982), and can be learned. The process definition of leadership is consistent with the definition of leadership that we have set forth in this chapter.

Assigned Versus Emergent Leadership

Some people are leaders because of their formal position in an organization, whereas others are leaders because of the way other group members respond to them. These two common forms of leadership are called *assigned leadership* and *emergent leadership*. Leadership that is based on occupying a position in an organization is assigned leadership. Team leaders, plant managers, department heads, directors, and administrators are all examples of assigned leadership.

Yet the person assigned to a leadership position does not always become the real leader in a particular setting. When others perceive an individual as the most influential member of a group or an organization, regardless of the individual's title, the person is exhibiting emergent leadership. The individual acquires emergent leadership through other people in the organization who support and accept that individual's behavior. This type of leadership is not assigned by position; rather, it emerges over a period through communication. Some of the positive communication behaviors that account for successful leader emergence include *being verbally involved, being informed, seeking others' opinions, initiating new ideas,* and *being firm but not rigid* (Fisher, 1974).

In addition to communication behaviors, researchers have found that personality plays a role in leadership emergence. For example, Smith and Foti (1998) found that certain personality traits were related to leadership emergence in a sample of 160 male college students. The individuals who were more dominant, more intelligent, and more confident about their own performance (general self-efficacy) were more likely to be identified as leaders by other members of their task group. Although it is uncertain whether these findings apply to women as well, Smith and Foti suggested that these three traits could be used to identify individuals perceived to be emergent leaders.

N Leadership: Skill or Process?

Figure 1.1   The Different Views of Leadership

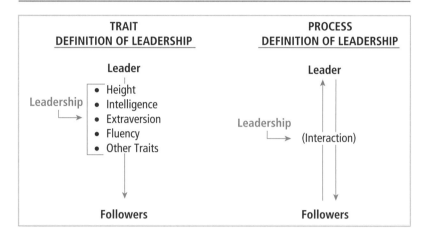

SOURCE: Adapted from *A Force for Change: How Leadership Differs From Management* (pp. 3–8), by J. P. Kotter, 1990, New York: Free Press.

Leadership emergence may also be affected by gender-biased perceptions. In a study of 40 mixed-sex college groups, Watson and Hoffman (2004) found that women who were urged to persuade their task groups to adopt high-quality decisions succeeded with the same frequency as men with identical instructions. Although women were equally influential leaders in their groups, they were rated significantly lower than comparable men were on leadership. Furthermore, these influential women were also rated as significantly less likable than comparably influential men were. These results suggest that there continue to be barriers to women's emergence as leaders in some settings.

A unique perspective on leadership emergence is provided by social identity theory (Hogg, 2001). From this perspective, leadership emergence is the degree to which a person fits with the identity of the group as a whole. As groups develop over time, a group prototype also develops. Individuals emerge as leaders in the group when they become most like the group prototype. Being similar to the prototype makes leaders attractive to the group and gives them influence with the group.

The leadership approaches we discuss in the subsequent chapters of this book apply equally to assigned leadership and emergent leadership. When a person is engaged in leadership, that person is a leader, whether leadership

 Ordinary Leaders

Table 1.1 Six Bases of Power

Referent Power	Based on followers' identification and liking for the leader. A teacher who is adored by students has referent power.
Expert Power	Based on followers' perceptions of the leader's competence. A tour guide who is knowledgeable about a foreign country has expert power.
Legitimate Power	Associated with having status or formal job authority. A judge who administers sentences in the courtroom exhibits legitimate power.
Reward Power	Derived from having the capacity to provide rewards to others. A supervisor who gives rewards to employees who work hard is using reward power.
Coercive Power	Derived from having the capacity to penalize or punish others. A coach who sits players on the bench for being late to practice is using coercive power.
Information Power	Derived from possessing knowledge that others want or need. A boss who has information regarding new criteria to decide employee promotion eligibility has information power.

SOURCE: Adapted from "The Bases of Social Power," by J. R. French Jr. and B. Raven, 1962, in D. Cartwright (Ed.), *Group Dynamics: Research and Theory* (pp. 259–269), New York: Harper & Row; and "Social Influence and Power," by B. H. Raven, 1965, in I. D. Steiner & M. Fishbein (Eds.), *Current Studies in Social Psychology* (pp. 371–382), New York: Holt, Rinehart, & Winston.

was assigned or emerged. This book focuses on the leadership process that occurs when any individual is engaged in influencing other group members in their efforts to reach a common goal.

Leadership and Power

The concept of power is related to leadership because it is part of the influence process. Power is the capacity or potential to influence. People have power when they have the ability to affect others' beliefs, attitudes, and courses of action. Judges, doctors, coaches, and teachers are all examples of people who have the potential to influence us. When they do, they are using their power, the resource they draw on to effect change in us.

Although there are no explicit theories in the research literature about power and leadership, power is a concept that people often associate with leadership. It is common for people to view leaders (both good and bad) and people in positions of leadership as individuals who wield power over others, and as a result, power is often thought of as synonymous with leadership. In addition, people are often intrigued by how leaders use their power. Studying

 Power and Leadership

 Bases of Power

Table 1.2   Types and Bases of Power

	Position Power	Personal Power
	Legitimate	Referent
	Reward	Expert
	Coercive	
	Information	

SOURCE: Adapted from *A Force for Change: How Leadership Differs From Management* (pp. 3–8), by J. P. Kotter, 1990, New York: Free Press.

how famous leaders, such as Hitler or Alexander the Great, use power to effect change in others is titillating to many people because it underscores that power can indeed effectuate change and maybe if they had power they too could effectuate change. But regardless of people's general interest in power and leadership, power has not been a major variable in theories of leadership. Clearly it is a component in the overall leadership process, but research on its role is limited.

In her recent book, *The End of Leadership* (2012), Kellerman argues there has been a shift in leadership power during the last 40 years. Power used to be the domain of leaders, but that is diminishing and shifting to followers. Changes in culture have meant followers demand more from leaders, and leaders have responded. Access to technology has empowered followers, given them access to huge amounts of information, and made leaders more transparent. The result is a decline in respect of leaders and leaders' legitimate power. In effect, followers have used information power to level the playing field. Power is no longer synonymous with leadership, and in the social contract between leaders and followers, leaders wield less power, according to Kellerman.

In college courses today, the most widely cited research on power is French and Raven's (1959) work on the bases of social power. In their work, they conceptualized power from the framework of a dyadic relationship that included both the person influencing and the person being influenced. French and Raven identified five common and important bases of power—referent, expert, legitimate, reward, and coercive—and Raven (1965) identified a sixth, information power (Table 1.1). Each of these bases of power increases a leader's capacity to influence the attitudes, values, or behaviors of others.

In organizations, there are two major kinds of power: position power and personal power. *Position power* is the power a person derives from a particular office or rank in a formal organizational system. It is the influence

 Types of Power

capacity a leader derives from having higher status than the followers have. Vice presidents and department heads have more power than staff personnel do because of the positions they hold in the organization. Position power includes legitimate, reward, coercive, and information power (Table 1.2).

Personal power is the influence capacity a leader derives from being seen by followers as likable and knowledgeable. When leaders act in ways that are important to followers, it gives leaders power. For example, some managers have power because their followers consider them to be good role models. Others have power because their followers view them as highly competent or considerate. In both cases, these managers' power is ascribed to them by others, based on how they are seen in their relationships with others. Personal power includes referent and expert power (Table 1.2).

In discussions of leadership, it is not unusual for leaders to be described as wielders of power, as individuals who dominate others. In these instances, power is conceptualized as a tool that leaders use to achieve their own ends. Contrary to this view of power, Burns (1978) emphasized power from a relationship standpoint. For Burns, power is not an entity that leaders use over others to achieve their own ends; instead, power occurs in relationships. It should be used by leaders and followers to promote their collective goals.

In this text, our discussions of leadership treat power as a relational concern for both leaders and followers. We pay attention to how leaders work with followers to reach common goals.

Leadership and Coercion

Coercive power is one of the specific kinds of power available to leaders. Coercion involves the use of force to effect change. *To coerce* means to influence others to do something against their will and may include manipulating penalties and rewards in their work environment. Coercion often involves the use of threats, punishment, and negative reward schedules. Classic examples of coercive leaders are Adolf Hitler in Germany, the Taliban leaders in Afghanistan, Jim Jones in Guyana, and North Korea's Supreme Leader Kim Jong-il, each of whom has used power and restraint to force followers to engage in extreme behaviors.

It is important to distinguish between coercion and leadership because it allows us to separate out from our examples of leadership the behaviors of individuals such as Hitler, the Taliban, and Jones. In our discussions of leadership, coercive people are not used as models of ideal leadership. Our

 Leadership and Coercion

definition suggests that leadership is reserved for those who influence a group of individuals toward a common goal. Leaders who use coercion are interested in their own goals and seldom are interested in the wants and needs of followers. Using coercion runs counter to working *with* followers to achieve a common goal.

Leadership and Management

Leadership is a process that is similar to management in many ways. Leadership involves influence, as does management. Leadership entails working with people, which management entails as well. Leadership is concerned with effective goal accomplishment, and so is management. In general, many of the functions of management are activities that are consistent with the definition of leadership we set forth at the beginning of this chapter.

But leadership is also different from management. Whereas the study of leadership can be traced back to Aristotle, management emerged around the turn of the 20th century with the advent of our industrialized society. Management was created as a way to reduce chaos in organizations, to make them run more effectively and efficiently. The primary functions of management, as first identified by Fayol (1916), were planning, organizing, staffing, and controlling. These functions are still representative of the field of management today.

In a book that compared the functions of management with the functions of leadership, Kotter (1990) argued that the functions of the two are quite dissimilar (Figure 1.2). The overriding function of management is to provide order and consistency to organizations, whereas the primary function of leadership is to produce change and movement. Management is about seeking order and stability; leadership is about seeking adaptive and constructive change.

As illustrated in Figure 1.2, the major activities of management are played out differently than the activities of leadership. Although they are different in scope, Kotter (1990, pp. 7–8) contended that both management and leadership are essential if an organization is to prosper. For example, if an organization has strong management without leadership, the outcome can be stifling and bureaucratic. Conversely, if an organization has strong leadership without management, the outcome can be meaningless or misdirected change for change's sake. To be effective, organizations need to nourish both competent management and skilled leadership.

▶ Managers Require; Leaders Inspire

Figure 1.2 Functions of Management and Leadership

Management Produces Order and Consistency	Leadership Produces Change and Movement
Planning and Budgeting • Establish agendas • Set timetables • Allocate resources	Establishing Direction • Create a vision • Clarify big picture • Set strategies
Organizing and Staffing • Provide structure • Make job placements • Establish rules and procedures	Aligning People • Communicate goals • Seek commitment • Build teams and coalitions
Controlling and Problem Solving • Develop incentives • Generate creative solutions • Take corrective action	Motivating and Inspiring • Inspire and energize • Empower followers • Satisfy unmet needs

SOURCE: Adapted from *A Force for Change: How Leadership Differs From Management* (pp. 3–8), by J. P. Kotter, 1990, New York: Free Press.

Many scholars, in addition to Kotter (1990), argue that leadership and management are distinct constructs. For example, Bennis and Nanus (1985) maintained that there is a significant difference between the two. *To manage* means to accomplish activities and master routines, whereas *to lead* means to influence others and create visions for change. Bennis and Nanus made the distinction very clear in their frequently quoted sentence, "Managers are people who do things right and leaders are people who do the right thing" (p. 221).

Rost (1991) has also been a proponent of distinguishing between leadership and management. He contended that leadership is a multidirectional influence relationship and management is a unidirectional authority relationship. Whereas leadership is concerned with the process of developing mutual purposes, management is directed toward coordinating activities in order to get a job done. Leaders and followers work together to create real change, whereas managers and subordinates join forces to sell goods and services (Rost, 1991, pp. 149–152).

In a recent study, Simonet and Tett (2012) explored how leadership and management are best conceptualized by having 43 experts identify the overlap and differences between leadership and management in regard to 63 different competencies. They found a large number of competencies (22)

Leadership in the NHS

descriptive of both leadership and management (e.g., productivity, customer focus, professionalism, and goal setting), but they also found several unique descriptors for each. Specifically, they found leadership was distinguished by motivating intrinsically, creative thinking, strategic planning, tolerance of ambiguity, and being able to read people, and management was distinguished by rule orientation, short-term planning, motivating extrinsically, orderliness, safety concerns, and timeliness.

Approaching the issue from a narrower viewpoint, Zaleznik (1977) went so far as to argue that leaders and managers themselves are distinct, and that they are basically different types of people. He contended that managers are reactive and prefer to work with people to solve problems but do so with low emotional involvement. They act to limit choices. Zaleznik suggested that leaders, on the other hand, are emotionally active and involved. They seek to shape ideas instead of responding to them and act to expand the available options to solve long-standing problems. Leaders change the way people think about what is possible.

Although there are clear differences between management and leadership, the two constructs overlap. When managers are involved in influencing a group to meet its goals, they are involved in leadership. When leaders are involved in planning, organizing, staffing, and controlling, they are involved in management. Both processes involve influencing a group of individuals toward goal attainment. For purposes of our discussion in this book, we focus on the leadership process. In our examples and case studies, we treat the roles of managers and leaders similarly and do not emphasize the differences between them.

PLAN OF THE BOOK

This book is user-friendly. It is based on substantive theories but is written to emphasize practice and application. Each chapter in the book follows the same format. The first section of each chapter briefly describes the leadership approach and discusses various research studies applicable to the approach. The second section of each chapter evaluates the approach, highlighting its strengths and criticisms. Special attention is given to how the approach contributes or fails to contribute to an overall understanding of the leadership process. The next section uses case studies to prompt discussion of how the approach can be applied in ongoing organizations. Finally, each chapter provides a leadership questionnaire along with a discussion of how the questionnaire measures the reader's leadership style. Each chapter ends with a summary and references.

Leadership and Nursing Theory

SUMMARY

Leadership is a topic with universal appeal; in the popular press and academic research literature, much has been written about leadership. Despite the abundance of writing on the topic, leadership has presented a major challenge to practitioners and researchers interested in understanding the nature of leadership. It is a highly valued phenomenon that is very complex.

Through the years, leadership has been defined and conceptualized in many ways. The component common to nearly all classifications is that leadership is an influence process that assists groups of individuals toward goal attainment. Specifically, in this book leadership is defined as a process whereby an individual influences a group of individuals to achieve a common goal.

Because both leaders and followers are part of the leadership process, it is important to address issues that confront followers as well as issues that confront leaders. Leaders and followers should be understood in relation to each other.

In prior research, many studies have focused on leadership as a trait. The trait perspective suggests that certain people in our society have special inborn qualities that make them leaders. This view restricts leadership to those who are believed to have special characteristics. In contrast, the approach in this text suggests that leadership is a process that can be learned, and that it is available to everyone.

Two common forms of leadership are *assigned* and *emergent*. *Assigned leadership* is based on a formal title or position in an organization. *Emergent leadership* results from what one does and how one acquires support from followers. Leadership, as a process, applies to individuals in both assigned roles and emergent roles.

Related to leadership is the concept of power, the potential to influence. There are two major kinds of power: position and personal. Position power, which is much like assigned leadership, is the power an individual derives from having a title in a formal organizational system. It includes legitimate, reward, information, and coercive power. Personal power comes from followers and includes referent and expert power. Followers give it to leaders because followers believe leaders have something of value. Treating power as a shared resource is important because it deemphasizes the idea that leaders are power wielders.

While coercion has been a common power brought to bear by many individuals in charge, it should not be viewed as ideal leadership. Our definition of leadership stresses *using influence* to bring individuals toward a common goal, while coercion involves the use of threats and punishment to *induce change* in followers for the sake of the leaders. Coercion runs counter to leadership because it does not treat leadership as a process that emphasizes working *with* followers to achieve shared objectives.

Leadership and management are different concepts that overlap. They are different in that management traditionally focuses on the activities of planning, organizing, staffing, and controlling, whereas leadership emphasizes the general influence process. According to some researchers, management is concerned with creating order and stability, whereas leadership is about adaptation and constructive change. Other researchers go so far as to argue that managers and leaders are different types of people, with managers being more reactive and less emotionally involved and leaders being more proactive and more emotionally involved. The overlap between leadership and management is centered on how both involve influencing a group of individuals in goal attainment.

In this book, we discuss leadership as a complex process. Based on the research literature, we describe selected approaches to leadership and assess how they can be used to improve leadership in real situations.

Sharpen your skills with SAGE edge at **edge.sagepub.com/northouse7e**

REFERENCES

Bass, B. M. (1990). *Bass and Stogdill's handbook of leadership: A survey of theory and research.* New York: Free Press.

Bennis, W. G., & Nanus, B. (1985). *Leaders: The strategies for taking charge.* New York: Harper & Row.

Bryman, A. (1992). *Charisma and leadership in organizations.* London: SAGE.

Bryman, A., Collinson, D., Grint, K., Jackson, G., & Uhl-Bien, M. (Eds.). (2011). *The SAGE handbook of leadership.* London: SAGE.

Burns, J. M. (1978). *Leadership.* New York: Harper & Row.

Copeland, N. (1942). *Psychology and the soldier.* Harrisburg, PA: Military Service Publications.

Day, D. V., & Antonakis, J. (Eds.). (2012). *The nature of leadership* (2nd ed.). Thousand Oaks, CA: SAGE.

Fayol, H. (1916). *General and industrial management.* London: Pitman.

Fisher, B. A. (1974). *Small group decision making: Communication and the group process.* New York: McGraw-Hill.

Fleishman, E. A., Mumford, M. D., Zaccaro, S. J., Levin, K. Y., Korotkin, A. L., & Hein, M. B. (1991). Taxonomic efforts in the description of leader behavior: A synthesis and functional interpretation. *Leadership Quarterly, 2*(4), 245–287.

French, J. R., Jr., & Raven, B. H. (1959). The bases of social power. In D. Cartwright (Ed.), *Studies in social power* (pp. 259–269). Ann Arbor, MI: Institute for Social Research.

Gardner, J. W. (1990). *On leadership.* New York: Free Press.

Heller, T., & Van Til, J. (1983). Leadership and followership: Some summary propositions. *Journal of Applied Behavioral Science, 18,* 405–414.

Hemphill, J. K. (1949). *Situational factors in leadership.* Columbus: Ohio State University, Bureau of Educational Research.

Hickman, G. R. (Ed.). (2009). *Leading organizations: Perspectives for a new era* (2nd ed.). Thousand Oaks, CA: SAGE.

Hogg, M. A. (2001). A social identity theory of leadership. *Personality and Social Psychology Review, 5,* 184–200.

Hollander, E. P. (1992). Leadership, followership, self, and others. *Leadership Quarterly, 3*(1), 43–54.

Jago, A. G. (1982). Leadership: Perspectives in theory and research. *Management Science, 28*(3), 315–336.

Kellerman, B. (2012). *The end of leadership.* New York: HarperCollins.

Kotter, J. P. (1990). *A force for change: How leadership differs from management.* New York: Free Press.

Moore, B. V. (1927). The May conference on leadership. *Personnel Journal, 6,* 124–128.

Mumford, M. D. (2006). *Pathways to outstanding leadership: A comparative analysis of charismatic, ideological, and pragmatic leaders.* Mahwah, NJ: Lawrence Erlbaum.

Peters, T. J., & Waterman, R. H. (1982). *In search of excellence: Lessons from America's best-run companies.* New York: Warner Books.

Raven, B. H. (1965). Social influence and power. In I. D. Steiner & M. Fishbein (Eds.), *Current studies in social psychology* (pp. 371–382). New York: Holt, Rinehart, & Winston.

Rost, J. C. (1991). *Leadership for the twenty-first century.* New York: Praeger.

Seeman, M. (1960). *Social status and leadership.* Columbus: Ohio State University, Bureau of Educational Research.

Simonet, D. V., & Tett, R. P. (2012). Five perspectives on the leadership-management relationship: A competency-based evaluation and integration. *Journal of Leadership & Organizational Studies, 20*(2), 199–213.

Smith, J. A., & Foti, R. J. (1998). A pattern approach to the study of leader emergence. *Leadership Quarterly, 9*(2), 147–160.

Stogdill, R. M. (1974). *Handbook of leadership: A survey of theory and research.* New York: Free Press.

Watson, C., & Hoffman, L. R. (2004). The role of task-related behavior in the emergence of leaders. *Group & Organization Management, 29*(6), 659–685.

Zaleznik, A. (1977, May–June). Managers and leaders: Are they different? *Harvard Business Review, 55,* 67–78.

2

Trait Approach

DESCRIPTION

Of interest to scholars throughout the 20th century, the trait approach was one of the first systematic attempts to study leadership. In the early 20th century, leadership traits were studied to determine what made certain people great leaders. The theories that were developed were called "great man" theories because they focused on identifying the innate qualities and characteristics possessed by great social, political, and military leaders (e.g., Catherine the Great, Mohandas Gandhi, Indira Gandhi, Abraham Lincoln, Joan of Arc, and Napoleon Bonaparte). It was believed that people were born with these traits, and that only the "great" people possessed them. During this time, research concentrated on determining the specific traits that clearly differentiated leaders from followers (Bass, 1990; Jago, 1982).

In the mid-20th century, the trait approach was challenged by research that questioned the universality of leadership traits. In a major review, Stogdill (1948) suggested that no consistent set of traits differentiated leaders from nonleaders across a variety of situations. An individual with leadership traits who was a leader in one situation might not be a leader in another situation. Rather than being a quality that individuals possess, leadership was reconceptualized as a relationship between people in a social situation. Personal factors related to leadership continued to be important, but researchers contended that these factors were to be considered as relative to the requirements of the situation.

The trait approach has generated much interest among researchers for its explanation of how traits influence leadership (Bryman, 1992). For example, an analysis of much of the previous trait research by Lord, DeVader, and

▶ Heroic Women   Ⓝ What Traits Do Leaders Have?

Alliger (1986) found that traits were strongly associated with individuals' perceptions of leadership. Similarly, Kirkpatrick and Locke (1991) went so far as to claim that effective leaders are actually distinct types of people in several key respects.

The trait approach has earned new interest through the current emphasis given by many researchers to visionary and charismatic leadership (see Bass, 1990; Bennis & Nanus, 1985; Nadler & Tushman, 1989; Zaccaro, 2007; Zaleznik, 1977). Charismatic leadership catapulted to the forefront of public attention with the 2008 election of the United States' first African American president, Barack Obama, who is perceived by many to be charismatic, among many other attributes. In a study to determine what distinguishes charismatic leaders from others, Jung and Sosik (2006) found that charismatic leaders consistently possess traits of self-monitoring, engagement in impression management, motivation to attain social power, and motivation to attain self-actualization. In short, the trait approach is alive and well. It began with an emphasis on identifying the qualities of great persons, shifted to include the impact of situations on leadership, and, currently, has shifted back to reemphasize the critical role of traits in effective leadership.

Although the research on traits spanned the entire 20th century, a good overview of this approach is found in two surveys completed by Stogdill (1948, 1974). In his first survey, Stogdill analyzed and synthesized more than 124 trait studies conducted between 1904 and 1947. In his second study, he analyzed another 163 studies completed between 1948 and 1970. By taking a closer look at each of these reviews, we can obtain a clearer picture of how individuals' traits contribute to the leadership process.

Stogdill's first survey identified a group of important leadership traits that were related to how individuals in various groups became leaders. His results showed that the average individual in the leadership role is different from an average group member with regard to the following eight traits: intelligence, alertness, insight, responsibility, initiative, persistence, self-confidence, and sociability.

The findings of Stogdill's first survey also indicated that an individual does not become a leader solely because that individual possesses certain traits. Rather, the traits that leaders possess must be relevant to situations in which the leader is functioning. As stated earlier, leaders in one situation may not necessarily be leaders in another situation. Findings showed that leadership was not a passive state but resulted from a working relationship between the leader and other group members. This research marked the beginning of a

▶ Great Man Theory   Impression Management

new approach to leadership research that focused on leadership behaviors and leadership situations.

Stogdill's second survey, published in 1974, analyzed 163 new studies and compared the findings of these studies to the findings he had reported in his first survey. The second survey was more balanced in its description of the role of traits and leadership. Whereas the first survey implied that leadership is determined principally by situational factors and not traits, the second survey argued more moderately that both traits and situational factors were determinants of leadership. In essence, the second survey validated the original trait idea that a leader's characteristics are indeed a part of leadership.

Similar to the first survey, Stogdill's second survey also identified traits that were positively associated with leadership. The list included the following 10 characteristics:

1. drive for responsibility and task completion;

2. vigor and persistence in pursuit of goals;

3. risk taking and originality in problem solving;

4. drive to exercise initiative in social situations;

5. self-confidence and sense of personal identity;

6. willingness to accept consequences of decision and action;

7. readiness to absorb interpersonal stress;

8. willingness to tolerate frustration and delay;

9. ability to influence other people's behavior; and

10. capacity to structure social interaction systems to the purpose at hand.

Mann (1959) conducted a similar study that examined more than 1,400 findings regarding traits and leadership in small groups, but he placed less emphasis on how situational factors influenced leadership. Although tentative in his conclusions, Mann suggested that certain traits could be used to distinguish leaders from nonleaders. His results identified leaders as strong in the following six traits: intelligence, masculinity, adjustment, dominance, extraversion, and conservatism.

 Everyday Leaders   Trait Leadership

Table 2.1 Studies of Leadership Traits and Characteristics

Stogdill (1948)	Mann (1959)	Stogdill (1974)	Lord, DeVader, and Alliger (1986)	Kirkpatrick and Locke (1991)	Zaccaro, Kemp, and Bader (2004)
intelligence	intelligence	achievement	intelligence	drive	cognitive abilities
alertness	masculinity	persistence	masculinity	motivation	extraversion
insight	adjustment	insight	dominance	integrity	conscientiousness
responsibility	dominance	initiative		confidence	emotional stability
initiative	extraversion	self-confidence		cognitive	openness
persistence	conservatism	responsibility		ability	agreeableness
self-confidence		cooperativeness		task	motivation
sociability		tolerance		knowledge	social intelligence
		influence			self-monitoring
		sociability			emotional intelligence
					problem solving

SOURCES: Adapted from "The Bases of Social Power," by J. R. P. French, Jr., and B. Raven, 1962, in D. Cartwright (Ed.), *Group Dynamics: Research and Theory* (pp. 259–269), New York: Harper and Row; Zaccaro, Kemp, & Bader (2004).

Lord et al. (1986) reassessed Mann's (1959) findings using a more sophisticated procedure called meta-analysis. Lord et al. found that intelligence, masculinity, and dominance were significantly related to how individuals perceived leaders. From their findings, the authors argued strongly that traits could be used to make discriminations consistently across situations between leaders and nonleaders.

Both of these studies were conducted during periods in American history where male leadership was prevalent in most aspects of business and society. In Chapter 15, we explore more contemporary research regarding the role of gender in leadership, and we look at whether traits such as masculinity and dominance still bear out as important factors in distinguishing between leaders and nonleaders.

Yet another review argues for the importance of leadership traits: Kirkpatrick and Locke (1991, p. 59) contended that "it is unequivocally clear that leaders are not like other people." From a qualitative synthesis of earlier research, Kirkpatrick and Locke postulated that leaders differ from nonleaders on six traits: drive, motivation, integrity, confidence, cognitive ability, and task knowledge. According to these writers, individuals can be born with these traits, they can learn them, or both. It is these six traits that make up the

🎙 Leadership Presence   📖 Florence Nightingale

Table 2.2 Major Leadership Traits

• Intelligence	• Integrity
• Self-confidence	• Sociability
• Determination	

"right stuff" for leaders. Kirkpatrick and Locke contended that leadership traits make some people different from others, and this difference should be recognized as an important part of the leadership process.

In the 1990s, researchers began to investigate the leadership traits associated with "social intelligence," characterized as those abilities to understand one's own and others' feelings, behaviors, and thoughts and to act appropriately (Marlowe, 1986). Zaccaro (2002) defined social intelligence as having such capacities as social awareness, social acumen, self-monitoring, and the ability to select and enact the best response given the contingencies of the situation and social environment. A number of empirical studies showed these capacities to be a key trait for effective leaders. Zaccaro, Kemp, and Bader (2004) included such social abilities in the categories of leadership traits they outlined as important leadership attributes (see Table 2.1).

Table 2.1 provides a summary of the traits and characteristics that were identified by researchers from the trait approach. It illustrates clearly the breadth of traits related to leadership. Table 2.1 also shows how difficult it is to select certain traits as definitive leadership traits; some of the traits appear in several of the survey studies, whereas others appear in only one or two studies. Regardless of the lack of precision in Table 2.1, however, it represents a general convergence of research regarding which traits are leadership traits.

What, then, can be said about trait research? What has a century of research on the trait approach given us that is useful? The answer is an extended list of traits that individuals might hope to possess or wish to cultivate if they want to be perceived by others as leaders. Some of the traits that are central to this list include intelligence, self-confidence, determination, integrity, and sociability (Table 2.2).

Intelligence

Intelligence or intellectual ability is positively related to leadership. Based on their analysis of a series of recent studies on intelligence and various indices of leadership, Zaccaro et al. (2004) found support for the finding that leaders tend to have higher intelligence than nonleaders. Having strong verbal

 Emotional and Other Intelligences

ability, perceptual ability, and reasoning appears to make one a better leader. Although it is good to be bright, the research also indicates that a leader's intellectual ability should not differ too much from that of the subordinates. If the leader's IQ is very different from that of the followers, it can have a counterproductive impact on leadership. Leaders with higher abilities may have difficulty communicating with followers because they are preoccupied or because their ideas are too advanced for their followers to accept.

An example of a leader for whom intelligence was a key trait was Steve Jobs, founder and CEO of Apple who died in 2011. Jobs once said, "I have this really incredible product inside me and I have to get it out" (Sculley, 2011, p. 27). Those visionary products, first the Apple II and Macintosh computers and then the iMac, iPod, iPhone, and iPad, have revolutionized the personal computer and electronic device industry, changing the way people play and work.

In the next chapter of this text, which addresses leadership from a skills perspective, intelligence is identified as a trait that significantly contributes to a leader's acquisition of complex problem-solving skills and social judgment skills. Intelligence is described as having a positive impact on an individual's capacity for effective leadership.

Self-Confidence

Self-confidence is another trait that helps one to be a leader. Self-confidence is the ability to be certain about one's competencies and skills. It includes a sense of self-esteem and self-assurance and the belief that one can make a difference. Leadership involves influencing others, and self-confidence allows the leader to feel assured that his or her attempts to influence others are appropriate and right.

Again, Steve Jobs is a good example of a self-confident leader. When Jobs described the devices he wanted to create, many people said they weren't possible. But Jobs never doubted his products would change the world, and, despite resistance, he did things the way he thought best. "Jobs was one of those CEOs who ran the company like he wanted to. He believed he knew more about it than anyone else, and he probably did," said a colleague (Stone, 2011).

Determination

Many leaders also exhibit determination. Determination is the desire to get the job done and includes characteristics such as initiative, persistence,

 Political Leadership   Steve Jobs

dominance, and drive. People with determination are willing to assert themselves, are proactive, and have the capacity to persevere in the face of obstacles. Being determined includes showing dominance at times and in situations where followers need to be directed.

Dr. Paul Farmer has shown determination in his efforts to secure health care and eradicate tuberculosis for the very poor of Haiti and other third world countries. He began his efforts as a recent college graduate, traveling and working in Cange, Haiti. While there, he was accepted to Harvard Medical School. Knowing that his work in Haiti was invaluable to his training, he managed to do both: spending months traveling back and forth between Haiti and Cambridge, Massachusetts, for school. His first effort in Cange was to establish a one-room clinic where he treated "all comers" and trained local health care workers. Farmer found that there was more to providing health care than just dispensing medicine: He secured donations to build schools, houses, and communal sanitation and water facilities in the region. He spearheaded vaccinations of all the children in the area, dramatically reducing malnutrition and infant mortality. In order to keep working in Haiti, he returned to America and founded Partners In Health, a charitable foundation that raises money to fund these efforts. Since its founding, PIH not only has succeeded in improving the health of many communities in Haiti but now has projects in Haiti, Lesotho, Malawi, Peru, Russia, Rwanda, and the United States, and supports other projects in Mexico and Guatemala (Kidder, 2004; Partners In Health, 2014).

Integrity

Integrity is another of the important leadership traits. Integrity is the quality of honesty and trustworthiness. People who adhere to a strong set of principles and take responsibility for their actions are exhibiting integrity. Leaders with integrity inspire confidence in others because they can be trusted to do what they say they are going to do. They are loyal, dependable, and not deceptive. Basically, integrity makes a leader believable and worthy of our trust.

In our society, integrity has received a great deal of attention in recent years. For example, as a result of two situations—the position taken by President George W. Bush regarding Iraq's alleged weapons of mass destruction and the impeachment proceedings during the Clinton presidency—people are demanding more honesty of their public officials. Similarly, scandals in the corporate world (e.g., Enron and WorldCom) have led people to become skeptical of leaders who are not highly ethical. In the educational arena, new

 Terry Fox   Consultant Nurses

K–12 curricula are being developed to teach character, values, and ethical leadership. (For instance, see the Character Counts! program developed by the Josephson Institute of Ethics in California at www.charactercounts.org, and the Pillars of Leadership program taught at the J. W. Fanning Institute for Leadership in Georgia at www.fanning.uga.edu.) In short, society is demanding greater integrity of character in its leaders.

Sociability

A final trait that is important for leaders is sociability. Sociability is a leader's inclination to seek out pleasant social relationships. Leaders who show sociability are friendly, outgoing, courteous, tactful, and diplomatic. They are sensitive to others' needs and show concern for their well-being. Social leaders have good interpersonal skills and create cooperative relationships with their followers.

An example of a leader with great sociability skills is Michael Hughes, a university president. Hughes prefers to walk to all his meetings because it gets him out on campus where he greets students, staff, and faculty. He has lunch in the dorm cafeterias or student union and will often ask a table of strangers if he can sit with them. Students rate him as very approachable, while faculty say he has an open-door policy. In addition, he takes time to write personal notes to faculty, staff, and students to congratulate them on their successes.

Although our discussion of leadership traits has focused on five major traits (i.e., intelligence, self-confidence, determination, integrity, and sociability), this list is not all-inclusive. While other traits indicated in Table 2.1 are associated with effective leadership, the five traits we have identified contribute substantially to one's capacity to be a leader.

Until recently, most reviews of leadership traits have been qualitative. In addition, they have lacked a common organizing framework. However, the research described in the following section provides a quantitative assessment of leadership traits that is conceptually framed around the five-factor model of personality. It describes how five major personality traits are related to leadership.

Five-Factor Personality Model and Leadership

Over the past 25 years, a consensus has emerged among researchers regarding the basic factors that make up what we call personality (Goldberg, 1990;

 Extraversion

Table 2.3 Big Five Personality Factors

Neuroticism	The tendency to be depressed, anxious, insecure, vulnerable, and hostile
Extraversion	The tendency to be sociable and assertive and to have positive energy
Openness	The tendency to be informed, creative, insightful, and curious
Agreeableness	The tendency to be accepting, conforming, trusting, and nurturing
Conscientiousness	The tendency to be thorough, organized, controlled, dependable, and decisive

SOURCE: Goldberg, L. R. (1990). An alternative "description of personality": The big-five factor structure. *Journal of Personality and Social Psychology, 59,* 1216–1229.

McCrae & Costa, 1987). These factors, commonly called the *Big Five,* are neuroticism, extraversion (surgency), openness (intellect), agreeableness, and conscientiousness (dependability). (See Table 2.3.)

To assess the links between the Big Five and leadership, Judge, Bono, Ilies, and Gerhardt (2002) conducted a major meta-analysis of 78 leadership and personality studies published between 1967 and 1998. In general, Judge et al. found a strong relationship between the Big Five traits and leadership. It appears that having certain personality traits is associated with being an effective leader.

Specifically, in their study, *extraversion* was the factor most strongly associated with leadership. It is the most important trait of effective leaders. Extraversion was followed, in order, by *conscientiousness, openness,* and *low neuroticism.* The last factor, *agreeableness,* was found to be only weakly associated with leadership.

Emotional Intelligence

Another way of assessing the impact of traits on leadership is through the concept of emotional intelligence, which emerged in the 1990s as an important area of study in psychology. It has been widely studied by researchers, and has captured the attention of many practitioners (Caruso & Wolfe, 2004; Goleman, 1995, 1998; Mayer & Salovey, 1995, 1997; Mayer, Salovey, & Caruso, 2000; Shankman & Allen, 2008).

 Emotional Intelligence

As the two words suggest, emotional intelligence has to do with our emotions (affective domain) and thinking (cognitive domain), and the interplay between the two. Whereas *intelligence* is concerned with our ability to learn *information* and apply it to life tasks, *emotional intelligence* is concerned with our ability to understand *emotions* and apply this understanding to life's tasks. Specifically, *emotional intelligence* can be defined as the ability to perceive and express emotions, to use emotions to facilitate thinking, to understand and reason with emotions, and to effectively manage emotions within oneself and in relationships with others (Mayer, Salovey, & Caruso, 2000).

There are different ways to measure emotional intelligence. One scale is the Mayer-Salovey-Caruso Emotional Intelligence Test (MSCEIT; Mayer, Caruso, & Salovey, 2000). The MSCEIT measures emotional intelligence as a set of mental abilities, including the abilities to perceive, facilitate, understand, and manage emotion.

Goleman (1995, 1998) takes a broader approach to emotional intelligence, suggesting that it consists of a set of personal and social competencies. Personal competence consists of self-awareness, confidence, self-regulation, conscientiousness, and motivation. Social competence consists of empathy and social skills such as communication and conflict management.

Shankman and Allen (2008) developed a practice-oriented model of emotionally intelligent leadership, which suggests that leaders must be conscious of three fundamental facets of leadership: context, self, and others. In the model, emotionally intelligent leaders are defined by 21 capacities to which a leader should pay attention, including group savvy, optimism, initiative, and teamwork.

There is a debate in the field regarding how big a role emotional intelligence plays in helping people be successful in life. Some researchers, such as Goleman (1995), suggested that emotional intelligence plays a major role in whether people are successful at school, home, and work. Others, such as Mayer, Salovey, and Caruso (2000), made softer claims for the significance of emotional intelligence in meeting life's challenges.

As a leadership ability or trait, emotional intelligence appears to be an important construct. The underlying premise suggested by this framework is that people who are more sensitive to their emotions and the impact of their emotions on others will be leaders who are more effective. As more research is conducted on emotional intelligence, the intricacies of how emotional intelligence relates to leadership will be better understood.

Emergent Leadership

HOW DOES THE TRAIT APPROACH WORK? ————————

The trait approach is very different from the other approaches discussed in subsequent chapters because it focuses exclusively on the leader, not on the followers or the situation. This makes the trait approach theoretically more straightforward than other approaches. In essence, the trait approach is concerned with what traits leaders exhibit and who has these traits.

The trait approach does not lay out a set of hypotheses or principles about what kind of leader is needed in a certain situation or what a leader should do, given a particular set of circumstances. Instead, this approach emphasizes that having a leader with a certain set of traits is crucial to having effective leadership. It is the leader and the leader's traits that are central to the leadership process.

The trait approach suggests that organizations will work better if the people in managerial positions have designated leadership profiles. To find the right people, it is common for organizations to use trait assessment instruments. The assumption behind these procedures is that selecting the right people will increase organizational effectiveness. Organizations can specify the characteristics or traits that are important to them for particular positions and then use trait assessment measures to determine whether an individual fits their needs.

The trait approach is also used for personal awareness and development. By analyzing their own traits, managers can gain an idea of their strengths and weaknesses, and can get a feel for how others in the organization see them. A trait assessment can help managers determine whether they have the qualities to move up or to move to other positions in the company.

A trait assessment gives individuals a clearer picture of who they are as leaders and how they fit into the organizational hierarchy. In areas where their traits are lacking, leaders can try to make changes in what they do or where they work to increase their traits' potential impact.

Near the end of the chapter, a leadership instrument is provided that you can use to assess your leadership traits. This instrument is typical of the kind of assessments that companies use to evaluate individuals' leadership potential. As you will discover by completing this instrument, trait measures are a good way to assess your own characteristics.

 Introvert Contributions

STRENGTHS

The trait approach has several identifiable strengths. First, the trait approach is intuitively appealing. It fits clearly with our notion that leaders are the individuals who are out front and leading the way in our society. The image in the popular press and community at large is that leaders are a special kind of people—people with gifts who can do extraordinary things. The trait approach is consistent with this perception because it is built on the premise that leaders are different, and their difference resides in the special traits they possess. People have a need to see their leaders as gifted people, and the trait approach fulfills this need.

A second strength of the trait approach is that it has a century of research to back it up. No other theory can boast of the breadth and depth of studies conducted on the trait approach. The strength and longevity of this line of research give the trait approach a measure of credibility that other approaches lack. Out of this abundance of research has emerged a body of data that points to the important role of various traits in the leadership process.

Another strength, more conceptual in nature, results from the way the trait approach highlights the leader component in the leadership process. Leadership is composed of leaders, followers, and situations, but the trait approach is devoted to only the first of these—leaders. Although this is also a potential weakness, by focusing exclusively on the role of the leader in leadership the trait approach has been able to provide us with a deeper and more intricate understanding of how the leader and the leader's traits are related to the leadership process.

Last, the trait approach has given us some benchmarks for what we need to look for if we want to be leaders. It identifies what traits we should have and whether the traits we do have are the best traits for leadership. Based on the findings of this approach, trait assessment procedures can be used to offer invaluable information to supervisors and managers about their strengths and weaknesses and ways to improve their overall leadership effectiveness.

CRITICISMS

In addition to its strengths, the trait approach has several weaknesses. First and foremost is the failure of the trait approach to delimit a definitive list of leadership traits. Although an enormous number of studies have been conducted over the past 100 years, the findings from these studies have

 Character Traits

been ambiguous and uncertain at times. Furthermore, the list of traits that has emerged appears endless. This is obvious from Table 2.1, which lists a multitude of traits. In fact, these are only a sample of the many leadership traits that were studied.

Another criticism is that the trait approach has failed to take situations into account. As Stogdill (1948) pointed out more than 60 years ago, it is difficult to isolate a set of traits that are characteristic of leaders without also factoring situational effects into the equation. People who possess certain traits that make them leaders in one situation may not be leaders in another situation. Some people may have the traits that help them emerge as leaders but not the traits that allow them to maintain their leadership over time. In other words, the situation influences leadership. It is therefore difficult to identify a universal set of leadership traits in isolation from the context in which the leadership occurs.

A third criticism, derived from the prior two criticisms, is that this approach has resulted in highly subjective determinations of the most important leadership traits. Because the findings on traits have been so extensive and broad, there has been much subjective interpretation of the meaning of the data. This subjectivity is readily apparent in the many self-help, practice-oriented management books. For example, one author might identify ambition and creativity as crucial leadership traits; another might identify empathy and calmness. In both cases, it is the author's subjective experience and observations that are the basis for the identified leadership traits. These books may be helpful to readers because they identify and describe important leadership traits, but the methods used to generate these lists of traits are weak. To respond to people's need for a set of definitive traits of leaders, authors have set forth lists of traits, even if the origins of these lists are not grounded in strong, reliable research.

Research on traits can also be criticized for failing to look at traits in relationship to leadership outcomes. This research has emphasized the identification of traits, but has not addressed how leadership traits affect group members and their work. In trying to ascertain universal leadership traits, researchers have focused on the link between specific traits and leader emergence, but they have not tried to link leader traits with other outcomes such as productivity or employee satisfaction. For example, trait research does not provide data on whether leaders who might have high intelligence and strong integrity have better results than leaders without these traits. The trait approach is weak in describing how leaders' traits affect the outcomes of groups and teams in organizational settings.

Effective and Ineffective Leaders

A final criticism of the trait approach is that it is not a useful approach for training and development for leadership. Even if definitive traits could be identified, teaching new traits is not an easy process because traits are not easily changed. For example, it is not reasonable to send managers to a training program to raise their IQ or to train them to become extraverted. The point is that traits are largely fixed psychological structures, and this limits the value of teaching and leadership training.

APPLICATION

Despite its shortcomings, the trait approach provides valuable information about leadership. It can be applied by individuals at all levels and in all types of organizations. Although the trait approach does not provide a definitive set of traits, it does provide direction regarding which traits are good to have if one aspires to a leadership position. By taking trait assessments and other similar questionnaires, people can gain insight into whether they have certain traits deemed important for leadership, and they can pinpoint their strengths and weaknesses with regard to leadership.

As we discussed previously, managers can use information from the trait approach to assess where they stand in their organization and what they need to do to strengthen their position. Trait information can suggest areas in which their personal characteristics are very beneficial to the company and areas in which they may want to get more training to enhance their overall approach. Using trait information, managers can develop a deeper understanding of who they are and how they will affect others in the organization.

CASE STUDIES

In this section, three case studies (Cases 2.1, 2.2, and 2.3) are provided to illustrate the trait approach and to help you understand how the trait approach can be used in making decisions in organizational settings. The settings of the cases are diverse—directing research and development at a large snack food company, running an office supply business, and being head of recruitment for a large bank—but all of the cases deal with trait leadership. At the end of each case, you will find questions that will help in analyzing the cases.

N What Are My Traits?

CASE 2.1

Choosing a New Director of Research

Sandra Coke is vice president for research and development at Great Lakes Foods (GLF), a large snack food company that has approximately 1,000 employees. As a result of a recent reorganization, Sandra must choose the new director of research. The director will report directly to Sandra and will be responsible for developing and testing new products. The research division of GLF employs about 200 people. The choice of directors is important because Sandra is receiving pressure from the president and board of GLF to improve the company's overall growth and productivity.

Sandra has identified three candidates for the position. Each candidate is at the same managerial level. She is having difficulty choosing one of them because each has very strong credentials. Alexa Smith is a longtime employee of GLF who started part-time in the mailroom while in high school. After finishing school, Alexa worked in as many as 10 different positions throughout the company to become manager of new product marketing. Performance reviews of Alexa's work have repeatedly described her as being very creative and insightful. In her tenure at GLF, Alexa has developed and brought to market four new product lines. Alexa is also known throughout GLF as being very persistent about her work: When she starts a project, she stays with it until it is finished. It is probably this quality that accounts for the success of each of the four new products with which she has been involved.

A second candidate for the new position is Kelsey Metts, who has been with GLF for 5 years and is manager of quality control for established products. Kelsey has a reputation for being very bright. Before joining GLF, she received her MBA at Harvard, graduating at the top of her class. People talk about Kelsey as the kind of person who will be president of her own company someday. Kelsey is also very personable. On all her performance reviews, she received extra-high scores on sociability and human relations. There isn't a supervisor in the company who doesn't have positive things to say about how comfortable it is to work with Kelsey. Since joining GLF, Kelsey has been instrumental in bringing two new product lines to market.

Thomas Santiago, the third candidate, has been with GLF for 10 years and is often consulted by upper management regarding strategic planning and corporate direction setting. Thomas has been very involved in establishing the vision for GLF and is a company person all the way. He believes in the values of GLF, and actively promotes its mission. The two

(Continued)

(Continued)

qualities that stand out above the rest in Thomas's performance reviews are his honesty and integrity. Employees who have worked under his supervision consistently report that they feel they can trust Thomas to be fair and consistent. Thomas is highly respected at GLF. In his tenure at the company, Thomas has been involved in some capacity with the development of three new product lines.

The challenge confronting Sandra is to choose the best person for the newly established director's position. Because of the pressure she feels from upper management, Sandra knows she must select the best leader for the new position.

Questions

1. Based on the information provided about the trait approach in Tables 2.1 and 2.2, if you were Sandra, whom would you select?

2. In what ways is the trait approach helpful in this type of selection?

3. In what ways are the weaknesses of the trait approach highlighted in this case?

CASE 2.2

A Remarkable Turnaround

Carol Baines was married for 20 years to the owner of the Baines Company until he died in a car accident. After his death, Carol decided not to sell the business but to try to run it herself. Before the accident, her only involvement in the business was in informal discussions with her husband over dinner, although she has a college degree in business, with a major in management.

Baines Company was one of three office supply stores in a city with a population of 200,000 people. The other two stores were owned by national chains. Baines was not a large company, and employed only five people. Baines had stable sales of about $200,000 a year, serving mostly the smaller companies in the city. The firm had not grown in a number of years and was beginning to feel the pressure of the advertising and lower prices of the national chains.

For the first 6 months, Carol spent her time familiarizing herself with the employees and the operations of the company. Next, she did a citywide analysis of companies that had reason to purchase office supplies. Based on her understanding of the company's capabilities and her assessment of the potential market for their products and services, Carol developed a specific set of short-term and long-term goals for the company. Behind all of her planning, Carol had a vision that Baines could be a viable, healthy, and competitive company. She wanted to carry on the business that her husband had started, but more than that she wanted it to grow.

Over the first 5 years, Carol invested significant amounts of money in advertising, sales, and services. These efforts were well spent because the company began to show rapid growth immediately. Because of the growth, the company hired another 20 people.

The expansion at Baines was particularly remarkable because of another major hardship Carol had to confront. Carol was diagnosed with breast cancer a year after her husband died. The treatment for her cancer included 2 months of radiation therapy and 6 months of strong chemotherapy. Although the side effects included hair loss and fatigue, Carol continued to manage the company throughout the ordeal. Despite her difficulties, Carol was successful. Under the strength of her leadership, the growth at Baines continued for 10 consecutive years.

Interviews with new and old employees at Baines revealed much about Carol's leadership. Employees said that Carol was a very solid person. She cared deeply about others and was fair and considerate. They said she created a family-like atmosphere at Baines. Few employees had quit Baines since Carol took over. Carol was devoted to all the employees, and she supported their interests. For example, the company sponsored a softball team in the summer and a basketball team in the winter. Others described Carol as a strong person. Even though she had cancer, she continued to be positive and interested in them. She did not get depressed about the cancer and its side effects, even though coping with cancer was difficult. Employees said she was a model of strength, goodness, and quality.

At age 55, Carol turned the business over to her two sons. She continues to act as the president but does not supervise the day-to-day operations. The company is doing more than $3.1 million in sales, and it outpaces the two chain stores in the city.

Questions

1. How would you describe Carol's leadership traits?

2. How big a part did Carol's traits play in the expansion of the company?

3. Would Carol be a leader in other business contexts?

CASE 2.3

Recruiting for the Bank

Pat Nelson is the assistant director of human resources in charge of recruitment for Central Bank, a large, full-service banking institution. One of Pat's major responsibilities each spring is to visit as many college campuses as he can to interview graduating seniors for credit analyst positions in the commercial lending area at Central Bank. Although the number varies, he usually ends up hiring about 20 new people, most of whom come from the same schools, year after year.

Pat has been doing recruitment for the bank for more than 10 years, and he enjoys it very much. However, for the upcoming spring he is feeling increased pressure from management to be particularly discriminating about whom he recommends hiring. Management is concerned about the retention rate at the bank because in recent years as many as 25% of the new hires have left. Departures after the first year have meant lost training dollars and strain on the staff who remain. Although management understands that some new hires always leave, the executives are not comfortable with the present rate, and they have begun to question the recruitment and hiring procedures.

The bank wants to hire people who can be groomed for higher-level leadership positions. Although certain competencies are required of entry-level credit analysts, the bank is equally interested in skills that will allow individuals to advance to upper management positions as their careers progress.

In the recruitment process, Pat always looks for several characteristics. First, applicants need to have strong interpersonal skills, they need to be confident, and they need to show poise and initiative. Next, because banking involves fiduciary responsibilities, applicants need to have proper ethics, including a strong sense of the importance of confidentiality. In addition, to do the work in the bank, they need to have strong analytical and technical skills, and experience in working with computers. Last, applicants need to exhibit a good work ethic, and they need to show commitment and a willingness to do their job even in difficult circumstances.

Pat is fairly certain that he has been selecting the right people to be leaders at Central Bank, yet upper management is telling him to reassess his hiring criteria. Although he feels that he has been doing the right thing, he is starting to question himself and his recruitment practices.

Questions

1. Based on ideas described in the trait approach, do you think Pat is looking for the right characteristics in the people he hires?

2. Could it be that the retention problem raised by upper management is unrelated to Pat's recruitment criteria?

3. If you were Pat, would you change your approach to recruiting?

LEADERSHIP INSTRUMENT ─────────────────

Organizations use a wide variety of questionnaires to measure individuals' traits. In many organizations, it is common practice to use standard trait measures such as the Minnesota Multiphasic Personality Inventory or the Myers-Briggs Type Indicator®. These measures provide valuable information to the individual and the organization about the individual's unique attributes for leadership and where the individual could best serve the organization.

In this section, the Leadership Trait Questionnaire (LTQ) is provided as an example of a measure that can be used to assess your personal leadership characteristics. The LTQ quantifies the perceptions of the individual leader and selected observers, such as subordinates or peers. It measures an individual's traits and points the individual to the areas in which that individual may have special strengths or weaknesses.

By taking the LTQ, you can gain an understanding of how trait measures are used for leadership assessment. You can also assess your own leadership traits.

Leadership Trait Questionnaire (LTQ)

Instructions: The purpose of this questionnaire is to measure personal characteristics of leadership. The questionnaire should be completed by the leader and five people who are familiar with the leader.

Make five copies of this questionnaire. This questionnaire should be completed by you and five people you know (e.g., roommates, coworkers, relatives, friends). Using the following scale, have each individual indicate the degree to which he or she agrees or disagrees with each of the 14 statements below. Do not forget to complete one for yourself.

_____ (leader's name) is

Key: 1 = Strongly   2 = Disagree   3 = Neutral   4 = Agree   5 = Strongly
          disagree   agree

1. **Articulate**: Communicates effectively with others	1 2 3 4 5
2. **Perceptive**: Is discerning and insightful	1 2 3 4 5
3. **Self-confident**: Believes in himself/herself and his/her ability	1 2 3 4 5
4. **Self-assured**: Is secure with self, free of doubts	1 2 3 4 5
5. **Persistent**: Stays fixed on the goals, despite interference	1 2 3 4 5
6. **Determined**: Takes a firm stand, acts with certainty	1 2 3 4 5
7. **Trustworthy**: Is authentic and inspires confidence	1 2 3 4 5
8. **Dependable**: Is consistent and reliable	1 2 3 4 5
9. **Friendly**: Shows kindness and warmth	1 2 3 4 5
10. **Outgoing**: Talks freely, gets along well with others	1 2 3 4 5
11. **Conscientious**: Is thorough, organized, and controlled	1 2 3 4 5
12. **Diligent**: Is persistent, hardworking	1 2 3 4 5
13. **Sensitive**: Shows tolerance, is tactful and sympathetic	1 2 3 4 5
14. **Empathic**: Understands others, identifies with others	1 2 3 4 5

Scoring

1. Enter the responses for Raters 1, 2, 3, 4, and 5 in the appropriate columns as shown in Example 2.1. The example provides hypothetical ratings to help explain how the questionnaire can be used.

2. For each of the 14 items, compute the average for the five raters and place that number in the "average rating" column.

3. Place your own scores in the "self-rating" column.

Example 2.1 Leadership Traits Questionnaire Ratings

	Rater 1	Rater 2	Rater 3	Rater 4	Rater 5	Average rating	Self-rating
1. Articulate	4	4	3	2	4	3.4	4
2. Perceptive	2	5	3	4	4	3.6	5
3. Self-confident	4	4	5	5	4	4.4	4
4. Self-assured	5	5	5	5	5	5	5
5. Persistent	4	4	3	3	3	3.4	3
6. Determined	4	4	4	4	4	4	4
7. Trustworthy	5	5	5	5	5	5	5
8. Dependable	4	5	4	5	4	4.4	4
9. Friendly	5	5	5	5	5	5	5
10. Outgoing	5	4	5	4	5	4.6	4
11. Conscientious	2	3	2	3	3	2.6	4
12. Diligent	3	3	3	3	3	3	4
13. Sensitive	4	4	5	5	5	4.6	3
14. Empathic	5	5	4	5	4	4.6	3

Scoring Interpretation

The scores you received on the LTQ provide information about how you see yourself and how others see you as a leader. The chart allows you to see where your perceptions are the same as those of others and where they differ.

The example ratings show how the leader self-rated higher than the observers did on the characteristic *articulate*. On the second characteristic, *perceptive*, the leader self-rated substantially higher than others. On the *self-confident* characteristic, the leader self-rated quite close to others' ratings but lower. There are no best ratings on this questionnaire. The purpose of the instrument is to give you a way to assess your strengths and weaknesses and to evaluate areas where your perceptions are congruent with those of others and where there are discrepancies.

SUMMARY

The trait approach has its roots in leadership theory that suggested that certain people were born with special traits that made them great leaders. Because it was believed that leaders and nonleaders could be differentiated by a universal set of traits, throughout the 20th century researchers were challenged to identify the definitive traits of leaders.

Around the mid-20th century, several major studies questioned the basic premise that a unique set of traits defined leadership. As a result, attention shifted to incorporating the impact of situations and of followers on leadership. Researchers began to study the interactions between leaders and their context instead of focusing only on leaders' traits. More recently, there have been signs that trait research has come full circle, with a renewed interest in focusing directly on the critical traits of leaders.

From the multitude of studies conducted through the years on personal characteristics, it is clear that many traits contribute to leadership. Some of the important traits that are consistently identified in many of these studies are intelligence, self-confidence, determination, integrity, and sociability. In addition, researchers have found a strong relationship between leadership and the traits described by the *five-factor personality model*. *Extraversion* was the trait most strongly associated with leadership, followed by *conscientiousness, openness, low neuroticism,* and *agreeableness*. Another recent line of research has focused on *emotional intelligence* and its relationship to leadership. This research suggests that leaders who are sensitive to their emotions and to the impact of their emotions on others may be leaders who are more effective.

On a practical level, the trait approach is concerned with which traits leaders exhibit and who has these traits. Organizations use personality assessment instruments to identify how individuals will fit within their organizations. The trait approach is also used for personal awareness and development because it allows managers to analyze their strengths and weaknesses and to gain a clearer understanding of how they should try to change to enhance their leadership.

There are several advantages to viewing leadership from the trait approach. First, it is intuitively appealing because it fits clearly into the popular idea that leaders are special people who are out front, leading the way in society. Second, a great deal of research validates the basis of this perspective. Third, by focusing exclusively on the leader, the trait approach provides an in-depth understanding of the leader component in the leadership process. Last, it has provided some benchmarks against which individuals can evaluate their own personal leadership attributes.

On the negative side, the trait approach has failed to provide a definitive list of leadership traits. In analyzing the traits of leaders, the approach has failed to take into account the impact of situations. In addition, the approach has resulted in subjective lists of the most important leadership traits, which are not necessarily grounded in strong, reliable research.

Furthermore, the trait approach has not adequately linked the traits of leaders with other outcomes such as group and team performance. Last, this approach is not particularly useful for training and development for leadership because individuals' personal attributes are largely stable and fixed, and their traits are not amenable to change.

Sharpen your skills with SAGE edge at **edge.sagepub.com/northouse7e**

REFERENCES

Bass, B. M. (1990). *Bass and Stogdill's handbook of leadership: A survey of theory and research.* New York: Free Press.

Bennis, W. G., & Nanus, B. (1985). *Leaders: The strategies for taking charge.* New York: Harper & Row.

Bryman, A. (1992). *Charisma and leadership in organizations.* London: SAGE.

Caruso, D. R., & Wolfe, C. J. (2004). Emotional intelligence and leadership development. In D. V. Day, S. J. Zaccaro, & S. M. Halpin (Eds.), *Leader development for transforming organizations: Growing leaders for tomorrow* (pp. 237–266). Mahwah, NJ: Lawrence Erlbaum.

Goldberg, L. R. (1990). An alternative "description of personality": The big-five factor structure. *Journal of Personality and Social Psychology, 59,* 1216–1229.

Goleman, D. (1995). *Emotional intelligence.* New York: Bantam.

Goleman, D. (1998). *Working with emotional intelligence.* New York: Bantam.

Jago, A. G. (1982). Leadership: Perspectives in theory and research. *Management Science, 28*(3), 315–336.

Judge, T. A., Bono, J. E., Ilies, R., & Gerhardt, M. W. (2002). Personality and leadership: A qualitative and quantitative review. *Journal of Applied Psychology, 87,* 765–780.

Jung, D., & Sosik, J. J. (2006). Who are the spellbinders? Identifying personal attributes of charismatic leaders. *Journal of Leadership & Organizational Studies, 12,* 12–27.

Kidder, T. (2004). *Mountains beyond mountains: The quest of Dr. Paul Farmer, a man who would cure the world.* New York: Random House.

Kirkpatrick, S. A., & Locke, E. A. (1991). Leadership: Do traits matter? *The Executive, 5,* 48–60.

Lord, R. G., DeVader, C. L., & Alliger, G. M. (1986). A meta-analysis of the relation between personality traits and leadership perceptions: An application of validity generalization procedures. *Journal of Applied Psychology, 71,* 402–410.

Mann, R. D. (1959). A review of the relationship between personality and performance in small groups. *Psychological Bulletin, 56,* 241–270.

Marlowe, H. A. (1986). Social intelligence: Evidence for multidimensionality and construct independence. *Journal of Educational Psychology, 78,* 52–58.

Mayer, J. D., Caruso, D. R., & Salovey, P. (2000). Selecting a measure of emotional intelligence: The case for ability scales. In R. Bar-On & J. D. A. Parker (Eds.), *The handbook of emotional intelligence* (pp. 320–342). San Francisco: Jossey-Bass.

Mayer, J. D., & Salovey, P. (1995). Emotional intelligence and the construction and regulation of feelings. *Applied & Preventive Psychology, 4,* 197–208.

Mayer, J. D., & Salovey, P. (1997). What is emotional intelligence? In P. Salovey & D. Sluyter (Eds.), *Emotional development and emotional intelligence: Implications for educators* (pp. 3–31). New York: Basic Books.

Mayer, J. D., Salovey, P., & Caruso, D. R. (2000). Models of emotional intelligence. In R. J. Sternberg (Ed.), *Handbook of intelligence* (pp. 396–420). Cambridge: Cambridge University Press.

McCrae, R. R., & Costa, P. T. (1987). Validation of the five-factor model of personality across instruments and observers. *Journal of Personality and Social Psychology, 52,* 81–90.

Nadler, D. A., & Tushman, M. L. (1989). What makes for magic leadership? In W. E. Rosenbach & R. L. Taylor (Eds.), *Contemporary issues in leadership* (pp. 135–139). Boulder, CO: Westview.

Partners In Health. (2014). *Our work.* Retrieved from http://www.pih.org/our-work

Sculley, J. (2011, October 10). No bozos. Ever. *Bloomberg Businessweek, 4249,* 27.

Shankman, M. L., & Allen, S. J. (2008). *Emotionally intelligent leadership: A guide for college students.* San Francisco: Jossey-Bass.

Stogdill, R. M. (1948). Personal factors associated with leadership: A survey of the literature. *Journal of Psychology, 25,* 35–71.

Stogdill, R. M. (1974). *Handbook of leadership: A survey of theory and research.* New York: Free Press.

Stone, B. (2011, October 10). The return. *Bloomberg Businessweek, 4249,* 40.

Zaccaro, S. J. (2002). Organizational leadership and social intelligence. In R. Riggio (Ed.), *Multiple intelligence and leadership* (pp. 29–54). Mahwah, NJ: Lawrence Erlbaum.

Zaccaro, S. J. (2007). Trait-based perspectives of leadership. *American Psychologist, 62,* 6–16.

Zaccaro, S. J., Kemp, C., & Bader, P. (2004). Leader traits and attributes. In J. Antonakis, A. T. Cianciolo, & R. J. Sternberg (Eds.), *The nature of leadership* (pp. 101–124). Thousand Oaks, CA: SAGE.

Zaleznik, A. (1977, May–June). Managers and leaders: Are they different? *Harvard Business Review, 55,* 67–78.

3

Skills Approach

DESCRIPTION

Like the trait approach we discussed in Chapter 2, the skills approach takes a leader-centered perspective on leadership. However, in the skills approach we shift our thinking from a focus on personality characteristics, which usually are viewed as innate and largely fixed, to an emphasis on skills and abilities that can be learned and developed. Although personality certainly plays an integral role in leadership, the skills approach suggests that knowledge and abilities are needed for effective leadership.

Researchers have studied leadership skills directly or indirectly for a number of years (see Bass, 1990, pp. 97–109). However, the impetus for research on skills was a classic article published by Robert Katz in the *Harvard Business Review* in 1955, titled "Skills of an Effective Administrator." Katz's article appeared at a time when researchers were trying to identify a definitive set of leadership traits. Katz's approach was an attempt to transcend the trait problem by addressing leadership as a set of developable *skills.* More recently, a revitalized interest in the skills approach has emerged. Beginning in the early 1990s, a multitude of studies have been published that contend that a leader's effectiveness depends on the leader's ability to solve complex organizational problems. This research has resulted in a comprehensive skill-based model of leadership that was advanced by Mumford and his colleagues (Mumford, Zaccaro, Harding, Jacobs, & Fleishman, 2000; Yammarino, 2000).

In this chapter, our discussion of the skills approach is divided into two parts. First, we discuss the general ideas set forth by Katz regarding three basic administrative skills: technical, human, and conceptual. Second, we discuss the recent work of Mumford and colleagues that has resulted in a new skills-based model of organizational leadership.

Three-Skill Approach

Based on field research in administration and his own firsthand observations of executives in the workplace, Katz (1955, p. 34) suggested that effective administration (i.e., leadership) depends on three basic personal skills: technical, human, and conceptual. Katz argued that these skills are quite different from traits or qualities of leaders. *Skills* are what leaders *can accomplish*, whereas *traits* are who leaders *are* (i.e., their innate characteristics). Leadership skills are defined in this chapter as the ability to use one's knowledge and competencies to accomplish a set of goals or objectives. This chapter shows that these leadership skills can be acquired and leaders can be trained to develop them.

Technical Skill

Technical skill is knowledge about and proficiency in a specific type of work or activity. It includes competencies in a specialized area, analytical ability, and the ability to use appropriate tools and techniques (Katz, 1955). For example, in a computer software company, technical skill might include knowing software language and programming, the company's software products, and how to make these products function for clients. Similarly, in an accounting firm, technical skill might include understanding and having the ability to apply generally accepted accounting principles to a client's audit. In both these examples, technical skills involve a hands-on activity with a basic product or process within an organization. Technical skills play an essential role in producing the actual products a company is designed to produce.

As illustrated in Figure 3.1, technical skill is most important at lower and middle levels of management and less important in upper management. For leaders at the highest level, such as CEOs, presidents, and senior officers, technical competencies are not as essential. Individuals at the top level depend on skilled followers to handle technical issues of the physical operation.

Human Skill

Human skill is knowledge about and ability to work with *people*. It is quite different from technical skill, which has to do with working with *things*

 Applying Katz's Skills   Technical Skills

(Katz, 1955). Human skills are "people skills." They are the abilities that help a leader to work effectively with followers, peers, and superiors to accomplish the organization's goals. Human skills allow a leader to assist group members in working cooperatively as a group to achieve common goals. For Katz, it means being aware of one's own perspective on issues and, at the same time, being aware of the perspective of others. Leaders with human skills adapt their own ideas to those of others. Furthermore, they create an atmosphere of trust where employees can feel comfortable and secure and where they can feel encouraged to become involved in the planning of things that will affect them. Being a leader with human skills means being sensitive to the needs and motivations of others and taking into account others' needs in one's decision making. In short, human skill is the capacity to get along with others as you go about your work.

In Figure 3.1, human skills are important in all three levels of management. Although managers at lower levels may communicate with a far greater number of employees, human skills are equally important at middle and upper levels.

Conceptual Skill

Broadly speaking, conceptual skills are the ability to work with ideas and concepts. Whereas technical skills deal with *things* and human skills deal with *people*, conceptual skills involve the ability to work with *ideas*. A leader with conceptual skills is comfortable talking about the ideas that shape an organization and the intricacies involved. He or she is good at putting the company's goals into words and can understand and express the economic principles that affect the company. A leader with conceptual skills works easily with abstractions and hypothetical notions.

Conceptual skills are central to creating a vision and strategic plan for an organization. For example, it would take conceptual skills for a CEO in a struggling manufacturing company to articulate a vision for a line of new products that would steer the company into profitability. Similarly, it would take conceptual skill for the director of a nonprofit health organization to create a strategic plan that could compete successfully with for-profit health organizations in a market with scarce resources. The point of these examples is that conceptual skill has to do with the mental work of shaping the meaning of organizational or policy issues—understanding what a company stands for and where it is or should be going.

In Figure 3.1, conceptual skill is most important at the top management levels. In fact, when upper-level managers do not have strong conceptual

Figure 3.1 Management Skills Necessary at Various Levels of an Organization

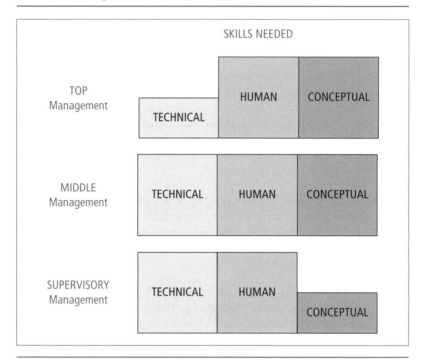

SOURCE: Adapted from "Skills of an Effective Administrator," by R. L. Katz, 1955, *Harvard Business Review,* 33(1), pp. 33–42.

skills, they can jeopardize the whole organization. Conceptual skills are also important in middle management; as we move down to lower management levels, conceptual skills become less important.

Summary of the Three-Skill Approach

To summarize, the three-skill approach includes technical, human, and conceptual skills. It is important for leaders to have all three skills; depending on where they are in the management structure, however, some skills are more important than others are.

Katz's work in the mid-1950s set the stage for conceptualizing leadership in terms of skills, but it was not until the mid-1990s that an empirically based skills approach received recognition in leadership research. In the next section, the comprehensive skill-based model of leadership is presented.

Skills Model

Beginning in the early 1990s, a group of researchers, with funding from the U.S. Army and Department of Defense, set out to test and develop a comprehensive theory of leadership based on problem-solving skills in organizations. The studies were conducted over a number of years using a sample of more than 1,800 Army officers, representing six grade levels, from second lieutenant to colonel. The project used a variety of new measures and tools to assess the skills of these officers, their experiences, and the situations in which they worked.

The researchers' main goal was to explain the underlying elements of effective performance. They addressed questions such as these: What accounts for why some leaders are good problem solvers and others are not? What specific skills do high-performing leaders exhibit? How do leaders' individual characteristics, career experiences, and environmental influences affect their job performance? As a whole, researchers wanted to identify the leadership factors that create exemplary job performance in an actual organization.

Based on the extensive findings from the project, Mumford and colleagues formulated a skill-based model of leadership. The model is characterized as a *capability* model because it examines the relationship between a leader's knowledge and skills (i.e., capabilities) and the leader's performance (Mumford, Zaccaro, Harding, et al., 2000, p. 12). Leadership capabilities can be developed over time through education and experience. Unlike the "great man" approach (discussed in this text, Chapter 2), which implies that leadership is reserved for only the gifted few, the skills approach suggests that many people have the potential for leadership. If people are capable of learning from their experiences, they can acquire leadership. The skills approach can also be distinguished from the leadership approaches we will discuss in subsequent chapters, which focus on behavioral patterns of leaders (e.g., the style approach, transformational leadership, or leader–member exchange theory). Rather than emphasizing *what leaders do*, the skills approach frames leadership as *the capabilities (knowledge and skills) that make effective leadership possible* (Mumford, Zaccaro, Harding, et al., 2000, p. 12).

The skill-based model of Mumford's group has five components: competencies, individual attributes, leadership outcomes, career experiences, and environmental influences. A portion of the model, illustrating three of these components, appears in Figure 3.2. This portion of the model is essential to understanding the overall skill-based leadership model.

 Career Experiences   Leadership Development

Figure 3.2   Three Components of the Skills Model

INDIVIDUAL ATTRIBUTES	COMPETENCIES	LEADERSHIP OUTCOMES
General Cognitive Ability Crystallized Cognitive Ability Motivation Personality	**Problem-Solving Skills** **Social Judgment Skills** **Knowledge**	Effective Problem Solving Performance

SOURCE: Adapted from "Leadership Skills for a Changing World: Solving Complex Social Problems," by M. D. Mumford, S. J. Zaccaro, F. D. Harding, T. O. Jacobs, and E. A. Fleishman, 2000, *Leadership Quarterly, 11*(1), 23.

Competencies

As can be observed in the middle box in Figure 3.2, problem-solving skills, social judgment skills, and knowledge are at the heart of the skills model. These three competencies are the key factors that account for effective performance.

Problem-Solving Skills. What are problem-solving skills? According to Mumford, Zaccaro, Harding, et al. (2000), problem-solving skills are a leader's creative ability to solve new and unusual, ill-defined organizational problems. The skills include being able to define significant problems, gather problem information, formulate new understandings about the problem, and generate prototype plans for problem solutions. These skills do not function in a vacuum, but are carried out in an organizational context. Problem-solving skills demand that leaders understand their own leadership capacities as they apply possible solutions to the unique problems in their organization (Mumford, Zaccaro, Connelly, & Marks, 2000).

Being able to construct solutions plays a special role in problem solving. In considering solutions to organizational problems, skilled leaders need to attend to the time frame for constructing and implementing a solution, short-term and long-term goals, career goals and organizational goals, and external issues, all of which could influence the solution (Mumford, Zaccaro, Harding, et al., 2000, p. 15).

 Conceptualizations of Skill   Shared Leadership

To clarify what is meant by problem-solving skills, conside   wing hypothetical situation. Imagine that you are the director of hu.. . .urces for a medium-sized company and you have been informed by the p . 'ent that you have to develop a plan to reduce the company's health care costs. In deciding what you will do, you could demonstrate problem-solving skills in the following ways. First, you identify the full ramifications for employees of changing their health insurance coverage. What is the impact going to be? Second, you gather information about how benefits can be scaled back. What other companies have attempted a similar change, and what were their results? Third, you find a way to teach and inform the employees about the needed change. How can you frame the change in such a way that it is clearly understood? Fourth, you create possible scenarios for how the changes will be instituted. How will the plan be described? Fifth, you look closely at the solution itself. How will implementing this change affect the company's mission and your own career? Last, are there issues in the organization (e.g., union rules) that may affect the implementation of these changes?

As illustrated by this example, the process of dealing with novel, ill-defined organizational problems is complex and demanding for leaders. In many ways, it is like a puzzle to be solved. For leaders to solve such puzzles, the skill-based model suggests that problem-solving skills are essential.

Social Judgment Skills. In addition to problem-solving skills, effective leadership performance also requires social judgment skills (see Figure 3.2). In general, social judgment skills are the capacity to understand people and social systems (Zaccaro, Mumford, Connelly, Marks, & Gilbert, 2000, p. 46). They enable leaders to *work with others* to solve problems and to marshal support to implement change within an organization. Social judgment skills are the people skills that are necessary to solve unique organizational problems.

Conceptually, social judgment skills are similar to Katz's (1955) early work on the role of human skills in management. In contrast to Katz's work, Mumford and colleagues have delineated social judgment skills into the following: perspective taking, social perceptiveness, behavioral flexibility, and social performance.

Perspective taking means understanding the attitudes that *others* have toward a particular problem or solution. It is empathy applied to problem solving. Perspective taking means being sensitive to other people's perspectives and goals—being able to understand their point of view on different issues. Included in perspective taking is knowing how different constituencies in an

Problem-Solving Approaches   Emotional Intelligence Skills

organization view a problem and possible solutions. According to Zaccaro, Gilbert, Thor, and Mumford (1991), perspective-taking skills can be likened to *social intelligence*. These skills are concerned with knowledge about people, the social fabric of organizations, and the interrelatedness of each of them.

Social perceptiveness is insight and awareness into how others in the organization function. What is important to others? What motivates them? What problems do they face, and how do they react to change? Social perceptiveness means understanding the unique needs, goals, and demands of different organizational constituencies (Zaccaro et al., 1991). A leader with social perceptiveness has a keen sense of how followers will respond to any proposed change in the organization. In a sense, you could say it allows the leader to know the pulse of followers on any issue at any time.

In addition to understanding others accurately, social judgment skills also involve reacting to others with flexibility. *Behavioral flexibility* is the capacity to change and adapt one's behavior in light of an understanding of others' perspectives in the organization. Being flexible means one is not locked into a singular approach to a problem. One is not dogmatic but rather maintains an openness and willingness to change. As the circumstances of a situation change, a flexible leader changes to meet the new demands.

Social performance includes a wide range of leadership competencies. Based on an understanding of followers' perspectives, leaders need to be able to communicate their own vision to others. Skill in persuasion and communicating change is essential to do this. When there is resistance to change or interpersonal conflict about change, leaders need to function as mediators. To this end, skill in conflict resolution is an important aspect of social performance competency. In addition, social performance sometimes requires that leaders coach followers, giving them direction and support as they move toward selected organizational goals. In all, social performance includes many related skills that may come under the umbrella of communication.

To review, social judgment skills are about being sensitive to how your ideas fit in with others. Can you understand others' perspectives and their unique needs and motivations? Are you flexible, and can you adapt your own ideas to others? Can you work with others even when there is resistance and conflict? Social judgment skills are the people skills needed to advance change in an organization.

Knowledge. As shown in the model (see Figure 3.2), the third aspect of competencies is knowledge. Knowledge is inextricably related to the

 Flexibility

application and implementation of problem-solving skills in organizations. It directly influences a leader's capacity to define complex organizational problems and to attempt to solve them (Mumford, Zaccaro, Harding, et al., 2000). *Knowledge* is the accumulation of information and the mental structures used to organize that information. Such a mental structure is called a *schema* (a summary, a diagrammatic representation, or an outline). Knowledge results from having developed an assortment of complex schemata for learning and organizing data.

For example, all of us take various kinds of facts and information into our minds. As we organize that information into categories or schemata, the information becomes more meaningful. Knowledge emerges from the facts *and* the organizational structures we apply to them. People with a lot of knowledge have more complex organizing structures than those with less knowledge. These knowledgeable people are called *experts.*

Consider the following baseball example. A baseball expert knows a lot of facts about the game; the expert knows the rules, strategies, equipment, players, and much, much more. The expert's knowledge about baseball includes the facts, but it also includes the complex mental structures used in organizing and structuring those facts. That person knows not only the season and lifetime statistics for each player, but also that player's quirks and injuries, the personality of the manager, the strengths and weaknesses of available substitutes, and so on. The expert knows baseball because she or he comprehends the complexities and nuances of the game. The same is true for leadership in organizations. Leaders with knowledge know much about the products, the tasks, the people, the organization, and all the different ways these elements are related to each other. A knowledgeable leader has many mental structures with which to organize the facts of organizational life.

Knowledge has a positive impact on how leaders engage in problem solving. It is knowledge and expertise that make it possible for people to think about complex system issues and identify possible strategies for appropriate change. Furthermore, this capacity allows people to use prior cases and incidents in order to plan for needed change. It is knowledge that allows people to use the past to constructively confront the future.

To summarize, the skills model consists of three competencies: problem-solving skills, social judgment skills, and knowledge. Collectively, these three components are positively related to effective leadership performance (see Figure 3.2).

 Evidence-Based Practice

Individual Attributes

Returning to Figure 3.2, the box on the left identifies four individual attributes that have an impact on leadership skills and knowledge: general cognitive ability, crystallized cognitive ability, motivation, and personality. These attributes play important roles in the skills model. Complex problem solving is a very difficult process and becomes more difficult as people move up in the organization. These attributes support people as they apply their leadership competencies.

General Cognitive Ability. General cognitive ability can be thought of as a person's intelligence. It includes perceptual processing, information processing, general reasoning skills, creative and divergent thinking capacities, and memory skills. General cognitive ability is linked to biology, not to experience.

General cognitive ability is sometimes described as fluid intelligence, a type of intelligence that usually grows and expands up through early adulthood and then declines with age. In the skills model, intelligence is described as having a positive impact on the leader's acquisition of complex problem-solving skills and the leader's knowledge.

Crystallized Cognitive Ability. Crystallized cognitive ability is intellectual ability that is learned or acquired over time. It is the store of knowledge we acquire through experience. We learn and increase our capacities over a lifetime, increasing our leadership potential (e.g., problem-solving skills, conceptual ability, and social judgment skills). In normally functioning adults, this type of cognitive ability grows continuously and typically does not fall off in adulthood. It includes being able to comprehend complex information and learn new skills and information, as well as being able to communicate to others in oral and written forms (Connelly et al., 2000, p. 71). Stated another way, crystallized cognitive ability is acquired intelligence: the ideas and mental abilities people learn through experience. Because it stays fairly stable over time, this type of intelligence is not diminished as people get older.

Motivation. Motivation is listed as the third attribute in the model. Although the model does not purport to explain the many ways in which motivation may affect leadership, it does suggest three aspects of motivation that are essential to developing leadership skills (Mumford, Zaccaro, Harding, et al., 2000, p. 22): First, leaders must be *willing* to tackle complex organizational problems. This first step is critical. For leadership to occur, a

 Role of Emotions

person wants to lead. Second, leaders must be willing to express *dominance*—to exert their influence, as we discussed in Chapter 2. In influencing others, the leader must take on the responsibility of dominance because the influence component of leadership is inextricably bound to dominance. Third, leaders must be committed to the *social good* of the organization. The *social good* is a broad term that can refer to a host of outcomes. However, in the skills model it refers to the leader's willingness to take on the responsibility of trying to advance the overall human good and value of the organization. Taken together, these three aspects of motivation (willingness, dominance, and social good) prepare people to become leaders.

Personality. Personality is the fourth individual attribute in the skills model. Placed where it is in the model, this attribute reminds us that our personality has an impact on the development of our leadership skills. For example, openness, tolerance for ambiguity, and curiosity may affect a leader's motivation to try to solve some organizational problems. Or, in conflict situations, traits such as confidence and adaptability may be beneficial to a leader's performance. The skills model hypothesizes that any personality characteristic that helps people to cope with complex organizational situations probably is related to leader performance (Mumford, Zaccaro, Harding, et al., 2000).

Leadership Outcomes

In the right-hand box in Figure 3.2, effective problem solving and performance are the outcomes of leadership. These outcomes are strongly influenced by the leader's competencies (i.e., problem-solving skills, social judgment skills, and knowledge). When leaders exhibit these competencies, they increase their chances of problem solving and overall performance.

Effective Problem Solving. As we discussed earlier, the skills model is a *capability model,* designed to explain why some leaders are good problem solvers and others are not. Problem solving is the keystone in the skills approach. In the model (see Figure 3.2), problem-solving skills, as competencies, lead to effective problem solving as a leadership outcome. The criteria for good problem solving are determined by the originality and the quality of expressed solutions to problems. Good problem solving involves creating solutions that are logical, effective, and unique, and that go beyond given information (Zaccaro et al., 2000).

Performance. In the model, performance outcomes reflect how well the leader has done her or his job. To measure performance, standard external

 Managerial Leadership

criteria are used. If the leader has done well and been successful, the leader's evaluations will be positive. Leaders who are effective receive good annual performance reviews, get merit raises, and are recognized by superiors and followers as competent leaders. In the end, performance is the degree to which a leader has successfully performed the assigned duties.

Taken together, effective problem solving and performance are the two ways to assess leadership effectiveness using the skills model. Furthermore, good problem solving and good performance go hand in hand. A full depiction of the comprehensive skills model appears in Figure 3.3. It contains two other components, not depicted in Figure 3.2, that contribute to overall leadership performance: career experiences and environmental influences.

Career Experiences

As you can see in Figure 3.3, career experiences have an impact on the characteristics and competencies of leaders. The skills model suggests that the experiences acquired in the course of leaders' careers influence their knowledge and skills to solve complex problems. Mumford, Zaccaro, Harding, et al. (2000, p. 24) pointed out that leaders can be helped through challenging job assignments, mentoring, appropriate training, and hands-on experience in solving new and unusual problems. In addition, the authors think that career experiences can positively affect the individual characteristics of leaders. For example, certain on-the-job assignments could enhance a leader's motivation or intellectual ability.

In the first section of this chapter, we discussed Katz's (1955) work, which notes that conceptual skills are essential for upper-level administrators. This is consistent with Mumford, Zaccaro, Harding, et al.'s (2000) skills model, which contends that leaders develop competencies over time. Career experience helps leaders to improve their skills and knowledge over time. Leaders learn and develop higher levels of conceptual capacity if the kinds of problems they confront are progressively more complex and more long term as they ascend the organizational hierarchy (Mumford, Zaccaro, Connelly, et al., 2000). Similarly, upper-level leaders, as opposed to first-line supervisors, develop new competencies because they are required to address problems that are more novel, that are more poorly defined, and that demand more human interaction. As these people move through their careers, higher levels of problem-solving and social judgment skills become increasingly important (Mumford & Connelly, 1991).

 Mentoring and Coaching

So the skills and knowledge of leaders are shaped by their career experiences as they address increasingly complex problems in the organization. This notion of developing leadership skills is unique and quite different from other leadership perspectives. If we say, "Leaders are shaped by their experiences," then it means leaders are not born to be leaders (Mumford, Zaccaro, Harding, et al., 2000). Leaders can develop their abilities through experience, according to the skills model.

Environmental Influences

The final component of the skills model is environmental influences, which is illustrated at the bottom of Figure 3.3. Environmental influences represent factors that lie outside the leader's competencies, characteristics, and experiences. These environmental influences can be *internal* and *external.*

Internal environmental influences affecting leadership performance can include such factors as technology, facilities, expertise of subordinates, and communication. For example, an aging factory or one lacking in high-speed technology could have a major impact on the nature of problem-solving activities. Another example might be the skill levels of followers: If a leader's followers are highly competent, they will definitely improve the group's problem solving and performance. Similarly, if a task is particularly complex or a group's communication poor, the leader's performance will be affected.

External environmental influences, including economic, political, and social issues, as well as natural disasters, can provide unique challenges to leaders. In March 2011, a massive earthquake and tsunami devastated large parts of Japan, crippling that nation's automobile manufacturing industry. Toyota Motor Corp. alone had more than 650 of its suppliers and component manufacturers wiped out, halting worldwide production of Toyota vehicles and devastating the company's sales. At the same time, this disaster was a boon to American carmakers, which increased shipments and began outselling Toyota, which had dominated the market. Leaders of these automobile companies, both Japanese and American, had to respond to unique challenges posed by external forces completely beyond their control.

The skills model does not provide an inventory of specific environmental influences. Instead, it acknowledges the existence of these factors and recognizes that they are indeed influences that can affect a leader's performance. In other words, environmental influences are a part of the skills model but not usually under the control of the leader.

 Veterans and Leadership

Figure 3.3 Skills Model of Leadership

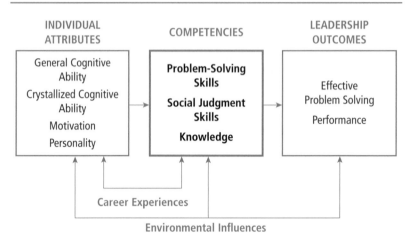

SOURCE: Adapted from "Leadership Skills for a Changing World: Solving Complex Social Problems," by M. D. Mumford, S. J. Zaccaro, F. D. Harding, T. O. Jacobs, and E. A. Fleishman, 2000, *Leadership Quarterly, 11*(1), 23.

Summary of the Skills Model

In summary, the skills model frames leadership by describing five components of leader performance. At the heart of the model are three competencies: *problem-solving skills, social judgment skills,* and *knowledge.* These three competencies are the central determinants of effective problem solving and performance, although individual attributes, career experiences, and environmental influences all have impacts on leader competencies. Through job experience and training, leaders can become better problem solvers and more effective leaders.

HOW DOES THE SKILLS APPROACH WORK?

The skills approach is primarily descriptive: It *describes* leadership from a skills perspective. Rather than providing prescriptions for success in leadership, the skills approach provides a structure for understanding the nature of effective leadership. In the previous sections, we discussed the skills perspective based on the work of Katz (1955) and Mumford, Zaccaro, Harding, et al. (2000). What does each of these bodies of work suggest about the structure and functions of leadership?

The three-skill approach of Katz suggests that the importance of certain leadership skills varies depending on where leaders are in a management hierarchy. For leaders operating at lower levels of management, technical and human skills are most important. When leaders move into middle management, it becomes important that they have all three skills: technical, human, and conceptual. At the upper management levels, it is paramount for leaders to exhibit conceptual and human skills.

This approach was reinforced in a 2007 study that examined the skills needed by executives at different levels of management. The researchers used a four-skill model, similar to Katz's approach, to assess cognitive skills, interpersonal skills, business skills, and strategic skills of 1,000 managers at the junior, middle, and senior levels of an organization. The results showed that interpersonal and cognitive skills were required more than business and strategic skills for those on the lower levels of management. As one climbed the career ladder, however, the execution of higher levels of all four of these leadership skills became necessary (Mumford, Campion, & Morgeson, 2007).

In their skills model, Mumford, Zaccaro, Harding, et al. (2000) provided a more complex picture of how skills relate to the manifestation of effective leadership. Their skills model contends that leadership outcomes are the direct result of a leader's competencies in problem-solving skills, social judgment skills, and knowledge. Each of these competencies includes a large repertoire of abilities, and each can be learned and developed. In addition, the model illustrates how individual attributes such as general cognitive ability, crystallized cognitive ability, motivation, and personality influence the leader's competencies. And finally, the model describes how career experiences and environmental influences play a direct or indirect role in leadership performance.

The skills approach works by providing a *map* for how to reach effective leadership in an organization: Leaders need to have problem-solving skills, social judgment skills, and knowledge. Workers can improve their capabilities in these areas through training and experience. Although each leader's personal attributes affect his or her skills, it is the leader's *skills* themselves that are most important in addressing organizational problems.

STRENGTHS

In several ways, the skills approach contributes positively to our understanding about leadership. First, it is a leader-centered model that stresses

 Leadership Skills Development

the importance of developing particular leadership skills. It is the first approach to conceptualize and create a structure of the process of leadership around *skills*. Whereas the early research on skills highlighted the importance of skills and the value of skills across different management levels, the later work placed learned skills at the center of effective leadership performance at *all* management levels.

Second, the skills approach is intuitively appealing. To describe leadership in terms of skills makes leadership available to everyone. Unlike personality traits, skills are competencies that people can learn or develop. It is like playing a sport such as tennis or golf. Even without natural ability in these sports, people can improve their games with practice and instruction. The same is true with leadership. When leadership is framed as a set of skills, it becomes a process that people can study and practice to become better at performing their jobs.

Third, the skills approach provides an expansive view of leadership that incorporates a wide variety of components, including problem-solving skills, social judgment skills, knowledge, individual attributes, career experiences, and environmental influences. Each of these components can further be subdivided into several subcomponents. The result is a picture of leadership that encompasses a multitude of factors. Because it includes so many variables, the skills approach can capture many of the intricacies and complexities of leadership not found in other models.

Last, the skills approach provides a structure that is very consistent with the curricula of most leadership education programs. Leadership education programs throughout the country have traditionally taught classes in creative problem solving, conflict resolution, listening, and teamwork, to name a few. The content of these classes closely mirrors many of the components in the skills model. Clearly, the skills approach provides a structure that helps to frame the curricula of leadership education and development programs.

CRITICISMS

Like all other approaches to leadership, the skills approach also has certain weaknesses. First, the breadth of the skills approach seems to extend beyond the boundaries of leadership. For example, by including motivation, critical thinking, personality, and conflict resolution, the skills approach addresses more than just leadership. Another example of the model's breadth is its inclusion of two types of intelligence (i.e., general cognitive ability and crystallized cognitive ability). Although both areas are studied widely in the field of cognitive psychology, they are seldom addressed in leadership research. By including so many components, the skills model of Mumford and others becomes more general and less precise in explaining leadership performance.

Second, related to the first criticism, the skills model is weak in predictive value. It does not explain specifically how variations in social judgment skills and problem-solving skills affect performance. The model suggests that these components are related, but it does not describe with any precision just how that works. In short, the model can be faulted because it does not explain *how* skills lead to effective leadership performance.

In addition, the skills approach can be criticized for claiming *not* to be a trait model when, in fact, a major component in the model includes individual attributes, which are trait-like. Although Mumford and colleagues describe cognitive abilities, motivation, and personality variables as factors contributing to competencies, these are also factors that are typically considered to be trait variables. The point is that the individual attributes component of the skills model is trait driven, and that shifts the model away from being strictly a skills approach to leadership.

The final criticism of the skills approach is that it may not be suitably or appropriately applied to other contexts of leadership. The skills model was constructed by using a large sample of military personnel and observing their performance in the armed services. This raises an obvious question: Can the results be generalized to other populations or organizational settings? Although some research suggests that these Army findings can be generalized to other groups (Mumford, Zaccaro, Connelly, et al., 2000), more research is needed to address this criticism.

APPLICATION

Despite its appeal to theorists and academics, the skills approach has not been widely used in applied leadership settings. For example, there are no training packages designed specifically to teach people leadership skills from this approach. Although many programs have been designed to teach leadership skills from a general self-help orientation, few of these programs are based on the conceptual frameworks set forth in this chapter.

Despite the lack of formal training programs, the skills approach offers valuable information about leadership. The approach provides a way to delineate the skills of the leader, and leaders at all levels in an organization can use it.

 Skills and Business Intelligence

In addition, this approach helps us to identify our strengths and weaknesses in regard to these technical, human, and conceptual skills. By taking a skills inventory such as the one provided at the end of this chapter, people can gain further insight into their own leadership competencies. Their scores allow them to learn about areas in which they may want to seek further training to enhance their overall contributions to their organization.

From a wider perspective, the skills approach may be used in the future as a template for the design of extensive leadership development programs. This approach provides the evidence for teaching leaders the important aspects of listening, creative problem solving, conflict resolution skills, and much more.

———— CASE STUDIES ————

The following three case studies (Cases 3.1, 3.2, and 3.3) describe leadership situations that can be analyzed and evaluated from the skills perspective. The first case involves the principal investigator of a federally funded research grant. The second case takes place in a military setting and describes how a lieutenant colonel handles the downsizing of a military base. In the third case, we learn about how the owner of an Italian restaurant has created his own recipe for success.

As you read each case, try to apply the principles of the skills approach to the leaders and their situations. At the end of each case are questions that will assist you in analyzing the case.

CASE 3.1

A Strained Research Team

Dr. Adam Wood is the principal investigator on a 3-year, $1 million federally funded research grant to study health education programs for older populations, called the Elder Care Project. Unlike previous projects, in which Dr. Wood worked alone or with one or two other investigators, on this project Dr. Wood has 11 colleagues. His project team is made up of two co-investigators (with PhDs), four intervention staff (with MAs), and five general staff members (with BAs). One year into the project, it has become apparent to Dr. Wood and the team that the project is underbudgeted and has too few resources. Team members are spending 20%–30% more time on the project than has been budgeted to pay

🌐 Training Skills

them. Regardless of the resource strain, all team members are committed to the project; they believe in its goals and the importance of its outcomes. Dr. Wood is known throughout the country as the foremost scholar in this area of health education research. He is often asked to serve on national review and advisory boards. His publication record is second to none. In addition, his colleagues in the university know Dr. Wood as a very competent researcher. People come to Dr. Wood for advice on research design and methodology questions. They also come to him for questions about theoretical formulations. He has a reputation as someone who can see the big picture on research projects.

Despite his research competence, there are problems on Dr. Wood's research team. Dr. Wood worries there is a great deal of work to be done but that the members of the team are not devoting sufficient time to the Elder Care Project. He is frustrated because many of the day-to-day research tasks of the project are falling into his lap. He enters a research meeting, throws his notebook down on the table, and says, "I wish I'd never taken this project on. It's taking way too much of my time. The rest of you aren't pulling your fair share." Team members feel exasperated at Dr. Wood's comments. Although they respect his competence, they find his leadership style frustrating. His negative comments at staff meetings are having a demoralizing effect on the research team. Despite their hard work and devotion to the project, Dr. Wood seldom compliments or praises their efforts. Team members believe that they have spent more time than anticipated on the project and have received less pay or credit than expected. The project is sucking away a lot of staff energy, yet Dr. Wood does not seem to understand the pressures confronting his staff.

The research staff is starting to feel burned out, but members realize they need to keep trying because they are under time constraints from the federal government to do the work promised. The team needs to develop a pamphlet for the participants in the Elder Care Project, but the pamphlet costs are significantly more than budgeted in the grant. Dr. Wood has been very adept at finding out where they might find small pockets of money to help cover those costs.

Although team members are pleased that he is able to obtain the money, they are sure he will use this as just another example of how he was the one doing most of the work on the project.

Questions

1. Based on the skills approach, how would you assess Dr. Wood's leadership and his relationship to the members of the Elder Care Project team? Will the project be successful?

(Continued)

(Continued)

2. Does Dr. Wood have the skills necessary to be an effective leader of this research team?

3. The skills model describes three important competencies for leaders: problem-solving skills, social judgment skills, and knowledge. If you were to coach Dr. Wood using this model, what competencies would you address with him? What changes would you suggest that he make in his leadership?

CASE 3.2

A Shift for Lieutenant Colonel Adams

Lt. Col. John Adams was an aeronautical engineer in the Air Force who was recognized as an accomplished officer; he rose quickly through the ranks of lieutenant, captain, and major. In addition, he successfully completed a number of professional development courses in the Air Force and received a master's degree in engineering. In the earlier part of his service, his career assignments required overseeing 15- to 20-person shifts that were responsible for routine maintenance schedules for squadron and base aircraft. As he progressed in rank, he moved to engineering projects, which were supported by small technical staffs.

Based on his strong performance, Major Adams was promoted to lieutenant colonel earlier than his peers. Instead of moving him into another engineering position, the personnel bureau and his assignment officer decided that Lieutenant Colonel Adams would benefit from a tour in which he could expand his professional background and experience. Consequently, he was assigned to Base X as the commanding officer of the administration branch. Base X was an airbase with approximately 5,000 military and civilian personnel.

As the administration officer, Adams was the senior human resource officer and the principal adviser to the base commander on all human resource issues. Adams and his staff of 135 civilian and military personnel were responsible for personnel issues, food services, recreation, family support, and medical services. In addition, Lieutenant Colonel Adams was assigned to chair the Labor–Management Relations Committee for the base.

At the end of the Cold War, as part of the declared peace dividend, the government decided to reduce its defense budget. In February, barely 6 months after Adams took over command of the administration branch, the federal government announced a significant reduction in the size of the military and the closure of many bases. Base X was to be closed as an air base and reassigned to the Army. The closure was to take place within 1 year, and the base was to be prepared for the arrival of the first Army troops in 2 years. As part of the reduction program, the federal government initiated voluntary retirement programs for civilian and military personnel. Those wanting to retire had until April 1 to decide.

Orders for the conversion of the airbase included the following:

- The base will continue normal operations for 6 months.
- The squadrons—complete with aircrews, equipment, and families (1,000)—must be relocated to their new bases and operational by August 1.
- The remaining base personnel strength, both civilian and military, must be reduced by 30%.
- The base must continue to provide personnel for operational missions.
- The reduction of personnel must be consistent with federal voluntary early-retirement programs.
- The base must be prepared with a support structure to accept 2,000 new soldiers, expected to arrive in 2 years.

Adams was assigned to develop a human resource plan that would meet the imposed staff levels for the entire base while ensuring that the base was still able to perform the operational tasks it had been given. Faced with this daunting task, Adams conducted an extensive review of all of the relevant orders concerning the base transformation, and he familiarized himself with all of the rules concerning the early-retirement program. After a series of initial meetings with the other base branch chiefs, he laid out a plan that could be accomplished by the established deadlines. At the same time, he chaired a number of meetings with his own staff about how to meet the mandated reductions within his own branch.

After considering the target figures for the early-retirement program, it was clear that the mandated numbers could not be reached. Simply allowing everyone who had applied for early retirement to leave was not considered an option because doing so would devastate entire sections of the base. More job cuts were required, and choices had to be made as to who would stay, why, and in what areas. Adams met stiff resistance in the meetings to determine what sections would bear the brunt of the additional cutbacks.

Adams conducted his own independent analysis of his own branch before consulting with his staff. Based on his thorough examination of the data, he mandated further reductions in his sections. Specifically targeted were personnel in base housing, single-person accommodations, family services, and recreational sections. He also mandated a further 10% cut of military positions in his sections.

After meeting the mandated reduction targets, Lieutenant Colonel Adams was informed that the federal government would accept all personnel who applied for early retirement, which was an unexpected decision. When superimposed on the already mandated reductions, this move

(Continued)

(Continued)

caused critical shortages in key areas. Within weeks of implementation of the plan, the base commander was receiving mounting complaints from both civilian and military members over the implementation of the plan.

Incidents of stress, frustration, and discontent rose dramatically. Families trying to move found support services cut back or nonexistent. Members of the transition staff were forced to work evenings and weekends. Family support services were swamped and asking for additional help.

Despite spending a large amount of overtime trying to address the diverse issues both base-wide and within his branch, Adams found himself struggling to keep his head above water. To make matters worse, the base was having difficulty meeting its operational mission, and vital sections were critically understaffed. The base commander wanted answers. When pressed, Adams stated that his plan met all of the required deadlines and targets, and the plan conformed to all of the guidelines of the early retirement programs. "Maybe so," replied the base commander, "but you forgot about the bigger picture."

Questions

1. Based on the skills model, how would you assess Lt. Col. John Adams's ability to meet the challenges of the base administration position?

2. How would you assess his ability to meet the additional tasks he faced regarding the conversion of the base?

3. If you were to coach Adams on how he could improve his leadership, what would you tell him?

CASE 3.3

Andy's Recipe

Andy Garafallo owns an Italian restaurant that sits in the middle of a cornfield near a large Midwestern city. On the restaurant's far wall is an elaborate mural of the canals of Venice. A gondola hangs on the opposite wall, up by the ceiling. Along another wall is a row of real potted lemon trees. "My ancestors are from Sicily," says Andy. "In fact, I can remember seeing my grandfather take a bite out of a lemon, just like the ones hanging on those trees."

Andy is very confident about his approach to this restaurant, and he should be, because the restaurant is celebrating its 25th anniversary. "I'm darned sure of what I want to do. I'm not trying different fads to get people to come here. People come here because they know they will get great food. They also want to support someone with whom they can connect. This is my approach. Nothing more, nothing less." Although other restaurants have folded, Andy seems to have found a recipe for success.

Since opening his restaurant, Andy has had a number of managers. Currently, he has three: Kelly, Danielle, and Patrick. Kelly is a kitchen (food prep) manager who is known as very honest and dependable. She loves her work, and is efficient, good with ordering, and good with preparation. Andy really likes Kelly but is frustrated with her because she has such difficulty getting along with the salespeople, delivery people, and waitstaff.

Danielle, who works out front in the restaurant, has been with Andy the longest, 6 years. Danielle likes working at Garafallo's—she lives and breathes the place. She fully buys into Andy's approach of putting customers first. In fact, Andy says she has a knack for knowing what customers need even before they ask. Although she is very hospitable, Andy says she is lousy with numbers. She just doesn't seem to catch on to that side of the business.

Patrick, who has been with Andy for 4 years, usually works out front but can work in the kitchen as well. Although Patrick has a strong work ethic and is great with numbers, he is weak on the people side. For some reason, Patrick treats customers as if they are faceless, coming across as very unemotional. In addition, Patrick tends to approach problems with an either–or perspective. This has gotten him into trouble on more than one occasion. Andy wishes that Patrick would learn to lighten up. "He's a good manager, but he needs to recognize that some things just aren't that important," says Andy.

Andy's approach to his managers is that of a teacher and coach. He is always trying to help them improve. He sees part of his responsibility as teaching them every aspect of the restaurant business. Andy's stated goal is that he wants his managers to be "A" players when they leave his business to take on jobs elsewhere. Helping people to become the best they can be is Andy's goal for his restaurant employees.

Although Andy works 12 hours a day, he spends little time analyzing the numbers. He does not think about ways to improve his profit margin by cutting corners, raising an item price here, or cutting quality there. Andy says, "It's like this: The other night I got a call from someone who said they wanted to come in with a group and wondered if they could bring along a cake. I said 'yes' with one stipulation. . . . I get a piece! Well the people came and spent a lot of money. Then they told me that they had actually wanted to go to another restaurant but the other place would not allow them to bring in their own cake." Andy believes very strongly in his approach. "You get business by being what you should be." Compared with other restaurants, his restaurant is doing quite well. Although many places are happy to net 5%–7% profit, Andy's Italian restaurant nets 30% profit, year in and year out.

(Continued)

(Continued)

Questions

1. What accounts for Andy's success in the restaurant business?

2. From a skills perspective, how would you describe the three managers, Kelly, Danielle, and Patrick? What does each of them need to do to improve his or her skills?

3. How would you describe Andy's competencies? Does Andy's leadership suggest that one does not need all three skills in order to be effective?

LEADERSHIP INSTRUMENT

Many questionnaires assess an individual's skills for leadership. A quick search of the Internet provides a host of these questionnaires. Almost all of them are designed to be used in training and development to give people a feel for their leadership abilities. Surveys have been used for years to help people understand and improve their leadership style, but most questionnaires are not used in research because they have not been tested for reliability and validity. Nevertheless, they are useful as self-help instruments because they provide specific information to people about their leadership skills.

In this chapter, we present a comprehensive skills model that is based on many empirical studies of leaders' skills. Although the questionnaires used in these studies are highly reliable and are valid instruments, they are not suitable for our more pragmatic discussion of leadership in this text. In essence, they are too complex and involved. For example, Mumford, Zaccaro, Harding, et al. (2000) used measures that included open-ended responses and very sophisticated scoring procedures. Though critically important for validating the model, these complicated measures are less valuable as self-instruction questionnaires.

A skills inventory is provided in the next section to assist you in understanding how leadership skills are measured and what your own skills might be. Your scores on the inventory will give you a sense of your own leadership competencies. You may be strong in all three skills, or you may be stronger in some skills than in others. The questionnaire will give you a sense of your own skills profile. If you are stronger in one skill and weaker in another, this may help you determine where you want to improve in the future.

Skills Inventory

Instructions: Read each item carefully and decide whether the item describes you as a person. Indicate your response to each item by circling one of the five numbers to the right of each item.

Key: 1 = Not   2 = Seldom   3 = Occasionally   4 = Somewhat   5 = Very
           true   true   true   true   true

1. I enjoy getting into the details of how things work.	1 2 3 4 5
2. As a rule, adapting ideas to people's needs is easy for me.	1 2 3 4 5
3. I enjoy working with abstract ideas.	1 2 3 4 5
4. Technical things fascinate me.	1 2 3 4 5
5. Being able to understand others is the most important part of my work.	1 2 3 4 5
6. Seeing the big picture comes easy for me.	1 2 3 4 5
7. One of my skills is being good at making things work.	1 2 3 4 5
8. My main concern is to have a supportive communication climate.	1 2 3 4 5
9. I am intrigued by complex organizational problems.	1 2 3 4 5
10. Following directions and filling out forms comes easily for me.	1 2 3 4 5
11. Understanding the social fabric of the organization is important to me.	1 2 3 4 5
12. I would enjoy working out strategies for my organization's growth.	1 2 3 4 5
13. I am good at completing the things I've been assigned to do.	1 2 3 4 5
14. Getting all parties to work together is a challenge I enjoy.	1 2 3 4 5
15. Creating a mission statement is rewarding work.	1 2 3 4 5
16. I understand how to do the basic things required of me.	1 2 3 4 5
17. I am concerned with how my decisions affect the lives of others.	1 2 3 4 5
18. Thinking about organizational values and philosophy appeals to me.	1 2 3 4 5

Scoring

The skills inventory is designed to measure three broad types of leadership skills: technical, human, and conceptual. Score the questionnaire by doing the following. First, sum the responses on items 1, 4, 7, 10, 13, and 16. This is your technical skill score. Second, sum the responses on items 2, 5, 8, 11, 14, and 17. This is your human skill score. Third, sum the responses on items 3, 6, 9, 12, 15, and 18. This is your conceptual skill score.

Total scores: Technical skill _____ Human skill _____ Conceptual skill _____

Scoring Interpretation

23–30 High Range

14–22 Moderate Range

6–13 Low Range

The scores you received on the skills inventory provide information about your leadership skills in three areas. By comparing the differences between your scores, you can determine where you have leadership strengths and where you have leadership weaknesses. Your scores also point toward the level of management for which you might be most suited.

SUMMARY

The skills approach is a leader-centered perspective that emphasizes the competencies of leaders. It is best represented in the early work of Katz (1955) on the *three-skill approach* and the more recent work of Mumford and his colleagues (Mumford, Zaccaro, Harding, et al., 2000), who initiated the development of a comprehensive *skills model of leadership.*

In the three-skill approach, effective leadership depends on three basic personal skills: technical, human, and conceptual. Although all three skills are important for leaders, the importance of each skill varies between management levels. At lower management levels, technical and human skills are most important. For middle managers, the three different skills are equally important. At upper management levels, conceptual and human skills are most important, and technical skills become less important. Leaders are more effective when their skills match their management level.

In the 1990s, the skills model was developed to explain the capabilities (knowledge and skills) that make effective leadership possible. Far more complex than Katz's paradigm, this model delineated five components of effective leader performance: competencies, individual attributes, leadership outcomes, career experiences, and environmental influences. The leader competencies at the heart of the model are problem-solving skills, social judgment skills, and knowledge. These competencies are directly affected by the leader's individual attributes, which include the leader's general cognitive ability, crystallized cognitive ability, motivation, and personality. The leader's competencies are also affected by his or her career experiences and the environment. The model postulates that effective problem solving and performance can be explained by the leader's basic competencies and that these competencies are in turn affected by the leader's attributes, experience, and environment.

There are several strengths in conceptualizing leadership from a skills perspective. First, it is a leader-centered model that stresses the importance of the leader's abilities, and it places learned skills at the center of effective leadership performance. Second, the skills approach describes leadership in such a way that it makes it available to everyone. Skills are competencies that we all can learn to develop and improve. Third, the skills approach provides a sophisticated map that explains how effective leadership performance can be achieved. Based on the model, researchers can develop complex plans for studying the leadership process. Last, this approach provides a structure for leadership education and development programs that include creative problem solving, conflict resolution, listening, and teamwork.

In addition to the positive features, there are also some negative aspects to the skills approach. First, the breadth of the model seems to extend beyond the boundaries of leadership, including, for example, conflict management, critical thinking, motivation theory, and personality theory. Second, the skills model is weak in predictive value. It does not explain how a person's competencies lead to effective leadership performance.

Third, the skills model claims not to be a trait approach; nevertheless, individual traits such as cognitive abilities, motivation, and personality play a large role in the model. Finally, the skills model is weak in general application because it was constructed using data only from military personnel. Until the model has been tested with other populations, such as small and large organizations and businesses, its basic tenets must still be questioned.

Sharpen your skills with SAGE edge at **edge.sagepub.com/northouse7e**

REFERENCES

Bass, B. M. (1990). *Bass & Stogdill's handbook of leadership: Theory, research, and managerial application* (3rd ed.). New York: Free Press.

Connelly, M. S., Gilbert, J. A., Zaccaro, S. J., Threlfall, K. V., Marks, M. A., & Mumford, M. D. (2000). Exploring the relationship of leadership skills and knowledge to leader performance. *Leadership Quarterly, 11*(1), 65–86.

Katz, R. L. (1955). Skills of an effective administrator. *Harvard Business Review, 33*(1), 33–42.

Mumford, M. D., & Connelly, M. S. (1991). Leaders as creators: Leader performance and problem solving in ill-defined domains. *Leadership Quarterly, 2,* 289–315.

Mumford, M. D., Zaccaro, S. J., Connelly, M. S., & Marks, M. A. (2000). Leadership skills: Conclusions and future directions. *Leadership Quarterly, 11*(1), 155–170.

Mumford, M. D., Zaccaro, S. J., Harding, F. D., Jacobs, T. O., & Fleishman, E. A. (2000). Leadership skills for a changing world: Solving complex social problems. *Leadership Quarterly, 11*(1), 11–35.

Mumford, T. V., Campion, M. A., & Morgeson, F. P. (2007). The leadership skills strataplex: Leadership skill requirements across organizational levels. *Leadership Quarterly, 18,* 154–166.

Yammarino, F. J. (2000). Leadership skills: Introduction and overview. *Leadership Quarterly, 11*(1), 5–9.

Zaccaro, S. J., Gilbert, J., Thor, K. K., & Mumford, M. D. (1991). Leadership and social intelligence: Linking social perceptiveness and behavioral flexibility to leader effectiveness. *Leadership Quarterly, 2,* 317–331.

Zaccaro, S. J., Mumford, M. D., Connelly, M. S., Marks, M. A., & Gilbert, J. A. (2000). Assessment of leader problem-solving capabilities. *Leadership Quarterly, 11*(1), 37–64.

4

Behavioral Approach

DESCRIPTION

The style approach emphasizes the behavior of the leader. This distinguishes it from the trait approach (Chapter 2), which emphasizes the personality characteristics of the leader, and the skills approach (Chapter 3), which emphasizes the leader's capabilities. The behavioral approach focuses exclusively on what leaders do and how they act. In shifting the study of leadership to leader behaviors, the behavioral approach expanded the research of leadership to include the actions of leaders toward followers in various contexts.

Researchers studying the behavioral approach determined that leadership is composed of two general kinds of behaviors: *task behaviors* and *relationship behaviors*. Task behaviors facilitate goal accomplishment: They help group members to achieve their objectives. Relationship behaviors help followers feel comfortable with themselves, with each other, and with the situation in which they find themselves. The central purpose of the behavioral approach is to explain how leaders combine these two kinds of behaviors to influence followers in their efforts to reach a goal.

Many studies have been conducted to investigate the behavioral approach. Some of the first studies to be done were conducted at The Ohio State University in the late 1940s, based on the findings of Stogdill's (1948) work, which pointed to the importance of considering more than leaders' traits in leadership research. At about the same time, another group of researchers at the University of Michigan was conducting a series of studies that explored how leadership functioned in small groups. A third line of research was begun by Blake and Mouton in the early 1960s; it explored how managers used task and relationship behaviors in the organizational setting.

N What is the Behavior Approach?   Hip-Hop Leader Behaviors

Although many research studies could be categorized under the heading of the behavioral approach, the Ohio State studies, the Michigan studies, and the studies by Blake and Mouton (1964, 1978, 1985) are strongly representative of the ideas in this approach. By looking closely at each of these groups of studies, we can draw a clearer picture of the underpinnings and implications of the behavioral approach.

The Ohio State Studies

A group of researchers at Ohio State believed that the results of studying leadership as a personality trait seemed fruitless and decided to analyze how individuals *acted* when they were leading a group or an organization. This analysis was conducted by having followers complete questionnaires about their leaders. On the questionnaires, followers had to identify the number of times their leaders engaged in certain types of behaviors.

The original questionnaire used in these studies was constructed from a list of more than 1,800 items describing different aspects of leader behavior. From this long list of items, a questionnaire composed of 150 questions was formulated; it was called the Leader Behavior Description Questionnaire (LBDQ; Hemphill & Coons, 1957). The LBDQ was given to hundreds of people in educational, military, and industrial settings, and the results showed that certain clusters of behaviors were typical of leaders. Six years later, Stogdill (1963) published a shortened version of the LBDQ. The new form, which was called the LBDQ-XII, became the most widely used instrument in leadership research. A questionnaire similar to the LBDQ, which you can use to assess your own leadership behavior, appears later in this chapter.

Researchers found that followers' responses on the questionnaire clustered around two general types of leader behaviors: *initiating structure* and *consideration* (Stogdill, 1974). Initiating structure behaviors are essentially task behaviors, including such acts as organizing work, giving structure to the work context, defining role responsibilities, and scheduling work activities. Consideration behaviors are essentially relationship behaviors and include building camaraderie, respect, trust, and liking between leaders and followers.

The two types of behaviors identified by the LBDQ-XII represent the core of the behavioral approach and are central to what leaders do: Leaders provide structure for followers, and they nurture them. The Ohio State studies viewed these two behaviors as distinct and independent. They were thought of not as two points along a single continuum, but as two different

Leadership Behavior   Different Leadership Behaviors

continua. For example, a leader can be high in initiating structure and high or low in task behavior. Similarly, a leader can be low in setting structure and low or high in consideration behavior. The degree to which a leader exhibits one behavior is not related to the degree to which she or he exhibits the other behavior.

Many studies have been done to determine which leadership behavior is most effective in a particular situation. In some contexts, high consideration has been found to be most effective, but in other situations, high initiating structure is most effective. Some research has shown that being high in both behaviors is the best form of leadership. Determining how a leader optimally mixes task and relationship behaviors has been the central task for researchers from the behavioral approach. The path–goal approach, which is discussed in Chapter 6, exemplifies a leadership theory that attempts to explain how leaders should integrate consideration and structure into their behaviors.

The University of Michigan Studies

Whereas researchers at Ohio State were developing the LBDQ , researchers at the University of Michigan were also exploring leadership behavior, giving special attention to the impact of leaders' behaviors on the performance of small groups (Cartwright & Zander, 1960; Katz & Kahn, 1951; Likert, 1961, 1967).

The program of research at Michigan identified two types of leadership behaviors: *employee orientation* and *production orientation.* Employee orientation is the behavior of leaders who approach subordinates with a strong human relations emphasis. They take an interest in workers as human beings, value their individuality, and give special attention to their personal needs (Bowers & Seashore, 1966). Employee orientation is very similar to the cluster of behaviors identified as consideration in the Ohio State studies.

Production orientation consists of leadership behaviors that stress the technical and production aspects of a job. From this orientation, workers are viewed as a means for getting work accomplished (Bowers & Seashore, 1966). Production orientation parallels the initiating structure cluster found in the Ohio State studies.

Unlike the Ohio State researchers, the Michigan researchers, in their initial studies, conceptualized employee and production orientations as opposite ends of a single continuum. This suggested that leaders who were oriented toward production were less oriented toward employees, and those who were

Aesthetic Leadership Behavior Approach: An Example

employee oriented were less production oriented. As more studies were completed, however, the researchers reconceptualized the two constructs, as in the Ohio State studies, as two independent leadership orientations (Kahn, 1956). When the two behaviors are treated as independent orientations, leaders are seen as being able to be oriented toward both production and employees at the same time.

In the 1950s and 1960s, a multitude of studies were conducted by researchers from both Ohio State and the University of Michigan to determine how leaders could best combine their task and relationship behaviors to maximize the impact of these behaviors on the satisfaction and performance of followers. In essence, the researchers were looking for a universal theory of leadership that would explain leadership effectiveness in every situation. The results that emerged from this large body of literature were contradictory and unclear (Yukl, 1994). Although some of the findings pointed to the value of a leader being both highly task oriented and highly relationship oriented in all situations (Misumi, 1985), the preponderance of research in this area was inconclusive.

Blake and Mouton's Managerial (Leadership) Grid

Perhaps the best known model of managerial behavior is the Managerial Grid®, which first appeared in the early 1960s and has been refined and revised several times (Blake & McCanse, 1991; Blake & Mouton, 1964, 1978, 1985). It is a model that has been used extensively in organizational training and development. The Managerial Grid, which has been renamed the Leadership Grid®, was designed to explain how leaders help organizations to reach their purposes through two factors: *concern for production* and *concern for people*. Although these factors are described as leadership orientations in the model, they closely parallel the task and relationship leadership behaviors we have been discussing throughout this chapter.

Concern for production refers to how a leader is concerned with achieving organizational tasks. It involves a wide range of activities, including attention to policy decisions, new product development, process issues, workload, and sales volume, to name a few. Not limited to an organization's manufactured product or service, concern for production can refer to whatever the organization is seeking to accomplish (Blake & Mouton, 1964).

Concern for people refers to how a leader attends to the people in the organization who are trying to achieve its goals. This concern includes

 Likeable Leaders

building organizational commitment and trust, promoting the personal worth of followers, providing good working conditions, maintaining a fair salary structure, and promoting good social relations (Blake & Mouton, 1964).

The Leadership (Managerial) Grid joins concern for production and concern for people in a model that has two intersecting axes (Figure 4.1). The horizontal axis represents the leader's concern for results, and the vertical axis represents the leader's concern for people. Each of the axes is drawn as a 9-point scale on which a score of 1 represents *minimum concern* and 9 represents *maximum concern.* By plotting scores from each of the axes, various leadership styles can be illustrated. The Leadership Grid portrays five major leadership styles: authority–compliance (9,1), country-club management (1,9), impoverished management (1,1), middle-of-the-road management (5,5), and team management (9,9).

Authority–Compliance (9,1)

The 9,1 style of leadership places heavy emphasis on task and job requirements, and less emphasis on people, except to the extent that people are tools for getting the job done. Communicating with subordinates is not emphasized except for the purpose of giving instructions about the task. This style is result driven, and people are regarded as tools to that end. The 9,1 leader is often seen as controlling, demanding, hard driving, and overpowering.

Country-Club Management (1,9)

The 1,9 style represents a low concern for task accomplishment coupled with a high concern for interpersonal relationships. Deemphasizing production, 1,9 leaders stress the attitudes and feelings of people, making sure the personal and social needs of followers are met. They try to create a positive climate by being agreeable, eager to help, comforting, and uncontroversial.

Impoverished Management (1,1)

The 1,1 style is representative of a leader who is unconcerned with both the task and interpersonal relationships. This type of leader goes through the motions of being a leader but acts uninvolved and withdrawn. The 1,1 leader

Leadership Trust

Figure 4.1 The Leadership Grid

SOURCE: The Leadership Grid© figure, Paternalism figure, and Opportunism figure from *Leadership Dilemmas—Grid Solutions,* by Robert R. Blake and Anne Adams McCanse. (Formerly the Managerial Grid by Robert R. Blake and Jane S. Mouton.) Houston: Gulf Publishing Company (Grid figure: p. 29, Paternalism figure: p. 30, Opportunism figure: p. 31). Copyright 1991 by Scientific Methods, Inc. Reproduced by permission of the owners.

often has little contact with followers and could be described as indifferent, noncommittal, resigned, and apathetic.

Middle-of-the-Road Management (5,5)

The 5,5 style describes leaders who are compromisers, who have an intermediate concern for the task and an intermediate concern for the people who do the task. They find a balance between taking people into account and still emphasizing the work requirements. Their compromising style

 Negative Leadership

gives up some of the push for production and some of the attention to employee needs. To arrive at an equilibrium, the 5,5 leader avoids conflict and emphasizes moderate levels of production and interpersonal relationships. This type of leader often is described as one who is expedient, prefers the middle ground, soft-pedals disagreement, and swallows convictions in the interest of "progress."

Team Management (9,9)

The 9,9 style places a strong emphasis on both tasks and interpersonal relationships. It promotes a high degree of participation and teamwork in the organization and satisfies a basic need in employees to be involved and committed to their work. The following are some of the phrases that could be used to describe the 9,9 leader: *stimulates participation, acts determined, gets issues into the open, makes priorities clear, follows through, behaves open-mindedly,* and *enjoys working.*

In addition to the five major styles described in the Leadership Grid, Blake and his colleagues have identified two other behaviors that incorporate multiple aspects of the grid.

Paternalism/Maternalism

Paternalism/maternalism refers to a leader who uses both 1,9 and 9,1 styles but does not integrate the two (Figure 4.2). This is the "benevolent dictator" who acts graciously but does so for the purpose of goal accomplishment. In essence, the paternalistic/maternalistic style treats people as if they were dissociated from the task. Paternalistic/maternalistic leaders are often described as "fatherly" or "motherly" toward their followers; regard the organization as a "family"; make most of the key decisions; and reward loyalty and obedience while punishing noncompliance.

Opportunism

Opportunism refers to a leader who uses any combination of the basic five styles for the purpose of personal advancement (Figure 4.3). An opportunistic leader will adapt and shift his or her leadership behavior to gain personal advantage, putting self-interest ahead of other priorities. Both the performance and the effort of the leader are to realize personal gain. Some phrases used to describe this leadership behavior include *ruthless, cunning,*

 Charisma   Paternalistic Leadership

Figure 4.2 Paternalism/Maternalism

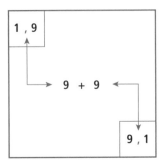

SOURCE: The Leadership Grid© figure, Paternalism figure, and Opportunism figure from *Leadership Dilemmas—Grid Solutions,* by Robert R. Blake and Anne Adams McCanse. (Formerly the Managerial Grid by Robert R. Blake and Jane S. Mouton.) Houston: Gulf Publishing Company (Grid figure: p. 29, Paternalism figure: p. 30, Opportunism figure: p. 31). Copyright 1991 by Scientific Methods, Inc. Reproduced by permission of the owners.

and *self-motivated,* while some could argue that these types of leaders are *adaptable* and *strategic.*

Blake and Mouton (1985) indicated that people usually have a dominant grid style (which they use in most situations) and a backup style. The backup style is what the leader reverts to when under pressure, when the usual way of accomplishing things does not work.

In summary, the Leadership Grid is an example of a practical model of leadership that is based on the two major leadership behaviors: task and relationship. It closely parallels the ideas and findings that emerged in the Ohio State and University of Michigan studies. It is used in consulting for organizational development throughout the world.

HOW DOES THE BEHAVIORAL APPROACH WORK?

Unlike many of the other approaches discussed in the book, the behavioral approach is not a refined theory that provides a neatly organized set of prescriptions for effective leadership behavior. Rather, the behavioral approach provides a framework for assessing leadership in a broad way, as behavior with a task and relationship dimension. The behavioral approach

Perspectives on Leadership

Figure 4.3 Opportunism

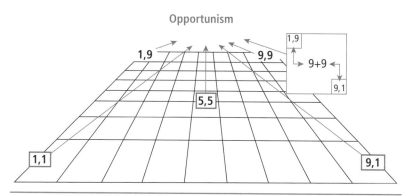

SOURCE: The Leadership Grid© figure, Paternalism figure, and Opportunism figure from *Leadership Dilemmas—Grid Solutions,* by Robert R. Blake and Anne Adams McCanse. (Formerly the Managerial Grid by Robert R. Blake and Jane S. Mouton.) Houston: Gulf Publishing Company (Grid figure: p. 29, Paternalism figure: p. 30, Opportunism figure: p. 31). Copyright 1991 by Scientific Methods, Inc. Reproduced by permission of the owners.

works not by telling leaders how to behave, but by describing the major components of their behavior.

The behavioral approach reminds leaders that their actions toward others occur on a task level and a relationship level. In some situations, leaders need to be more task oriented, whereas in others they need to be more relationship oriented. Similarly, some followers need leaders who provide a lot of direction, whereas others need leaders who can show them a great deal of nurturance and support. The behavioral approach gives the leader a way to look at his or her own behavior by subdividing it into two dimensions.

An example may help explain how the behavioral approach works. Imagine two college classrooms on the first day of class and two professors with entirely different styles. Professor Smith comes to class, introduces herself, takes attendance, goes over the syllabus, explains the first assignment, and dismisses the class. Professor Jones comes to class and, after introducing herself and handing out the syllabus, tries to help the students to get to know one another by having each of the students describe a little about themselves, their majors, and their favorite nonacademic activities. The leadership behaviors of professors Smith and Jones are quite different. The preponderance of what Professor Smith does could be labeled task behavior, and the majority of what Professor Jones does could be labeled relationship

 Personal Leadership Behaviors

behavior. The behavioral approach provides a way to inform the professors about the differences in their behaviors. Depending on the response of the students to their leadership behaviors, the professors may want to change their behavior to improve their teaching on the first day of class.

Overall, the behavioral approach offers a means of assessing in a general way the behaviors of leaders. It reminds leaders that their impact on others occurs through the tasks they perform as well as in the relationships they create.

STRENGTHS

The behavioral approach makes several positive contributions to our understanding of the leadership process. First, the behavioral approach marked a major shift in the general focus of leadership research. Before the inception of this approach, researchers treated leadership exclusively as a trait (see Chapter 2). The behavioral approach broadened the scope of leadership research to include the behaviors of leaders and what they do in various situations. No longer was the focus of leadership on the personal characteristics of leaders: It was expanded to include what leaders did and how they acted.

Second, a wide range of studies on leadership behavior validates and gives credibility to the basic tenets of the approach. First formulated and reported by researchers from The Ohio State University and the University of Michigan, and subsequently reported in the works of Blake and Mouton (1964, 1978, 1985) and Blake and McCanse (1991), the behavioral approach is substantiated by a multitude of research studies that offer a viable approach to understanding the leadership process.

Third, on a conceptual level, researchers of the behavioral approach have ascertained that a leader's style consists primarily of two major types of behaviors: task and relationship. The significance of this idea is not to be understated. Whenever leadership occurs, the leader is acting out both task and relationship behaviors; the key to being an effective leader often rests on how the leader balances these two behaviors. Together they form the core of the leadership process.

Fourth, the behavioral approach is heuristic. It provides us with a broad conceptual map that is worthwhile to use in our attempts to understand the complexities of leadership. Leaders can learn a lot about themselves and how they come across to others by trying to see their behaviors in light of the task and relationship dimensions. Based on the behavioral approach, leaders can

 Leadership Theories

assess their actions and determine how they may want to change to improve their leadership behaviors.

CRITICISMS

Along with its strengths, the behavioral approach also has several weaknesses. First, the research on the behavioral approach has not adequately shown how leaders' behaviors are associated with performance outcomes (Bryman, 1992; Yukl, 1994). Researchers have not been able to establish a consistent link between task and relationship behaviors and outcomes such as morale, job satisfaction, and productivity. According to Yukl (1994, p. 75), the "results from this massive research effort have been mostly contradictory and inconclusive." He further pointed out that the only strong finding about leadership behaviors is that leaders who are considerate have followers who are more satisfied.

Another criticism is that this approach has failed to find a universal style of leadership that could be effective in almost every situation. The overarching goal for researchers studying the behavioral approach appeared to be the identification of a universal set of leadership behaviors that would consistently result in effective outcomes. Because of inconsistencies in the research findings, this goal was never reached. Similar to the trait approach, which was unable to identify the definitive personal characteristics of leaders, the behavioral approach has been unable to identify the universal behaviors that are associated with effective leadership.

A final criticism of the behavioral approach is that it implies that the most effective leadership style is the high–high style (i.e., high task and high relationship). Although some researchers (e.g., Blake & McCanse, 1991; Misumi, 1985) suggested that high–high managers are most effective, that may not be the case in all situations. In fact, the full range of research findings provides only limited support for a universal high–high style (Yukl, 1994). Certain situations may require different leadership styles; some may be complex and require high-task behavior, and others may be simple and require supportive behavior. At this point in the development of research on the behavioral approach, it remains unclear whether the high–high style is the best style of leadership.

APPLICATION

The behavioral approach can be applied easily in ongoing leadership settings. At all levels in all types of organizations, managers are continually

 College Graduate Behaviors

 Behavioral Strategies

engaged in task and relationship behaviors. By assessing their own behaviors, managers can determine how they are coming across to others and how they could change their behaviors to be more effective. In essence, the behavioral approach provides a mirror for managers that is helpful in answering the frequently asked question, "How am I doing as a leader?"

Many leadership training and development programs throughout the country are structured along the lines of the behavioral approach. Almost all are designed similarly and include giving managers questionnaires that assess in some way their task and relationship behaviors toward followers. Participants use these assessments to improve their overall leadership behavior.

An example of a training and development program that deals exclusively with leader behaviors is Blake and Mouton's Leadership Grid (formerly Managerial Grid) seminar. Grid seminars are about increasing productivity, improving morale, and gaining employee commitment. They are offered by Grid International, an international organization development company (www.gridinternational.com). At grid seminars, self-assessments, small-group experiences, and candid critiques allow managers to learn how to define effective leadership, how to manage for optimal results, and how to identify and change ineffective leadership behaviors. The conceptual framework around which the grid seminars are structured is the behavioral approach to leadership.

In short, the behavioral approach applies to nearly everything a leader does. It is an approach that is used as a model by many training and development companies to teach managers how to improve their effectiveness and organizational productivity.

CASE STUDIES

In this section, you will find three case studies (Cases 4.1, 4.2, and 4.3) that describe the leadership behaviors of three different managers, each of whom is working in a different organizational setting. The first case is about a maintenance director in a large hospital, the second deals with a supervisor in a small sporting goods store, and the third is concerned with the director of marketing and communications at a college. At the end of each case are questions that will help you to analyze the case from the perspective of the style approach.

 Organic Leadership Behaviors

CASE 4.1

A Drill Sergeant at First

Mark Young is the head of the painting department in a large hospital; 20 union employees report to him. Before coming on board at the hospital, he had worked as an independent contractor. At the hospital, he took a position that was newly created because the hospital believed change was needed in how painting services were provided.

Upon beginning his job, Mark did a 4-month analysis of the direct and indirect costs of painting services. His findings supported the perceptions of his administrators that painting services were inefficient and costly. As a result, Mark completely reorganized the department, designed a new scheduling procedure, and redefined the expected standards of performance.

Mark says that when he started out in his new job he was "all task," like a drill sergeant who didn't seek any input from his subordinates. From Mark's point of view, the hospital environment did not leave much room for errors, so he needed to be strict about getting painters to do a good job within the constraints of the hospital environment.

As time went along, Mark relaxed his style and was less demanding. He delegated some responsibilities to two crew leaders who reported to him, but he always stayed in close touch with each of the employees. On a weekly basis, Mark was known to take small groups of workers to the local sports bar for burgers on the house. He loved to banter with the employees and could take it as well as dish it out.

Mark is very proud of his department. He says he always wanted to be a coach, and that's how he feels about running his department. He enjoys working with people; in particular, he says he likes to see the glint in their eyes when they realize that they've done a good job and they have done it on their own.

Because of Mark's leadership, the painting department has improved substantially and is now seen by workers in other departments as the most productive department in hospital maintenance. Painting services received a customer rating of 92%, which is the highest of any service in the hospital.

Questions

1. From the behavioral perspective, how would you describe Mark's leadership?

2. How did his behavior change over time?

3. In general, do you think he is more task oriented or more relationship oriented?

4. What score do you think he would get on Blake and Mouton's grid?

CASE 4.2

Eating Lunch Standing Up

Susan Parks is the part–owner and manager of Marathon Sports, an athletic equipment store that specializes in running shoes and accessories. The store employs about 10 people, most of whom are college students who work part-time during the week and full-time on weekends. Marathon Sports is the only store of its kind in a college town with a population of 125,000. The annual sales figures for the store have shown 15% growth each year.

Susan has a lot invested in the store, and she works very hard to make sure the store continues to maintain its reputation and pattern of growth. She works 50 hours a week at the store, where she wears many hats, including those of buyer, scheduler, trainer, planner, and salesperson. There is never a moment when Susan is not doing something. Rumor has it that she eats her lunch standing up.

Employees' reactions to Susan are strong and varied. Some people like her style, and others do not. Those who like her style talk about how organized and efficient the store is when she is in charge. Susan makes the tasks and goals for everyone very clear. She keeps everyone busy; when they go home at night, they feel as if they have accomplished something. They like to work for Susan because she knows what she is doing. Those who do not like her style complain that she is too driven. It seems that her sole purpose for being at the store is to get the job done. She seldom, if ever, takes a break or just hangs out with the staff. These people say Susan is pretty hard to relate to, and as a result it is not much fun working at Marathon Sports.

Susan is beginning to sense that employees have a mixed reaction to her leadership style. This bothers her, but she does not know what to do about it. In addition to her work at the store, Susan struggles hard to be a good spouse and mother of three children.

Questions

1. According to the behavioral approach, how would you describe Susan's leadership?

2. Why does her leadership behavior create such a pronounced reaction from her subordinates?

3. Do you think she should change her behavior?

4. Would she be effective if she changed?

CASE 4.3

We Are Family

Betsy Moore has been hired as the director of marketing and communications for a medium-sized college in the Midwest. With a long history of success as a marketing and public relations professional, she was the unanimous choice of the hiring committee. Betsy is excited to be working for Marianne, the vice president of college advancement, who comes from a similar background to Betsy's. In a meeting with Marianne, Betsy is told the college needs an aggressive plan to revamp and energize the school's marketing and communications efforts. Betsy and Marianne seem in perfect sync with the direction they believe is right for the college's program. Marianne also explains that she has established a departmental culture of teamwork and empowerment and that she is a strong advocate of being a mentor to her subordinates rather than a manager.

Betsy has four direct reports: two writers, Bridget and Suzanne, who are young women in their 20s; and Carol and Francine, graphic designers who are in their 50s. In her first month, Betsy puts together a meeting with her direct reports to develop a new communications plan for the college, presenting the desired goals to the team and asking for their ideas on initiatives and improvements to meet those goals. Bridget and Suzanne provide little in the way of suggested changes, with Bridget asking pointedly, "Why do we need to change anything?"

In her weekly meeting with the vice president, Betsy talks about the resistance to change she encountered from the team. Marianne nods, saying she heard some of the team members' concerns when she went to lunch with them earlier in the week. When Betsy looks surprised, Marianne gives her a knowing smile. "We are like a family here; we have close relationships outside of work. I go to lunch or the movies with Suzanne and Bridget at least once a week. But don't worry; I am only a sounding board for them, and encourage them to come to you to resolve their issues. They know you are their boss."

But they don't come to Betsy. Soon, Bridget stops coming to work at 8 a.m., showing up at 10 a.m. daily. As a result, she misses the weekly planning meetings. When Betsy approaches her about it, Bridget tells her, "It's OK with Marianne; she says as long as I am using the time to exercise and improve my health she supports it."

Betsy meets with Suzanne to implement some changes to Suzanne's pet project, the internal newsletter. Suzanne gets blustery and tearful, accusing Betsy of insulting her work. Later, Betsy watches Suzanne and Marianne leave the office together for lunch. A few hours later, Marianne

(Continued)

(Continued)

comes into Betsy's office and tells her, "Go easy on the newsletter changes. Suzanne is an insecure person, and she is feeling criticized and put down by you right now."

Betsy's relationship with the other two staff members is better. Neither seems to have the close contact with Marianne that the younger team members have. They seem enthusiastic and supportive of the new direction Betsy wants to take the program in.

As the weeks go by, Marianne begins having regular "Mentor Meetings" with Bridget and Suzanne, going to lunch with both women at least twice a week. After watching the three walk out together one day, Francine asks Betsy if it troubles her. Betsy replies, as calmly as she can, "It is part of Marianne's mentoring program."

Francine rolls her eyes and says, "Marianne's not mentoring anyone; she just wants someone to go to lunch with every day."

After 4 months on the job, Betsy goes to Marianne and outlines the challenges that the vice president's close relationships with Bridget and Suzanne have presented to the progress of the marketing and communications program. She asks her directly, "Please stop."

Marianne gives her the knowing, motherly smile again. "I see a lot of potential in Bridget and Suzanne and want to help foster that," she explains. "They are still young in their careers, and my relationship with them is important because I can provide the mentoring and guidance to develop their abilities."

"But it's creating problems between them and me," Betsy points out. "I can't manage them if they can circumvent me every time they disagree with me. We aren't getting any work done. You and I have to be on the same team."

Marianne shakes her head. "The problem is that we have very different leadership styles. I like to empower people, and you like to boss them around."

Questions

1. Marianne and Betsy do indeed have different leadership styles. What style would you ascribe to Betsy? To Marianne?

2. Does Betsy need to change her leadership style to improve the situation with Bridget and Suzanne? Does Marianne need to change her style of leadership?

3. How can Marianne and Betsy work together?

LEADERSHIP INSTRUMENT

Researchers and practitioners alike have used many different instruments to assess the behaviors of leaders. The two most commonly used measures have been the LBDQ (Stogdill, 1963) and the Leadership Grid (Blake & McCanse, 1991). Both of these measures provide information about the degree to which a leader acts task directed or people directed. The LBDQ was designed primarily for research and has been used extensively since the 1960s. The Leadership Grid was designed primarily for training and development; it continues to be used today for training managers and supervisors in the leadership process.

To assist you in developing a better understanding of how leadership behaviors are measured and what your own behavior might be, a leadership behavior questionnaire is included in this section. This questionnaire is made up of 20 items that assess two orientations: *task* and *relationship*. By scoring the Leadership Behavior Questionnaire, you can obtain a general profile of your leadership behavior.

Leadership Behavior Questionnaire

Instructions: Read each item carefully and think about how often you (or the person you are evaluating) engage in the described behavior. Indicate your response to each item by circling one of the five numbers to the right of each item.

Key: 1 = Never   2 = Seldom   3 = Occasionally   4 = Often   5 = Always

1.	Tells group members what they are supposed to do.	1	2	3	4	5
2.	Acts friendly with members of the group.	1	2	3	4	5
3.	Sets standards of performance for group members.	1	2	3	4	5
4.	Helps others in the group feel comfortable.	1	2	3	4	5
5.	Makes suggestions about how to solve problems.	1	2	3	4	5
6.	Responds favorably to suggestions made by others.	1	2	3	4	5
7.	Makes his or her perspective clear to others.	1	2	3	4	5
8.	Treats others fairly.	1	2	3	4	5
9.	Develops a plan of action for the group.	1	2	3	4	5
10.	Behaves in a predictable manner toward group members.	1	2	3	4	5
11.	Defines role responsibilities for each group member.	1	2	3	4	5
12.	Communicates actively with group members.	1	2	3	4	5
13.	Clarifies his or her own role within the group.	1	2	3	4	5
14.	Shows concern for the well-being of others.	1	2	3	4	5
15.	Provides a plan for how the work is to be done.	1	2	3	4	5
16.	Shows flexibility in making decisions.	1	2	3	4	5
17.	Provides criteria for what is expected of the group.	1	2	3	4	5
18.	Discloses thoughts and feelings to group members.	1	2	3	4	5
19.	Encourages group members to do high-quality work.	1	2	3	4	5
20.	Helps group members get along with each other.	1	2	3	4	5

Scoring

The Leadership Behavior Questionnaire is designed to measure two major types of leadership behaviors: task and relationship. Score the questionnaire by doing the following: First, sum the responses on the odd-numbered items. This is your task score. Second, sum the responses on the even-numbered items. This is your relationship score.

Total scores: Task _____ Relationship _____

Scoring Interpretation

45–50	Very high range
40–44	High range
35–39	Moderately high range
30–34	Moderately low range
25–29	Low range
10–24	Very low range

The score you receive for task refers to the degree to which you help others by defining their roles and letting them know what is expected of them. This factor describes your tendencies to be task directed toward others when you are in a leadership position. The score you receive for relationship is a measure of the degree to which you try to make subordinates feel comfortable with themselves, each other, and the group itself. It represents a measure of how people oriented you are.

Your results on the Leadership Behavior Questionnaire give you data about your task orientation and people orientation. What do your scores suggest about your leadership style? Are you more likely to lead with an emphasis on task or with an emphasis on relationship? As you interpret your responses to the Leadership Behavior Questionnaire, ask yourself if there are ways you could change your behavior to shift the emphasis you give to tasks and relationships. To gain more information about your style, you may want to have four or five of your coworkers fill out the questionnaire based on their perceptions of you as a leader. This will give you additional data to compare and contrast to your own scores about yourself.

SUMMARY

The behavioral approach is strikingly different from the trait and skills approaches to leadership because the behavioral approach focuses on what leaders do rather than who leaders are. It suggests that leaders engage in two primary types of behaviors: task behaviors and relationship behaviors. How leaders combine these two types of behaviors to influence others is the central focus of the behavioral approach.

The behavioral approach originated from three different lines of research: the Ohio State studies, the University of Michigan studies, and the work of Blake and Mouton on the Managerial Grid.

Researchers at Ohio State developed a leadership questionnaire called the Leader Behavior Description Questionnaire (LBDQ), which identified *initiation of structure* and *consideration* as the core leadership behaviors. The Michigan studies provided similar findings but called the leader behaviors *production orientation* and *employee orientation.*

Using the Ohio State and Michigan studies as a basis, much research has been carried out to find the best way for leaders to combine task and relationship behaviors. The goal has been to find a universal set of leadership behaviors capable of explaining leadership effectiveness in every situation. The results from these efforts have not been conclusive, however. Researchers have had difficulty identifying one best style of leadership.

Blake and Mouton developed a practical model for training managers that described leadership behaviors along a grid with two axes: concern for results and concern for people. How leaders combine these orientations results in five major leadership styles: authority–compliance (9,1), country-club management (1,9), impoverished management (1,1), middle-of-the-road management (5,5), and team management (9,9).

The behavioral approach has several strengths and weaknesses. On the positive side, it has broadened the scope of leadership research to include the study of the behaviors of leaders rather than only their personal traits or characteristics. Second, it is a reliable approach because it is supported by a wide range of studies. Third, the behavioral approach is valuable because it underscores the importance of the two core dimensions of leadership behavior: task and relationship. Fourth, it has heuristic value in that it provides us with a broad conceptual map that is useful in gaining an understanding of our own leadership behaviors. On the negative side, researchers have not been able to associate the behaviors of leaders (task and relationship) with outcomes such as morale, job satisfaction, and productivity. In addition, researchers from the behavioral approach have not been able to identify a universal set of leadership behaviors that would consistently result in effective leadership. Last, the behavioral approach implies but fails to support fully the idea that the most effective leadership style is a high–high style (i.e., high task and high relationship).

Overall, the behavioral approach is not a refined theory that provides a neatly organized set of prescriptions for effective leadership behavior. Rather, the behavioral approach provides a valuable framework for assessing leadership in a broad way as assessing behavior with task and relationship dimensions. Finally, the behavioral approach reminds leaders that their impact on others occurs along both dimensions.

Sharpen your skills with SAGE edge at **edge.sagepub.com/northouse7e**

REFERENCES

Blake, R. R., & McCanse, A. A. (1991). *Leadership dilemmas: Grid solutions.* Houston, TX: Gulf Publishing Company.

Blake, R. R., & Mouton, J. S. (1964). *The Managerial Grid.* Houston, TX: Gulf Publishing Company.

Blake, R. R., & Mouton, J. S. (1978). *The new Managerial Grid.* Houston, TX: Gulf Publishing Company.

Blake, R. R., & Mouton, J. S. (1985). *The Managerial Grid III.* Houston, TX: Gulf Publishing Company.

Bowers, D. G., & Seashore, S. E. (1966). Predicting organizational effectiveness with a four-factor theory of leadership. *Administrative Science Quarterly, 11,* 238–263.

Bryman, A. (1992). *Charisma and leadership in organizations.* London: SAGE.

Cartwright, D., & Zander, A. (1960). *Group dynamics research and theory.* Evanston, IL: Row, Peterson.

Hemphill, J. K., & Coons, A. E. (1957). Development of the Leader Behavior Description Questionnaire. In R. M. Stogdill & A. E. Coons (Eds.), *Leader behavior: Its description and measurement* (Research Monograph No. 88). Columbus: Ohio State University, Bureau of Business Research.

Kahn, R. L. (1956). The prediction of productivity. *Journal of Social Issues, 12,* 41–49.

Katz, D., & Kahn, R. L. (1951). Human organization and worker motivation. In L. R. Tripp (Ed.), *Industrial productivity* (pp. 146–171). Madison, WI: Industrial Relations Research Association.

Likert, R. (1961). *New patterns of management.* New York: McGraw-Hill.

Likert, R. (1967). *The human organization: Its management and value.* New York: McGraw-Hill.

Misumi, J. (1985). *The behavioral science of leadership: An interdisciplinary Japanese research program.* Ann Arbor: University of Michigan Press.

Stogdill, R. M. (1948). Personal factors associated with leadership: A survey of the literature. *Journal of Psychology, 25,* 35–71.

Stogdill, R. M. (1963). *Manual for the Leader Behavior Description Questionnaire form XII.* Columbus: Ohio State University, Bureau of Business Research.

Stogdill, R. M. (1974). *Handbook of leadership: A survey of theory and research.* New York: Free Press.

Yukl, G. (1994). *Leadership in organizations* (3rd ed.). Englewood Cliffs, NJ: Prentice Hall.

5

Situational Approach

DESCRIPTION

One of the more widely recognized approaches to leadership is the situational approach, which was developed by Hersey and Blanchard (1969a) based on Reddin's (1967) 3-D management style theory. The situational approach has been refined and revised several times since its inception (see Blanchard, Zigarmi, & Nelson, 1993; Blanchard, Zigarmi, & Zigarmi, 1985; Hersey & Blanchard, 1977, 1988), and it has been used extensively in organizational leadership training and development.

As the name of the approach implies, the situational approach focuses on leadership in situations. The premise of the theory is that different situations demand different kinds of leadership. From this perspective, to be an effective leader requires that a person adapt his or her style to the demands of different situations.

The situational approach is illustrated in the model developed by Blanchard (1985) and Blanchard et al. (1985; 2013), called the Situational Leadership® II (SLII®) model (Figure 5.1). The model is an extension and refinement of the original model developed by Hersey and Blanchard (1969a). This chapter focuses on the SLII® model.

The situational approach stresses that leadership is composed of both a directive and a supportive dimension, and that each has to be applied appropriately in a given situation. To determine what is needed in a particular situation, a leader must evaluate her or his followers and assess how competent and committed they are to perform a given goal. Based on the assumption that followers' skills and motivation vary over time, situational leadership

Situational Leadership®   Creating Compelling Vision

suggests that leaders should change the degree to which they are directive or supportive to meet the changing needs of followers.

In brief, the essence of the situational approach demands that leaders match their style to the competence and commitment of the followers. Effective leaders are those who can recognize what followers need and then adapt their own style to meet those needs.

The dynamics of this approach are clearly illustrated in the SLII® model which is comprised of two major dimensions: *leadership style* and *development level of followers.*

Leadership Styles

Leadership style consists of the behavior pattern of a person who attempts to influence others. It includes both *directive behaviors* and *supportive behaviors.* Directive behaviors help group members accomplish goals by giving directions, establishing goals and methods of evaluation, setting timelines, defining roles, and showing how the goals are to be achieved. Directive behaviors clarify, often with one-way communication, what is to be done, how it is to be done, and who is responsible for doing it. Supportive behaviors help group members feel comfortable about themselves, their coworkers, and the situation. Supportive behaviors involve two-way communication and responses that show social and emotional support to others. Examples of supportive behaviors include asking for input, solving problems, praising, sharing information about oneself, and listening. Supportive behaviors are mostly job related.

Leadership styles can be classified further into four distinct categories of directive and supportive behaviors (see Figure 5.1). The first style (S1) is a *high directive–low supportive* style, which is also called a *directing* style. In this approach, the leader focuses communication on goal achievement, and spends a smaller amount of time using supportive behaviors. Using this style, a leader gives instructions about what and how goals are to be achieved by the followers and then supervises them carefully.

The second style (S2) is called a *coaching* approach and is a *high directive– high supportive* style. In this approach, the leader focuses communication on both achieving goals and meeting followers' socioemotional needs. The coaching style requires that the leader involve himself or herself with followers by giving encouragement and soliciting follower input. However, coaching is an extension of S1 in that it still requires that the leader make the final decision on the *what* and *how* of goal accomplishment.

Ken Blanchard   Cultural Situational Leadership®

Figure 5.1 Situational Leadership® II

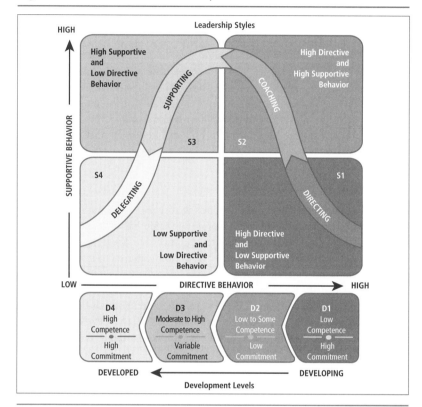

SOURCE: From *Leadership and the One Minute Manager: Increasing Effectiveness Through Situational Leadership® II,* by K. Blanchard, P. Zigarmi, and D. Zigarmi, 2013, New York: William Morrow. Used with permission. This model cannot be used without the expressed, written consent of The Ken Blanchard Companies. To learn more, visit http://www .kenblanchard.com/

Style 3 (S3) is a *supporting* approach that requires that the leader take a *high supportive–low directive* style. In this approach, the leader does not focus exclusively on goals but uses supportive behaviors that bring out followers' skills around the goal to be accomplished. The supportive style includes listening, praising, asking for input, and giving feedback. A leader using this style gives followers control of day-to-day decisions but remains available to facilitate problem solving. An S3 leader is quick to give recognition and social support to followers.

Last, S4 is called the *low supportive–low directive* style, or a *delegating* approach. In this approach, the leader offers less goal input and social support, facilitating followers' confidence and motivation in reference to the goal. The delegative

 Adjusting Behavioral Style   Task Leadership

leader lessens involvement in planning, control of details, and goal clarification. After the group agrees on what it is to do, this style lets followers take responsibility for getting the job done the way they see fit. A leader using S4 gives control to followers and refrains from intervening with unnecessary social support.

The SLII® model (see Figure 5.1) illustrates how directive and supportive leadership behaviors combine for each of the four different leadership styles. As shown by the arrows on the bottom and left side of the model, directive behaviors are high in the S1 and S2 quadrants and low in S3 and S4, whereas supportive behaviors are high in S2 and S3 and low in S1 and S4.

Development Levels

A second major part of the SLII® model concerns the development level of followers. Development level is the degree to which followers have the competence and commitment necessary to accomplish a given goal or activity (Blanchard et al., 1985). Stated another way, it indicates whether a person has mastered the skills to achieve a specific goal and whether a person has developed a positive attitude regarding the goal (Blanchard et al., 1993). Followers are at a high development level if they are interested and confident in their work and know how to achieve the goal. Followers are at a developing level if they have little skill for the goal at hand but believe that they have the motivation or confidence to get the job done.

The levels of development are illustrated in the lower portion of the diagram in Figure 5.1. The levels describe various combinations of commitment and competence for followers on a given goal. They are intended to be goal specific and are not intended to be used for the purpose of labeling followers.

On a particular goal, followers can be classified into four categories: D1, D2, D3, and D4, from developing to developed. Specifically, D1 followers are low in competence and high in commitment. They are new to a goal and do not know exactly how to do it, but they are excited about the challenge of it. D2 followers are described as having some competence but low commitment. They have started to learn a job, but they also have lost some of their initial motivation about the job. D3 represents followers who have moderate to high competence but may have variable commitment. They have essentially developed the skills for the job, but they are uncertain as to whether they can accomplish the goal by themselves. Finally, D4 followers are the highest in development, having both a high degree of competence and a high degree of commitment to getting the job done. They have the skills to do the job and the motivation to get it done.

N The Situational Approach   **in** Decisional Involvement

HOW DOES THE SITUATIONAL APPROACH WORK?

The situational approach is constructed around the idea that followers move forward and backward along the developmental continuum, which represents the relative competence and commitment of followers. For leaders to be effective, it is essential that they determine where followers are on the developmental continuum and adapt their leadership styles so they directly match their style to that development level.

In a given situation, the first task for a leader is to determine the nature of the situation. Questions such as the following must be addressed: What goal are followers being asked to achieve? How complex is the goal? Are the followers sufficiently skilled to accomplish the goal? Do they have the desire to complete the job once they start it? Answers to these questions will help leaders to identify correctly the specific developmental level at which their followers are functioning. For example, new followers who are very excited but lack understanding of job requirements would be identified as D1-level followers. Conversely, seasoned followers with proven abilities and great devotion to an organization would be identified as functioning at the D4 level.

Having identified the correct development level, the second task for the leader is to adapt his or her style to the prescribed leadership style represented in the SLII® model. There is a one-to-one relationship between the development level of followers (D1, D2, etc.) and the leader's style (S1, S2, etc.). For example, if followers are at the first level of development, D1, the leader needs to adopt a high-directive and low-supportive leadership style (S1, or directing). If followers are more advanced and at the second development level, D2, the leader needs to adopt a high directive–high supportive leadership style (S2, or coaching). For each level of development, there is a specific style of leadership that the leader should adopt.

An example of this would be Rene Martinez, who owns a house painting business. Rene specializes in restoration of old homes and over 30 years has acquired extensive knowledge of the specialized abilities required including understanding old construction, painting materials and techniques, plaster repair, carpentry, and window glazing. Rene has three employees: Ashley, who has worked for him for seven years and whom he trained from the beginning of her career; Levi, who worked for a commercial painter for four years before being hired by Rene two years ago; and Anton, who is just starting out.

Because of Ashley's years of experience and training, Rene would classify her as primarily D3. She is very competent, but still seeks Rene's insight on some

N More on the Situational Approach   Leadership Programs

tasks. She is completely comfortable prepping surfaces for painting and directing the others, but has some reluctance to taking on jobs that involve carpentry. Depending on the work he assigns Ashley, Rene moves between S3 (supporting) and S4 (delegating) leadership behaviors.

When it comes to painting, Levi is a developed follower needing little direction or support from Rene. But Levi has to be trained in many other aspects of home restoration, making him a D1 or D2 in those skills. Levi is a quick learner, and Rene finds he only needs to be shown or told how to do something once before he is able to complete it easily. In most situations, Rene uses an S2 (coaching) leadership behavior with Levi. If the goal is more complicated and requires detailed training, Rene moves back into the S1 (directing) behavior with Levi.

Anton is completely new to this field, developing his skills but at the D1 level. What he lacks in experience he more than makes up for in energy. He is always willing to jump in and do whatever he's asked to do. He is not as careful as he needs to be, however, often neglecting the proper prepping techniques and cleanup about which Rene is a stickler. Rene finds that not only he, but also Ashley, uses an S1 (directing) behavior with Anton. Because Levi is also fairly new, he finds it difficult to be directive with Anton, but likes to give him help when he seems unsure of himself, falling into the S3 (supporting) behavior.

This example illustrates how followers can move back and forth along the development continuum, requiring leaders to be flexible in their leadership behavior. Followers may move from one development level to another rather quickly over a short period (e.g., a day or a week), or more slowly on goals that proceed over much longer periods of time (e.g., a month). Leaders cannot use the same style in all contexts; rather, they need to adapt their style to followers and their unique situations. Unlike the trait and contingency approaches, which advocate a fixed style for leaders, the situational approach demands that leaders demonstrate a high degree of flexibility.

STRENGTHS

The situational approach to leadership has several strengths, particularly for practitioners. The first strength is that it has a history of usefulness in the marketplace. Situational Leadership® is well known and frequently used for training leaders within organizations. Hersey and Blanchard (1993) reported that it has been a factor in training programs of more than 400 of the Fortune 500 companies. It is perceived by corporations as offering a useful model for training people to become effective leaders.

▶ Situational Leadership® in Practice

A second strength of the approach is its practicality. Situational Leadership® is easy to understand, intuitively sensible, and easily applied in a variety of settings. Whereas some leadership approaches provide complex and sophisticated ways to assess your own leadership behavior (e.g., the decision-making approach in Vroom & Yetton, 1973), Situational Leadership® provides a straightforward approach that is easily used. Because it is described at an abstract level that is easily grasped, the ideas behind the approach are quickly acquired. In addition, the principles suggested by this approach are easy to apply across a variety of settings, including work, school, and family.

Closely akin to the strength of practicality is a third strength: it has prescriptive value. Whereas many theories of leadership are descriptive in nature, the situational approach is prescriptive. It tells you what you should and should not do in various contexts. For example, if your followers are very low in competence, Situational Leadership® prescribes a directing style for you as the leader. On the other hand, if your followers appear to be competent but lack confidence, the situational approach suggests that you lead with a supporting style. These prescriptions provide leaders with a valuable set of guidelines that can facilitate and enhance leadership.

A fourth strength of Situational Leadership® is that it emphasizes leader flexibility (Graeff, 1983; Yukl, 1989). The approach stresses that leaders need to find out about their followers' needs and then adapt their leadership style accordingly. Leaders cannot lead using a single style: They must be willing to change their style to meet the requirements of the situation. This approach recognizes that followers act differently when doing different goals, and that they may act differently during different stages of the same goal. Effective leaders are those who can change their own style based on the goal requirements and the followers' needs, even in the middle of a project.

Finally, Situational Leadership® reminds us to treat each follower differently based on the goal at hand and to seek opportunities to help followers learn new skills and become more confident in their work (Fernandez & Vecchio, 1997; Yukl, 1998). Overall, this approach underscores that followers have unique needs and deserve our help in trying to become better at doing their work.

CRITICISMS

Despite its history of use in leadership training and development, Situational Leadership® has several limitations. The following criticisms point out

 Creative Leadership   Leader Effectiveness

several weaknesses in this approach and help to provide a more balanced picture of the general utility of this approach in studying and practicing leadership.

The first criticism of Situational Leadership® is that only a few research studies have been conducted to justify the assumptions and propositions set forth by the approach. Although many doctoral dissertations address dimensions of Situational Leadership,® most of these research studies have not been published. The lack of a strong body of research on this approach raises questions about the theoretical basis of the approach (Fernandez & Vecchio, 1997; Graeff, 1997; Vecchio & Boatwright, 2002; Vecchio, Bullis, & Brazil, 2006). Can we be sure it is a valid approach? Is it certain that this approach does indeed improve performance? Does this approach compare favorably with other leadership approaches in its impact on followers? It is difficult to give firm answers to these questions when the testing of this approach has not resulted in a significant amount of published research findings.

A second criticism that can be directed at the situational approach concerns the ambiguous conceptualization in the model of followers' development levels. The authors of the model do not make clear how commitment is combined with competence to form four distinct levels of development (Graeff, 1997; Yukl, 1989). In one of the earliest versions of the model, Hersey and Blanchard (1969b) defined the four levels of commitment (maturity) as unwilling and unable (Level 1), willing and unable (Level 2), unwilling and able (Level 3), and willing and able (Level 4). In a more recent version, represented by the SLII® model, development level is described as high commitment and low competence in D1, low commitment and some competence in D2, variable commitment and high competence in D3, and high commitment and high competence in D4.

The authors of Situational Leadership® do not explain the theoretical basis for these changes in the composition of each of the development levels. Furthermore, they do not explain how competence and commitment are weighted across different development levels. As pointed out by Blanchard et al. (1993), there is a need for further research to establish how competence and commitment are conceptualized for each development level. Closely related to the general criticism of ambiguity about followers' development levels is a concern with how commitment itself is conceptualized in the model. For example, Graeff (1997) suggested the conceptualization is very unclear. Blanchard et al. (1985) stated that followers' commitment is composed of confidence and motivation, but it is not clear how confidence and motivation combine to define commitment. According to the SLII® model, commitment starts out

Situational Leadership® Theory

high in D1, moves down in D2, becomes variable in D3, and rises again in D4. Intuitively, it appears more logical to describe follower commitment as existing on a continuum moving from low to moderate to high.

The argument provided by Blanchard et al. (1993) for how commitment varies in the SLII® model is that followers usually start out motivated and eager to learn, and then they may become discouraged and disillusioned. Next, they may begin to lack confidence or motivation, or both, and last they become highly confident and motivated. But why is this so? Why do followers who learn a task become less committed? Why is there a decrease in commitment at Development Levels 2 and 3? Without research findings to substantiate the way follower commitment is conceptualized, this dimension of Situational Leadership® remains unclear.

A fourth criticism of the situational approach has to do with how the model matches leader style with follower development levels—the prescriptions of the model. To determine the validity of the prescriptions suggested by the Hersey and Blanchard approach, Vecchio (1987) conducted a study of more than 300 high school teachers and their principals. He found that newly hired teachers were more satisfied and performed better under principals who had highly structured leadership styles, but that the performance of more experienced and mature teachers was unrelated to the style their principals exhibited.

Vecchio and his colleagues have replicated this study twice: first in 1997, using university employees (Fernandez & Vecchio, 1997), and most recently in 2006, studying more than 800 U.S. Military Academy cadets (Vecchio et al., 2006). Both studies failed to find strong evidence to support the basic prescriptions suggested in the situational approach.

To further test the assumptions and validity of the Situational Leadership® model, Thompson and Vecchio (2009) analyzed the original and revised versions of the model using data collected from 357 banking employees and 80 supervisors. They found no clear empirical support for the model in any of its versions. At best, they found some evidence to support leaders being more directive with newer employees, and being more supportive and less directive as employees become more senior.

A fifth criticism of Situational Leadership® is that it fails to account for how certain demographic characteristics (e.g., education, experience, age, and gender) influence the leader–follower prescriptions of the model. For example, a study conducted by Vecchio and Boatwright (2002) showed that level of education and job experience were inversely related to directive leadership and were not related to supportive leadership. In other words, followers with more education and more work experience desired less structure. An interesting finding is that age was positively related to desire for structure: The older followers desired more structure than the younger followers did. In addition, their findings indicated that female and male followers had different preferences for styles of leadership. Female followers expressed a stronger preference for supportive leadership, whereas male followers had a stronger desire for directive leadership. These findings indicate that demographic characteristics may affect followers' preferences for a particular leadership style. However, these characteristics are not considered in the Situational Leadership® approach.

Situational Leadership® can also be criticized from a practical standpoint because it does not fully address the issue of one-to-one versus group leadership in an organizational setting. For example, should a leader with a group of 20 followers lead by matching her or his style to the overall development level of the group or to the development level of individual members of the group? Carew, Parisi-Carew, and Blanchard (1990) suggested that groups go through development stages that are similar to individuals', and that therefore leaders should try to match their styles to the group's development level. However, if the leader matches her or his style to the mean development level of a group, how will this affect the individuals whose development levels are quite different from those of their colleagues? Existing research on Situational Leadership® does not answer this question. More research is needed to explain how leaders can adapt their styles simultaneously to the development levels of individual group members and to the group as a whole.

A final criticism of Situational Leadership® can be directed at the leadership questionnaires that accompany the model. Questionnaires on the situational approach typically ask respondents to analyze various work situations and select the best leadership style for each situation. The questionnaires are constructed to force respondents to describe leadership style in terms of four specific parameters (i.e., directing, coaching, supporting, and delegating) rather than in terms of other leadership behaviors. Because the best answers available to respondents have been predetermined, the questionnaires are biased in favor of Situational Leadership® (Graeff, 1983; Yukl, 1989).

APPLICATION

As we discussed earlier in this chapter, Situational Leadership® is used in consulting because it is an approach that is easy to conceptualize and apply.

 Practice of Corporate Hiring

The straightforward nature of Situational Leadership® makes it practical for managers to use.

The principles of this approach can be applied at many different levels in an organization. They can apply to how a CEO of a large corporation works with a board of directors, and they can also apply to how a crew chief in an assembly plant leads a small group of production workers. Middle managers can use Situational Leadership® to direct staff meetings, and heads of departments can use this approach in planning structural changes within an organization. There is no shortage of opportunities for using Situational Leadership®.

Situational Leadership® applies during the initial stages of a project, when idea formation is important, and during the various subsequent phases of a project, when implementation issues are important. The fluid nature of situational Leadership® makes it ideal for applying to followers as they move forward or go backward (regress) on various projects. Because Situational Leadership® stresses adapting to followers, it is ideal for use with followers whose commitment and competence change over the course of a project.

Given the breadth of the situational approach, it is applicable in almost any type of organization, at any level, for nearly all types of goals. It is an encompassing model with a wide range of applications.

CASE STUDIES

To see how Situational Leadership® can be applied in different organizational settings, you may want to assess Cases 5.1, 5.2, and 5.3. For each of these cases, ask yourself what you would do if you found yourself in a similar situation. At the end of each case, there are questions that will help you analyze the context from the perspective of Situational Leadership®.

CASE 5.1

Marathon Runners at Different Levels

David Abruzzo is the newly elected president of the Metrocity Striders Track Club (MSTC). One of his duties is to serve as the coach for runners

(Continued)

 Emergency Situations

(Continued)

who hope to complete the New York City Marathon. Because David has run many marathons and ultramarathons successfully, he feels quite comfortable assuming the role and responsibilities of coach for the marathon runners.

The training period for runners intending to run New York is 16 weeks. During the first couple of weeks of training, David was pleased with the progress of the runners and had little difficulty in his role as coach. However, when the runners reached Week 8, the halfway mark, some things began to occur that raised questions in David's mind regarding how best to help his runners. The issues of concern seemed quite different from those that David had expected to hear from runners in a marathon-training program. All in all, the runners and their concerns could be divided into three different groups.

One group of runners, most of whom had never run a marathon, peppered the coach with all kinds of questions. They were very concerned about how to do the marathon and whether they had the ability to complete such a challenging event successfully. They asked questions about how far to run in training, what to eat, how much to drink, and what kind of shoes to wear. One runner wanted to know what to eat the night before the marathon, and another wanted to know whether it was likely that he would pass out when he crossed the finish line. For David the questions were never-ending and rather basic. He wanted to treat the runners like informed adults, but they seemed to be acting immature, and rather childish.

The second group of runners, all of whom had finished the New York City Marathon in the previous year, seemed most concerned about the effects of training on their running. For example, they wanted to know precisely how their per-week running mileage related to their possible marathon finishing time. Would running long practice runs help them through the wall at the 20-mile mark? Would taking a rest day during training actually help their overall conditioning? Basically, the runners in this group seemed to want assurances from David that they were training in the right way for New York. For David, talking to this group was easy because he enjoyed giving them encouragement and motivational pep talks.

A third group was made up of seasoned runners, most of whom had run several marathons and many of whom had finished in the top 10 of their respective age divisions. Sometimes they complained of feeling flat and acted a bit moody and down about training. Even though they had confidence in their ability to compete and finish well, they lacked an element of excitement about running in the New York event. The occasional questions they raised usually concerned such things as whether their overall training strategy was appropriate or whether their training would help them in other races besides the New York City Marathon. Because of his running experience, David liked to offer running tips to this group. However, when he did, he felt like the runners ignored and discounted his suggestions. He was concerned that they may not appreciate him or his coaching.

Questions

1. Based on the principles of the SLII® model, how would you describe the runners in Group 1? What kind of leadership do they want from David, and what kind of leadership does David seem prepared to give them?

2. How would you describe the fit between the runners in Group 2 and David's coaching style? Discuss.

3. The experienced runners in Group 3 appear to be a challenge to David. Using SLII®, explain why David appears ineffective with this group.

4. If you were helping David with his coaching, how would you describe his strengths and weaknesses? What suggestions would you make to him about how to improve?

CASE 5.2

Why Aren't They Listening?

Jim Anderson is a training specialist in the human resource department of a large pharmaceutical company. In response to a recent company-wide survey, Jim specifically designed a 6-week training program on listening and communication skills to encourage effective management in the company. Jim's goals for the seminar are twofold: for participants to learn new communication behaviors and for participants to enjoy the seminar so they will want to attend future seminars.

The first group to be offered the program was middle-level managers in research and development. This group consisted of about 25 people, nearly all of whom had advanced degrees. Most of this group had attended several in-house training programs in the past, so they had a

(Continued)

(Continued)

sense of how the seminar would be designed and run. Because the previous seminars had not always been very productive, many of the managers felt a little disillusioned about coming to the seminar. As one of the managers said, "Here we go again: a fancy in-house training program from which we will gain nothing."

Because Jim recognized that the managers were very experienced, he did not put many restrictions on attendance and participation. He used a variety of presentation methods and actively solicited involvement from the managers in the seminar. Throughout the first two sessions, he went out of his way to be friendly with the group. He gave them frequent coffee breaks during the sessions; during these breaks, he promoted socializing and networking.

During the third session, Jim became aware of some difficulties with the seminar. Rather than the full complement of 25 managers, attendance had dropped to about only 15 managers. Although the starting time was established at 8:30, attendees had been arriving as late as 10:00. During the afternoon sessions, some of the managers were leaving the sessions to return to their offices at the company.

As he approached the fourth session, Jim was apprehensive about why things had been going poorly. He had become quite uncertain about how he should approach the group. Many questions were running through his mind: Had he treated the managers in the wrong way? Had he been too easy regarding attendance at the sessions? Should he have said something about the managers skipping out in the afternoon? Were the participants taking the seminar seriously? Jim was certain that the content of the seminars was innovative and substantive, but he could not figure out what he could change to make the program more successful. He sensed that his style was not working for this group, but he didn't have a clue as to how he should change what he was doing to make the sessions better.

Questions

1. According to the SLII® model (see Figure 5.1), what style of leadership is Jim using to run the seminars?

2. At what level are the managers?

3. From a leadership perspective, what is Jim doing wrong?

4. What specific changes could Jim implement to improve the seminars?

CASE 5.3

Getting the Message Across

Ann Caldera is the program director of a college campus radio station (WCBA) that is supported by the university. WCBA has a long history and is viewed favorably by students, faculty, the board of trustees, and the people in the community.

Ann does not have a problem getting students to work at WCBA. In fact, it is one of the most sought-after university-related activities. The few students who are accepted to work at WCBA are always highly motivated because they value the opportunity to get hands-on media experience. In addition, those who are accepted tend to be highly confident (sometimes naïvely so) of their own radio ability. Despite their eagerness, most of them lack a full understanding of the legal responsibilities of being on the air.

One of the biggest problems that confronts Ann every semester is how to train new students to follow the rules and procedures of WCBA when they are doing on-air announcing for news, sports, music, and other radio programs. It seems as if every semester numerous incidents arise in which an announcer violates in no small way the Federal Communications Commission (FCC) rules for appropriate airtime communication. For example, rumor has it that one year a first-year student disc jockey on the evening shift announced that a new band was playing in town, the cover was $10, and everyone should go to hear the group. Making an announcement such as this is a clear violation of FCC rules: It is illegal.

Ann is frustrated with her predicament but cannot seem to figure out why it keeps occurring. She puts a lot of time and effort into helping new DJs, but they just do not seem to get the message that working at WCBA is a serious job and that obeying the FCC rules is an absolute necessity. Ann wonders whether her leadership style is missing the mark.

Each semester, Ann gives the students a very complete handout on policies and procedures. In addition, she tries to get to know each of the new students personally. Because she wants everybody to be happy at WCBA, she tries very hard to build a relational climate at the station. Repeatedly, students say that Ann is the nicest adviser on campus. Because she recognizes the quality of her students, Ann mostly lets them do what they want at the station.

Questions

1. What's the problem at WCBA?

(Continued)

(Continued)

2. Using SLII® as a basis, what would you advise Ann to do differently at the station?

3. Based on Situational Leadership®, what creative schemes could Ann use to reduce FCC infractions at WCBA?

LEADERSHIP INSTRUMENT

Although different versions of instruments have been developed to measure Situational Leadership®, nearly all of them are constructed similarly. As a rule, the questionnaires provide 12 to 20 work-related situations and ask respondents to select their preferred style for each situation from four alternatives. The situations and styles are written to directly represent the leadership styles of the four quadrants in the model. Questionnaire responses are scored to give respondents information about their primary and secondary leadership styles, their flexibility, and their leadership effectiveness.

The brief questionnaire provided in this section illustrates how leadership style is measured in questionnaires of Situational Leadership®. For each situation on the questionnaire, you have to identify the development level of the followers in the situation and then select one of the four response alternatives that indicate the style of leadership you would use in that situation.

Expanded versions of the brief questionnaire give respondents an overall profile of their leadership style. By analyzing the alternatives a respondent makes on the questionnaire, one can determine that respondent's primary and secondary leadership styles. By analyzing the range of choices a respondent makes, one can determine that respondent's leadership flexibility. Leadership effectiveness and diagnostic ability can be measured by analyzing the number of times the respondent made accurate assessments of a preferred leadership style.

In addition to these self-scored questionnaires, Situational Leadership® uses similar forms to tap the concurrent perceptions that bosses, associates, and followers have of a person's leadership style. These questionnaires give respondents a wide range of feedback on their leadership styles and the opportunity to compare their own views of leadership with the way others view them in a leadership role.

Situational Leadership® Questionnaire: Sample Items

Instructions: Look at the following four leadership situations and indicate what the development level is in each situation, which leadership style each response represents, and which leadership style is needed in the situation (i.e., action A, B, C, or D).

Situation 1

Because of budget restrictions imposed on your department, it is necessary to consolidate. You are thinking of asking a highly capable and experienced member of your department to take charge of the consolidation. This person has worked in all areas of your department and has the trust and respect of most of the staff. She is very willing to help with the consolidation.

A. Assign the project to her and let her determine how to accomplish it.

B. Assign the task to her, indicate to her precisely what must be done, and supervise her work closely.

C. Assign the task to her and provide support and encouragement as needed.

D. Assign the task to her and indicate to her precisely what needs to be done but make sure you incorporate her suggestions.

Development level _____ Action _____

Situation 2

You have recently been made a department head of the new regional office. In getting to know your departmental staff, you have noticed that one of your inexperienced employees is not following through on assigned tasks. She is enthusiastic about her new job and wants to get ahead in the organization.

A. Discuss the lack of follow-through with her and explore the alternative ways this problem can be solved.

B. Specify what she must do to complete the tasks but incorporate any suggestions she may have.

C. Define the steps necessary for her to complete the assigned tasks and monitor her performance frequently.

D. Let her know about the lack of follow-through and give her more time to improve her performance.

Development level _____ Action _____

Situation 3

Because of a new and very important unit project, for the past 3 months you have made sure that your staff members understood their responsibilities and expected level of performance, and you have supervised them closely. Due to some recent project setbacks, your staff members have become somewhat discouraged. Their morale has dropped, and so has their performance.

A. Continue to direct and closely supervise their performance.

B. Give the group members more time to overcome the setbacks but occasionally check their progress.

C. Continue to define group activities but involve the group members more in decision making and incorporate their ideas.

D. Participate in the group members' problem-solving activities and encourage and support their efforts to overcome the project setbacks.

Development level _____ Action _____

Situation 4

As a director of the sales department, you have asked a member of your staff to take charge of a new sales campaign. You have worked with this person on other sales campaigns, and you know he has the job knowledge and experience to be successful at new assignments. However, he seems a little unsure about his ability to do the job.

A. Assign the new sales campaign to him and let him function on his own.

B. Set goals and objectives for this new assignment but consider his suggestions and involve him in decision making.

C. Listen to his concerns but assure him he can do the job and support his efforts.

D. Tell him exactly what the new campaign involves and what you expect of him, and supervise his performance closely.

Development level _____ Action _____

SOURCE: Adapted from *Game Plan for Leadership and the One Minute Manager* (Figure 5.20, Learning Activity, p. 5), by K. Blanchard, P. Zigarmi, and D. Zigarmi, 1992, Escondido, CA: Blanchard Training and Development (phone 760-489-5005). Used with permission.

Scoring Interpretation

A short discussion of the correct answers to the brief questionnaire will help to explain the nature of Situational Leadership® questionnaires.

Situation 1 in the brief questionnaire describes a common problem faced by organizations during downsizing: the need to consolidate. In this particular situation, the leader has identified a person to direct the downsizing project who appears to be highly competent, experienced, and motivated. According to the SLII® model, this person is at Developmental Level 4, which calls for a delegative approach. Of the four response alternatives, it is the (A) response, "Assign the project to her and let her determine how to accomplish it," that best represents delegating (S4): low supportive–low directive leadership.

Situation 2 describes a problem familiar to leaders at all levels in nearly all organizations: lack of follow-through by an enthusiastic follower. In the given example, the follower falls in Developmental Level 1 because she lacks the experience to do the job even though she is highly motivated to succeed. The SLII® approach prescribes directing (S1) leadership for this type of follower. She needs to be told when and how to do her specific job. After she is given directions, her performance should be supervised closely. The correct response is (C), "Define the steps necessary to complete the assigned tasks and monitor her performance frequently."

Situation 3 describes a very different circumstance. In this situation, the followers seem to have developed some experience and an understanding of what is required of them, but they have lost some of their motivation to complete the goal. Their performance and commitment have stalled because of recent setbacks, even though the leader has been directing them closely. According to SLII®, the correct response for the leader is to shift to a more supportive coaching style (S2) of leadership. The action response that reflects coaching is (C), "Continue to define group activities but involve the group members more in decision making and incorporate their ideas."

Situation 4 describes some of the concerns that arise for a director attempting to identify the correct person to head a new sales campaign. The person identified for the position obviously has the skills necessary to do a good job with the new sales campaign, but he appears apprehensive about his own abilities. In this context, SLII® suggests that the director should use a supportive style (S3), which is consistent with leading followers who are competent but lacking a certain degree of confidence. A supportive style is represented by action response (C), "Listen to his concerns but assure him he can do the job and support his efforts."

Now select two of your own followers. Diagnose their current development level on three different goals and your style of leadership in each situation. Is there a match? If not, what specifically can you do for them as a leader to ensure that they have what they need to succeed?

SUMMARY

Situational Leadership® is a prescriptive approach to leadership that suggests how leaders can become effective in many different types of organizational settings involving a wide variety of organizational goals. This approach provides a model that suggests to leaders how they should behave based on the demands of a particular situation.

Situational Leadership® II classifies leadership into four styles: S1 is high directive–low supportive, S2 is high directive–high supportive, S3 is low directive–high supportive, and S4 is low directive–low supportive. The model describes how each of the four leadership styles applies to followers who work at different levels of development, from D1 (low in competence and high in commitment), to D2 (low to some competence and low in commitment), to D3 (moderately competent but lacking commitment), to D4 (a great deal of competence and a high degree of commitment).

Effective leadership occurs when the leader can accurately diagnose the development level of followers in a goal situation and then exhibit the prescribed leadership style that matches that situation.

Leadership is measured in this approach with questionnaires that ask respondents to assess a series of work-related situations. The questionnaires provide information about the leader's diagnostic ability, flexibility, and effectiveness. They are useful in helping leaders to learn about how they can change their leadership style to become more effective across different situations.

There are four major strengths to the situational approach. First, it is recognized by many as a standard for training leaders. Second, it is a practical approach, which is easily understood and easily applied. Third, this approach sets forth a clear set of prescriptions for how leaders should act if they want to enhance their leadership effectiveness. Fourth, Situational Leadership® recognizes and stresses that there is not one best style of leadership; instead, leaders need to be flexible and adapt their style to the requirements of the situation.

Criticisms of Situational Leadership® suggest that it also has limitations. Unlike many other leadership theories, this approach does not have a strong body of research findings to justify and support the theoretical underpinnings on which it stands. As a result, there is ambiguity regarding how the approach conceptualizes certain aspects of leadership. It is not clear in explaining how followers move from developing levels to developed levels, nor is it clear on how commitment changes over time for followers. Without the basic research findings, the validity of the basic prescriptions for matching leaders' styles to followers' development levels must be questioned. In addition, the model does not address how demographic characteristics affect followers' preferences for leadership. Finally, the model does not provide guidelines for how leaders can use this approach in group settings as opposed to one-to-one contexts.

Sharpen your skills with SAGE edge at **edge.sagepub.com/northouse7e**

REFERENCES

Blanchard, K. H. (1985). *SLII®: A situational approach to managing people.* Escondido, CA: Blanchard Training and Development.

Blanchard, K., Zigarmi, D., & Nelson, R. (1993). Situational Leadership® after 25 years: A retrospective. *Journal of Leadership Studies, 1*(1), 22–36.

Blanchard, K., Zigarmi, P., & Zigarmi, D. (2013). *Leadership and the one minute manager: Increasing effectiveness through Situational Leadership® II.* New York: William Morrow.

Blanchard, K., Zigarmi, P., & Zigarmi, D. (1992). *Game plan for leadership and the one minute manager.* Escondido, CA: Blanchard Training and Development.

Carew, P., Parisi-Carew, E., & Blanchard, K. H. (1990). *Group development and Situational Leadership II.* Escondido, CA: Blanchard Training and Development.

Fernandez, C. F., & Vecchio, R. P. (1997). Situational Leadership theory revisited: A test of an across-jobs perspective. *Leadership Quarterly, 8*(1), 67–84.

Graeff, C. L. (1983). The Situational Leadership theory: A critical view. *Academy of Management Review, 8,* 285–291.

Graeff, C. L. (1997). Evolution of Situational Leadership theory: A critical review. *Leadership Quarterly, 8*(2), 153–170.

Hersey, P., & Blanchard, K. H. (1969a). Life-cycle theory of leadership. *Training and Development Journal, 23,* 26–34.

Hersey, P., & Blanchard, K. H. (1969b). *Management of organizational behavior: Utilizing human resources.* Englewood Cliffs, NJ: Prentice Hall.

Hersey, P., & Blanchard, K. H. (1977). *Management of organizational behavior: Utilizing human resources* (3rd ed.). Englewood Cliffs, NJ: Prentice Hall.

Hersey, P., & Blanchard, K. H. (1988). *Management of organizational behavior: Utilizing human resources* (5th ed.). Englewood Cliffs, NJ: Prentice Hall.

Hersey, P., & Blanchard, K. H. (1993). *Management of organizational behavior: Utilizing human resources* (6th ed.). Englewood Cliffs, NJ: Prentice Hall.

Reddin, W. J. (1967, April). The 3-D management style theory. *Training and Development Journal,* pp. 8–17.

Thompson, G., & Vecchio, R. P. (2009). Situational Leadership theory: A test of three versions. *Leadership Quarterly, 20,* 837–848.

Vecchio, R. P. (1987). Situational Leadership theory: An examination of a prescriptive theory. *Journal of Applied Psychology, 72*(3), 444–451.

Vecchio, R. P., & Boatwright, K. J. (2002). Preferences for idealized style of supervision. *Leadership Quarterly, 13,* 327–342.

Vecchio, R. P., Bullis, R. C., & Brazil, D. M. (2006). The utility of Situational Leadership theory: A replication in a military setting. *Small Group Leadership, 37,* 407–424.

Vroom, V. H., & Yetton, P. W. (1973). *Leadership and decision-making.* Pittsburgh, PA: University of Pittsburgh Press.

Yukl, G. A. (1989). *Leadership in organizations* (2nd ed.). Englewood Cliffs, NJ: Prentice Hall.

Yukl, G. A. (1998). *Leadership in organizations* (4th ed.). Upper Saddle River, NJ: Prentice Hall.

6

Path–Goal Theory

DESCRIPTION

Path–goal theory is about how leaders motivate followers to accomplish designated goals. Drawing heavily from research on what motivates followers, path–goal theory first appeared in the leadership literature in the early 1970s in the works of Evans (1970), House (1971), House and Dessler (1974), and House and Mitchell (1974). The stated goal of this leadership theory is to enhance follower performance and follower satisfaction by focusing on follower motivation.

In contrast to the situational approach, which suggests that a leader must adapt to the development level of followers (see Chapter 5), path–goal theory emphasizes the relationship between the leader's style and the characteristics of the followers and the organizational setting. For the leader, the imperative is to use a leadership style that best meets followers' motivational needs. This is done by choosing behaviors that complement or supplement what is missing in the work setting. Leaders try to enhance followers' goal attainment by providing information or rewards in the work environment (Indvik, 1986); leaders provide followers with the elements they think followers need to reach their goals.

According to House and Mitchell (1974), leadership generates motivation when it increases the number and kinds of payoffs that followers receive from their work. Leadership also motivates when it makes the path to the goal clear and easy to travel through coaching and direction, removing obstacles and roadblocks to attaining the goal, and making the work itself more personally satisfying (Figure 6.1).

Figure 6.1 The Basic Idea Behind Path–Goal Theory

Path–Goal Leadership

- Defines goals
- Clarifies path
- Removes obstacles
- Provides support

In brief, path–goal theory is designed to explain how leaders can help followers along the path to their goals by selecting specific behaviors that are best suited to followers' needs and to the situation in which followers are working. By choosing the appropriate style, leaders increase followers' expectations for success and satisfaction.

Within path-goal theory, motivation is conceptualized from the perspective of the expectancy theory of motivation (Vroom, 1964). The underlying assumption of expectancy theory is that followers will be motivated if they think they are capable of performing their work, if they believe their efforts will result in a certain outcome, and if they believe that the payoffs for doing their work are worthwhile. The challenge for a leader using ideas from expectancy theory is to understand fully the goals of each follower and the rewards associated with the goals. Followers want to feel efficacious, like they can accomplish what they set out to do. But, they also want to know that they will be rewarded if they can accomplish their work. A leader needs to find out what is rewarding to followers about their work and then make those rewards available to them when they accomplish the requirements of their work. Expectancy theory is about the goals that followers choose and how leaders help them and reward them for meeting those goals.

Conceptually, path–goal theory is complex. It is useful to break it down into smaller units so we can better understand the complexities of this approach.

Figure 6.2 illustrates the different components of path–goal theory, including leader behaviors, follower characteristics, task characteristics, and motivation. Path–goal theory suggests that each type of leader behavior has a different kind of impact on followers' motivation. Whether a particular leader behavior is motivating to followers is contingent on the followers' characteristics and the characteristics of the task.

 Motivation is Contagious   Path-Goal Theory

Figure 6.2 Major Components of Path–Goal Theory

Leader Behaviors

Although many different leadership behaviors could have been selected to be a part of path–goal theory, this approach has so far examined *directive, supportive, participative,* and *achievement-oriented* leadership behaviors (House & Mitchell, 1974, p. 83). Path–goal theory is explicitly left open to the inclusion of other variables.

Directive Leadership

Directive leadership is similar to the "initiating structure" concept described in the Ohio State studies (Halpin & Winer, 1957) and the "telling" style described in Situational Leadership®. It characterizes a leader who gives followers instructions about their task, including what is expected of them, how it is to be done, and the timeline for when it should be completed. A directive leader sets clear standards of performance and makes the rules and regulations clear to followers.

Supportive Leadership

Supportive leadership resembles the consideration behavior construct that was identified by the Ohio State studies discussed in Chapter 4. Supportive leadership consists of being friendly and approachable as a leader and

 Hope and Leadership   Steve Jobs

includes attending to the well-being and human needs of followers. Leaders using supportive behaviors go out of their way to make work pleasant for followers. In addition, supportive leaders treat followers as equals and give them respect for their status.

Participative Leadership

Participative leadership consists of inviting followers to share in the decision making. A participative leader consults with followers, obtains their ideas and opinions, and integrates their suggestions into the decisions about how the group or organization will proceed.

Achievement-Oriented Leadership

Achievement-oriented leadership is characterized by a leader who challenges followers to perform work at the highest level possible. This leader establishes a high standard of excellence for followers and seeks continuous improvement. In addition to expecting a lot from followers, achievement-oriented leaders show a high degree of confidence that followers are capable of establishing and accomplishing challenging goals.

House and Mitchell (1974) suggested that leaders might exhibit any or all of these four styles with various followers and in different situations. Path–goal theory is not a trait approach that locks leaders into only one kind of leadership. Leaders should adapt their styles to the situation or to the motivational needs of their followers. For example, if followers need participative leadership at one point in a task and directive leadership at another, the leader can change her or his style as needed. Different situations may call for different types of leadership behavior. Furthermore, there may be instances when it is appropriate for a leader to use more than one style at the same time.

In addition to leader behaviors, Figure 6.2 illustrates two other major components of path–goal theory: follower characteristics and task characteristics. Each of these two sets of characteristics influences the way leaders' behaviors affect follower motivation. In other words, the impact of leadership is *contingent* on the characteristics of both followers and their task.

Follower Characteristics

Follower characteristics determine how a leader's behavior is interpreted by followers in a given work context. Researchers have focused on followers'

 Followers as Individuals

needs for affiliation, preferences for structure, desires for control, and *self-perceived level of task ability.* These characteristics and many others determine the degree to which followers find the behavior of a leader an immediate source of satisfaction or instrumental to some future satisfaction.

Path–goal theory predicts that followers who have strong *needs for affiliation* prefer supportive leadership because friendly and concerned leadership is a source of satisfaction. For followers who are dogmatic and authoritarian and have to work in uncertain situations, path–goal theory suggests directive leadership because that provides psychological *structure* and task clarity. Directive leadership helps these followers by clarifying the path to the goal, making it less ambiguous. The authoritarian type of follower feels more comfortable when the leader provides a greater sense of certainty in the work setting.

Followers' *desires for control* have received special attention in path–goal research through studies of a personality construct locus of control that can be subdivided into internal and external dimensions. Followers with an *internal locus of control* believe that they are in charge of the events that occur in their life, whereas those with an *external locus of control* believe that chance, fate, or outside forces determine life events. Path–goal theory suggests that for followers with an internal locus of control participative leadership is most satisfying because it allows them to feel in charge of their work and to be an integral part of decision making. For followers with an external locus of control, path–goal theory suggests that directive leadership is best because it parallels followers' feelings that outside forces control their circumstances.

Another way in which leadership affects follower motivation is the followers' *perceptions of their own abilities* to perform a specific task. As followers' perceptions of their abilities and competence goes up, the need for directive leadership goes down. In effect, directive leadership becomes redundant and perhaps excessively controlling when followers feel competent to complete their own work.

Task Characteristics

In addition to follower characteristics, task characteristics also have a major impact on the way a leader's behavior influences followers' motivation (see Figure 6.2). Task characteristics include the design of the *follower's task,* the *formal authority system* of the organization, and the *primary work group* of followers. Collectively, these characteristics in themselves can provide motivation for followers. When a situation provides a clearly structured task, strong group norms, and an established authority system, followers will find

Path-Goal Leadership   Motivating Volunteers

the paths to desired goals apparent and will not need a leader to clarify goals or coach them in how to reach these goals. Followers will feel as if they can accomplish their work and that their work is of value. Leadership in these types of contexts could be seen as unnecessary, unempathic, and excessively controlling.

In some situations, however, the *task characteristics* may call for leadership involvement. Tasks that are unclear and ambiguous call for leadership input that provides structure. In addition, highly repetitive tasks call for leadership that gives support in order to maintain followers' motivation. In work settings where the *formal authority* system is weak, leadership becomes a tool that helps followers by making the rules and work requirements clear. In contexts where the *group norms* are weak or nonsupportive, leadership assists in building cohesiveness and role responsibility.

A special focus of path–goal theory is helping followers overcome obstacles. Obstacles could be just about anything in the work setting that gets in the way of followers. Specifically, obstacles create excessive uncertainties, frustrations, or threats for followers. In these settings, path–goal theory suggests that it is the leader's responsibility to help followers by removing these obstacles or helping them around them. Helping followers around these obstacles will increase followers' expectations that they can complete the task and increase their sense of job satisfaction.

In 1996, House published a reformulated path–goal theory that extends his original work to include eight classes of leadership behaviors. Besides the four leadership behaviors discussed previously in this chapter—(a) directive, (b) supportive, (c) participative, and (d) achievement-oriented behavior—the new theory adds (e) work facilitation, (f) group-oriented decision process, (g) work-group representation and networking, and (h) value-based leadership behavior. The essence of the new theory is the same as the original: To be effective, leaders need to help followers by giving them what is missing in their environment and by helping them compensate for deficiencies in their abilities.

HOW DOES PATH–GOAL THEORY WORK? ────────

Path–goal theory is an approach to leadership that is not only theoretically complex, but also pragmatic. In theory, it provides a set of assumptions about how various leadership styles interact with characteristics of followers and the work setting to affect the motivation of followers. In practice, the theory

Motivation in Work Settings   Role-Play Exercise

provides direction about how leaders can help followers to accomplish their work in a satisfactory manner. Table 6.1 illustrates how leadership behaviors are related to follower and task characteristics in path–goal theory.

Table 6.1 Path–Goal Theory: How It Works

Leadership Behavior	Follower Characteristics	Task Characteristics
Directive Provides guidance and psychological structure	Dogmatic Authoritarian	Ambiguous Unclear rules Complex
Supportive Provides nurturance	Unsatisfied Need affiliation Need human touch	Repetitive Unchallenging Mundane
Participative Provides involvement	Autonomous Need for control Need for clarity	Ambiguous Unclear Unstructured
Achievement Oriented Provides challenges	High expectations Need to excel	Ambiguous Challenging Complex

Theoretically, the path–goal approach suggests that leaders need to choose a leadership style that best fits the needs of followers and the work they are doing. The theory predicts that a directive style of leadership is best in situations in which followers are dogmatic and authoritarian, the task demands are ambiguous, the organizational rules are unclear, and the task is complex. In these situations, directive leadership complements the work by providing guidance and psychological structure for followers (House & Mitchell, 1974, p. 90).

For tasks that are structured, unsatisfying, or frustrating, path–goal theory suggests that leaders should use a supportive style. The supportive style provides what is missing by nurturing followers when they are engaged in tasks that are repetitive and unchallenging. Supportive leadership offers a sense of human touch for followers engaged in mundane, mechanized activity.

Participative leadership is considered best when a task is ambiguous: Participation gives greater clarity to how certain paths lead to certain goals, and helps followers learn what leads to what (House & Mitchell, 1974, p. 92).

 Motivation and Rewards   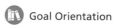 Goal Orientation

In addition, participative leadership has a positive impact when followers are autonomous and have a strong need for control because this kind of follower responds favorably to being involved in decision making and in the structuring of work.

Furthermore, path–goal theory predicts that achievement-oriented leadership is most effective in settings in which followers are required to perform ambiguous tasks. In settings such as these, leaders who challenge and set high standards for followers raise followers' confidence that they have the ability to reach their goals. In effect, achievement-oriented leadership helps followers feel that their efforts will result in effective performance. In settings where the task is more structured and less ambiguous, however, achievement-oriented leadership appears to be unrelated to followers' expectations about their work efforts.

Pragmatically, path–goal theory is straightforward. An effective leader has to attend to the needs of followers. The leader should help followers to define their goals and the paths they want to take in reaching those goals. When obstacles arise, the leader needs to help followers confront them. This may mean helping the follower around the obstacle, or it may mean removing the obstacle. The leader's job is to help followers reach their goals by directing, guiding, and coaching them along the way.

STRENGTHS

Path–goal theory has several positive features. First, path–goal theory provides a useful theoretical framework for understanding how various leadership behaviors affect followers' satisfaction and work performance. It was one of the first theories to specify four conceptually distinct varieties of leadership (e.g., directive, supportive, participative, and achievement oriented), expanding the focus of prior research, which dealt exclusively with task- and relationship-oriented behaviors (Jermier, 1996). The path–goal approach was also one of the first situational contingency theories of leadership to explain how task and follower characteristics affect the impact of leadership on follower performance. The framework provided in path–goal theory informs leaders about how to choose an appropriate leadership style based on the various demands of the task and the type of followers being asked to do the task.

A second positive feature of path–goal theory is that it attempts to integrate the motivation principles of expectancy theory into a theory of leadership.

 Motivation Theories   Dispersed Leadership

This makes path–goal theory unique because no other leadership approach deals directly with motivation in this way. Path–goal theory forces us continually to ask questions such as these about follower motivation: How can I motivate followers to feel that they have the ability to do the work? How can I help them feel that if they successfully do their work, they will be rewarded? What can I do to improve the payoffs that followers expect from their work? Path–goal theory is designed to keep these kinds of questions, which address issues of motivation, at the forefront of the leader's mind.

A third strength, and perhaps its greatest, is that path–goal theory provides a model that in certain ways is very practical. The representation of the model (see Figure 6.1) underscores and highlights the important ways leaders help followers. It shouts out for leaders to clarify the paths to the goals and remove or help followers around the obstacles to the goals. In its simplest form, the theory reminds leaders that the overarching purpose of leadership is to guide and coach followers as they move along the path to achieve a goal.

CRITICISMS

Although path–goal theory has various strengths, it also has several identifiable weaknesses. First, path–goal theory is so complex and incorporates so many different aspects of leadership that interpreting the theory can be confusing. For example, path–goal theory makes predictions about which of four different leadership styles is appropriate for tasks with different degrees of structure, for goals with different levels of clarity, for followers at different levels of ability, and for organizations with different degrees of formal authority. To say the least, it is a daunting task to incorporate all of these factors simultaneously into one's selection of a preferred leadership style. Because the scope of path–goal theory is so broad and encompasses so many different interrelated sets of assumptions, it is difficult to use this theory fully in trying to improve the leadership process in a given organizational context.

A second limitation of path–goal theory is that it has received only partial support from the many empirical research studies that have been conducted to test its validity (House & Mitchell, 1974; Indvik, 1986; Schriesheim, Castro, Zhou, & DeChurch, 2006; Schriesheim & Kerr, 1977; Schriesheim & Schriesheim, 1980; Stinson & Johnson, 1975; Wofford & Liska, 1993). For example, some research supports the prediction that leader directiveness is positively related to follower satisfaction when tasks are ambiguous, but

 Rewards

other research has failed to confirm this relationship. Furthermore, not all aspects of the theory have been given equal attention. A great deal of research has been designed to study directive and supportive leadership, but fewer studies address participative and achievement-oriented leadership. The claims of path–goal theory remain tentative because the research findings to date do not provide a full and consistent picture of the basic assumptions and corollaries of path–goal theory (Evans, 1996; Jermier, 1996; Schriesheim & Neider, 1996).

Another criticism of path–goal theory is that it fails to explain adequately the relationship between leadership behavior and follower motivation. Path–goal theory is unique in that it incorporates the tenets of expectancy theory; however, it does not go far enough in explicating how leadership is related to these tenets. The principles of expectancy theory suggest that followers will be motivated if they feel competent and trust that their efforts will get results, but path–goal theory does not describe how a leader could use various styles directly to help followers feel competent or assured of success. For example, path–goal theory does not explain how directive leadership during ambiguous tasks increases follower motivation. Similarly, it does not explain how supportive leadership during tedious work relates to follower motivation. The result is that the practitioner is left with an inadequate understanding of how her or his leadership will affect followers' expectations about their work.

A final criticism that can be made of path–goal theory concerns a practical outcome of the theory. Path–goal theory suggests that it is important for leaders to provide coaching, guidance, and direction for followers, to help followers define and clarify goals, and to help followers around obstacles as they attempt to reach their goals. In effect, this approach treats leadership as a one-way event: The leader affects the follower. The potential difficulty in this type of "helping" leadership is that followers may easily become dependent on the leader to accomplish their work. Path–goal theory places a great deal of responsibility on leaders and much less on followers. Over time, this kind of leadership could be counterproductive because it promotes dependency and fails to recognize the full abilities of followers.

APPLICATION

Path–goal theory is not an approach to leadership for which many management training programs have been developed. You will not find many seminars with titles such as "Improving Your Path–Goal Leadership" or

N How to Use Path-Goal Theory

"Assessing Your Skills in Path–Goal Leadership," either. Nevertheless, path–goal theory does offer significant insights that can be applied in ongoing settings to improve one's leadership.

Path–goal theory provides a set of general recommendations based on the characteristics of followers and tasks for how leaders should act in various situations if they want to be effective. It informs us about when to be directive, supportive, participative, or achievement oriented. For instance, the theory suggests that leaders should be directive when tasks are complex, and the leader should give support when tasks are dull. Similarly, it suggests that leaders should be participative when followers need control and that leaders should be achievement oriented when followers need to excel. In a general way, path–goal theory offers leaders a road map that gives directions about ways to improve follower satisfaction and performance.

The principles of path–goal theory can be used by leaders at all levels in the organization and for all types of tasks. To apply path–goal theory, a leader must carefully assess the followers and their tasks, and then choose an appropriate leadership style to match those characteristics. If followers are feeling insecure about doing a task, the leader needs to adopt a style that builds follower confidence. For example, in a university setting where a junior faculty member feels apprehensive about his or her teaching and research, a department chair should give supportive leadership. By giving care and support, the chair helps the junior faculty member gain a sense of confidence about his or her ability to perform the work (Bess & Goldman, 2001). If followers are uncertain whether their efforts will result in reaching their goals, the leader needs to prove to them that their efforts will be rewarded. As discussed earlier in the chapter, path–goal theory is useful because it continually reminds leaders that their central purpose is to help followers define their goals and then to help followers reach their goals in the most efficient manner.

CASE STUDIES

The following cases provide descriptions of various situations in which a leader is attempting to apply path–goal theory. Two of the cases, Cases 6.1 and 6.2, are from traditional business contexts; the third, Case 6.3, is from an academic perspective of teaching orchestra students. As you read the cases, try to apply the principles of path–goal theory to determine the degree to which you think the leaders in the cases have done a good job of using this theory.

 Empowerment

CASE 6.1

Three Shifts, Three Supervisors

Brako is a small manufacturing company that produces parts for the automobile industry. The company has several patents on parts that fit in the brake assembly of nearly all domestic and foreign cars. Each year, the company produces 3 million parts that it ships to assembly plants throughout the world. To produce the parts, Brako runs three shifts with about 40 workers on each shift.

The supervisors for the three shifts (Art, Bob, and Carol) are experienced employees, and each has been with the company for more than 20 years. The supervisors appear satisfied with their work and have reported no major difficulty in supervising employees at Brako.

Art supervises the first shift. Employees describe him as being a very hands-on type of leader. He gets very involved in the day-to-day operations of the facility. Workers joke that Art knows to the milligram the amount of raw materials the company has on hand at any given time. Art often can be found walking through the plant and reminding people of the correct procedures to follow in doing their work. Even for those working on the production line, Art always has some directions and reminders.

Workers on the first shift have few negative comments to make about Art's leadership. However, they are negative about many other aspects of their work. Most of the work on this shift is very straightforward and repetitive; as a result, it is monotonous. The rules for working on the production line or in the packaging area are all clearly spelled out and require no independent decision making on the part of workers. Workers simply need to show up and go through the motions. On lunch breaks, workers often are heard complaining about how bored they are doing the same old thing over and over. Workers do not criticize Art, but they do not think he really understands their situation.

Bob supervises the second shift. He really enjoys working at Brako and wants all the workers on the afternoon shift to enjoy their work as well. Bob is a people-oriented supervisor whom workers describe as very genuine and caring. Hardly a day goes by that Bob does not post a message about someone's birthday or someone's personal accomplishment. Bob works hard at creating camaraderie, including sponsoring a company softball team, taking people out to lunch, and having people over to his house for social events.

Despite Bob's personableness, absenteeism and turnover are highest on the second shift. The second shift is responsible for setting up the machines and equipment when changes are made from making one part to making another. In addition, the second shift is responsible for the complex computer programs that monitor the machines. Workers on the second shift take a lot of heat from others at Brako for not doing a good job.

Workers on the second shift feel pressure because it is not always easy to figure out how to do their tasks. Each setup is different and entails different procedures. Although the computer is extremely helpful when it is calibrated appropriately to the task, it can be extremely problematic when the software it uses is off the mark. Workers have complained to Bob and upper management many times about the difficulty of their jobs.

Carol supervises the third shift. Her style is different from that of the others at Brako. Carol routinely has meetings, which she labels trouble-shooting sessions, for the purpose of identifying problems workers are experiencing. Any time there is a glitch on the production line, Carol wants to know about it so she can help workers find a solution. If workers cannot do a particular job, she shows them how. For those who are uncertain of their competencies, Carol gives reassurance. Carol tries to spend time with each worker and help the workers focus on their personal goals. In addition, she stresses company goals and the rewards that are available if workers are able to make the grade.

People on the third shift like to work for Carol. They find she is good at helping them do their job. They say she has a wonderful knack for making everything fall into place. When there are problems, she addresses them. When workers feel down, she builds them up. Carol was described by one worker as an interesting mixture of part parent, part coach, and part manufacturing expert. Upper management at Brako is pleased with Carol's leadership, but they have experienced problems repeatedly when workers from Carol's shift have been rotated to other shifts at Brako.

Questions

1. Based on the principles of path–goal theory, describe why Art and Bob appear to be less effective than Carol.

2. How does the leadership of each of the three supervisors affect the motivation of their respective followers?

3. If you were consulting with Brako about leadership, what changes and recommendations would you make regarding the supervision of Art, Bob, and Carol?

CASE 6.2

Direction for Some, Support for Others

Daniel Shivitz is the manager of a small business called The Copy Center, which is located near a large university. The Copy Center employs about 18 people, most of whom work part-time while going to school full-time. The store caters to the university community by specializing in course packs, but it also provides desktop publishing and standard copying services. It has three large, state-of-the-art copy machines and several computer workstations.

There are two other national chain copy stores in the immediate vicinity of The Copy Center, yet this store does more business than both of the other stores combined. A major factor contributing to the success of this store is Daniel's leadership style.

One of the things that stand out about Daniel is the way he works with his part-time staff. Most of them are students, who have to schedule their work hours around their class schedules, and Daniel has a reputation of being really helpful with working out schedule conflicts. No conflict is too small for Daniel, who is always willing to juggle schedules to meet the needs of everyone. Students talk about how much they feel included and like the spirit at The Copy Center. It is as if Daniel makes the store like a second family for them.

Work at The Copy Center divides itself into two main areas: duplicating services and desktop publishing. In both areas, Daniel's leadership is effective.

Duplicating is a straightforward operation that entails taking a customer's originals and making copies of them. Because this job is tedious, Daniel goes out of his way to help the staff make it tolerable. He promotes a friendly work atmosphere by doing such things as letting the staff wear casual attire, letting them choose their own background music, and letting them be a bit wild on the job. Daniel spends a lot of time each day conversing informally with each employee; he also welcomes staff talking with each other. Daniel has a knack for making each worker feel significant even when the work is insignificant. He promotes camaraderie among his staff, and he is not afraid to become involved in their activities.

The desktop publishing area is more complex than duplicating. It involves creating business forms, advertising pieces, and résumés for customers. Working in desktop publishing requires skills in writing, editing, design, and layout. It is challenging work because it is not always easy to satisfy customers' needs. Most of the employees in this area are full-time workers.

Through the years, Daniel has found that employees who work best in desktop publishing are a unique type of person, very different from those who work in duplicating. They are usually quite independent, self-assured, and self-motivated. In supervising them, Daniel gives them a lot of space, is available when they need help, but otherwise leaves them alone.

Daniel likes the role of being the resource person for these employees. For example, if an employee is having difficulty on a customer's project, he willingly joins the employee in troubleshooting the problem. Similarly, if one of the staff is having problems with a software program, Daniel is quick to offer his technical expertise. Because the employees in desktop publishing are self-directed, Daniel spends far less time with them than with those who work in duplicating.

Overall, Daniel feels successful with his leadership at The Copy Center. Profits for the store continue to grow each year, and its reputation for high-quality service is widespread.

Questions

1. According to path–goal theory, why is Daniel an effective leader?
2. How does his leadership style affect the motivation of employees at The Copy Center?
3. How do characteristics of the task and the followers influence Daniel's leadership?
4. One of the principles of path–goal theory is to make the end goal valuable to workers. What could Daniel do to improve follower motivation in this area?

CASE 6.3

Playing in the Orchestra

Martina Bates is the newly hired orchestra teacher at Middletown School District in rural Sparta, Kansas. After graduating from the Juilliard School of Music, Martina had intended to play violin professionally, but when no jobs became available, she accepted an offer to teach orchestra in her hometown, believing it would be a good place to hone her skills until a professional position became available.

(Continued)

(Continued)

Being the orchestra instructor at Middletown is challenging because it involves teaching music classes, directing the high school orchestra, and directing both the middle school and grade school orchestra programs. When classes started, Martina hit the ground running and found she liked teaching, exhilarated by her work with students. After her first year, however, she is having misgivings about her decision to teach. Most of all, she is feeling troubled by how different students are in each of the three programs, and how her leadership does not seem to be effective with all the students.

Running the elementary orchestra program is demanding, but fun. A lot of parents want their children to play an instrument, so the turnout for orchestra is really strong, and it is the largest of the three Middletown programs. Many students have never held an instrument before, so teaching them is quite a challenge. Learning to make the cornet sound like a cornet or moving the bow of a cello so it sounds like a cello is a huge undertaking. Whether it is drums, bass viol, clarinet, or saxophone, Martina patiently shows the kids how to play and consistently compliments them every small step of the way. First and foremost, she wants each child to feel like he or she can "do it." She instructs her students with great detail about how to hold the instruments, position their tongues, and read notes. They respond well to Martina's kindness and forbearance, and the parents are thrilled. The orchestra's spring concert had many wild sounds but was also wildly successful, with excited children and happy parents.

The middle school orchestra is somewhat smaller in size and presents different challenges for Martina. The students in this orchestra are starting to sound good on their instruments and are willing to play together as a group, but some of them are becoming disinterested and want to quit. Martina uses a different style of leadership with the middle schoolers, stressing practice and challenging students to improve their skills. At this level, students are placed in "chairs" for each instrument. The best players sit in the first chair, the next best are second chair, and so on down to the last chair. Each week, the students engage in "challenges" for the chairs. If students practice hard and improve, they can advance to a higher chair; students who don't practice can slip down to a lower chair. Martina puts up charts to track students' practice hours, and when they reach established goals, they can choose a reward from "the grab bag of goodies," which has candy, trinkets, and gift cards. Never knowing what their prize will be motivates the students, especially as they all want to get the gift cards. Although some kids avoid practice because they find it tedious and boring, many enjoy it because it improves their performance, to say nothing about the chance to get a prize. The spring concert for this group is Martina's favorite, because the sounds are better and the students are interested in playing well.

Middletown's high school orchestra is actually very small, which is surprising to Martina. Why does she have nearly a hundred kids in the elementary orchestra and less than half that number in the high school program? She likes teaching the high school students, but they do not seem too excited about playing. Because she is highly trained herself, Martina likes to show students advanced techniques and give them challenging music to play. She spends hours listening to each student play, providing individualized feedback that, unfortunately in many cases, doesn't seem to have any impact on the students. For example, Chris Trotter, who plays third-chair trumpet, is considering dropping orchestra to go out for cross-country. Similarly, Lisa Weiss, who is first-chair flute, seems bored and may quit the orchestra to get a part-time job. Martina is frustrated and baffled; why would these students want to quit? They are pretty good musicians, and most of them are willing to practice. The students have such wonderful potential but don't seem to want to use it. Students profess to liking Martina, but many of them just don't seem to want to be in the orchestra.

Questions

1. Path–goal leadership is about how leaders can help followers reach their goals. Generally, what are the goals for the students in each of the different orchestras? What obstacles do they face? In what way does Martina help them address obstacles and reach their goals?

2. Based on the principles of expectancy theory described in the chapter, why is Martina effective with the elementary and middle school orchestras? Why do both of these groups seem motivated to play for her? In what ways did she change her leadership style for the middle schoolers?

3. Martina's competencies as a musician do not seem to help her with the students who are becoming disinterested in orchestra. Why? Using ideas from expectancy theory, what would you advise her to do to improve her leadership with the high school orchestra?

4. Achievement-oriented leadership is one of the four major kinds of path–goal leadership. For which of the three orchestras do you think this style would be most effective? Discuss.

LEADERSHIP INSTRUMENT

Because the path–goal theory was developed as a complex set of theoretical assumptions to direct researchers in developing new leadership theory, it has used many different instruments to measure the leadership process. The Path–Goal Leadership Questionnaire has been useful in measuring and learning about important aspects of path–goal leadership (Indvik, 1985, 1988). This questionnaire provides information for respondents about four different leadership styles: directive, supportive, participative, and achievement oriented. Respondents' scores on each of the different styles provide them with information on their strong and weak styles and the relative importance they place on each of the styles.

To understand the path–goal questionnaire better, it may be useful to analyze a hypothetical set of scores. For example, hypothesize that your scores on the questionnaire were 29 for directive, which is high; 22 for supportive, which is low; 21 for participative, which is average; and 25 for achievement, which is high. These scores suggest that you are a leader who is typically more directive and achievement oriented than most other leaders, less supportive than other leaders, and quite similar to other leaders in the degree to which you act participatively.

According to the principles of path–goal theory, if your scores matched these hypothetical scores, you would be effective in situations where the tasks and procedures are unclear and your followers have a need for certainty. You would be less effective in work settings that are structured and unchallenging. In addition, you would be moderately effective in ambiguous situations with followers who want control. Last, you would do very well in uncertain situations where you could set high standards, challenge followers to meet these standards, and help them feel confident in their abilities.

In addition to the Path–Goal Leadership Questionnaire, leadership researchers have commonly used multiple instruments to study path–goal theory, including measures of task structure, locus of control, follower expectancies, and follower satisfaction. Although the primary use of these instruments has been for theory building, many of the instruments offer valuable information related to practical leadership issues.

Path–Goal Leadership Questionnaire

Instructions: This questionnaire contains questions about different styles of path–goal leadership. Indicate how often each statement is true of your own behavior.

Key: 1 = Never   2 = Hardly ever   3 = Seldom   4 = Occasionally   5 = Often
        6 = Usually   7 = Always

1. I let followers know what is expected of them.   1 2 3 4 5 6 7
2. I maintain a friendly working relationship   1 2 3 4 5 6 7
    with followers.
3. I consult with followers when facing a problem. 1 2 3 4 5 6 7
4. I listen receptively to followers' ideas and   1 2 3 4 5 6 7
    suggestions.
5. I inform followers about what needs to be   1 2 3 4 5 6 7
    done and how it needs to be done.
6. I let followers know that I expect them to per-   1 2 3 4 5 6 7
    form at their highest level.
7. I act without consulting my followers.   1 2 3 4 5 6 7
8. I do little things to make it pleasant to be a   1 2 3 4 5 6 7
    member of the group.
9. I ask followers to follow standard rules and   1 2 3 4 5 6 7
    regulations.
10. I set goals for followers' performance that are   1 2 3 4 5 6 7
    quite challenging.
11. I say things that hurt followers' personal feel-   1 2 3 4 5 6 7
    ings.
12. I ask for suggestions from followers concern-   1 2 3 4 5 6 7
    ing how to carry out assignments.
13. I encourage continual improvement in follow-   1 2 3 4 5 6 7
    ers' performance.
14. I explain the level of performance that is   1 2 3 4 5 6 7
    expected of followers.
15. I help followers overcome problems that stop   1 2 3 4 5 6 7
    them from carrying out their tasks.
16. I show that I have doubts about followers'   1 2 3 4 5 6 7
    ability to meet most objectives.
17. I ask followers for suggestions on what assign-   1 2 3 4 5 6 7
    ments should be made.
18. I give vague explanations of what is expected   1 2 3 4 5 6 7
    of followers on the job.
19. I consistently set challenging goals for follow-   1 2 3 4 5 6 7
    ers to attain.
20. I behave in a manner that is thoughtful of fol-   1 2 3 4 5 6 7
    lowers' personal needs.

Scoring

1. Reverse the scores for Items 7, 11, 16, and 18.

2. Directive style: Sum of scores on Items 1, 5, 9, 14, and 18.

3. Supportive style: Sum of scores on Items 2, 8, 11, 15, and 20.

4. Participative style: Sum of scores on Items 3, 4, 7, 12, and 17.

5. Achievement-oriented style: Sum of scores on Items 6, 10, 13, 16, and 19.

Scoring Interpretation

- Directive style: A common score is 23, scores above 28 are considered high, and scores below 18 are considered low.
- Supportive style: A common score is 28, scores above 33 are considered high, and scores below 23 are considered low.
- Participative style: A common score is 21, scores above 26 are considered high, and scores below 16 are considered low.
- Achievement-oriented style: A common score is 19, scores above 24 are considered high, and scores below 14 are considered low.

The scores you received on the Path–Goal Leadership Questionnaire provide information about which styles of leadership you use most often and which you use less often. In addition, you can use these scores to assess your use of each style relative to your use of the other styles.

SOURCES: Adapted from *A Path–Goal Theory Investigation of Superior–Subordinate Relationships,* by J. Indvik, unpublished doctoral dissertation, University of Wisconsin–Madison, 1985; and Indvik (1988). Based on the work of House and Dessler (1974) and House (1977) cited in Fulk and Wendler (1982). Used by permission.

SUMMARY

Path–goal theory was developed to explain how leaders motivate followers to be productive and satisfied with their work. It is a contingency approach to leadership because effectiveness depends on the fit between the leader's behavior and the characteristics of followers and the task.

The basic principles of path–goal theory are derived from expectancy theory, which suggests that followers will be motivated if they feel competent, if they think their efforts will be rewarded, and if they find the payoff for their work valuable. A leader can help followers by selecting a style of leadership (directive, supportive, participative, or achievement oriented) that provides what is missing for followers in a particular work setting. In simple terms, it is the leader's responsibility to help followers reach their goals by directing, guiding, and coaching them along the way.

Path–goal theory offers a large set of predictions for how a leader's style interacts with followers' needs and the nature of the task. Among other things, it predicts that directive leadership is effective with ambiguous tasks, that supportive leadership is effective for repetitive tasks, that participative leadership is effective when tasks are unclear and followers are autonomous, and that achievement-oriented leadership is effective for challenging tasks.

Path–goal theory has three major strengths. First, it provides a theoretical framework that is useful for understanding how directive, supportive, participative, and achievement-oriented styles of leadership affect the productivity and satisfaction of followers. Second, path–goal theory is unique in that it integrates the motivation principles of expectancy theory into a theory of leadership. Third, it provides a practical model that underscores the important ways in which leaders help followers.

On the negative side, four criticisms can be leveled at path–goal theory. First, the scope of path–goal theory encompasses so many interrelated sets of assumptions that it is hard to use this theory in a given organizational setting. Second, research findings to date do not support a full and consistent picture of the claims of the theory. Furthermore, path–goal theory does not show in a clear way how leader behaviors directly affect follower motivation levels. Last, path–goal theory is very leader oriented and fails to recognize the interactional nature of leadership. It does not promote follower involvement in the leadership process.

Sharpen your skills with SAGE edge at **edge.sagepub.com/northouse7e**

REFERENCES

Bess, J. L., & Goldman, P. (2001). Leadership ambiguity in universities and K–12 schools and the limits of contemporary leadership theory. *Leadership Quarterly, 12*, 419–450.

Evans, M. G. (1970). The effects of supervisory behavior on the path–goal relationship. *Organizational Behavior and Human Performance, 5*, 277–298.

Evans, M. G. (1996). R. J. House's "A path–goal theory of leader effectiveness." *Leadership Quarterly, 7*(3), 305–309.

Fulk, J., & Wendler, E. R. (1982). Dimensionality of leader–subordinate interactions: A path–goal investigation. *Organizational Behavior and Human Performance, 30*, 241–264.

Halpin, A. W., & Winer, B. J. (1957). A factorial study of the leader behavior descriptions. In R. M. Stogdill & A. E. Coons (Eds.), *Leader behavior: Its description and measurement.* Columbus: Ohio State University, Bureau of Business Research.

House, R. J. (1971). A path–goal theory of leader effectiveness. *Administrative Science Quarterly, 16*, 321–328.

House, R. J. (1977). A 1976 theory of charismatic leadership. In J. G. Hunt & L. L. Larson (Eds.), *Leadership: The cutting edge* (pp. 189–207). Carbondale: Southern Illinois University Press.

House, R. J. (1996). Path–goal theory of leadership: Lessons, legacy, and a reformulated theory. *Leadership Quarterly, 7*(3), 323–352.

House, R. J., & Dessler, G. (1974). The path–goal theory of leadership: Some post hoc and a priori tests. In J. Hunt & L. Larson (Eds.), *Contingency approaches in leadership* (pp. 29–55). Carbondale: Southern Illinois University Press.

House, R. J., & Mitchell, R. R. (1974). Path–goal theory of leadership. *Journal of Contemporary Business, 3*, 81–97.

Indvik, J. (1985). *A path–goal theory investigation of superior–subordinate relationships.* Unpublished doctoral dissertation, University of Wisconsin–Madison.

Indvik, J. (1986). Path–goal theory of leadership: A meta-analysis. In *Proceedings of the Academy of Management Meeting* (pp. 189–192). Briarcliff Manor, NY: Academy of Management.

Indvik, J. (1988). *A more complete testing of path–goal theory.* Paper presented at the Academy of Management, Anaheim, CA.

Jermier, J. M. (1996). The path–goal theory of leadership: A subtextual analysis. *Leadership Quarterly, 7*(3), 311–316.

Schriesheim, C. A., Castro, S. L., Zhou, X., & DeChurch, L. A. (2006). An investigation of path-goal and transformational leadership theory predictions at the individual level of analysis. *Leadership Quarterly, 17*, 21–38.

Schriesheim, C. A., & Kerr, S. (1977). Theories and measures of leadership: A critical appraisal. In J. G. Hunt & L. L. Larson (Eds.), *Leadership: The cutting edge* (pp. 9–45). Carbondale: Southern Illinois University Press.

Schriesheim, C. A., & Neider, L. L. (1996). Path–goal leadership theory: The long and winding road. *Leadership Quarterly, 7*(3), 317–321.

Schriesheim, J. R., & Schriesheim, C. A. (1980). A test of the path–goal theory of leadership and some suggested directions for future research. *Personnel Psychology, 33*, 349–370.

Stinson, J. E., & Johnson, R. W. (1975). The path–goal theory of leadership: A partial test and suggested refinement. *Academy of Management Journal, 18*, 242–252.

Vroom, V. H. (1964). *Work and motivation.* New York: McGraw Hill.

Wofford, J. C., & Liska, L. Z. (1993). Path–goal theories of leadership: A meta-analysis. *Journal of Management, 19*(4), 857–876.

7

Leader–Member Exchange Theory

DESCRIPTION

Most of the leadership theories discussed thus far in this book have emphasized leadership from the point of view of the leader (e.g., trait approach, skills approach, and style approach) or the follower and the context (e.g., Situational Leadership® and path–goal theory). Leader–member exchange (LMX) theory takes still another approach and conceptualizes leadership as a process that is centered on the *interactions* between leaders and followers. As Figure 7.1 illustrates, LMX theory makes the *dyadic relationship* between leaders and followers the focal point of the leadership process.

Before LMX theory, researchers treated leadership as something leaders did toward all of their followers. This assumption implied that leaders treated followers in a collective way, as a group, using an average leadership style. LMX theory challenged this assumption and directed researchers' attention to the differences that might exist between the leader and each of the leader's followers.

Early Studies

In the first studies of exchange theory, which was then called vertical dyad linkage (VDL) theory, researchers focused on the nature of the *vertical linkages* leaders formed with each of their followers (Figure 7.2). A leader's relationship to the work unit as a whole was viewed as a series of vertical dyads (Figure 7.3).

Figure 7.1   Dimensions of Leadership

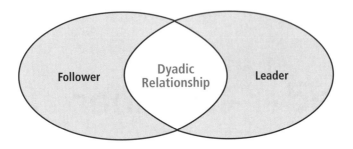

NOTE: LMX theory was first described 28 years ago in the works of Dansereau, Graen, and Haga (1975), Graen (1976), and Graen and Cashman (1975). Since it first appeared, it has undergone several revisions, and it continues to be of interest to researchers who study the leadership process.

In assessing the characteristics of these vertical dyads, researchers found two general types of linkages (or relationships): those that were based on expanded and negotiated role responsibilities (extra-roles), which were called the *in-group*, and those that were based on the formal employment contract (defined roles), which were called the *out-group* (Figure 7.4).

Within an organizational work unit, followers become a part of the in-group or the out-group based on how well they work with the leader and how well the leader works with them. Personality and other personal characteristics are related to this process (Dansereau, Graen, & Haga, 1975). In addition, membership in one group or the other is based on how followers involve themselves in expanding their role responsibilities with the leader (Graen, 1976). Followers who are interested in negotiating with the leader what they are willing to do for the group can become a part of the in-group. These negotiations involve exchanges in which followers do certain activities that go beyond their formal job descriptions, and the leader, in turn, does more for these followers. If followers are not interested in taking on new and different job responsibilities, they become a part of the out-group.

Followers in the in-group receive more information, influence, confidence, and concern from their leaders than do out-group followers (Dansereau et al., 1975). In addition, they are more dependable, more highly involved,

 In and Out Functions   Out-Group Members

and more communicative than out-group followers (Dansereau et al., 1975). Whereas in-group members do extra things for the leader and the leader does the same for them, followers in the out-group are less compatible with the leader and usually just come to work, do their job, and go home.

Figure 7.2   The Vertical Dyad

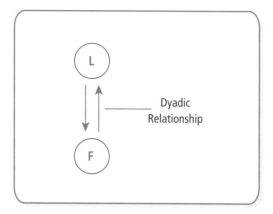

NOTE: The leader (L) forms an individualized working relationship with each of his or her followers (F). The exchanges (both content and process) between the leader and follower define their dyadic relationship.

Figure 7.3   Vertical Dyads

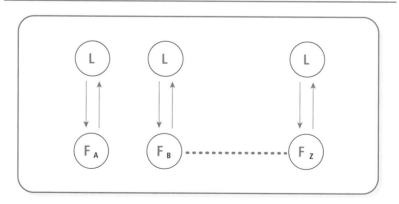

NOTE: The leader (L) forms special relationships with all of his or her followers (F). Each of these relationships is special and has its own unique characteristics.

 What is LMX About?   In-Groups and Out-Groups

Figure 7.4   In-Groups and Out-Groups

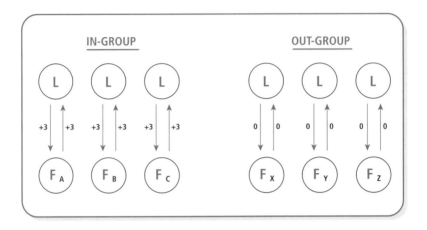

NOTE: A leader (L) and his or her followers (F) form unique relationships. Relationships within the in-group are marked by mutual trust, respect, liking, and reciprocal influence. Relationships within the out-group are marked by formal communication based on job descriptions. Plus 3 is a high-quality relationship, and zero is a stranger.

Later Studies

After the first set of studies, there was a shift in the focus of LMX theory. Whereas the initial studies of this theory addressed primarily the nature of the differences between in-groups and out-groups, a subsequent line of research addressed how LMX theory was related to organizational effectiveness.

Specifically, these studies focus on how the quality of leader–member exchanges was related to positive outcomes for leaders, followers, groups, and the organization in general (Graen & Uhl-Bien, 1995).

Researchers found that high-quality leader–member exchanges produced less employee turnover, more positive performance evaluations, higher frequency of promotions, greater organizational commitment, more desirable work assignments, better job attitudes, more attention and support from the leader, greater participation, and faster career progress over 25 years (Graen & Uhl-Bien, 1995; Liden, Wayne, & Stilwell, 1993).

In a meta-analysis of 164 LMX studies, Gerstner and Day (1997) found that LMX was consistently related to member job performance, satisfaction (overall and supervisory), commitment, role conflict and clarity, and turnover

📖 Examining Outcomes with LMX

intentions. In addition, they found strong support in these studies for the psychometric properties of the LMX 7 Questionnaire. For purposes of research, they highlighted the importance of measuring LMX from the perspective of both the leader and the follower.

Based on a review of 130 studies of LMX research conducted since 2002, Anand, Hu, Liden, and Vidyarthi (2011) found that interest in studying leader–member exchange has not diminished. A large majority of these studies (70%) examined the antecedents and outcomes of leader–member exchange. The research trends show increased attention to the context surrounding LMX relationships (e.g., group dynamics), analyzing leader–member exchange from individual and group levels, and studying leader–member exchange with non-U.S. samples.

For example, using a sample of employees in a variety of jobs in Israeli organizations, Atwater and Carmeli (2009) examined the connection between employees' perceptions of leader–member exchange and their energy and creativity at work. They found that perceived high-quality leader–member exchange was positively related to feelings of energy in employees, which, in turn, was related to greater involvement in creative work. LMX theory was not directly associated with creativity, but it served as a mechanism to nurture people's feelings, which then enhanced their creativity.

Ilies, Nahrgang, and Morgeson (2007) did a meta-analysis of 51 research studies that examined the relationship between LMX and employee citizenship behaviors. Citizenship behaviors are discretionary employee behaviors that go beyond the prescribed role, job description, or reward system (Katz, 1964; Organ, 1988). They found a positive relationship between the quality of leader–member relationships and citizenship behaviors. In other words, followers who had higher-quality relationships with their leaders were more likely to engage in more discretionary (positive "payback") behaviors that benefited the leader and the organization.

Researchers have also studied how LMX theory is related to empowerment. Harris, Wheeler, and Kacmar (2009) explored how empowerment moderates the impact of leader–member exchange on job outcomes such as job satisfaction, turnover, job performance, and organizational citizenship behaviors. Based on two samples of college alumni, they found that empowerment and leader–member exchange quality had a slight synergistic effect on job outcomes. The quality of leader–member exchange mattered most for employees who felt little empowerment. For these employees, high-quality leader–member exchange appeared to compensate for the drawbacks of not being empowered.

📖 Empowerment Through LMX   🌐 Empowering Employees

In essence, the aforementioned findings clearly illustrate that organizations stand to gain much from having leaders who can create good working relationships. When leaders and followers have good exchanges, they feel better and accomplish more, and the organization prospers.

Leadership Making

Research of LMX theory has also focused on how exchanges between leaders and followers can be used for leadership making (Graen & Uhl-Bien, 1991). Leadership making is a prescriptive approach to leadership emphasizing that leaders should develop high-quality exchanges with all of their followers rather than just a few. It attempts to make every follower feel as if he or she is a part of the in-group and, by so doing, avoids the inequities and negative implications of being in an out-group. In general, leadership making promotes partnerships in which the leader tries to build effective dyads with all followers in the work unit (Graen & Uhl-Bien, 1995). In addition, leadership making suggests that leaders can create networks of partnerships throughout the organization, which will benefit the organization's goals and the leader's own career progress.

Graen and Uhl-Bien (1991) suggested that leadership making develops progressively over time in three phases: (1) the stranger phase, (2) the acquaintance phase, and (3) the mature partnership phase (Table 7.1). During Phase 1, the stranger phase, the interactions in the leader–follower dyad generally are rule bound, relying heavily on contractual relationships. Leaders and followers relate to each other within prescribed organizational roles. They have lower-quality exchanges, similar to those of out-group members discussed earlier in the chapter. The follower complies with the formal leader, who has hierarchical status for the purpose of achieving the economic rewards the leader controls. The motives of the follower during the stranger phase are directed toward self-interest rather than toward the good of the group (Graen & Uhl-Bien, 1995).

In a study of the early stages of leader–member relationship development, Nahrgang, Morgeson, and Ilies (2009) found that leaders look for followers who exhibit enthusiasm, participation, gregariousness, and extraversion. In contrast, followers look for leaders who are pleasant, trusting, cooperative, and agreeable. Leader extraversion did not influence relationship quality for the followers, and follower agreeableness did not influence relationship quality for the leaders. A key predictor of relationship quality for both leaders and followers was behaviors such as performance.

Phase 2, the acquaintance phase, begins with an offer by the leader or the follower for improved career-oriented social exchanges, which involve sharing more resources and personal or work-related information. It is a testing period

 Leader Follower Interaction   Changing Relationships

Table 7.1 Phases in Leadership Making

	Phase 1 Stranger	Phase 2 Acquaintance	Phase 3 Partnership
Roles	Scripted	Tested	Negotiated
Influences	One way	Mixed	Reciprocal
Exchanges	Low quality	Medium quality	High quality
Interests	Self	Self and other	Group
		Time	

SOURCE: Adapted from "Relationship-Based Approach to Leadership: Development of Leader–Member Exchange (LMX) Theory of Leadership Over 25 Years: Applying a Multi-Level, Multi-Domain Perspective," by G. B. Graen and M. Uhl-Bien, 1995, *Leadership Quarterly, 6*(2), 231.

for both the leader and the follower to assess whether the follower is interested in taking on more roles and responsibilities and to assess whether the leader is willing to provide new challenges for followers. During this time, dyads shift away from interactions that are governed strictly by job descriptions and defined roles and move toward new ways of relating. As measured by LMX theory, it could be said that the quality of their exchanges has improved to medium quality. Successful dyads in the acquaintance phase begin to develop greater trust and respect for each other. They also tend to focus less on their own self-interests and more on the purposes and goals of the group.

Phase 3, mature partnership, is marked by high-quality leader–member exchanges. People who have progressed to this stage in their relationships experience a high degree of mutual trust, respect, and obligation toward each other. They have tested their relationship and found that they can depend on each other. In mature partnerships, there is a high degree of reciprocity between leaders and followers: Each affects and is affected by the other. For example, in a study of 75 bank managers and 58 engineering managers, Schriesheim, Castro, Zhou, and Yammarino (2001) found that good leader–member relations were more egalitarian and that influence and control were more evenly balanced between the supervisor and the follower. In addition, during Phase 3, members may depend on each other for favors and special assistance. For example, leaders may rely on followers to do extra assignments, and followers may rely on leaders for needed support or encouragement. The point is that leaders and followers are tied together in productive ways that go well beyond a traditional hierarchically defined work relationship. They

 Relationships   Mature Partnership

have developed an extremely effective way of relating that produces positive outcomes for themselves and the organization. In effect, partnerships are transformational in that they assist leaders and followers in moving beyond their own self-interests to accomplish the greater good of the team and organization (see Chapter 8).

The benefits for employees who develop high-quality leader–member relationships include preferential treatment, increased job-related communication, ample access to supervisors, and increased performance-related feedback (Harris et al., 2009). The disadvantages for those with low-quality leader–member relationships include limited trust and support from supervisors and few benefits outside the employment contract (Harris et al., 2009). To evaluate leader–member exchanges, researchers typically use a brief questionnaire that asks leaders and followers to report on the effectiveness of their working relationships. The questionnaire assesses the degree to which respondents express respect, trust, and obligation in their exchanges with others. At the end of this chapter, a version of the LMX questionnaire is provided for you to take for the purpose of analyzing some of your own leader–member relationships.

HOW DOES LMX THEORY WORK?

LMX theory works in two ways: It describes leadership, and it prescribes leadership. In both instances, the central concept is the dyadic relationship that a leader forms with each of the leader's followers. Descriptively, LMX theory suggests that it is important to recognize the existence of in-groups and out-groups within a group or an organization.

The differences in how goals are accomplished by in-groups and out-groups are substantial. Working with an in-group allows a leader to accomplish more work in a more effective manner than he or she can accomplish working without one. In-group members are willing to do more than is required in their job description and look for innovative ways to advance the group's goals. In response to their extra effort and devotion, leaders give them more responsibilities and more opportunities. Leaders also give in-group members more of their time and support.

Out-group members act quite differently than in-group members. Rather than trying to do extra work, out-group members operate strictly within their prescribed organizational roles. They do what is required of them but nothing more. Leaders treat out-group members fairly and according to the formal contract, but they do not give them special attention. For their efforts, out-group members receive the standard benefits as defined in the job description.

Prescriptively, LMX theory is best understood within the leadership-making model of Graen and Uhl-Bien (1991). Graen and Uhl-Bien advocated that leaders should create a special relationship with all followers, similar to the relationships described as in-group relationships. Leaders should offer each follower the opportunity to take on new roles and responsibilities. Furthermore, leaders should nurture high-quality exchanges with their followers. Rather than focusing on the differences between in-group and out-group members, the leadership-making model suggests that leaders should look for ways to build trust and respect with all of their followers, thus making the entire work unit an in-group. In addition, leaders should look beyond their own work unit and create high-quality partnerships with people throughout the organization.

Whether descriptive or prescriptive, LMX theory works by focusing our attention on the special, unique relationship that leaders can create with others. When these relationships are of high quality, the goals of the leader, the followers, and the organization are all advanced.

STRENGTHS

LMX theory makes several positive contributions to our understanding of the leadership process. First, it is a strong descriptive theory. Intuitively, it makes sense to describe work units in terms of those who contribute more and those who contribute less (or the bare minimum) to the organization. Anyone who has ever worked in an organization has felt the presence of in-groups and out-groups. Despite the potential harm of out-groups, we all know that leaders have special relationships with certain people who do more and get more. We may not like this because it seems unfair, but it is a reality, and the LMX theory has accurately described this situation. LMX theory validates our experience of how people within organizations relate to each other and the leader. Some contribute more and receive more; others contribute less and get less.

Second, LMX theory is unique because it is the only leadership approach that makes the concept of the dyadic relationship the centerpiece of the leadership process. Other approaches emphasize the characteristics of leaders, followers, contexts, or a combination of these, but none of them addresses the specific relationships between the leader and each follower. LMX theory

Leadership and Communication

underscores that effective leadership is contingent on effective leader–member exchanges.

Third, LMX theory is noteworthy because it directs our attention to the importance of communication in leadership. The high-quality exchanges advocated in LMX theory are inextricably bound to effective communication. Communication is the vehicle through which leaders and followers create, nurture, and sustain useful exchanges. Effective leadership occurs when the communication of leaders and followers is characterized by mutual trust, respect, and commitment.

Fourth, LMX theory provides an important alert for leaders. It warns leaders to avoid letting their conscious or unconscious biases influence who is invited into the in-group (e.g., biases regarding race, gender, ethnicity, religion, or age). The principles outlined in LMX theory serve as a good reminder for leaders to be fair and equal in how they approach each of their followers.

Finally, a large body of research substantiates how the practice of LMX theory is related to positive organizational outcomes. In a review of this research, Graen and Uhl-Bien (1995) pointed out that leader–member exchange is related to performance, organizational commitment, job climate, innovation, organizational citizenship behavior, empowerment, procedural and distributive justice, career progress, and many other important organizational variables. By linking the use of LMX theory to real outcomes, researchers have been able to validate the theory and increase its practical value.

CRITICISMS

LMX theory also has some limitations. First, on the surface, leader–member exchange in its initial formulation (vertical dyad linkage theory) runs counter to the basic human value of fairness. Throughout our lives, beginning when we are very young, we are taught to try to get along with everyone and to treat everyone equally. We have been taught that it is wrong to form in-groups or cliques because they are harmful to those who cannot be a part of them. Because LMX theory divides the work unit into two groups and one group receives special attention, it gives the appearance of discrimination against the out-group.

Our culture is replete with examples of people of different genders, ages, cultures, and abilities who have been discriminated against. Although LMX theory was not designed to do so, it supports the development of privileged

 Attribution Biases

groups in the workplace. In so doing, it appears unfair and discriminatory. Furthermore, as reported by McClane (1991), the existence of in-groups and out-groups may have undesirable effects on the group as a whole.

Whether LMX theory actually creates inequalities is questionable (cf. Harter & Evanecky, 2002; Scandura, 1999). If a leader does not intentionally keep out-group members "out," and if they are free to become members of the in-group, then LMX theory may not create inequalities. However, the theory does not elaborate on strategies for how one gains access to the in-group if one chooses to do so.

Furthermore, LMX theory does not address other fairness issues, such as followers' perceptions of the fairness of pay increases and promotion opportunities (distributive justice), decision-making rules (procedural justice), or communication of issues within the organization (interactional justice) (Scandura, 1999). There is a need for further research on how these types of fairness issues affect the development and maintenance of LMX relationships.

A second criticism of LMX theory is that the basic ideas of the theory are not fully developed. For example, the theory does not fully explain how high-quality leader–member exchanges are created (Anand et al., 2011). In the early studies, it was implied that they were formed when a leader found certain followers more compatible in regard to personality, interpersonal skills, or job competencies, but these studies never described the relative importance of these factors or how this process worked (Yukl, 1994). Research has suggested that leaders should work to create high-quality exchanges with all followers, but the guidelines for how this is done are not clearly spelled out. For example, the model on leadership making highlights the importance of role making, incremental influence, and type of reciprocity (see Table 7.1), but it does not explain how these concepts function to build mature partnerships. Similarly, the model strongly promotes building trust, respect, and obligation in leader–follower relationships, but it does not describe the means by which these factors are developed in relationships.

Based on an examination of 147 studies of leader–member exchange, Schriesheim, Castro, and Cogliser (1999) concluded that improved theorization about leader–member exchange and its basic processes is needed. Similarly, in a review of the research on relational leadership, Uhl-Bien, Maslyn, and Ospina (2012) point to the need for further understanding of how high- and low-quality relationships develop in leader–member exchange. Although many studies have been conducted on leader–member exchange, these studies have not resulted in a clear, refined set of definitions, concepts, and propositions about the theory.

 NGO Leadership

A third criticism of the theory is that researchers have not adequately explained the contextual factors that may have an impact on LMX relationships (Anand et al., 2011). Since leader–member exchange is often studied in isolation, researchers have not examined the potential impact of other variables on LMX dyads. For example, workplace norms and other organizational culture variables are likely to influence leader–member exchange. There is a need to explore how the surrounding constellations of social networks influence specific LMX relationships and the individuals in those relationships.

Finally, questions have been raised about the measurement of leader–member exchanges in LMX theory (Graen & Uhl-Bien, 1995; Schriesheim, Castro, & Cogliser, 1999; Schriesheim, Castro, Zhou, et al., 2001). For example, no empirical studies have used dyadic measures to analyze the LMX process (Schriesheim, Castro, Zhou, et al., 2001). In addition, leader–member exchanges have been measured with different versions of leader–member exchange scales and with different levels of analysis, so the results are not always directly comparable. Furthermore, the content validity and dimensionality of the scales have been questioned (Graen & Uhl-Bien, 1995; Schriesheim, Castro, Zhou, et al., 2001).

APPLICATION

Although LMX theory has not been packaged in a way to be used in standard management training and development programs, it offers many insights that leaders could use to improve their own leadership behavior. Foremost, LMX theory directs leaders to assess their leadership from a relationship perspective. This assessment will sensitize leaders to how in-groups and out-groups develop within their own organization. In addition, LMX theory suggests ways in which leaders can improve their organization by building strong leader–member exchanges with all of their followers.

The ideas set forth in LMX theory can be used by leaders at all levels within an organization. For example, LMX theory could be used to explain how CEOs develop special relationships with select individuals in upper management to develop new strategic and tactical corporate goals. A presidential cabinet is a good example of this. A U.S. president will handpick the 15 people that serve as his or her closest advisers. The cabinet includes the vice president and the heads of 15 executive departments—the secretaries of the Departments of Agriculture, Commerce, Defense, Education, Energy, Health and Human Services, Homeland Security, Housing and Urban Development, Interior, Labor, State, Transportation, Treasury, and Veterans Affairs, as well

N Using LMX

as the attorney general. These individuals, in turn, run their own departments in accordance with the goals and philosophy of the president.

On a lower level, LMX theory could be used to explain how line managers in a manufacturing plant use a select few workers to accomplish the production quotas of their work unit. The point is that the ideas presented in LMX theory are applicable throughout organizations.

In addition, the ideas of LMX theory can be used to explain how individuals create leadership networks throughout an organization to help them accomplish work more effectively (Graen & Scandura, 1987). A person with a network of high-quality partnerships can call on many people to help solve problems and advance the goals of the organization.

LMX theory can also be applied in different types of organizations. It applies in volunteer settings as well as traditional business, education, and government settings. Imagine a community leader who heads a volunteer program that assists older adults. To run the program effectively, the leader depends on a few of the volunteers who are more dependable and committed than the rest of the volunteers. This process of working closely with a small cadre of trusted volunteers is explained by the principles of LMX theory. Similarly, a manager in a traditional business setting might use certain individuals to achieve a major change in the company's policies and procedures. The way the manager goes about this process is explicated in LMX theory.

In summary, LMX theory tells us to be aware of how we relate to our followers. It tells us to be sensitive to whether some followers receive special attention and some followers do not. In addition, it tells us to be fair to all followers and allow each of them to become as involved in the work of the unit as they want to be. LMX theory tells us to be respectful and to build trusting relationships with all of our followers, recognizing that each follower is unique and wants to relate to us in a special way.

CASE STUDIES

In the following section, three case studies (Cases 7.1, 7.2, and 7.3) are presented to clarify how LMX theory can be applied to various group settings. The first case is about the creative director at an advertising agency, the second is about a production manager at a mortgage company, and the third is about the leadership of the manager of a district office of the Social Security Administration. After each case, there are questions that will help you analyze it, using the ideas from LMX theory.

CASE 7.1

His Team Gets the Best Assignments

Carly Peters directs the creative department of the advertising agency of Mills, Smith, & Peters. The agency has about 100 employees, 20 of whom work for Carly in the creative department. Typically, the agency maintains 10 major accounts and a number of smaller accounts. It has a reputation for being one of the best advertising and public relations agencies in the country.

In the creative department, there are four major account teams. Each is led by an associate creative director, who reports directly to Carly. In addition, each team has a copywriter, an art director, and a production artist. These four account teams are headed by Jack, Terri, Julie, and Sarah.

Jack and his team get along really well with Carly, and they have done excellent work for their clients at the agency. Of all the teams, Jack's team is the most creative and talented and the most willing to go the extra mile for Carly. As a result, when Carly has to showcase accounts to upper management, she often uses the work of Jack's team. Jack and his team members are comfortable confiding in Carly and she in them. Carly is not afraid to allocate extra resources to Jack's team or to give them free rein on their accounts because they always come through for her.

Terri's team also performs well for the agency, but Terri is unhappy with how Carly treats her team. She feels that Carly is not fair because she favors Jack's team. For example, Terri's team was counseled out of pursuing an ad campaign because the campaign was too risky, whereas Jack's group was praised for developing a very provocative campaign. Terri feels that Jack's team is Carly's pet: His team gets the best assignments, accounts, and budgets. Terri finds it hard to hold back the animosity she feels toward Carly.

Like Terri, Julie is concerned that her team is not in the inner circle, close to Carly. She has noticed repeatedly that Carly favors the other teams. For example, whenever additional people are assigned to team projects, it is always the other teams who get the best writers and art directors. Julie is mystified as to why Carly doesn't notice her team or try to help it with its work. She feels Carly undervalues her team because Julie knows the quality of her team's work is indisputable.

Although Sarah agrees with some of Terri's and Julie's observations about Carly, she does not feel any antagonism about Carly's leadership. Sarah has worked for the agency for nearly 10 years, and nothing seems to bother her. Her account teams have never been earthshaking, but they have never been problematic either. Sarah views her team and its work more as a nuts-and-bolts operation in which the team is given an assignment and carries it out. Being in Carly's inner circle would entail putting in extra time in the evening or on weekends and would create more headaches for Sarah. Therefore, Sarah is happy with her role as it is, and she has little interest in trying to change the way the department works.

Questions

1. Based on the principles of LMX theory, what observations would you make about Carly's leadership at Mills, Smith, & Peters?

2. Is there an in-group and out-group, and if so, which are they?

3. In what way is Carly's relationship with the four groups productive or counterproductive to the overall goals of the agency?

4. Do you think Carly should change her approach toward the associate directors? If so, what should she do differently?

CASE 7.2

Working Hard at Being Fair

City Mortgage is a medium-size mortgage company that employs about 25 people. Jenny Hernandez, who has been with the company for 10 years, is the production manager who oversees its day-to-day operations.

Reporting to Jenny are loan originators (salespeople), closing officers, mortgage underwriters, and processing and shipping personnel. Jenny is proud of the company and feels as if she has contributed substantially to its steady growth and expansion.

The climate at City Mortgage is very positive. People like to come to work because the office environment is comfortable. They respect each other at the company and show tolerance for those who are different from themselves.

Whereas at many mortgage companies it is common for resentments to build between people who earn different incomes, this is not the case at City Mortgage.

Jenny's leadership has been instrumental in shaping the success of City Mortgage. Her philosophy stresses listening to employees and then determining how each employee can best contribute to the mission of the company. She makes a point of helping each person explore her or his own talents, and challenges each one to try new things.

(Continued)

(Continued)

At the annual holiday party, Jenny devised an interesting event that symbolizes her leadership style. She bought a large piece of colorful glass and had it cut into 25 pieces and handed out one piece to each person. Then she asked each employee to come forward with the piece of glass and briefly state what he or she liked about City Mortgage and how he or she had contributed to the company in the past year. After the statements were made, the pieces of glass were formed into a cut glass window that hangs in the front lobby of the office. The glass is a reminder of how each individual contributes his or her uniqueness to the overall purpose of the company.

Another characteristic of Jenny's style is her fairness. She does not want to give anyone the impression that certain people have the inside track, and she goes to great lengths to prevent this from happening. For example, she avoids social lunches because she thinks they foster the perception of favoritism. Similarly, even though her best friend is one of the loan originators, she is seldom seen talking with her, and if she is, it is always about business matters.

Jenny also applies her fairness principle to how information is shared in the office. She does not want anyone to feel as if he or she is out of the loop, so she tries very hard to keep her employees informed on all the matters that could affect them. Much of this she does through her open-door office policy. Jenny does not have a special group of employees with whom she confides her concerns; rather, she shares openly with each of them.

Jenny is very committed to her work at City Mortgage. She works long hours and carries a beeper on the weekend. At this point in her career, her only concern is that she could be burning out.

Questions

1. Based on the LMX model, how would you describe Jenny's leadership?

2. How do you think the employees at City Mortgage respond to Jenny?

3. If you were asked to follow in Jenny's footsteps, do you think you could or would want to manage City Mortgage with a similar style?

CASE 7.3

Taking on Additional Responsibilities

Jim Madison is manager of a district office for the Social Security Administration. The office serves a community of 200,000 people and has a staff of 30 employees, most of whom work as claim representatives.

The primary work of the office is to provide the public with information about Social Security benefits and to process retirement, survivor, disability, and Medicare claims.

Jim has been the manager of the office for 6 years; during that time, he has made many improvements in the overall operations of the office. People in the community have a favorable view of the office and have few complaints about the services it provides. On the annual survey of community service organizations, the district office receives consistently high marks for overall effectiveness and customer satisfaction.

Almost all of the employees who work for Jim have been employed at the district office for 6 years or more; one employee has been there for 22 years. Although Jim takes pride in knowing all of them personally, he calls on a few of them more frequently than others to help him accomplish his goals.

When it comes to training staff members about new laws affecting claim procedures, Jim relies heavily on two particular claim representatives, Shirley and Patti, both of whom are very knowledgeable and competent. Shirley and Patti view the additional training responsibilities as a challenge. This helps Jim: He does not need to do the job himself or supervise them closely because they are highly respected people within the office, and they have a history of being mature and conscientious about their work. Shirley and Patti like the additional responsibility because it gives them greater recognition and increased benefits from receiving positive job appraisals.

To showcase the office's services to the community, Jim calls on two other employees, Ted and Jana. Ted and Jana serve as field representatives for the office and give presentations to community organizations about the nature of Social Security and how it serves the citizens of the district. In addition, they speak on local radio stations, answering call-in questions about the various complexities of Social Security benefits.

Although many of the claim people in the office could act as field representatives, Jim typically calls on Ted and Jana because of their willingness to take on the public relations challenge and because of their special capabilities in this area. This is advantageous for Jim for two reasons: First, these people do an outstanding job in representing the office to the public. Second, Jim is a reticent person, and he finds it quite threatening to be in the public eye. Ted and Jana like to take on this additional role because it gives them added prestige and greater freedom. Being a field representative has its perks because field staff can function as their own bosses when they are not in the office; they can set their own schedules and come and go as they please.

A third area in which Jim calls on a few representatives for added effort is in helping him supervise the slower claim representatives, who seem to be continually behind in writing up the case reports of their clients.

(Continued)

(Continued)

When even a few staff members get behind with their work, it affects the entire office operation. To ameliorate this problem, Jim calls on Glenda and Annie, who are both highly talented, to help the slower staff complete their case reports. Although it means taking on more work themselves, Glenda and Annie do it to be kind and to help the office run more smoothly. Other than personal satisfaction, no additional benefits accrue to them for taking on the additional responsibilities.

Overall, the people who work under Jim's leadership are satisfied with his supervision. There are some who feel that he caters too much to a few special representatives, but most of the staff think Jim is fair and impartial. Even though he depends more on a few, Jim tries very hard to attend to the wants and needs of his entire staff.

Questions

1. From an LMX theory point of view, how would you describe Jim's relationships with his employees at the district Social Security office?

2. Can you identify an in-group and an out-group?

3. Do you think the trust and respect Jim places in some of his staff are productive or counterproductive? Why?

4. As suggested in the chapter, *leadership making* recommends that the leader build high-quality relationships with all of the followers. How would you evaluate Jim's leadership in regards to leadership making? Discuss.

LEADERSHIP INSTRUMENT

Researchers have used many different questionnaires to study LMX theory. All of them have been designed to measure the quality of the working relationship between leaders and followers. We have chosen to include in this chapter the LMX 7, a seven-item questionnaire that provides a reliable and valid measure of the quality of leader–member exchanges (Graen & Uhl-Bien, 1995).

The LMX 7 is designed to measure three dimensions of leader–member relationships: respect, trust, and obligation. It assesses the degree to which leaders and followers have mutual respect for each other's capabilities, feel a deepening sense of reciprocal trust, and have a strong sense of obligation to one another. Taken together, these dimensions are the ingredients of strong partnerships.

LMX 7 Questionnaire

Instructions: This questionnaire contains items that ask you to describe your relationship with either your leader or one of your followers. For each of the items, indicate the degree to which you think the item is true for you by circling one of the responses that appear below the item.

1. Do you know where you stand with your leader (follower) . . . [and] do you usually know how satisfied your leader (follower) is with what you do?

Rarely	Occasionally	Sometimes	Fairly often	Very often
1	2	3	4	5

2. How well does your leader (follower) understand your job problems and needs?

Not a bit	A little	A fair amount	Quite a bit	A great deal
1	2	3	4	5

3. How well does your leader (follower) recognize your potential?

Not at all	A little	Moderately	Mostly	Fully
1	2	3	4	5

4. Regardless of how much formal authority your leader (follower) has built into his or her position, what are the chances that your leader (follower) would use his or her power to help you solve problems in your work?

None	Small	Moderate	High	Very high
1	2	3	4	5

5. Again, regardless of the amount of formal authority your leader (follower) has, what are the chances that he or she would "bail you out" at his or her expense?

None	Small	Moderate	High	Very high
1	2	3	4	5

6. I have enough confidence in my leader (follower) that I would defend and justify his or her decision if he or she were not present to do so.

Strongly disagree	Disagree	Neutral	Agree	Strongly agree
1	2	3	4	5

7. How would you characterize your working relationship with your leader (follower)?

Extremely ineffective	Worse than average	Average	Better than average	Extremely effective
1	2	3	4	5

By completing the LMX 7, you can gain a fuller understanding of how LMX theory works. The score you obtain on the questionnaire reflects the quality of your leader–member relationships, and indicates the degree to which your relationships are characteristic of partnerships, as described in the LMX model.

You can complete the questionnaire both as a leader and as a follower. In the leader role, you would complete the questionnaire multiple times, assessing the quality of the relationships you have with each of your followers. In the follower role, you would complete the questionnaire based on the leaders to whom you report.

Scoring Interpretation

Although the LMX 7 is most commonly used by researchers to explore theoretical questions, you can also use it to analyze your own leadership style. You can interpret your LMX 7 scores using the following guidelines: very high = 30–35, high = 25–29, moderate = 20–24, low = 15–19, and very low = 7–14. Scores in the upper ranges indicate stronger, higher-quality leader–member exchanges (e.g., in-group members), whereas scores in the lower ranges indicate exchanges of lesser quality (e.g., out-group members).

SOURCE: Reprinted from "Relationship-Based Approach to Leadership: Development of Leader–Member Exchange (LMX) Theory of Leadership Over 25 Years: Applying a Multi-Level, Multi-Domain Perspective," by G. B. Graen and M. Uhl-Bien, 1995, *Leadership Quarterly, 6*(2), 219–247. Copyright © 1995. Reprinted with permission from Elsevier Science.

N The LMX Score

SUMMARY

Since it first appeared more than 30 years ago under the title "vertical dyad linkage (VDL) theory," LMX theory has been and continues to be a much-studied approach to leadership. LMX theory addresses leadership as a process centered on the interactions between leaders and followers. It makes the leader–member relationship the pivotal concept in the leadership process.

In the early studies of LMX theory, a leader's relationship to the overall work unit was viewed as a series of vertical dyads, categorized as being of two different types: Leader–member dyads based on expanded role relationships were called the leader's in-group, and those based on formal job descriptions were called the leader's out-group. It is believed that followers become in-group members based on how well they get along with the leader and whether they are willing to expand their role responsibilities. Followers who maintain only formal hierarchical relationships with their leader are out-group members. Whereas in-group members receive extra influence, opportunities, and rewards, out-group members receive standard job benefits.

Subsequent studies of LMX theory were directed toward how leader–member exchanges affect organizational performance. Researchers found that high-quality exchanges between leaders and followers produced multiple positive outcomes (e.g., less employee turnover, greater organizational commitment, and more promotions). In general, researchers determined that good leader–member exchanges result in followers feeling better, accomplishing more, and helping the organization prosper.

A select body of LMX research focuses on leadership making, which emphasizes that leaders should try to develop high-quality exchanges with all of their followers. Leadership making develops over time and includes a stranger phase, an acquaintance phase, and a mature partnership phase. By taking on and fulfilling new role responsibilities, followers move through these three phases to develop mature partnerships with their leaders. These partnerships, which are marked by a high degree of mutual trust, respect, and obligation, have positive payoffs for the individuals themselves, and help the organization run more effectively.

There are several positive features to LMX theory. First, LMX theory is a strong descriptive approach that explains how leaders use some followers (in-group members) more than others (out-group members) to accomplish organizational goals effectively. Second, LMX theory is unique in that, unlike other approaches, it makes the leader–member relationship the focal

LMX Explanation

point of the leadership process. Related to this focus, LMX theory is note-worthy because it directs our attention to the importance of effective com-munication in leader–member relationships. In addition, it reminds us to be evenhanded in how we relate to our followers. Last, LMX theory is sup-ported by a multitude of studies that link high-quality leader–member exchanges to positive organizational outcomes.

There are also negative features in LMX theory. First, the early formulation of LMX theory (VDL theory) runs counter to our principles of fairness and justice in the workplace by suggesting that some members of the work unit receive special attention and others do not. The perceived inequalities cre-ated by the use of in-groups can have a devastating impact on the feelings, attitudes, and behavior of out-group members. Second, LMX theory empha-sizes the importance of leader–member exchanges but fails to explain the intricacies of how one goes about creating high-quality exchanges. Although the model promotes building trust, respect, and commitment in relation-ships, it does not fully explicate how this takes place. Third, researchers have not adequately explained the contextual factors that influence LMX rela-tionships. Finally, there are questions about whether the measurement pro-cedures used in LMX research are adequate to fully capture the complexities of the leader–member exchange process.

Sharpen your skills with SAGE edge at **edge.sagepub.com/northouse7e**

REFERENCES

Anand, S., Hu, J., Liden, R. C., & Vidyarthi, P. R. (2011). Leader-member exchange: Recent research findings and prospects for the future. In A. Bryman, D. Collinson, K. Grint, G. Jackson, & B. Uhl-Bien (Eds.), *The SAGE handbook of leadership* (pp. 311–325). London: SAGE.

Atwater, L., & Carmeli, A. (2009). Leader-member exchange, feelings of energy, and involvement in creative work. *Leadership Quarterly, 20,* 264–275.

Dansereau, F., Graen, G. B., & Haga, W. (1975). A vertical dyad linkage approach to leadership in formal organizations. *Organizational Behavior and Human Perfor-mance, 13,* 46–78.

Gerstner, C. R., & Day, D. V. (1997). Meta-analytic review of leader-member exchange theory: Correlates and construct issues. *Journal of Applied Psychology, 82,* 827–844.

Graen, G. B. (1976). Role-making processes within complex organizations. In M. D. Dunnette (Ed.), *Handbook of industrial and organizational psychology* (pp. 1202–1245). Chicago: Rand McNally.

Graen, G. B., & Cashman, J. (1975). A role-making model of leadership in formal organizations: A developmental approach. In J. G. Hunt & L. L. Larson (Eds.), *Leadership frontiers* (pp. 143–166). Kent, OH: Kent State University Press.

Graen, G. B., & Scandura, T. A. (1987). Toward a psychology of dyadic organizing. In B. Staw & L. L. Cumming (Eds.), *Research in organizational behavior* (Vol. 9, pp. 175–208). Greenwich, CT: JAI.

Graen, G. B., & Uhl-Bien, M. (1991). The transformation of professionals into self-managing and partially self-designing contributions: Toward a theory of leadership making. *Journal of Management Systems, 3*(3), 33–48.

Graen, G. B., & Uhl-Bien, M. (1995). Relationship-based approach to leadership: Development of leader–member exchange (LMX) theory of leadership over 25 years: Applying a multi-level, multi-domain perspective. *Leadership Quarterly, 6*(2), 219–247.

Harris, K. J., Wheeler, A. R., & Kacmar, K. M. (2009). Leader-member exchange and empowerment: Direct and interactive effects on job satisfaction, turnover intentions, and performance. *Leadership Quarterly, 20,* 371–382.

Harter, N., & Evanecky, D. (2002). Fairness in leader–member exchange theory: Do we all belong on the inside? *Leadership Review, 2*(2), 1–7.

Ilies, R., Nahrgang, J. D., & Morgeson, F. P. (2007). Leader-member exchange and citizenship behaviors: A meta-analysis. *Journal of Applied Psychology, 92*(1), 269–277.

Katz, D. (1964). Motivational basis of organizational behavior. *Behavioral Science, 9* 131–146.

Liden, R. C., Wayne, S. J., & Stilwell, D. (1993). A longitudinal study on the early development of leader–member exchange. *Journal of Applied Psychology, 78,* 662–674.

McClane, W. E. (1991). Implications of member role differentiation: Analysis of a key concept in the LMX model of leadership. *Group & Organization Studies, 16*(1), 102–113.

Nahrgang, J. D., Morgeson, R. P., & Ilies, R. (2009). The development of leader-member exchanges: Exploring how personality and performance influence leader and member relationships over time. *Organizational Behavior and Human Decision Processes, 108,* 256–266.

Organ, D. W. (1988). *Organizational citizenship behavior: The good soldier syndrome.* Lexington, MA: Lexington Books.

Scandura, T. A. (1999). Rethinking leader–member exchange: An organizational justice perspective. *Leadership Quarterly, 10*(1), 25–40.

Schriesheim, C. A., Castro, S. L., & Cogliser, C. C. (1999). Leader–member exchange (LMX) research: A comprehensive review of theory, measurement, and data-analytic practices. *Leadership Quarterly, 10,* 63–113.

Schriesheim, C. A., Castro, S. L., Zhou, X., & Yammarino, F. J. (2001). The folly of theorizing "A" but testing "B": A selective level-of-analysis review of the field and a detailed leader–member exchange illustration. *Leadership Quarterly, 12,* 515–551.

Uhl-Bien, M., Maslyn, J., & Ospina, S. (2012). The nature of relational leadership: A multitheoretical lens on leadership relationships and processes. In D. V. Day & J. Antonakis (Eds.), *The nature of leadership* (2nd ed., pp. 289–330). Thousand Oaks, CA: SAGE.

Yukl, G. (1994). *Leadership in organizations* (3rd ed.). Englewood Cliffs, NJ: Prentice Hall.

8

Transformational Leadership

DESCRIPTION

One of the current and most popular approaches to leadership that has been the focus of much research since the early 1980s is the transformational approach. Transformational leadership is part of the "New Leadership" paradigm (Bryman, 1992), which gives more attention to the charismatic and affective elements of leadership. In a content analysis of articles published in *Leadership Quarterly*, Lowe and Gardner (2001) found that one third of the research was about transformational or charismatic leadership. Similarly, Antonakis (2012) found that the number of papers and citations in the field has grown at an increasing rate, not only in traditional areas like management and social psychology, but in other disciplines such as nursing, education, and industrial engineering. Bass and Riggio (2006) suggested that transformational leadership's popularity might be due to its emphasis on intrinsic motivation and follower development, which fits the needs of today's work groups, who want to be inspired and empowered to succeed in times of uncertainty. Clearly, many scholars are studying transformational leadership, and it occupies a central place in leadership research.

As its name implies, transformational leadership is a process that changes and transforms people. It is concerned with emotions, values, ethics, standards, and long-term goals. It includes assessing followers' motives, satisfying their needs, and treating them as full human beings. Transformational leadership involves an exceptional form of influence that moves followers to accomplish more than what is usually expected of them. It is a process that often incorporates charismatic and visionary leadership.

N Transformational Leadership

An encompassing approach, transformational leadership can be used to describe a wide range of leadership, from very specific attempts to influence followers on a one-to-one level, to very broad attempts to influence whole organizations and even entire cultures. Although the transformational leader plays a pivotal role in precipitating change, followers and leaders are inextricably bound together in the transformation process.

Transformational Leadership Defined

The term *transformational leadership* was first coined by Downton (1973). Its emergence as an important approach to leadership began with a classic work by political sociologist James MacGregor Burns titled *Leadership* (1978). In his work, Burns attempted to link the roles of leadership and followership. He wrote of leaders as people who tap the motives of followers in order to better reach the goals of leaders and followers (p. 18). For Burns, leadership is quite different from power because it is inseparable from followers' needs.

Transformational vs. Transactional Leadership. Burns distinguished between two types of leadership: *transactional* and *transformational.* Transactional leadership refers to the bulk of leadership models, which focus on the exchanges that occur between leaders and their followers. Politicians who win votes by promising "no new taxes" are demonstrating transactional leadership. Similarly, managers who offer promotions to employees who surpass their goals are exhibiting transactional leadership. In the classroom, teachers are being transactional when they give students a grade for work completed. The exchange dimension of transactional leadership is very common and can be observed at many levels throughout all types of organizations.

In contrast to transactional leadership, transformational leadership is the process whereby a person engages with others and creates a connection that raises the level of motivation and morality in both the leader and the follower. This type of leader is attentive to the needs and motives of followers and tries to help followers reach their fullest potential. Burns points to Mohandas Gandhi as a classic example of transformational leadership. Gandhi raised the hopes and demands of millions of his people, and, in the process, was changed himself.

Another good example of transformational leadership can be observed in the life of Ryan White. This teenager raised the American people's awareness about AIDS and in the process became a spokesperson for increasing government support of AIDS research. In the organizational world, an example of transformational leadership would be a manager who attempts to change

 James MacGregor Burns

his or her company's corporate values to reflect a more humane standard of fairness and justice. In the process, both the manager and the followers may emerge with a stronger and higher set of moral values.

Pseudotransformational Leadership. Because the conceptualization of transformational leadership set forth by Burns (1978) includes raising the level of morality in others, it is difficult to use this term when describing leaders such as Adolf Hitler and Saddam Hussein, who were transforming but in a negative way. To deal with this problem Bass (1998) coined the term *pseudotransformational leadership.* This term refers to leaders who are self-consumed, exploitive, and power oriented, with warped moral values (Bass & Riggio, 2006). Pseudotransformational leadership is considered personalized leadership, which focuses on the leader's own interests rather than on the interests of others (Bass & Steidlmeier, 1999). Authentic transformational leadership is socialized leadership, which is concerned with the collective good. Socialized transformational leaders transcend their own interests for the sake of others (Howell & Avolio, 1993).

In a series of four experimental studies, Christie, Barling, and Turner (2011) set forth a preliminary model of pseudotransformational leadership that reflected four components of transformational leadership discussed later in this chapter: *idealized influence, inspirational motivation, intellectual stimulation,* and *individualized consideration.* This model helps to clarify the meaning of pseudotransformational leadership. It suggests that pseudotransformational leadership is inspired leadership that is self-serving, is unwilling to encourage independent thought in followers, and exhibits little general caring for others. A pseudotransformational leader has strong inspirational talent and appeal but is manipulative and dominates and directs followers toward his or her own values. It is leadership that is threatening to the welfare of followers because it ignores the common good.

To sort out the complexities related to the "moral uplifting" component of authentic transformational leadership, Zhu, Avolio, Riggio, and Sosik (2011) proposed a theoretical model examining how authentic transformational leadership influences the ethics of individual followers and groups. The authors hypothesize that authentic transformational leadership positively affects followers' moral identities and moral emotions (e.g., empathy and guilt) and this, in turn, leads to moral decision making and moral action by the followers. Furthermore, the authors theorize that authentic transformational leadership is positively associated with group ethical climate, decision making, and moral action. In the future, research is needed to test the validity of the assumptions laid out in this model.

 Transformational Leadership

Transformational Leadership and Charisma

At about the same time Burns's book was published, House (1976) published a theory of charismatic leadership. Since its publication, charismatic leadership has received a great deal of attention by researchers (e.g., Conger, 1999; Hunt & Conger, 1999). It is often described in ways that make it similar to, if not synonymous with, transformational leadership.

The word *charisma* was first used to describe a special gift that certain individuals possess that gives them the capacity to do extraordinary things. Weber (1947) provided the most well-known definition of charisma as a special personality characteristic that gives a person superhuman or exceptional powers and is reserved for a few, is of divine origin, and results in the person being treated as a leader. Despite Weber's emphasis on charisma as a personality characteristic, he also recognized the important role played by followers in validating charisma in these leaders (Bryman, 1992; House, 1976).

In his theory of charismatic leadership, House suggested that charismatic leaders act in unique ways that have specific charismatic effects on their followers (Table 8.1). For House, the personality characteristics of a charismatic leader include being dominant, having a strong desire to influence others, being self-confident, and having a strong sense of one's own moral values.

In addition to displaying certain personality characteristics, charismatic leaders also demonstrate specific types of behaviors. First, they are strong role models for the beliefs and values they want their followers to adopt. For example, Gandhi advocated nonviolence and was an exemplary role model of civil disobedience. Second, charismatic leaders appear competent to followers. Third, they articulate ideological goals that have moral overtones. Martin Luther King, Jr.'s famous "I Have a Dream" speech is an example of this type of charismatic behavior.

Fourth, charismatic leaders communicate high expectations for followers, and they exhibit confidence in followers' abilities to meet these expectations. The impact of this behavior is to increase followers' sense of competence and self-efficacy (Avolio & Gibbons, 1988), which in turn improves their performance.

Fifth, charismatic leaders arouse task-relevant motives in followers that may include affiliation, power, or esteem. For example, former U.S. President John F. Kennedy appealed to the human values of the American people when he stated, "Ask not what your country can do for you; ask what you can do for your country."

 Teaching Charisma

Table 8.1 Personality Characteristics, Behaviors, and Effects on Followers of Charismatic Leadership

Personality Characteristics	Behaviors	Effects on Followers
Dominant	Sets strong role model	Trust in leader's ideology
Desire to influence	Shows competence	Belief similarity between leader and follower
Self-confident	Articulates goals	
Strong moral values	Communicates high expectations	Unquestioning acceptance
		Affection toward leader
	Expresses confidence	Obedience
	Arouses motives	Identification with leader
		Emotional involvement
		Heightened goals
		Increased confidence

According to House's charismatic theory, several effects are the direct result of charismatic leadership. They include follower trust in the leader's ideology, similarity between the followers' beliefs and the leader's beliefs, unquestioning acceptance of the leader, expression of affection toward the leader, follower obedience, identification with the leader, emotional involvement in the leader's goals, heightened goals for followers, and increased follower confidence in goal achievement. Consistent with Weber, House contends that these charismatic effects are more likely to occur in contexts in which followers feel distress because in stressful situations followers look to leaders to deliver them from their difficulties.

House's charismatic theory has been extended and revised through the years (see Conger, 1999; Conger & Kanungo, 1998). One major revision to the theory was made by Shamir, House, and Arthur (1993). They postulated that charismatic leadership transforms followers' self-concepts and tries to link the identity of followers to the collective identity of the organization. Charismatic leaders forge this link by emphasizing the intrinsic rewards of work and deemphasizing the extrinsic rewards. The hope is that followers will view work as an expression of themselves. Throughout the process, leaders express high expectations for followers and help them gain a sense of confidence and self-efficacy. In summary, charismatic leadership works because it ties followers and their self-concepts to the organizational identity.

 Romance of Leadership

A Model of Transformational Leadership

In the mid-1980s, Bass (1985) provided a more expanded and refined version of transformational leadership that was based on, but not fully consistent with, the prior works of Burns (1978) and House (1976). In his approach, Bass extended Burns's work by giving more attention to followers' rather than leaders' needs, by suggesting that transformational leadership could apply to situations in which the outcomes were not positive, and by describing transactional and transformational leadership as a single continuum (Figure 8.1) rather than mutually independent continua (Yammarino, 1993). Bass extended House's work by giving more attention to the emotional elements and origins of charisma and by suggesting that charisma is a necessary but not sufficient condition for transformational leadership (Yammarino, 1993).

Figure 8.1   Leadership Continuum From Transformational to Laissez-Faire Leadership

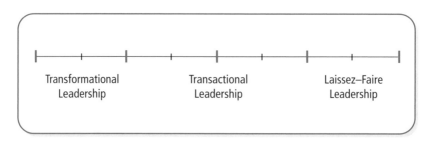

Bass (1985, p. 20) argued that transformational leadership motivates followers to do more than expected by (a) raising followers' levels of consciousness about the importance and value of specified and idealized goals, (b) getting followers to transcend their own self-interest for the sake of the team or organization, and (c) moving followers to address higher-level needs. An elaboration of the dynamics of the transformation process is provided in his model of transformational and transactional leadership (Bass, 1985, 1990; Bass & Avolio, 1993, 1994). Additional clarification of the model is provided by Avolio in his book *Full Leadership Development: Building the Vital Forces in Organizations* (1999).

As can be seen in Table 8.2, the model of transformational and transactional leadership incorporates seven different factors. These factors are also illustrated in the Full Range of Leadership model, which is provided in Figure 8.2 on page 168. A discussion of each of these seven factors will help

Transformational Leadership

to clarify Bass's model. This discussion will be divided into three parts: transformational factors (4), transactional factors (2), and the nonleadership, nontransactional factor (1).

Table 8.2 Leadership Factors

Transformational Leadership	Transactional Leadership	Laissez–Faire Leadership
Factor 1	Factor 5	Factor 7
Idealized influence	Contingent reward	Laissez–faire
Charisma	Constructive transactions	Nontransactional
Factor 2	Factor 6	
Inspirational motivation	Management-by-exception	
Factor 3	Active and passive	
Intellectual stimulation	Corrective transactions	
Factor 4		
Individualized consideration		

Transformational Leadership Factors

Transformational leadership is concerned with improving the performance of followers and developing followers to their fullest potential (Avolio, 1999; Bass & Avolio, 1990a). People who exhibit transformational leadership often have a strong set of internal values and ideals, and they are effective at motivating followers to act in ways that support the greater good rather than their own self-interests (Kuhnert, 1994).

Idealized Influence. Factor 1 is called *charisma* or *idealized influence.* It is the emotional component of leadership (Antonakis, 2012). Idealized influence describes leaders who act as strong role models for followers; followers identify with these leaders and want very much to emulate them. These leaders usually have very high standards of moral and ethical conduct and can be counted on to do the right thing. They are deeply respected by followers, who usually place a great deal of trust in them. They provide followers with a vision and a sense of mission.

The idealized influence factor is measured on two components: an *attributional component* that refers to the attributions of leaders made by followers based on perceptions they have of their leaders, and a *behavioral component* that refers to followers' observations of leader behavior.

 Innovative Leader Behaviors

Figure 8.2 Full Range of Leadership Model

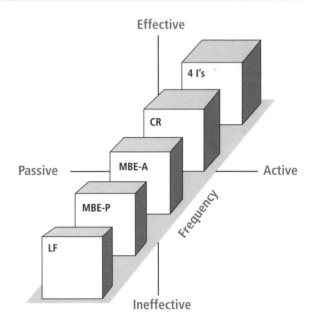

LEGEND

Nonleadership

    LF   Laissez-Faire

Transactional

    MBE-P   Management-by-Exception, Passive
    MBE-A   Management-by-Exception, Active
    CR   Contingent Reward

Transformational 4 I's

    Idealized Influence
    Inspirational Motivation
    Intellectual Stimulation
    Individualized Consideration

SOURCE: From Bass, B. M., & Avolio, B. J., *Improving Organizational Effectiveness Through Transformational Leadership,* © 1994, SAGE Publications, Inc. Reprinted with permission.

In essence, the charisma factor describes people who are special and who make others want to follow the vision they put forward. A person whose leadership exemplifies the charisma factor is Nelson Mandela, the first non-White president of South Africa. Mandela is viewed as a leader with high moral standards and a vision for South Africa that resulted in monumental change in how the people of South Africa would be governed. His charismatic qualities and the people's response to them transformed an entire nation.

Inspirational Motivation. Factor 2 is called *inspiration* or *inspirational motivation*. This factor is descriptive of leaders who communicate high expectations to followers, inspiring them through motivation to become committed to and a part of the shared vision in the organization. In practice, leaders use symbols and emotional appeals to focus group members' efforts to achieve more than they would in their own self-interest. Team spirit is enhanced by this type of leadership. An example of this factor would be a sales manager who motivates members of the sales force to excel in their work through encouraging words and pep talks that clearly communicate the integral role they play in the future growth of the company.

Intellectual Stimulation. Factor 3 is *intellectual stimulation*. It includes leadership that stimulates followers to be creative and innovative and to challenge their own beliefs and values as well as those of the leader and the organization.

This type of leadership supports followers as they try new approaches and develop innovative ways of dealing with organizational issues. It encourages followers to think things out on their own and engage in careful problem solving. An example of this type of leadership is a plant manager who promotes workers' individual efforts to develop unique ways to solve problems that have caused slowdowns in production.

Individualized Consideration. Factor 4 of transformational leadership is called *individualized consideration*. This factor is representative of leaders who provide a supportive climate in which they listen carefully to the individual needs of followers. Leaders act as coaches and advisers while trying to assist followers in becoming fully actualized. These leaders may use delegation to help followers grow through personal challenges. An example of this type of leadership is a manager who spends time treating each employee in a caring and unique way. To some employees, the leader may give strong affiliation; to others, the leader may give specific directives with a high degree of structure.

In essence, transformational leadership produces greater effects than transactional leadership (Figure 8.3). Whereas transactional leadership results in expected outcomes, transformational leadership results in performance that goes well beyond what is expected. In a meta-analysis of 39 studies in the transformational literature, for example, Lowe, Kroeck, and Sivasubramaniam (1996) found that people who exhibited transformational leadership were perceived to be more effective leaders with better work outcomes than those who exhibited only transactional leadership. These

 Additive Effect

 Mother Theresa

Figure 8.3 The Additive Effect of Transformational Leadership

TRANSFORMATIONAL LEADERSHIP

| Idealized Influence | + | Inspirational Motivation | + | Intellectual Stimulation | + | Individualized Consideration |

TRANSACTIONAL LEADERSHIP

Contingent Reward + Management-by-Exception → Expected Outcomes → Performance Beyond Expectations

SOURCE: Adapted from "The Implications of Transactional and Transformational Leadership for Individual, Team, and Organizational Development," by B. M. Bass and B. J. Avolio, 1990a, *Research in Organizational Change and Development*, 4, 231–272.

findings were true for higher- and lower-level leaders, and for leaders in both public and private settings. Transformational leadership moves followers to accomplish more than what is usually expected of them. They become motivated to transcend their own self-interests for the good of the group or organization (Bass & Avolio, 1990a).

In a study of 220 employees at a large public transport company in Germany, Rowold and Heinitz (2007) found that transformational leadership augmented the impact of transactional leadership on employees' performance and company profit. In addition, they found that transformational leadership and charismatic leadership were overlapping but unique constructs, and that both were different from transactional leadership.

Similarly, Nemanich and Keller (2007) examined the impact of transformational leadership on 447 employees from a large multinational firm who were going through a merger and being integrated into a new organization. They found that transformational leadership behaviors such as idealized influence, inspirational motivation, individualized consideration, and intellectual stimulation were positively related to acquisition acceptance, job satisfaction, and performance.

More recently, Tims, Bakker, and Xanthopoulou (2011) examined the relationship between transformational leadership and work engagement in

 Transformational or Transactional?

42 employees and their supervisors in two different organizations in the Netherlands. Findings revealed that employees became more engaged in their work (i.e., vigor, dedication, and absorption) when their supervisors were able to boost employees' optimism through a transformational leadership style. These findings underscore the important role played by personal characteristics (i.e., optimism) in the transformational leadership-performance process.

Transactional Leadership Factors

Transactional leadership differs from transformational leadership in that the transactional leader does not individualize the needs of followers or focus on their personal development. Transactional leaders exchange things of value with followers to advance their own and their followers' agendas (Kuhnert, 1994). Transactional leaders are influential because it is in the best interest of followers for them to do what the leader wants (Kuhnert & Lewis, 1987).

Contingent Reward. Factor 5, *contingent reward,* is the first of two transactional leadership factors (see Figure 8.2). It is an exchange process between leaders and followers in which effort by followers is exchanged for specified rewards. With this kind of leadership, the leader tries to obtain agreement from followers on what must be done and what the payoffs will be for the people doing it. An example of this type of transaction is a parent who negotiates with a child about how much television the child can watch after practicing the piano. Another example often occurs in the academic setting: A dean negotiates with a college professor about the number and quality of publications he or she needs to have written in order to receive tenure and promotion.

Management-by-Exception. Factor 6 is called *management-by-exception.* It is leadership that involves corrective criticism, negative feedback, and negative reinforcement. Management-by-exception takes two forms: active and passive. A leader using the active form of management-by-exception watches followers closely for mistakes or rule violations and then takes corrective action. An example of active management-by-exception can be illustrated in the leadership of a sales supervisor who daily monitors how employees approach customers. She quickly corrects salespeople who are slow to approach customers in the prescribed manner. A leader using the passive form intervenes only after standards have not been met or problems have arisen. An example of passive management-by-exception is illustrated in the leadership of a supervisor who gives an employee a poor performance evaluation without ever talking with the employee about her or his prior work performance. In essence, both the active and passive management types use more negative reinforcement patterns than the positive reinforcement pattern described in Factor 5 under contingent reward.

Nonleadership Factor

In the model, the nonleadership factor diverges farther from transactional leadership and represents behaviors that are nontransactional.

Laissez-Faire. Factor 7 describes leadership that falls at the far right side of the transactional–transformational leadership continuum (see Figure 8.1). This factor represents the absence of leadership. As the French phrase implies, the *laissez-faire* leader takes a "hands-off, let-things-ride" approach. This leader abdicates responsibility, delays decisions, gives no feedback, and makes little effort to help followers satisfy their needs. There is no exchange with followers or attempt to help them grow. An example of a laissez-faire leader is the president of a small manufacturing firm who calls no meetings with plant supervisors, has no long-range plan for the firm, acts detached, and makes little contact with employees.

Other Transformational Perspectives

In addition to Bass's (1985, 1990; Bass & Avolio, 1994) work, two other lines of research have contributed in unique ways to our understanding of the nature of transformational leadership. They are the research of Bennis and Nanus (1985) and the work of Kouzes and Posner (1987, 2002). These scholars used similar research methods. They identified a number of middle- or senior-level leaders and conducted interviews with them, using open-ended, semistructured questionnaires. From this information, they constructed their models of leadership.

Bennis and Nanus

Bennis and Nanus (1985) asked 90 leaders basic questions such as "What are your strengths and weaknesses?" "What past events most influenced your leadership approach?" and "What were the critical points in your career?" From the answers leaders provided to these questions, Bennis and

▶ Maxwell's Five Levels

Nanus identified four common strategies used by leaders in transforming organizations.

First, transforming leaders had a clear *vision* of the future state of their organizations. It was an image of an attractive, realistic, and believable future (Bennis & Nanus, 1985, p. 89). The vision usually was simple, understandable, beneficial, and energy creating. The compelling nature of the vision touched the experiences of followers and pulled them into supporting the organization. When an organization has a clear vision, it is easier for people within the organization to learn how they fit in with the overall direction of the organization and even the society in general. It empowers them because they feel they are a significant dimension of a worthwhile enterprise (pp. 90–91). Bennis and Nanus found that, to be successful, the vision had to grow out of the needs of the entire organization and to be claimed by those within it. Although leaders play a large role in articulating the vision, the emergence of the vision originates from both the leaders and the followers.

Second, transforming leaders were *social architects* for their organizations. This means they created a shape or form for the shared meanings people maintained within their organizations. These leaders communicated a direction that transformed their organization's values and norms. In many cases, these leaders were able to mobilize people to accept a new group identity or a new philosophy for their organizations.

Third, transforming leaders created *trust* in their organizations by making their own positions clearly known and then standing by them. Trust has to do with being predictable or reliable, even in situations that are uncertain. For organizations, leaders built trust by articulating a direction and then consistently implementing the direction even though the vision may have involved a high degree of uncertainty. Bennis and Nanus (1985) found that when leaders established trust in an organization, it gave the organization a sense of integrity analogous to a healthy identity (p. 48).

Fourth, transforming leaders used *creative deployment of self* through positive self-regard. Leaders knew their strengths and weaknesses, and they emphasized their strengths rather than dwelling on their weaknesses. Based on an awareness of their own competence, effective leaders were able to immerse themselves in their tasks and the overarching goals of their organizations. They were able to fuse a sense of self with the work at hand. Bennis and Nanus also found that positive self-regard in leaders had a reciprocal impact on followers, creating in them feelings of confidence and high expectations. In addition, leaders in the study were committed to learning and relearning, so in their organizations there was consistent emphasis on education.

 Workplace Civility

Kouzes and Posner

Kouzes and Posner (1987, 2002) developed their model by interviewing leaders about leadership. They interviewed more than 1,300 middle- and senior-level managers in private and public sector organizations and asked them to describe their "personal best" experiences as leaders. Based on a content analysis of these descriptions, Kouzes and Posner constructed a model of leadership.

The Kouzes and Posner model consists of five fundamental *practices* that enable leaders to get extraordinary things accomplished: model the way, inspire a shared vision, challenge the process, enable others to act, and encourage the heart. For each of the five practices of exemplary leadership, Kouzes and Posner also have identified two commitments that serve as strategies for practicing exemplary leadership.

Model the Way. To model the way, leaders need to be clear about their own values and philosophy. They need to find their own voice and express it to others. Exemplary leaders set a personal example for others by their own behaviors. They also follow through on their promises and commitments and affirm the common values they share with others.

Inspire a Shared Vision. Effective leaders create compelling visions that can guide people's behavior. They are able to visualize positive outcomes in the future and communicate them to others. Leaders also listen to the dreams of others and show them how their dreams can be realized. Through inspiring visions, leaders challenge others to transcend the status quo to do something for others.

Challenge the Process. Challenging the process means being willing to change the status quo and step into the unknown. It includes being willing to innovate, grow, and improve. Exemplary leaders are like pioneers: They want to experiment and try new things. They are willing to take risks to make things better. When exemplary leaders take risks, they do it one step at a time, learning from their mistakes as they go.

Enable Others to Act. Outstanding leaders are effective at working with people. They build trust with others and promote collaboration. Teamwork and cooperation are highly valued by these leaders. They listen closely to diverse points of view and treat others with dignity and respect. They also allow others to make choices, and they support the decisions that others make. In short, they create environments where people can feel good about their work and how it contributes to the greater community.

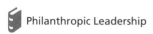 Philanthropic Leadership

Encourage the Heart. Leaders encourage the heart by rewarding others for their accomplishments. It is natural for people to want support and recognition. Effective leaders are attentive to this need and are willing to give praise to workers for jobs well done. They use authentic celebrations and rituals to show appreciation and encouragement to others. The outcome of this kind of support is greater collective identity and community spirit.

Overall, the Kouzes and Posner model emphasizes behaviors and has a prescriptive quality: It recommends what people need to do in order to become effective leaders. The five practices and their accompanying commitments provide a unique set of prescriptions for leaders. Kouzes and Posner (2002, p. 13) stressed that the five practices of exemplary leadership are available to everyone and are not reserved for those with "special" ability. The model is not about personality: It is about practice.

To measure the behaviors described in the model, Kouzes and Posner developed the Leadership Practices Inventory (LPI). The LPI is a 360-degree leadership assessment tool that consists of 30 questions that assess individual leadership competencies. It has been widely used in leadership training and development.

HOW DOES THE TRANSFORMATIONAL APPROACH WORK?

The transformational approach to leadership is a broad-based perspective that encompasses many facets and dimensions of the leadership process. In general, it describes how leaders can initiate, develop, and carry out significant changes in organizations. Although not definitive, the steps followed by transformational leaders usually take the following form.

Transformational leaders set out to empower followers and nurture them in change. They attempt to raise the consciousness in individuals and to get them to transcend their own self-interests for the sake of others. For example, Jung, Chow, and Wu (2003) studied upper-level leadership in 32 Taiwanese companies and found that transformational leadership was directly related to organizational innovation. Transformational leadership created a culture in which employees felt empowered and encouraged to freely discuss and try new things.

To create change, transformational leaders become strong role models for their followers. They have a highly developed set of moral values and a self-determined sense of identity (Avolio & Gibbons, 1988). They are confident,

 Achieving More Than Expected

competent, and articulate, and they express strong ideals. They listen to followers and are not intolerant of opposing viewpoints. A spirit of cooperation often develops between these leaders and their followers. Followers want to emulate transformational leaders because they learn to trust them and believe in the ideas for which they stand.

It is common for transformational leaders to create a vision. The vision emerges from the collective interests of various individuals and units in an organization. The vision is a focal point for transformational leadership. It gives the leader and the organization a conceptual map for where the organization is headed; it gives meaning and clarifies the organization's identity. Furthermore, the vision gives followers a sense of identity within the organization and also a sense of self-efficacy (Shamir et al., 1993).

The transformational approach also requires that leaders become social architects. This means that they make clear the emerging values and norms of the organization. They involve themselves in the culture of the organization and help shape its meaning. People need to know their roles and understand how they contribute to the greater purposes of the organization. Transformational leaders are out front in interpreting and shaping for organizations the shared meanings that exist within them.

Throughout the process, transformational leaders are effective at working with people. They build trust and foster collaboration with others. Transformational leaders encourage others and celebrate their accomplishments. In the end, transformational leadership results in people feeling better about themselves and their contributions to the greater common good.

STRENGTHS

In its present stage of development, the transformational approach has several strengths. First, transformational leadership has been widely researched from many different perspectives, including a series of qualitative studies of prominent leaders and CEOs in large, well-known organizations. It has also been the focal point for a large body of leadership research since its introduction in the 1970s. For example, content analysis of all the articles published in *Leadership Quarterly* from 1990 to 2000 showed that 34% of the articles were about transformational or charismatic leadership (Lowe & Gardner, 2001).

Second, transformational leadership has intuitive appeal. The transformational perspective describes how the leader is out front advocating change

 Inspiring Leaders

for others; this concept is consistent with society's popular notion of what leadership means. People are attracted to transformational leadership because it makes sense to them. It is appealing that a leader will provide a vision for the future.

Third, transformational leadership treats leadership as a process that occurs between followers and leaders. Because this process incorporates both the followers' and the leader's needs, leadership is not the sole responsibility of a leader but rather emerges from the interplay between leaders and followers. The needs of others are central to the transformational leader. As a result, followers gain a more prominent position in the leadership process because their attributions are instrumental in the evolving transformational process (Bryman, 1992, p. 176).

Fourth, the transformational approach provides a broader view of leadership that augments other leadership models. Many leadership models focus primarily on how leaders exchange rewards for achieved goals—the transactional process. The transformational approach provides an expanded picture of leadership that includes not only the exchange of rewards, but also leaders' attention to the needs and growth of followers (Avolio, 1999; Bass, 1985).

Fifth, transformational leadership places a strong emphasis on followers' needs, values, and morals. Burns (1978) suggested that transformational leadership involves attempts by leaders to move people to higher standards of moral responsibility. It includes motivating followers to transcend their own self-interests for the good of the team, organization, or community (Howell & Avolio, 1993; Shamir et al., 1993). Transformational leadership is fundamentally morally uplifting (Avolio, 1999). This emphasis sets the transformational approach apart from all other approaches to leadership because it suggests that leadership has a moral dimension. Therefore, the coercive uses of power by people such as Hitler, Jim Jones, and David Koresh can be disregarded as models of leadership.

Finally, there is substantial evidence that transformational leadership is an effective form of leadership (Yukl, 1999). In a critique of transformational and charismatic leadership, Yukl reported that in studies using the Multifactor Leadership Questionnaire (MLQ) to appraise leaders, transformational leadership was positively related to follower satisfaction, motivation, and performance. Furthermore, in studies that used interviews and observations, transformational leadership was shown to be effective in a variety of different situations.

 Morals Matter

CRITICISMS

Transformational leadership has several weaknesses. One criticism is that it lacks conceptual clarity. Because it covers such a wide range of activities and characteristics—including creating a vision, motivating, being a change agent, building trust, giving nurturance, and acting as a social architect, to name a few—it is difficult to define exactly the parameters of transformational leadership. Specifically, research by Tracey and Hinkin (1998) has shown substantial overlap between each of the Four *I*s (idealized influence, inspirational motivation, intellectual stimulation, and individualized consideration), suggesting that the dimensions are not clearly delimited. Furthermore, the parameters of transformational leadership often overlap with similar conceptualizations of leadership. Bryman (1992), for example, pointed out that transformational and charismatic leadership often are treated synonymously, even though in some models of leadership (e.g., Bass, 1985) charisma is only one component of transformational leadership.

Another criticism revolves around how transformational leadership is measured. Researchers typically have used some version of the MLQ to measure transformational leadership. However, some studies have challenged the validity of the MLQ. In some versions of the MLQ, the four factors of transformational leadership (the Four *I*s) correlate highly with each other, which means they are not distinct factors (Tejeda, Scandura, & Pillai, 2001). In addition, some of the transformational factors correlate with the transactional and laissez-faire factors, which means they may not be unique to the transformational model (Tejeda et al., 2001).

A third criticism is that transformational leadership treats leadership as a personality trait or personal predisposition rather than a behavior that people can learn (Bryman, 1992, pp. 100–102). If it is a trait, training people in this approach becomes more problematic because it is difficult to teach people how to change their traits. Even though many scholars, including Weber, House, and Bass, emphasized that transformational leadership is concerned with leader behaviors, such as how leaders involve themselves with followers, there is an inclination to see this approach from a trait perspective. Perhaps this problem is exacerbated because the word *transformational* creates images of one person being the most active component in the leadership process. For example, even though "creating a vision" involves follower input, there is a tendency to see transformational leaders as visionaries. There is also a tendency to see transformational leaders as people who have special qualities that *transform* others. These images accentuate a trait characterization of transformational leadership.

Comparing Leadership Theories

Fourth, researchers have not established that transformational leaders are actually able to transform individuals and organizations (Antonakis, 2012). There is evidence that indicates that transformational leadership is associated with positive outcomes, such as organizational effectiveness; however, studies have not yet clearly established a causal link between transformational leaders and changes in followers or organizations.

A fifth criticism some have made is that transformational leadership is elitist and antidemocratic (Avolio, 1999; Bass & Avolio, 1993). Transformational leaders often play a direct role in creating changes, establishing a vision, and advocating new directions. This gives the strong impression that the leader is acting independently of followers or putting himself or herself above the followers' needs. Although this criticism of elitism has been refuted by Bass and Avolio (1993) and Avolio (1999), who contended that transformational leaders can be directive and participative as well as democratic and authoritarian, the substance of the criticism raises valid questions about transformational leadership.

Related to this criticism, some have argued that transformational leadership suffers from a "heroic leadership" bias (Yukl, 1999). Transformational leadership stresses that it is the *leader* who moves *followers* to do exceptional things. By focusing primarily on the leader, researchers have failed to give attention to shared leadership or reciprocal influence. Followers can influence leaders just as leaders can influence followers. More attention should be directed toward how leaders can encourage followers to challenge the leader's vision and share in the leadership process.

A final criticism of transformational leadership is that it has the potential to be abused. Transformational leadership is concerned with changing people's values and moving them to a new vision. But who is to determine whether the new directions are good and more affirming? Who decides that a new vision is a better vision? If the values to which the leader is moving his or her followers are not better, and if the set of human values is not more redeeming, then the leadership must be challenged. However, the dynamics of how followers challenge leaders or respond to their visions is not fully understood.

There is a need to understand how transformational leaders affect followers psychologically and how leaders respond to followers' reactions. In fact, Burns argued that understanding this area (i.e., charisma and follower worship) is one of the central problems in leadership studies today (Bailey & Axelrod, 2001). The charismatic nature of transformational leadership presents significant risks for organizations because it can be used for destructive purposes (Conger, 1999; Howell & Avolio, 1993).

History is full of examples of charismatic individuals who used coercive power to lead people to evil ends. For this reason, transformational leadership puts a burden on individuals and organizations to be aware of how they are being influenced and in what directions they are being asked to go. Christie et al. (2011) warn that astute followers need to be vigilant and pay careful attention to the vision of their leader, whether it is collective or self-focused, whether the leader is tolerant of opposing viewpoints, and whether the leader is caring of followers. The potential for abuse of transformational leadership is mitigated when followers are aware and engaged in how they are being led.

APPLICATION

Rather than being a model that tells leaders what to do, transformational leadership provides a broad set of generalizations of what is typical of leaders who are transforming or who work in transforming contexts. Unlike other leadership approaches, such as Situational Leadership® (discussed in Chapter 5), transformational leadership does not provide a clearly defined set of assumptions about how leaders should act in a particular situation to be successful. Rather, it provides a general way of thinking about leadership that emphasizes ideals, inspiration, innovations, and individual concerns. Transformational leadership requires that leaders be aware of how their own behavior relates to the needs of their followers and the changing dynamics within their organizations.

Bass and Avolio (1990a) suggested that transformational leadership can be taught to people at all levels in an organization and that it can positively affect a firm's performance. It can be used in recruitment, selection and promotion, and training and development. It can also be used in improving team development, decision-making groups, quality initiatives, and reorganizations (Bass & Avolio, 1994).

Programs designed to develop transformational leadership usually require that leaders or their associates take the MLQ (Bass & Avolio, 1990b) or a similar questionnaire to determine the leader's particular strengths and weaknesses in transformational leadership. Taking the MLQ helps leaders pinpoint areas in which they could improve their leadership. For example, leaders might learn that it would be beneficial if they were more confident in expressing their goals, or that they need to spend more time nurturing followers, or that they need to be more tolerant of opposing viewpoints. The MLQ is the springboard to helping leaders improve a whole series of their leadership attributes.

One particular aspect of transformational leadership that has been given special emphasis in training programs is the process of building a vision. For

N Become a Transformational Leader

example, it has become quite common for training programs to have leaders write elaborate statements that describe their own five-year career plans and their perceptions of the future directions for their organizations. Working with leaders on vision statements is one way to help them enhance their transformational leadership behavior. Another important aspect of training is teaching leaders to exhibit greater individual consideration and promote intellectual stimulation for their followers. Lowe et al. (1996) found that this is particularly valuable for lower-level leaders in organizations.

The desire to provide effective training in how to be more successful in demonstrating transactional and transformational leadership resulted in the development of a guide by Sosik and Jung (2010). This comprehensive, evidence-based approach includes self-assessments, 360-degree feedback, and leadership development planning. Their work serves as a thorough training guide that explains how, when, and why the full range of leadership behaviors work.

Overall, transformational leadership provides leaders with information about a full range of their behaviors, from nontransactional to transactional to transformational. In the next section, we provide some actual leadership examples to which the principles of transformational leadership can be applied.

——————— CASE STUDIES ———————

In the following section, three brief case studies (Cases 8.1, 8.2, and 8.3) from very different contexts are provided. Each case describes a situation in which transformational leadership is present to some degree. The questions at the end of each case point to some of the unique issues surrounding the use of transformational leadership in ongoing organizations.

CASE 8.1

The Vision Failed

High Tech Engineering (HTE) is a 50-year-old family-owned manufacturing company with 250 employees that produces small parts for the aircraft industry. The president of HTE is Harold Barelli, who came to the company from a smaller business with strong credentials as a leader in

(Continued)

 Transformational Leadership in Education

(Continued)

advanced aircraft technology. Before Harold, the only other president of HTE was the founder and owner of the company. The organizational structure at HTE was very traditional, and it was supported by a very rich organizational culture.

As the new president, Harold sincerely wanted to transform HTE. He wanted to prove that new technologies and advanced management techniques could make HTE one of the best manufacturing companies in the country. To that end, Harold created a vision statement that was displayed throughout the company. The two-page statement, which had a strong democratic tone, described the overall purposes, directions, and values of the company.

During the first 3 years of Harold's tenure as president, several major reorganizations took place at the company. These were designed by Harold and a select few of his senior managers. The intention of each reorganization was to implement advanced organizational structures to bolster the declared HTE vision.

Yet the major outcome of each of the changes was to dilute the leadership and create a feeling of instability among the employees. Most of the changes were made from the top down, with little input from lower or middle management. Some of the changes gave employees more control in circumstances where they needed less, whereas other changes limited employee input in contexts where employees should have been given more input. There were some situations in which individual workers reported to three different bosses, and other situations in which one manager had far too many workers to oversee. Rather than feeling comfortable in their various roles at HTE, employees began to feel uncertain about their responsibilities and how they contributed to stated goals of the company. The overall effect of the reorganizations was a precipitous drop in worker morale and production.

In the midst of all the changes, the vision that Harold had for the company was lost. The instability that employees felt made it difficult for them to support the company's vision. People at HTE complained that although mission statements were displayed throughout the company, no one understood in which direction they were going.

To the employees at HTE, Harold was an enigma. HTE was an American company that produced U.S. products, but Harold drove a foreign car. Harold claimed to be democratic in his style of leadership, but he was arbitrary in how he treated people. He acted in a nondirective style toward some people, and he showed arbitrary control toward others. He wanted to be seen as a hands-on manager, but he delegated operational control of the company to others while he focused on external customer relations and matters of the board of directors.

At times Harold appeared to be insensitive to employees' concerns. He wanted HTE to be an environment in which everyone could feel empowered, but he often failed to listen closely to what employees were saying.

He seldom engaged in open, two-way communication. HTE had a long, rich history with many unique stories, but the employees felt that Harold either misunderstood or did not care about that history.

Four years after arriving at HTE, Harold stepped down as president after his operations officer ran the company into a large debt and cash-flow crisis. His dream of building HTE into a world-class manufacturing company was never realized.

Questions

1. If you were consulting with the HTE board of directors soon after Harold started making changes, what would you advise them regarding Harold's leadership from a transformational perspective?

2. Did Harold have a clear vision for HTE? Was he able to implement it?

3. How effective was Harold as a change agent and social architect for HTE?

4. What would you advise Harold to do differently if he had the chance to return as president of HTE?

CASE 8.2

An Exploration in Leadership

Every year, Dr. Cook, a college professor, leads a group of 25 college students to the Middle East on an archaeological dig that usually lasts about 8 weeks. The participants, who come from big and small colleges throughout the country, usually have little prior knowledge or background in what takes place during an excavation. Dr. Cook enjoys leading these expeditions because he likes teaching students about archaeology and because the outcomes of the digs actually advance his own scholarly work.

(Continued)

(Continued)

While planning for his annual summer excavation, Dr. Cook told the following story:

This summer will be interesting because I have 10 people returning from last year. Last year was quite a dig. During the first couple of weeks everything was very disjointed. Team members seemed unmotivated and tired. In fact, there was one time early on when it seemed as if nearly half the students were either physically ill or mentally exhausted. Students seemed lost and uncertain about the meaning of the entire project.

For example, it is our tradition to get up every morning at 4:30 a.m. to depart for the excavation site at 5:00 a.m. However, during the first weeks of the dig, few people were ever ready at 5, even after several reminders.

Every year it takes some time for people to learn where they fit with each other and with the purposes of the dig. The students all come from such different backgrounds. Some are from small, private, religious schools, and others are from large state universities. Each comes with a different agenda, different skills, and different work habits. One person may be a good photographer, another a good artist, and another a good surveyor. It is my job to complete the excavation with the resources available to us.

At the end of Week 2, I called a meeting to assess how things were going. We talked about a lot of things including personal things, how our work was progressing, and what we needed to change. The students seemed to appreciate the chance to talk at this meeting. Each of them described his or her special circumstances and hopes for the summer.

I told the students several stories about past digs; some were humorous, and others highlighted accomplishments. I shared my particular interests in this project and how I thought we as a group could accomplish the work that needed to be done at this important historical site. In particular, I stressed two points: (a) that they shared the responsibility for the successful outcome of the venture, and (b) that they had independent authority to design, schedule, and carry out the details of their respective assignments, with the director and other senior staff available at all times as advisers and resource persons. In regard to the departure time issue, I told the participants that the standard departure time on digs was 5:00 a.m.

Well, shortly after our meeting I observed a real shift in the group attitude and atmosphere. People seemed to become more involved in the work, there was less sickness, and there was more camaraderie. All assignments were completed without constant prodding and in a spirit of mutual support. Each morning at 5:00 a.m. everyone was ready to go.

I find that each year my groups are different. It's almost as if each of them has a unique personality. Perhaps that is why I find it so challenging. I try to listen to the students and use their particular strengths. It really is quite amazing how these students can develop in 8 weeks. They really become good at archaeology, and they accomplish a great deal.

This coming year will again be different because of the 10 returning "veterans."

Questions

1. How is this an example of transformational leadership?

2. Where are Dr. Cook's strengths on the Full Range of Leadership model (see Figure 8.2)?

3. What is the vision Dr. Cook has for the archaeology excavations?

CASE 8.3

Her Vision of a Model Research Center

Rachel Adams began as a researcher at a large pharmaceutical company. After several years of observing how clinical drug studies were conducted, she realized that there was a need and an opportunity for a research center not connected with a specific pharmaceutical company. In collaboration with other researchers, she launched a new company that was the first of its kind in the country. Within 5 years, Rachel had become president and CEO of the Independent Center for Clinical Research (ICCR). Under Rachel's leadership, ICCR has grown to a company with revenues of $6 million and profits of $1 million. ICCR employs 100 full-time employees, most of whom are women.

Rachel wants ICCR to continue its pattern of formidable growth. Her vision for the company is to make it a model research center that will blend credible science with efficient and cost-effective clinical trials. To that end, the company, which is situated in a large urban setting, maintains strong links to academia, industry, and the community.

Rachel and her style have a great deal to do with the success of ICCR. She is a freethinker who is always open to new ideas, opportunities,

(Continued)

(Continued)

and approaches. She is a positive person who enjoys the nuances of life, and she is not afraid to take risks. Her optimistic approach has had a significant influence on the company's achievements and its organizational climate. People employed at ICCR claim they have never worked at a place that is so progressive and so positive in how it treats its employees and customers. The women employees at ICCR feel particularly strongly about Rachel's leadership, and many of them use Rachel as a role model. It is not by accident that the majority (85%) of the people who work at ICCR are women. Her support for women's concerns is evident in the type of drug studies the company selects to conduct and in her service to national committees on women's health and research issues. Within ICCR, Rachel has designed an on-site day care program, flextime scheduling for mothers with young children, and a benefit package that gives full health coverage to part-time employees. At a time when most companies are searching for ways to include more women in decision making, ICCR has women in established leadership positions at all levels.

Although Rachel has been extremely effective at ICCR, the success of the company has resulted in many changes that have affected Rachel's leadership at the company.

Rapid growth of ICCR has required that Rachel spend a great deal of time traveling throughout the country. Because of her excessive travel, Rachel has begun to feel distant from the day-to-day operations of ICCR. She has begun to feel as if she is losing her handle on what makes the company tick. For example, although she used to give weekly pep talks to supervisors, she finds that she now gives two formal presentations a year. Rachel also complains of feeling estranged from employees at the company. At a recent directors' meeting, she expressed frustration that people no longer called her by her first name, and others did not even know who she was.

Growth at ICCR has also demanded that more planning and decision making be delegated to department heads. This has been problematic for Rachel, particularly in the area of strategic planning. Rachel finds that the department heads are beginning to shift the focus of ICCR in a direction that contradicts her ideal model of what the company should be and what it is best at doing. Rachel built the company on the idea that ICCR would be a strong blend of credible science and cost-effective clinical trials, and she does not want to give up that model. The directors, on the other hand, would like to see ICCR become similar to a standard pharmaceutical company dedicated primarily to the research and development of new drugs.

Questions

1. What is it about Rachel's leadership that clearly suggests that she is engaged in transformational leadership?

2. In what ways has the growth of ICCR had an impact on Rachel's leadership?

3. Given the problems Rachel is confronting as a result of the growth of the company, what should she do to reestablish herself as a transformational leader at ICCR?

LEADERSHIP INSTRUMENT

The most widely used measure of transformational leadership is the Multifactor Leadership Questionnaire (MLQ). An earlier version of the MLQ was developed by Bass (1985), based on a series of interviews he and his associates conducted with 70 senior executives in South Africa. These executives were asked to recall leaders who had raised their awareness to broader goals, moved them to higher motives, or inspired them to put others' interests ahead of their own. The executives were then asked to describe how these leaders behaved—what they did to effect change. From these descriptions and from numerous other interviews with both junior and senior executives, Bass constructed the questions that make up the MLQ. The questions measure followers' perceptions of a leader's behavior for each of the factors in the Full Range of Leadership model (see Figure 8.2).

Antonakis, Avolio, and Sivasubramaniam (2003) assessed the psychometric properties of the MLQ using a business sample of more than 3,000 raters and found strong support for the validity of the MLQ. They found that the MLQ (Form 5X) clearly distinguished nine factors in the Full Range of Leadership model. Similarly, Hinkin and Schriesheim (2008) examined the empirical properties of the transactional and the nonleadership factors on the MLQ and identified several ways to use the questionnaire to generate more reliable and valid results. Since the MLQ was first designed, it has gone through many revisions, and it continues to be refined to strengthen its reliability and validity.

Based on a summary analysis of a series of studies that used the MLQ to predict how transformational leadership relates to outcomes such as effectiveness, Bryman (1992) and Bass and Avolio (1994) have suggested that the charisma and motivation factors on the MLQ are the most likely to be related to positive effects. Individualized consideration, intellectual stimulation, and contingent reward are the next most important factors. Management-by-exception in its passive form has been found to be somewhat related to outcomes, and in its active form it has been found to be negatively related to outcomes. Generally, laissez-faire leadership has been found to be negatively related to outcomes such as effectiveness and satisfaction in organizations.

We present sample items from the MLQ (Form 5X-short) in this section so that you can explore your beliefs and perceptions about transformational, transactional, and nontransactional leadership. This questionnaire should give you a clearer picture of your own style and the complexity of transformational leadership itself.

Sample Items From the Multifactor Leadership Questionnaire (MLQ) Form 5X-Short

These questions provide examples of the items that are used to evaluate leadership style. The MLQ is provided in both Self and Rater forms. The Self form measures self-perception of leadership behaviors. The Rater form is used to measure leadership. By thinking about the leadership styles as exemplified below, you can get a sense of your own belief about your leadership.

Key: 0 = Not   1 = Once in   2 = Sometimes   3 = Fairly   4 = Frequently,
          at all   a while   often   if not always

Transformational Leadership Styles

Idealized Influence (Attributes)	I go beyond self-interest for the good of the group.	0 1 2 3 4
Idealized Influence (Behaviors)	I consider the moral and ethical consequences of decisions.	0 1 2 3 4
Inspirational Motivation	I talk optimistically about the future.	0 1 2 3 4
Intellectual Stimulation	I reexamine critical assumptions to question whether they are appropriate.	0 1 2 3 4
Individualized Consideration	I help others to develop their strengths.	0 1 2 3 4

Transactional Leadership Styles

Contingent Reward	I make clear what one can expect to receive when performance goals are achieved.	0 1 2 3 4
Management by Exception: Active	I keep track of all mistakes.	0 1 2 3 4

Passive/Avoidant Leadership Styles

Management by Exception: Passive	I wait for things to go wrong before taking action.	0 1 2 3 4
Laissez-Faire	I avoid making decisions.	0 1 2 3 4

SUMMARY

One of the most encompassing approaches to leadership—transformational leadership—is concerned with the process of how certain leaders are able to inspire followers to accomplish great things. This approach stresses that leaders need to understand and adapt to the needs and motives of followers. Transformational leaders are recognized as change agents who are good role models, who can create and articulate a clear vision for an organization, who empower followers to meet higher standards, who act in ways that make others want to trust them, and who give meaning to organizational life.

Transformational leadership emerged from and is rooted in the writings of Burns (1978) and Bass (1985). The works of Bennis and Nanus (1985) and Kouzes and Posner (1987) are also representative of transformational leadership.

Transformational leadership can be assessed through use of the Multifactor Leadership Questionnaire (MLQ), which measures a leader's behavior in seven areas: idealized influence (charisma), inspirational motivation, intellectual stimulation, individualized consideration, contingent reward, management-by-exception, and laissez-faire. High scores on individualized consideration and motivation factors are most indicative of strong transformational leadership.

There are several positive features of the transformational approach, including that it is a current model that has received a lot of attention by researchers, it has strong intuitive appeal, it emphasizes the importance of followers in the leadership process, it goes beyond traditional transactional models and broadens leadership to include the growth of followers, and it places strong emphasis on morals and values.

Balancing against the positive features of transformational leadership are several weaknesses. These include that the approach lacks conceptual clarity; it is based on the MLQ, which has been challenged by some research; it creates a framework that implies that transformational leadership has a trait-like quality; it is sometimes seen as elitist and undemocratic; it suffers from a "heroic leadership" bias; and it has the potential to be used counterproductively in negative ways by leaders. Despite the weaknesses, transformational leadership appears to be a valuable and widely used approach.

Sharpen your skills with SAGE edge at **edge.sagepub.com/northouse7e**

REFERENCES

Antonakis, J. (2012). Transformational and charismatic leadership. In D. V. Day & J. Antonakis (Eds.), *The nature of leadership* (2nd ed., pp. 256–288). Thousand Oaks, CA: SAGE.

Antonakis, J., Avolio, B. J., & Sivasubramaniam, N. (2003). Context and leadership: An examination of the nine-factor full-range leadership theory using the Multifactor Leadership Questionnaire. *Leadership Quarterly, 14*(3), 261–295.

Avolio, B. J. (1999). *Full leadership development: Building the vital forces in organizations.* Thousand Oaks, CA: SAGE.

Avolio, B. J., & Gibbons, T. C. (1988). Developing transformational leaders: A life span approach. In J. A. Conger, R. N. Kanungo, & Associates (Eds.), *Charismatic leadership: The elusive factor in organizational effectiveness* (pp. 276–308). San Francisco: Jossey-Bass.

Bailey, J., & Axelrod, R. H. (2001). Leadership lessons from Mount Rushmore: An interview with James MacGregor Burns. *Leadership Quarterly, 12,* 113–127.

Bass, B. M. (1985). *Leadership and performance beyond expectations.* New York: Free Press.

Bass, B. M. (1990). From transactional to transformational leadership: Learning to share the vision. *Organizational Dynamics, 18,* 19–31.

Bass, B. M. (1998). The ethics of transformational leadership. In J. Ciulla (Ed.), *Ethics: The heart of leadership* (pp. 169–192). Westport, CT: Praeger.

Bass, B. M., & Avolio, B. J. (1990a). The implications of transactional and transformational leadership for individual, team, and organizational development. *Research in Organizational Change and Development, 4,* 231–272.

Bass, B. M., & Avolio, B. J. (1990b). *Multifactor Leadership Questionnaire.* Palo Alto, CA: Consulting Psychologists Press.

Bass, B. M., & Avolio, B. J. (1993). Transformational leadership: A response to critiques. In M. M. Chemers & R. Ayman (Eds.), *Leadership theory and research: Perspectives and directions* (pp. 49–80). San Diego, CA: Academic Press.

Bass, B. M., & Avolio, B. J. (1994). *Improving organizational effectiveness through transformational leadership.* Thousand Oaks, CA: SAGE.

Bass, B. M., & Avolio, B. J. (1995). *Multifactor Leadership Questionnaire for research.* Menlo Park, CA: Mind Garden.

Bass, B. M., & Riggio, R. E. (2006). *Transformational leadership* (2nd ed.). Mahwah, NJ: Lawrence Erlbaum.

Bass, B. M., & Steidlmeier, P. (1999). Ethics, character, and authentic transformational leadership. *Leadership Quarterly, 10,* 181–217.

Bennis, W. G., & Nanus, B. (1985). *Leaders: The strategies for taking charge.* New York: Harper & Row.

Bryman, A. (1992). *Charisma and leadership in organizations.* London: SAGE.

Burns, J. M. (1978). *Leadership.* New York: Harper & Row.

Christie, A., Barling, J., & Turner, N. (2011). Pseudo-transformational leadership: Model specification and outcomes. *Journal of Applied Social Psychology, 44*(12), 2943–2984.

Conger, J. A. (1999). Charismatic and transformational leadership in organizations: An insider's perspective on these developing streams of research. *Leadership Quarterly, 10*(2), 145–179.

Conger, J. A., & Kanungo, R. N. (1998). *Charismatic leadership in organizations.* Thousand Oaks, CA: SAGE.

Downton, J. V. (1973). *Rebel leadership: Commitment and charisma in a revolutionary process.* New York: Free Press.

Hinkin, T. R., & Schriesheim, C. A. (2008). A theoretical and empirical examination of the transactional and non-leadership dimensions of the Multifactor Leadership Questionnaire (MLQ). *Leadership Quarterly, 19,* 501–513.

House, R. J. (1976). A 1976 theory of charismatic leadership. In J. G. Hunt & L. L. Larson (Eds.), *Leadership: The cutting edge* (pp. 189–207). Carbondale: Southern Illinois University Press.

Howell, J. M., & Avolio, B. J. (1993). The ethics of charismatic leadership: Submission or liberation? *Academy of Management Executive, 6*(2), 43–54.

Hunt, J. G., & Conger, J. A. (1999). From where we sit: An assessment of transformational and charismatic leadership research. *Leadership Quarterly, 10*(3), 335–343.

Jung, D. I., Chow, C., & Wu, A. (2003). The role of transformational leadership in enhancing organizational innovation: Hypotheses and some preliminary findings. *Leadership Quarterly, 14*(4–5), 525–544.

Kouzes, J. M., & Posner, B. Z. (1987). *The leadership challenge: How to get extraordinary things done in organizations.* San Francisco: Jossey-Bass.

Kouzes, J. M., & Posner, B. Z. (2002). *The leadership challenge* (3rd ed.). San Francisco: Jossey-Bass.

Kuhnert, K. W. (1994). Transforming leadership: Developing people through delegation. In B. M. Bass & B. J. Avolio (Eds.), *Improving organizational effectiveness through transformational leadership* (pp. 10–25). Thousand Oaks, CA: SAGE.

Kuhnert, K. W., & Lewis, P. (1987). Transactional and transformational leadership: A constructive/developmental analysis. *Academy of Management Review, 12*(4), 648–657.

Lowe, K. B., & Gardner, W. L. (2001). Ten years of the *Leadership Quarterly:* Contributions and challenges for the future. *Leadership Quarterly, 11*(4), 459–514.

Lowe, K. B., Kroeck, K. G., & Sivasubramaniam, N. (1996). Effectiveness correlates of transformational and transactional leadership: A meta-analytic review of the MLQ literature. *Leadership Quarterly, 7*(3), 385–425.

Nemanich, L. A., & Keller, R. T. (2007). Transformational leadership in an acquisition: A field study of employees. *Leadership Quarterly, 18,* 49–68.

Rowold, J., & Heinitz, K. (2007). Transformational and charismatic leadership: Assessing the convergent, divergent and criterion validity of the MLQ and the CKS. *Leadership Quarterly, 18,* 121–133.

Shamir, B., House, R. J., & Arthur, M. B. (1993). The motivational effects of charismatic leadership: A self-concept based theory. *Organization Science, 4*(4), 577–594.

Sosik, J. J., & Jung, D. I. (2010). *Full range leadership development: Pathways for people, profit, and planet.* New York: Psychology Press.

Tejeda, M. J., Scandura, T. A., & Pillai, R. (2001). The MLQ revisited: Psychometric properties and recommendations. *Leadership Quarterly, 12,* 31–52.

Tims, M., Bakker, A. B., & Xanthopoulou, D. (2011). Do transformational leaders enhance their followers' daily work engagement? *Leadership Quarterly, 22,* 121–131.

Tracey, J. B., & Hinkin, T. R. (1998). Transformational leadership or effective managerial practices? *Group & Organization Management, 23*(3), 220–236.

Weber, M. (1947). *The theory of social and economic organizations* (T. Parsons, Trans.). New York: Free Press.

Yammarino, F. J. (1993). Transforming leadership studies: Bernard Bass' leadership and performance beyond expectations. *Leadership Quarterly, 4*(3), 379–382.

Yukl, G. A. (1999). An evaluation of conceptual weaknesses in transformational and charismatic leadership theories. *Leadership Quarterly, 10*(2), 285–305.

Zhu, W., Avolio, B. J., Riggio, R. E., & Sosik, J. J. (2011). The effect of authentic transformational leadership on follower and group ethics. *Leadership Quarterly, 22,* 801–817.

9

Authentic Leadership

DESCRIPTION

Authentic leadership represents one of the newest areas of leadership research. It focuses on whether leadership is genuine and "real." As the title of this approach implies, authentic leadership is about the *authenticity* of leaders and their leadership. Unlike many of the theories that we have discussed in this book, authentic leadership is still in the formative phase of development. As a result, authentic leadership needs to be considered more tentatively: It is likely to change as new research about the theory is published.

In recent times, upheavals in society have energized a tremendous demand for authentic leadership. The destruction on 9/11, corporate scandals at companies like WorldCom and Enron, and massive failures in the banking industry have all created fear and uncertainty. People feel apprehensive and insecure about what is going on around them, and as a result, they long for bona fide leadership they can trust and for leaders who are honest and good. People's demands for trustworthy leadership make the study of authentic leadership timely and worthwhile.

In addition to the public's interest, authentic leadership has been intriguing to researchers: It was identified earlier in transformational leadership research but never fully articulated (Bass, 1990; Bass & Steidlmeier, 1999; Burns, 1978; Howell & Avolio, 1993). Furthermore, practitioners had developed approaches to authentic leadership that were not evidence based, and so needed further clarification and testing. In attempts to more fully explore authentic leadership, researchers set out to identify the parameters of authentic leadership and more clearly conceptualize it, efforts that continue today.

Ⓝ Authentic Leadership   ▶ Character and Purpose

Authentic Leadership Defined

On the surface, authentic leadership appears easy to define. In actuality, it is a complex process that is difficult to characterize. Among leadership scholars, there is no single accepted definition of authentic leadership. Instead, there are multiple definitions, each written from a different viewpoint and with a different emphasis (Chan, 2005).

One of those viewpoints is the *intrapersonal* perspective, which focuses closely on the leader and what goes on within the leader. It incorporates the leader's self-knowledge, self-regulation, and self-concept. In Shamir and Eilam's (2005) description of the intrapersonal approach, they suggest that authentic leaders exhibit genuine leadership, lead from conviction, and are originals, not copies. This perspective emphasizes a leader's life experiences and the meaning he or she attaches to those experiences as being critical to the development of the authentic leader.

A second way of defining authentic leadership is as an *interpersonal* process. This perspective outlines authentic leadership as relational, created by leaders and followers together (Eagly, 2005). It results not from the leader's efforts alone, but also from the response of followers. Authenticity emerges from the interactions between leaders and followers. It is a reciprocal process because leaders affect followers and followers affect leaders.

Finally, authentic leadership can be defined from a *developmental* perspective, which is exemplified in the work of Avolio and his associates (Avolio & Gardner, 2005; Gardner, Avolio, & Walumbwa, 2005; Walumbwa, Avolio, Gardner, Wernsing, & Peterson, 2008). This perspective, which underpins the approaches to authentic leadership discussed in the following section, views authentic leadership as something that can be nurtured in a leader, rather than as a fixed trait. Authentic leadership develops in people over a lifetime and can be triggered by major life events, such as a severe illness or a new career.

Taking a developmental approach, Walumbwa et al. (2008) conceptualized authentic leadership as a pattern of leader behavior that develops from and is grounded in the leader's positive psychological qualities and strong ethics. They suggest that authentic leadership is composed of four distinct but related components: self-awareness, internalized moral perspective, balanced processing, and relational transparency (Avolio, Walumbwa, & Weber, 2009). Over a lifetime, authentic leaders learn and develop each of these four types of behavior.

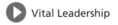 Building Authenticity   Vital Leadership

Approaches to Authentic Leadership

Formulations about authentic leadership can be differentiated into two areas: (1) the practical approach, which evolved from real-life examples and training and development literature; and (2) the theoretical approach, which is based on findings from social science research. Both approaches offer interesting insights about the complex process of authentic leadership.

Practical Approach

Books and programs about authentic leadership are popular today; people are interested in the basics of this type of leadership. Specifically, they want to know the "how to" steps to become an authentic leader. In this section, we will discuss Bill George's authentic leadership approach (2003).

Bill George's Authentic Leadership Approach. The authentic leadership approach developed by George (2003; George & Sims, 2007) focuses on the characteristics of authentic leaders. George describes, in a practical way, the essential qualities of authentic leadership and how individuals can develop these qualities if they want to become authentic leaders.

Based on his experience as a corporate executive and through interviews with a diverse sample of 125 successful leaders, George found that authentic leaders have a genuine desire to serve others, they know themselves, and they feel free to lead from their core values. Specifically, authentic leaders demonstrate five basic characteristics: (1) They understand their purpose, (2) they have strong values about the right thing to do, (3) they establish trusting relationships with others, (4) they demonstrate self-discipline and act on their values, and (5) they are passionate about their mission (i.e., act from their heart) (Figure 9.1; George, 2003).

Figure 9.1 illustrates five dimensions of authentic leadership identified by George: purpose, values, relationships, self-discipline, and heart. The figure also illustrates each of the related characteristics—passion, behavior, connectedness, consistency, and compassion—that individuals need to develop to become authentic leaders.

In his interviews, George found that authentic leaders have a real sense of *purpose*. They know what they are about and where they are going. In addition to knowing their purpose, authentic leaders are inspired and intrinsically motivated about their goals. They are *passionate* individuals who have a deep-seated interest in what they are doing and truly care about their work.

 The Authentic Leader

A good example of an authentic leader who exhibited passion about his goals was Terry Fox, a cancer survivor, whose leg was amputated after it was overcome by bone cancer. Using a special leg prosthesis, Terry attempted to run across Canada, from the Atlantic to the Pacific, to raise awareness and money for cancer research. Although he died before he finished his run, his courage and passion affected the lives of millions of people. He also accomplished his goals to increase cancer awareness and to raise money for cancer research. Today, the Terry Fox Foundation is going strong and has raised more than $400 million (Canadian) for cancer research (www.terryfox.org). Of the dimensions and characteristics in Figure 9.1, Terry Fox clearly demonstrated purpose and passion in his leadership.

Authentic leaders understand their own *values* and *behave* toward others based on these values. Stated another way, George suggests that authentic leaders know their "True North." They have a clear idea of who they are,

Figure 9.1 Authentic Leadership Characteristics

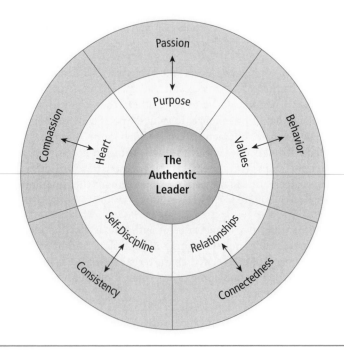

SOURCE: From *Authentic Leadership: Rediscovering the Secrets to Creating Lasting Value* by Bill George, copyright © 2003. Reproduced with permission of John Wiley & Sons, Inc.

where they are going, and what the right thing is to do. When tested in difficult situations, authentic leaders do not compromise their values, but rather use those situations to strengthen their values.

An example of a leader with a strong set of values is Nobel Peace Prize Laureate Nelson Mandela. Mandela was a deeply moral man with a strong conscience. While fighting to abolish apartheid in South Africa, he was unyielding in his pursuit of justice and equality for all. When he was in prison and offered early release in exchange for denouncing his viewpoint, he chose to remain incarcerated rather than compromise his position. Nelson Mandela knew who he was at his core. He knew his values, and his leadership reflected those values.

A third characteristic of authentic leadership in the George approach is strong *relationships*. Authentic leaders have the capacity to open themselves up and establish a *connection* with others. They are willing to share their own story with others and listen to others' stories. Through mutual disclosure, leaders and followers develop a sense of trust and closeness.

George argued that people today want to have access to their leaders and they want their leaders to be open with them. In a sense, people are asking leaders to soften the boundary around their leadership role and to be more transparent. People want to have a trusting relationship with their leaders. In exchange, people are willing to give leaders greater loyalty and commitment.

As we discussed in Chapter 7 (leader–member exchange theory), effective leader–follower relationships are marked by high-quality communication in which leaders and followers demonstrate a high degree of mutual trust, respect, and obligation toward each other. Leaders and followers are tied together in productive ways that go beyond the stereotypical leader–follower relationship. This results in strong leader–member relationships, greater understanding, and higher productivity.

Self-discipline is another dimension of authentic leadership, and is the quality that helps leaders to reach their goals. Self-discipline gives leaders focus and determination. When leaders establish objectives and standards of excellence, self-discipline helps them to reach these goals and to keep everyone accountable. Furthermore, self-discipline gives authentic leaders the energy to carry out their work in accordance with their values.

Like long-distance runners, authentic leaders with self-discipline are able to stay focused on their goals. They are able to listen to their inner compass and can discipline themselves to move forward, even in challenging circumstances. In stressful times, self-discipline allows authentic leaders to remain cool, calm, and *consistent*. Because disciplined leaders are predictable in their behavior, other people know what to expect and find it easier to communicate with them. When the leader is self-directed and "on course," it gives other people a sense of security.

Last, the George approach identifies *compassion* and *heart* as important aspects of authentic leadership. Compassion refers to being sensitive to the plight of others, opening one's self to others, and being willing to help them. George (2003, p. 40) argued that as leaders develop compassion, they learn to be authentic. Leaders can develop compassion by getting to know others' life stories, doing community service projects, being involved with other racial or ethnic groups, or traveling to developing countries (George, 2003). These activities increase the leader's sensitivity to other cultures, backgrounds, and living situations.

In summary, George's authentic leadership approach highlights five important features of authentic leaders. Collectively, these features provide a practical picture of what people need to do to become authentic in their leadership. Authentic leadership is a lifelong developmental process, which is formed and informed by each individual's life story.

Theoretical Approach

Although still in its initial stages of development, a theory of authentic leadership is emerging in social science literature. In this section, we identify the basic components of authentic leadership and describe how these components are related to one another.

Background to the Theoretical Approach. Although people's interest in "authenticity" is probably timeless, research on authentic leadership is very recent, with the first article appearing in 2003. The primary catalyst for this research was a leadership summit at the University of Nebraska. This summit was sponsored by the Gallup Leadership Institute, and focused on the nature of authentic leadership and its development. From the summit, two sets of publications emerged: (1) a special issue of *Leadership Quarterly* in the summer of 2005, and (2) *Monographs in Leadership and Management,* titled "Authentic Leadership Theory and Process: Origins, Effects and Development," also published in 2005. Prior to the summit, Luthans and Avolio (2003) published an article on authentic leadership development

▶ Authenticity and Brand

and positive organizational scholarship. The article also helped to ignite this area of research.

Interest in authentic leadership increased during a time in which there was a great deal of societal upheaval and instability in the United States. The attacks of 9/11, widespread corporate corruption, and a troubled economy all created a sense of uncertainty and anxiety in people about leadership. Widespread unethical and ineffective leadership necessitated the need for more humane, constructive leadership that served the common good (Fry & Whittington, 2005; Luthans & Avolio, 2003).

In addition, researchers felt the need to extend the work of Bass (1990) and Bass and Steidlmeier (1999) regarding the meaning of authentic transformational leadership. There was a need to operationalize the meaning of authentic leadership and create a theoretical framework to explain it. To develop a theory of authentic leadership, researchers drew from the fields of leadership, positive organizational scholarship, and ethics (Cooper, Scandura, & Schriesheim, 2005; Gardner et al., 2005).

A major challenge confronting researchers in developing a theory was to define the construct and identify its characteristics. As we discussed earlier in the chapter, authentic leadership has been defined in multiple ways, with each definition emphasizing a different aspect of the process. For this chapter, we have selected the definition set forth in an article by Walumbwa et al. (2008), who defined authentic leadership as "a pattern of leader behavior that draws upon and promotes both positive psychological capacities and a positive ethical climate, to foster greater self-awareness, an internalized moral perspective, balanced processing of information, and relational transparency on the part of leaders working with followers, fostering positive self-development" (p. 94). Although complex, this definition captures the current thinking of scholars regarding the phenomenon of authentic leadership and how it works.

In the research literature, different models have been developed to illustrate the process of authentic leadership. Gardner et al. (2005) created a model that frames authentic leadership around the developmental processes of leader and follower self-awareness and self-regulation. Ilies, Morgeson, and Nahrgang (2005) constructed a multicomponent model that discusses the impact of authenticity on leaders' and followers' happiness and well-being. In contrast, Luthans and Avolio (2003) formulated a model that explains authentic leadership as a developmental process. In this chapter, we will present a basic model of authentic leadership that is derived from the research literature that

Fostering Authenticity   CEOs and Positive Psychology

focuses on the core components of authentic leadership. Our discussion will focus on authentic leadership as a process.

Components of Authentic Leadership. In an effort to further our understanding of authentic leadership, Walumbwa and associates (2008) conducted a comprehensive review of the literature and interviewed groups of content experts in the field to determine what components constituted authentic leadership and to develop a valid measure of this construct. Their research identified four components: self-awareness, internalized moral perspective, balanced processing, and relational transparency (Figure 9.2). Together, these four components form the foundation for a theory of authentic leadership.

Self-awareness refers to the personal insights of the leader. It is not an end in itself but a process in which individuals understand themselves, including their strengths and weaknesses, and the impact they have on others. Self-awareness includes reflecting on your core values, identity, emotions, motives,

Figure 9.2 Authentic Leadership

SOURCE: Adapted from Luthans, F., & Avolio, B. J. (2003). Authentic leadership development. In K. S. Cameron, J. E. Dutton, & R. E. Quinn (Eds.), *Positive organizational scholarship* (pp. 241–258). San Francisco: Berrett-Koehler; and Gardner, W. L., Avolio, B. J., Luthans, F., May, D. R., & Walumbwa, F. O. (2005). "Can you see the real me?" A self-based model of authentic leader and follower development. *Leadership Quarterly, 16,* 343–372.

📚 Authenticity and Identity

and goals, and coming to grips with who you really are at the deepest level. In addition, it includes being aware of and trusting your own feelings (Kernis, 2003). When leaders know themselves and have a clear sense of who they are and what they stand for, they have a strong anchor for their decisions and actions (Gardner et al., 2005). Other people see leaders who have greater self-awareness as more authentic.

Internalized moral perspective refers to a self-regulatory process whereby individuals use their internal moral standards and values to guide their behavior rather than allow outside pressures to control them (e.g., group or societal pressure). It is a self-regulatory process because people have control over the extent to which they allow others to influence them. Others see leaders with an internalized moral perspective as authentic because their actions are consistent with their expressed beliefs and morals.

Balanced processing is also a self-regulatory behavior. It refers to an individual's ability to analyze information objectively and explore other people's opinions before making a decision. It also means avoiding favoritism about certain issues and remaining unbiased. Balanced processing includes soliciting viewpoints from those who disagree with you and fully considering their positions before taking your own action. Leaders with balanced processing are seen as authentic because they are open about their own perspectives, but are also objective in considering others' perspectives.

Relational transparency refers to being open and honest in presenting one's true self to others. It is self-regulatory because individuals can control their transparency with others. Relational transparency occurs when individuals share their core feelings, motives, and inclinations with others in an appropriate manner (Kernis, 2003). It includes the individuals showing both positive and negative aspects of themselves to others. In short, relational transparency is about communicating openly and being real in relationships with others.

Fundamentally, authentic leadership comprises the above four factors—self-awareness, internalized moral perspective, balanced processing, and relational transparency. These factors form the basis for authentic leadership.

Factors That Influence Authentic Leadership. There are other factors such as positive psychological capacities, moral reasoning, and critical life events that influence authentic leadership (Figure 9.2).

The four key *positive psychological attributes* that have an impact on authentic leadership—confidence, hope, optimism, and resilience—have been drawn from the fields of positive psychology and positive organizational behavior

 Leadership from Within

(Table 9.1; Luthans & Avolio, 2003). Positive attributes predispose or enhance a leader's capacity to develop the components of authentic leadership discussed in the previous section. Each of these attributes has a trait-like and a state-like quality. They are trait-like because they may characterize a relatively fixed aspect of someone's personality that has been evident throughout his or her life (e.g., extraversion), and they are state-like because, with training or coaching, individuals are capable of developing or changing their characteristics.

Table 9.1   Related Positive Psychological Capacities

- Confidence
- Hope
- Optimism
- Resilience

SOURCE: Luthans, F., & Avolio, B. J. (2003). Authentic leadership development. In K. S. Cameron, J. E. Dutton, & R. E. Quinn (Eds.), *Positive organizational scholarship* (pp. 241–258). San Francisco: Berrett-Koehler.

Confidence refers to having self-efficacy—the belief that one has the ability to successfully accomplish a specified task. Leaders who have confidence are more likely to be motivated to succeed, to be persistent when obstacles arise, and to welcome a challenge (Bandura, 1997; Luthans & Avolio, 2003). *Hope* is a positive motivational state based on willpower and goal planning (Luthans & Avolio, 2003). Authentic leaders with hope have goals they know can be accomplished; their hope inspires followers to trust them and believe in their goals. *Optimism* refers to the cognitive process of viewing situations from a positive light and having favorable expectations about the future. Leaders with optimism are positive about their capabilities and the outcomes they can achieve. They approach life with a sense of abundance rather than scarcity (Covey, 1990). *Resilience* is the capacity to recover from and adjust to adverse situations. It includes the ability to positively adapt to hardships and suffering. During difficult times, resilient people are able to bounce back from challenging situations and feel strengthened and more resourceful as a result of them (Sutcliffe & Vogus, 2003).

Moral reasoning is another factor that can influence authentic leadership (Figure 9.2). It is the capacity to make ethical decisions about issues of right or wrong and good or bad. Developing the capacity for moral reasoning is a lifelong process. Higher levels of moral reasoning make it possible for the authentic leader to make decisions that transcend individual differences and align individuals toward a common goal. They enable leaders to be selfless

Authentic Leadership

and make judgments that serve the greater good of the group, organization, or community. Moral reasoning capacity also enables authentic leaders to use this ability to promote justice and achieve what is right for a community.

A final factor related to authentic leadership is *critical life events* (Figure 9.2). Critical events are major events that shape people's lives. They can be positive events, like receiving an unexpected promotion, having a child, or reading an important book; or they can be negative events, like being diagnosed with cancer, getting a negative year-end evaluation, or having a loved one die. Critical life events act as catalysts for change. Shamir and Eilam (2005) argued that authentic leadership rests heavily on the insights people attach to their life experiences. When leaders tell their life stories, they gain greater self-knowledge, more clarity about who they are, and a better understanding of their role. By understanding their own life experiences, leaders become more authentic.

Critical life events also stimulate growth in individuals and help them become stronger leaders (Luthans & Avolio, 2003). For example, Howard Schultz (founder and CEO of Starbucks) tells a story about when he was little: His father, who was a delivery driver, fell and was hurt on the job. His father did not have health insurance or worker's compensation. Seeing the problems that resulted from his father's difficulties, when Schultz built Starbucks he provided comprehensive health insurance for employees who worked as few as 20 hours a week. Schultz's style of leadership was triggered by his childhood experience.

As the theory of authentic leadership develops further, other antecedent factors that influence the process may be identified. To date, however, it is positive psychological capacities, moral reasoning capacities, and critical life events that have been identified as factors that are influential in a person's ability to become an authentic leader.

HOW DOES AUTHENTIC LEADERSHIP THEORY WORK?

In this chapter, we have discussed authentic leadership from a practical and theoretical perspective. Both perspectives describe authentic leadership as a developmental process that forms in leaders over time; however, both perspectives provide different descriptions for how authentic leadership works.

The practical approach provides prescriptions for how to be authentic and how to develop authentic leadership. For example, the George approach (2003)

Authenticity

focuses on five characteristics leaders should develop to become authentic leaders. More specifically, George advocates that leaders become more *purposeful, value centered, relational, self-disciplined,* and *compassionate.* The essence of authentic leadership is being a leader who strongly demonstrates these five qualities.

Rather than simple prescriptions, the theoretical approach describes what authentic leadership is and what accounts for it. From this perspective, authentic leadership works because leaders demonstrate *self-awareness,* an *internalized moral perspective, balanced processing,* and *relational transparency.* Leaders develop these attributes through a lifelong process that is often influenced by critical life events. In addition, the literature suggests that positive psychological characteristics and moral reasoning have a significant impact on authentic leaders.

Authentic leadership is a complex process that emphasizes the development of qualities that help leaders to be perceived as trustworthy and believable by their followers. The leader's job is to learn to develop these qualities and apply them to the common good as he or she serves others.

STRENGTHS

Although it is in its early stages of development, the authentic leadership approach has several strengths. First, it fulfills an expressed need for trustworthy leadership in society. During the past 20 years, failures in public and private leadership have created distrust in people. Authentic leadership helps to fill a void and provides an answer to people who are searching for good and sound leadership in an uncertain world.

Second, authentic leadership provides broad guidelines for individuals who want to become authentic leaders. Both the practical and theoretical approaches clearly point to what leaders should do to become authentic leaders. Social science literature emphasizes that it is important for leaders to have self-awareness, an internalized moral perspective, balanced processing, and relational transparency to be authentic. Taken together, these approaches provide a map for becoming an authentic leader.

Third, similar to transformational and servant leadership, authentic leadership has an explicit moral dimension. Underlying both the practical and theoretical approaches is the idea that authenticity requires leaders to do what is "right" and "good" for their followers and society. Authentic leaders understand their own values, place followers' needs above their own, and

Authenticity Framework

work with followers to align their interests in order to create a greater common good.

Fourth, authentic leadership emphasizes that authentic values and behaviors can be developed in leaders over time. Authentic leadership is not an attribute that only some people exhibit: Everyone can develop authenticity and learn to be more authentic. For example, leaders can learn to become more aware and transparent, or they can learn to be more relational and other-directed. Leaders can also develop moral reasoning capacities. Furthermore, Luthans and Avolio (2003) contended that leaders could learn to develop positive psychological capacities such as confidence, hope, optimism, and resilience, and could use these to create a positive organizational climate. They contended that there are many ways that leaders can learn to become authentic leaders over a lifetime.

Finally, authentic leadership can be measured using the Authentic Leadership Questionnaire (ALQ). The ALQ is a validated, theory-based instrument comprising 16 items that measure four factors of authentic leadership (Avolio et al., 2009; Walumbwa et al., 2008). As research moves forward in refining authentic leadership theory, it is valuable to have an established instrument of this construct that is theory-based and can be used to measure authentic leadership in future research.

CRITICISMS

Authentic leadership is still in the formative stages of development, and a number of questions still need to be addressed about the theory. First, the concepts and ideas presented in George's practical approach are not fully substantiated. While the practical approach is interesting and offers insight on authentic leadership, it is not built on a broad empirical base, nor has it been tested for validity. Without research support, the ideas set forth in the practical approach should be treated cautiously as explanations of the authentic leadership process.

Second, the moral component of authentic leadership is not fully explained. Whereas authentic leadership implies that leaders are motivated by higher-order end values such as justice and community, the way that these values function to influence authentic leadership is not clear. For example, how are a leader's values related to a leader's self-awareness? Or, what is the path or underlying process through which moral values affect other components of authentic leadership? In its present form, authentic leadership does not offer thorough answers to these questions.

 Authentic Leadership Questionnaire

Third, researchers have questioned whether positive psychological capacities should be included as components of authentic leadership. Although there is an interest in the social sciences to study positive human potential and the best of the human condition (Cameron, Dutton, & Quinn, 2003), the rationale for including positive psychological capacities as an inherent part of authentic leadership has not been clearly explained by researchers. In addition, some have argued that the inclusion of positive leader capacities in authentic leadership broadens the construct of authentic leadership too much and makes it difficult to measure (Cooper et al., 2005). At this point in the development of research on authentic leadership, the role of positive psychological capacities in authentic leadership theory needs further clarification.

Finally, it is not clear how authentic leadership results in positive organizational outcomes. Given that it is a new area of research, it is not unexpected that there are few data on outcomes, but these data are necessary to substantiate the value of the theory. Although authentic leadership is intuitively appealing on the surface, questions remain about whether this approach is effective, in what contexts it is effective, and whether authentic leadership results in productive outcomes. Relatedly, it is also not clear in the research whether authentic leadership is sufficient to achieve organizational goals. For example, can an authentic leader who is disorganized and lacking in technical competence be an effective leader? Authenticity is important and valuable to good leadership, but how authenticity relates to effective leadership is unknown. Clearly, future research should be conducted to explore how authentic leadership is related to organizational outcomes.

APPLICATION

Because authentic leadership is still in the early phase of its development, there has been little research on strategies that people can use to develop or enhance authentic leadership behaviors. While there are prescriptions set forth in the practical approach, there is little evidence-based research on whether these prescriptions or how-to strategies actually increase authentic leadership behavior.

In spite of the lack of intervention research, there are common themes from the authentic leadership literature that may be applicable to organizational or practice settings. One theme common to all of the formulations of authentic leadership is that people have the capacity to learn to be authentic

▶ Teaching Authentic Leadership

leaders. In their original work on authentic leadership, Luthans and Avolio (2003) constructed a model of authentic leadership development. Conceptualizing it as a lifelong learning process, they argued that authentic leadership is a process that can be developed over time. This suggests that human resource departments may be able to foster authentic leadership behaviors in employees who move into leadership positions.

Another theme that can be applied to organizations is the overriding goal of authentic leaders to try to do the "right" thing, to be honest with themselves and others, and to work for the common good. Authentic leadership can have a positive impact in organizations. For example, Cianci, Hannah, Roberts, and Tsakumis (2014) investigated the impact of authentic leadership on followers' morality. Based on the responses of 118 MBA students, they found that authentic leaders significantly inhibited followers from making unethical choices in the face of temptation. Authentic leadership appears to be a critical contextual factor that morally strengthens followers. Cianci et al. suggest that the four components of authentic leadership (i.e., self-awareness, internalized moral perspective, balanced processing, and relational transparency) should be developed in organizational leadership to increase ethical organizational behavior.

Last, authentic leadership is shaped and reformed by critical life events that act as triggers to growth and greater authenticity. Being sensitive to these events and using them as springboards to growth may be relevant to many people who are interested in becoming leaders who are more authentic.

CASE STUDIES

The following section provides three case studies (Cases 9.1, 9.2, and 9.3) of individuals who demonstrate authentic leadership. The first case is about Sally Helgesen, author of *The Female Advantage: Women's Ways of Leadership* (1990). The second case is about Greg Mortenson and how his mission to promote schools and peace in Pakistan and Afghanistan came under fire when he was accused of lying and financial impropriety. The final case is about Betty Ford, former First Lady of the United States, and her work in the areas of breast cancer awareness and substance abuse treatment. At the end of each of the cases, questions are provided to help you analyze the case using ideas from authentic leadership.

CASE 9.1

Am I Really a Leader?

Sally Helgesen was born in the small Midwestern town of Saint Cloud, Minnesota. Her mother was a housewife who later taught English, and her father was a college professor of speech. After attending a local state college, where she majored in English and comparative religion, Sally spread her wings and moved to New York, inspired by the classic film *Breakfast at Tiffany's.*

Sally found work as a writer, first in advertising and then as an assistant to a columnist at the then-influential *Village Voice.* She contributed free-lance articles to magazines such as *Harper's, Glamour, Vogue, Fortune,* and *Inside Sports.* She also returned to school, completing a degree in classics at Hunter College and taking language courses at the city graduate center in preparation for a PhD in comparative religion. She envisioned herself as a college professor, but also enjoyed freelancing. She felt a strong dichotomy within her, part quiet scholar and part footloose dreamer. The conflict bothered her, and she wondered how she would resolve it. Choosing to be a writer—actually declaring herself to be one—seemed scary, grandiose, and fraudulent.

Then one day, while walking on a New York side street in the rain, Sally saw an adventuresome black cat running beside her. It reminded her of Holly Golightly's cat in *Breakfast at Tiffany's,* an emblem in the movie for Holly's dreamy temperament and rootlessness. It made her realize how much the freedom and independence offered by her "temporary" career as a writer suited her temperament. Sally told the cat she was a writer—she'd never been able to say the words before—and decided she was going to commit to full-time writing, at least for a time. When she saw the opportunity to cover a prominent murder trial in Fort Worth, Texas, she took it.

While covering the trial, Sally became intrigued with the culture of Texas, and decided she wanted to write a book on the role of independent oil producers in shaping the region. Doing so required a huge expenditure of time and money, and for almost a year Sally lived out of the trunk of her car, staying with friends in remote regions all over Texas. It was lonely and hard and exhilarating, but Sally was determined to see the project through. When the book, *Wildcatters* (1981), was published, it achieved little recognition, but Sally felt an enormous increase in confidence and commitment as a result of having finished the book. It strengthened her conviction that, for better or worse, she was a writer.

Sally moved back to New York and continued to write articles and search around for another book. She also began writing speeches for the CEO at a Fortune 500 company. She loved the work, and particularly enjoyed being an observer of office politics, even though she did not perceive herself to be a part of them. Sally viewed her role as being an "outsider looking in," an observer of the culture. She sometimes felt like an actor in a play about an office, but this detachment made her feel professional rather than fraudulent.

As a speechwriter, Sally spent a lot of time interviewing people in the companies she worked for. Doing so made her realize that men and women often approach their work in fundamentally different ways. She also became convinced that many of the skills and attitudes women brought to their work were increasingly appropriate for the ways in which organizations were changing, and that women had certain advantages as a result. She also noticed that the unique perspectives of women were seldom valued by CEOs or other organizational leaders, who could have benefited if they had better understood and been more attentive to what women had to offer.

These observations inspired Sally to write another book. In 1988, she signed a contract with a major publisher to write a book on what women had to contribute to organizations. Until then, almost everything written about women at work focused on how they needed to change and adapt. Sally felt strongly that if women were encouraged to emphasize the negative, they would miss a historic opportunity to help lead organizations in a time of change. The time was right for this message, and *The Female Advantage: Women's Ways of Leadership* (1990) became very successful, topping a number of best-seller charts and remaining steadily in print for nearly 20 years. The book's prominence resulted in numerous speaking and consulting opportunities, and Sally began traveling the world delivering seminars and working with a variety of clients.

This acclaim and visibility were somewhat daunting to Sally. While she recognized the value of her book, she also knew that she was not a social scientist with a body of theoretical data on women's issues. She saw herself as an author rather than an expert, and the old questions about fraudulence that she had dealt with in her early years in New York began to reassert themselves in a different form. Was she really being authentic? Could she take on the mantle of leadership and all it entailed? In short, she wondered if she could be the leader that people seemed to expect.

The path Sally took to answer these questions was simply to present herself for who she was. She was Sally Helgesen, an outsider looking in, a skilled and imaginative observer of current issues. For Sally, the path to leadership did not manifest itself in a step-by-step process. Sally's leadership began with her own journey of finding herself and accepting her personal authenticity. Through this self-awareness, she grew to trust her own expertise as a writer with a keen eye for current trends in organizational life.

(Continued)

(Continued)

Sally continues to be an internationally recognized consultant and speaker on contemporary issues, and has published five books. She remains uncertain about whether she will finish her degree in comparative religion and become a college professor, but always keeps in mind the career of I. F. Stone, an influential political writer in the 1950s and 1960s who went back to school and got an advanced degree in classics at the age of 75.

Questions

1. Learning about one's self is an essential step in becoming an authentic leader. What role did self-awareness play in Sally Helgesen's story of leadership?

2. How would you describe the authenticity of Sally Helgesen's leadership?

3. At the end of the case, Sally Helgesen is described as taking on the "mantle of leadership." Was this important for her leadership? How is taking on the mantle of leadership related to a leader's authenticity? Does every leader reach a point in his or her career where embracing the leadership role is essential?

CASE 9.2

A Leader Under Fire

(The previous edition of this book includes a case study outlining Greg Mortenson's creation of the Central Asia Institute and highlighting his authentic leadership qualities in more detail. For an additional perspective on Mortenson, you can access the original case study at www.sage pub.com/northouse6e.)

By 2011, there were few people who had never heard of Greg Mortenson. He was the subject of two best-selling books, *Three Cups of Tea* (2006, with David O. Relin) and *Stones Into Schools* (2009), which told how the former emergency trauma room nurse had become a hero who built schools in rural areas of Afghanistan and Pakistan.

His story was phenomenal: Lost and sick after attempting to scale K2, Greg was nursed back to health by the villagers of remote Korphe, Afghanistan. Greg promised to build the village a school, a monumental effort that took him three years as he learned to raise money, navigate the foreign culture, and build a bridge above a 60-foot-deep chasm. His success led him to create the Central Asia Institute (CAI), a nonprofit organization that "empowers communities of Central Asia through literacy and education, especially for girls, promotes peace through education, and conveys the importance of these activities globally." By 2011, the CAI had successfully established or supported more than 170 schools in Pakistan and Afghanistan, and helped to educate more than 68,000 students (CAI, 2011a).

Greg's story seemed too good to be true. In April 2011, television news show *60 Minutes* and author Jon Krakauer alleged that it was. *60 Minutes* accused Greg of misusing money and benefitting excessively from the CAI. The show's reporter visited schools the CAI had built overseas and claimed that he could not find six of the schools and that others were abandoned. The show featured an interview with Krakauer, who claimed Greg had fabricated parts of his best-selling book, *Three Cups of Tea.* When *60 Minutes* approached Greg for comment at a book signing, he refused to talk to the program.

The next day, Krakauer (*Into Thin Air* [1997] and *Under the Banner of Heaven* [2003]) published a short online book, *Three Cups of Deceit* (2011), in which he claimed Greg lied many times in *Three Cups of Tea,* starting with his initial tale of being in Korphe.

Greg and the CAI were caught in a firestorm of media and public scrutiny. An investigation into the alleged financial improprieties was launched by Montana's attorney general (the CAI is based in Bozeman), and two Montana legislators filed a $5 million class action lawsuit claiming Greg fooled 4 million people into buying his books.

Greg withdrew from the public eye. The day the *60 Minutes* program aired, he posted a letter on the CAI website saying he stood by his books and claiming the news show "paints a distorted picture using inaccurate information, innuendo and a microscopic focus on one year's (2009) IRS 990 financial, and a few points in the book *Three Cups of Tea* that occurred almost 18 years ago" (CAI, 2011b). Many criticized the organization's founder for not more aggressively defending himself.

What many people did not know, however, was that two days before the *60 Minutes* segment appeared, Greg had been diagnosed with a hole and a large aneurysm in his heart and was scheduled for open-heart surgery in the next few months. Meanwhile, the CAI worked to ensure its transparency by posting its tax returns and a master list of projects and their status. The report documented 210 schools, with 17 of those receiving "full support" from the CAI, which includes teachers' salaries, supplies, books, and furniture and monitoring by CAI contractors (Flandro, 2011).

(Continued)

(Continued)

The attorney general investigation concluded in 2012 and determined that Greg as well as CAI board members had mismanaged the CAI, and that Greg had personally profited from it. In a settlement, Greg agreed to pay $1 million to the CAI for expenses he incurred that were deemed as personal. The attorney general's conclusions did not address the allegations that Mortenson fabricated parts of his book. While he continues to be a CAI employee, Greg is not allowed to have any financial oversight for the organization or sit on its board of directors (Flandro, 2012).

Despite the controversy and subsequent finding of wrongdoing, former CAI board member Andrew Marcus hopes the public will consider what Greg and the organization have accomplished.

"It's hard to imagine anyone who's done more for education in that part of the world," Marcus has said. "It took a real human being to do that" (Flandro, 2011).

Questions

1. Would you describe Greg Mortenson as an authentic leader? Explain your answer.

2. In the chapter, we discussed moral reasoning and transparency as components of authentic leadership. Do you think Greg exhibited these components as part his leadership?

3. How was Greg's response to the allegations against him characteristic of an authentic leader?

4. How did the outcome of the investigation affect the authenticity of Greg Mortenson's leadership?

CASE 9.3

The Reluctant First Lady

Betty Ford admits that August 9, 1974, the day her husband was sworn in as the 38th President of the United States, was "the saddest day of my life" (Ford, 1978, p. 1).

Elizabeth Bloomer Ford was many things—a former professional dancer and dance teacher, the mother of four nearly grown children, the wife of 13-term U.S. Congressman Gerald "Jerry" R. Ford who was looking forward to their retirement—but she never saw being the country's First Lady as her destiny.

As she held the Bible her husband's hand rested on while he took the oath of office, Betty began a journey in which she would become many more things: a breast cancer survivor, an outspoken advocate of women's rights, a recovering alcoholic and addict, and cofounder and president of the Betty Ford Center, a nonprofit treatment center for substance abuse.

The Fords' path to the White House began in October 1973, when Jerry was tapped to replace then-U.S. Vice President Spiro Agnew who had resigned. After only 9 months in that role, Jerry became the U.S. President after Richard M. Nixon left office amidst the Watergate scandal.

In her first days as the First Lady, Betty became known for her openness and candor. At the time, women were actively fighting for equal rights in the workplace and in society. Less than half of American women were employed outside the home, and women's earnings were only 38% of their male counterparts' (Spraggins, 2005). Betty raised a number of eyebrows in her first press conference, when she spoke out in support of abortion rights, women in politics, and the Equal Rights Amendment.

Betty hadn't even been in the White House a month when she was diagnosed with breast cancer. She again broke with social conventions and spoke openly about the diagnosis and treatment for a disease that was not widely discussed in public. With her cooperation, *Newsweek* magazine printed a complete account of her surgery and treatment, which included a radical mastectomy. This openness helped raise awareness of breast cancer screening and treatment options and created an atmosphere of support and comfort for other women fighting the disease.

"Lying in the hospital, thinking of all those women going for cancer checkups because of me, I'd come to recognize more clearly the power of the woman in the White House," she said in her first autobiography, *The Times of My Life.* "Not my power, but the power of the position, a power which could be used to help" (Ford, 1978, p. 194).

After her recuperation, Betty made good use of that newfound power. She openly supported and lobbied for passage of the Equal Rights Amendment, a bill that would ensure that "equality of rights under the law shall not be denied or abridged by the United States or by any state on account of sex" (Francis, 2009).

In an interview with *60 Minutes*, Betty drew the ire of many conservatives when she candidly shared her views on the provocative issues of abortion rights, premarital sex, and marijuana use. After the interview aired,

(Continued)

(Continued)

public opinion of Betty plummeted, but her popularity quickly rebounded, and within months her approval rating had climbed to 75%.

At the same time, Betty was busy with the duties of First Lady, entertaining dignitaries and heads of state from countries across the globe. In 1975 she began actively campaigning for her husband for the 1976 presidential election, inspiring buttons that read "Vote for Betty's Husband." Ford lost the election to Jimmy Carter and, because he was suffering from laryngitis, Betty stepped into the spotlight to read Jerry's concession speech to the country, congratulating Carter on his victory. Betty's time as First Lady ended in January 1977, and the Fords retired to Rancho Mirage, California, and Vail, Colorado.

A little more than a year later, at the age of 60, Betty began another personal battle: overcoming alcoholism and an addiction to prescription medicine. Betty had a 14-year dependence on painkillers for chronic neck spasms, arthritis, and a pinched nerve, but refused to admit she was addicted to alcohol. After checking into the Long Beach Naval Hospital's Alcohol and Drug Rehabilitation Service, she found the strength to face her demons and, again, went public with her struggles.

"I have found that I am not only addicted to the medications I've been taking for my arthritis, but also to alcohol," she wrote in a statement released to the public. "I expect this treatment and fellowship to be a solution for my problems and I embrace it not only for me but for all the others who are here to participate" (Ford, 1978, p. 285).

Betty Ford found recovering from addiction was particularly daunting at a time when most treatment centers were geared toward treating men. "The female alcoholic has more emotional problems, more health problems, more parenting problems, makes more suicide attempts, than the alcoholic man," Betty explained in her second autobiography, *Betty, a Glad Awakening* (Ford, 1987, p. 129).

For this reason, Betty helped to establish the nonprofit Betty Ford Center in 1982 in Rancho Mirage. The center splits its space equally between male and female patients, but the treatment is gender specific with programs for the entire family system affected by addiction. The center's success has attracted celebrities as well as everyday people including middle-class moms, executives, college students, and laborers. Betty's activism in the field of recovery earned her the Presidential Medal of Freedom in 1991 and the Congressional Medal of Honor in 1999.

Speaking at an alumni reunion of Betty Ford Center patients, Betty said, "I'm really proud of this center. And I'm really grateful for my own recovery, because with my recovery, I was able to help some other people come forward and address their own addictions. And I don't think there's anything as wonderful in life as being able to help someone else" (Ford, 1987, p. 217).

Questions

1. How would you describe Betty Ford's leadership? In what ways could her leadership be described as authentic?

2. How did critical life events play a role in the development of her leadership?

3. Is there a clear moral dimension to Betty Ford's leadership? In what way is her leadership about serving the common good? Discuss.

4. As we discussed in the chapter, self-awareness and transparency are associated with authentic leadership. How does Betty Ford exhibit these qualities?

LEADERSHIP INSTRUMENT

Although still in its early phases of development, the Authentic Leadership Questionnaire (ALQ) was created by Walumbwa and associates (2008) to explore and validate the assumptions of authentic leadership. It is a 16-item instrument that measures four factors of authentic leadership: self-awareness, internalized moral perspective, balanced processing, and relational transparency. Based on samples in China, Kenya, and the United States, Walumbwa and associates validated the dimensions of the instrument and found it positively related to outcomes such as organizational citizenship, organizational commitment, and satisfaction with supervisor and performance. To obtain this instrument, contact Mind Garden, Inc., in Menlo Park, California, or visit www.mindgarden.com.

In this section, we provide an authentic leadership self-assessment to help you determine your own level of authentic leadership. This questionnaire will help you understand how authentic leadership is measured and provide you with your own scores on items that characterize authentic leadership. The questionnaire includes 16 questions that assess the four major components of authentic leadership discussed earlier in this chapter: self-awareness, internalized moral perspective, balanced processing, and relational transparency. Your results on this self-assessment questionnaire will give you information about your level of authentic leadership on these underlying dimensions of authentic leadership. This questionnaire is intended for practical applications to help you understand the complexities of authentic leadership. It is not designed for research purposes.

Authentic Leadership Self-Assessment Questionnaire

Instructions: This questionnaire contains items about different dimensions of authentic leadership. There are no right or wrong responses, so please answer honestly. Use the following scale when responding to each statement by writing the number from the scale below that you feel most accurately characterizes your response to the statement.

Key: 1 = Strongly   2 = Disagree   3 = Neutral   4 = Agree   5 = Strongly
disagree   agree

1. I can list my three greatest weaknesses.	1 2 3 4 5
2. My actions reflect my core values.	1 2 3 4 5
3. I seek others' opinions before making up my own mind.	1 2 3 4 5
4. I openly share my feelings with others.	1 2 3 4 5
5. I can list my three greatest strengths.	1 2 3 4 5
6. I do not allow group pressure to control me.	1 2 3 4 5
7. I listen closely to the ideas of those who disagree with me.	1 2 3 4 5
8. I let others know who I truly am as a person.	1 2 3 4 5
9. I seek feedback as a way of understanding who I really am as a person.	1 2 3 4 5
10. Other people know where I stand on controversial issues.	1 2 3 4 5
11. I do not emphasize my own point of view at the expense of others.	1 2 3 4 5
12. I rarely present a "false" front to others.	1 2 3 4 5
13. I accept the feelings I have about myself.	1 2 3 4 5
14. My morals guide what I do as a leader.	1 2 3 4 5
15. I listen very carefully to the ideas of others before making decisions.	1 2 3 4 5
16. I admit my mistakes to others.	1 2 3 4 5

Scoring

1. Sum the responses on items 1, 5, 9, and 13 (self-awareness).

2. Sum the responses on items 2, 6, 10, and 14 (internalized moral perspective).

3. Sum the responses on items 3, 7, 11, and 15 (balanced processing).

4. Sum the responses on items 4, 8, 12, and 16 (relational transparency).

Total Scores

Self-Awareness: _____

Internalized Moral Perspective: _____

Balanced Processing: _____

Relational Transparency: _____

Scoring Interpretation

This self-assessment questionnaire is designed to measure your authentic leadership by assessing four components of the process: self-awareness, internalized moral perspective, balanced processing, and relational transparency. By comparing your scores on each of these components, you can determine which are your stronger and which are your weaker components in each category. You can interpret your authentic leadership scores using the following guideline: high = 16–20 and low = 15 and below. Scores in the upper range indicate stronger authentic leadership, whereas scores in the lower range indicate weaker authentic leadership.

SUMMARY ——————————————————————

As a result of leadership failures in the public and private sectors, authentic leadership is emerging in response to societal demands for genuine, trustworthy, and good leadership. Authentic leadership describes leadership that is transparent, morally grounded, and responsive to people's needs and values. Even though authentic leadership is still in the early stages of development, the study of authentic leadership is timely and worthwhile, offering hope to people who long for true leadership.

Although there is no single accepted definition of authentic leadership, it can be conceptualized intrapersonally, developmentally, and interpersonally. The intrapersonal perspective focuses on the leader and the leader's knowledge, self-regulation, and self-concept. The interpersonal perspective claims that authentic leadership is a collective process, created by leaders and followers together. The developmental perspective emphasizes major components of authentic leadership that develop over a lifetime and are triggered by major life events.

The practical approach to authentic leadership provides basic "how to" steps to become an authentic leader. George's approach (2003) identifies five basic dimensions of authentic leadership and the corresponding behavioral characteristics individuals need to develop to become authentic leaders.

In the social science literature, a theoretical approach to authentic leadership is emerging. Drawing from the fields of leadership, positive organizational scholarship, and ethics, researchers have identified four major components of authentic leadership: self-awareness, internalized moral perspective, balanced processing, and relational transparency.

In addition, researchers have found that authentic leadership is influenced by a leader's positive psychological capacities, moral reasoning, and critical life events.

Authentic leadership has several positive features. First, it provides an answer to people who are searching for good and sound leadership in an uncertain world. Second, authentic leadership is prescriptive and provides a great deal of information about how leaders can learn to become authentic. Third, it has an explicit moral dimension that asserts that leaders need to do what is "right" and "good" for their followers and society. Fourth, it is framed as a process that is developed by leaders over time rather than as a fixed trait. Last, authentic leadership can be measured with a theory-based instrument.

There are also negative features to authentic leadership. First, the ideas set forth in the practical approach need to be treated cautiously because they have not been fully substantiated by research. Second, the moral component of authentic leadership is not fully explained. For example, it does not describe how values such as justice and community are related to authentic leadership. Third, the rationale for including positive psychological capacities as an inherent part of a model of authentic leadership has not been fully explicated. Finally, there is a lack of evidence regarding the effectiveness of authentic leadership and how it is related to positive organizational outcomes.

In summary, authentic leadership is a new and exciting area of research, which holds a great deal of promise. As more research is conducted on authentic leadership, a clearer picture will emerge about the true nature of the process and the assumptions and principles that it encompasses.

Sharpen your skills with SAGE edge at **edge.sagepub.com/northouse7e**

REFERENCES

Avolio, B. J., & Gardner, W. L. (2005). Authentic leadership development: Getting to the root of positive forms of leadership. *Leadership Quarterly, 16*, 315–338.

Avolio, B. J., Walumbwa, F. O., & Weber, T. J. (2009). Leadership: Current theories, research, and future directions. *Annual Review of Psychology, 60*, 421–449.

Bandura, A. (1997). *Self-efficacy: The exercise of control.* New York: Freeman.

Bass, B. M. (1990). *Handbook of leadership.* New York: Free Press.

Bass, B. M., & Steidlmeier, P. (1999). Ethics, character, and authentic transformational leadership. *Leadership Quarterly, 10*, 181–217.

Burns, J. M. (1978). *Leadership.* New York: Harper & Row.

Cameron, K. S., Dutton, J. E., & Quinn, R. E. (2003). Foundations of positive organizational scholarship. In K. S. Cameron, J. E. Dutton, & R. E. Quinn (Eds.), *Positive organizational scholarship* (pp. 3–13). San Francisco: Berrett-Koehler.

Central Asia Institute. (2011a). *Central Asia Institute.* Retrieved September 30, 2011, from https://www.ikat.org

Central Asia Institute. (2011b). *Executive Director Greg Mortenson's message to supporters 04/17/11.* Retrieved September 30, 2011, from https://www.ikat.org

Chan, A. (2005). Authentic leadership measurement and development: Challenges and suggestions. In W. L. Gardner, B. J. Avolio, & F. O. Walumbwa (Eds.), *Authentic leadership theory and practice: Origins, effects, and development* (pp. 227–251). Oxford: Elsevier Science.

Cianci, A. M., Hannah, S. T., Roberts, R. P., & Tsakumis, G. T. (2014). The effects of authentic leadership on followers' ethical decision-making in the face of temptation: An experimental study. *The Leadership Quarterly, 25,* 581–594.

Cooper, C., Scandura, T. A., & Schriesheim, C. A. (2005). Looking forward but learning from our past: Potential challenges to developing authentic leadership theory and authentic leaders. *Leadership Quarterly, 116,* 474–495.

Covey, S. R. (1990). *Principle-centered leadership.* New York: Fireside.

Eagly, A. H. (2005). Achieving relational authenticity in leadership: Does gender matter? *Leadership Quarterly, 16,* 459–474.

Flandro, C. (2011, September 25). *The rise, fall and future of humanitarian Greg Mortenson and the Central Asia Institute.* Retrieved September 27, 2011, from http://www.bozemandailychronicle.com/news/

Flandro, C. (2012, April 5). *Greg Mortenson, Central Asia Institute mismanaged money, reach $1M settlement with attorney general's office.* Retrieved August 12, 2014, from http://www.bozemandailychronicle.com/news/

Ford, B. (1978). *The times of my life.* New York: Harper & Row.

Ford, B. (1987). *Betty, a glad awakening.* Garden City, NY: Doubleday.

Francis, R. W. (2009). *The history of the equal rights amendment.* Retrieved May 29, 2009, from http://www.equalrightsamendment.org/

Fry, L. W., & Whittington, J. L. (2005). In search of authenticity: Spiritual leadership theory as a source for future theory, research, and practice on authentic leadership. In W. L. Gardner, B. J. Avolio, & F. O. Walumbwa (Eds.), *Authentic leadership theory and practice: Origins, effects, and development* (pp. 183–202). Oxford: Elsevier Science.

Gardner, W. L., Avolio, B. J., Luthans, F., May, D. R., & Walumbwa, F. O. (2005). "Can you see the real me?" A self-based model of authentic leader and follower development. *Leadership Quarterly, 16,* 343–372.

Gardner, W. L., Avolio, B. J., & Walumbwa, F. O. (2005). Authentic leadership development: Emergent trends and future directions. In W. L. Gardner, B. J. Avolio, & F. O. Walumbwa (Eds.), *Authentic leadership theory and practice: Origins, effects, and development* (pp. 387–406). Oxford: Elsevier Science.

George, B. (2003). *Authentic leadership: Rediscovering the secrets to creating lasting value.* San Francisco: Jossey-Bass.

George, B., & Sims, P. (2007). *True north: Discover your authentic leadership.* San Francisco: Jossey-Bass.

Helgesen, S. (1981). *Wildcatters: A story of Texans, oil, and money.* New York: Doubleday.

Helgesen, S. (1990). *The female advantage: Women's ways of leadership.* New York: Doubleday.

Howell, J. M., & Avolio, B. J. (1993). The ethics of charismatic leadership: Submission or liberation? *Academy of Management Executive, 6*(2), 43–54.

Ilies, R., Morgeson, F. P., & Nahrgang, J. D. (2005). Authentic leadership and eudaemonic well-being: Understanding leader-follower outcomes. *Leadership Quarterly, 16,* 373–394.

Kernis, M. H. (2003). Toward a conceptualization of optimal self-esteem. *Psychological Inquiry, 14,* 1–26.

Krakauer, J. (1997). *Into thin air: A personal account of the Mount Everest disaster.* New York: Villard Books.

Krakauer, J. (2003). *Under the banner of heaven: A story of violent faith.* New York: Doubleday.

Krakauer, J. (2011). *Three cups of deceit.* New York: Anchor Books.

Luthans, F., & Avolio, B. J. (2003). Authentic leadership development. In K. S. Cameron, J. E. Dutton, & R. E. Quinn (Eds.), *Positive organizational scholarship* (pp. 241–258). San Francisco: Berrett-Koehler.

Mortenson, G. (2009). *Stones into schools: Promoting peace with education in Afghanistan and Pakistan.* New York: Penguin Books.

Mortenson, G., & Relin, D. O. (2006). *Three cups of tea: One man's mission to promote peace . . . one school at a time.* New York: Penguin Books.

Shamir, B., & Eilam, G. (2005). "What's your story?" A life-stories approach to authentic leadership development. *Leadership Quarterly, 16,* 395–417.

Spraggins, R. E. (2005). *We the people: Men and women in the United States.* Retrieved May 30, 2009, from http://www.census.gov/prod/2005pubs/censr-20.pdf

Sutcliffe, K. M., & Vogus, T. J. (2003). Organizing for resilience. In K. S. Cameron, J. E. Dutton, & R. E. Quinn (Eds.), *Positive organizational scholarship* (pp. 94–110). San Francisco: Berrett-Koehler.

Walumbwa, F. O., Avolio, B. J., Gardner, W. L., Wernsing, T. S., & Peterson, S. J. (2008). Authentic leadership: Development and validation of a theory-based measure. *Journal of Management, 34*(1), 89–126.

10

Servant Leadership

DESCRIPTION

Servant leadership is a paradox—an approach to leadership that runs counter to common sense. Our everyday images of leadership do not coincide with leaders being servants. Leaders influence, and servants follow. How can leadership be both service *and* influence? How can a person be a leader *and* a servant at the same time? Although servant leadership seems contradictory and challenges our traditional beliefs about leadership, it is an approach that offers a unique perspective.

Servant leadership, which originated in the writings of Greenleaf (1970, 1972, 1977), has been of interest to leadership scholars for more than 40 years. Until recently, little empirical research on servant leadership has appeared in established peer-reviewed journals. Most of the academic and nonacademic writing on the topic has been prescriptive, focusing on how servant leadership should ideally be, rather than descriptive, focusing on what servant leadership actually is in practice (van Dierendonck, 2011). However, in the past 10 years, multiple publications have helped to clarify servant leadership and substantiate its basic assumptions.

Similar to earlier leadership theories discussed in this book (e.g., skills approach and behavioral approach), servant leadership is an approach focusing on leadership from the point of view of the leader and his or her behaviors. Servant leadership emphasizes that leaders be attentive to the concerns of their followers, empathize with them, and nurture them. Servant leaders put followers *first*, empower them, and help them develop their full personal capacities. Furthermore, servant leaders are ethical (see Chapter 13, "Leadership Ethics," for an extended discussion of this topic) and lead in

(N) Servant Leadership   (▶) Everyday Servant Leadership

ways that serve the greater good of the organization, community, and society at large.

Servant Leadership Defined

What is servant leadership? Scholars have addressed this approach from many different perspectives resulting in a variety of definitions of servant leadership. Greenleaf (1970) provides the most frequently referenced definition:

> [Servant leadership] begins with the natural feeling that one wants to serve, to serve *first*. Then conscious choice brings one to aspire to lead. . . . The difference manifests itself in the care taken by the servant—first to make sure that other people's highest priority needs are being served. The best test . . . is: do those served grow as persons; do they, *while being served,* become healthier, wiser, freer, more autonomous, more likely themselves to become servants? *And,* what is the effect on the least privileged in society; will they benefit, or, at least, will they not be further deprived? (p. 15)

Although complex, this definition sets forth the basic ideas of servant leadership that have been highlighted by current scholars. Servant leaders place the good of followers over their own self-interests and emphasize follower development (Hale & Fields, 2007). They demonstrate strong moral behavior toward followers (Graham, 1991; Walumbwa, Hartnell, & Oke, 2010), the organization, and other stakeholders (Ehrhart, 2004). Practicing servant leadership comes more naturally for some than others, but everyone can learn to be a servant leader (Spears, 2010). Although servant leadership is sometimes treated by others as a trait, in our discussion, servant leadership is viewed as a behavior.

Historical Basis of Servant Leadership

Robert K. Greenleaf coined the term *servant leadership* and is the author of the seminal works on the subject. Greenleaf's persona and writings have significantly influenced how servant leadership has developed on the practical and theoretical level. He founded the Center for Applied Ethics in 1964, now the Greenleaf Center for Servant Leadership, which provides a clearinghouse and focal point for research and writing on servant leadership.

Greenleaf worked for 40 years at AT&T and, after retiring, began exploring how institutions function and how they could better serve society. He was

 Being a Servant Leader   Serving on Southwest

intrigued by issues of power and authority and how individuals in organizations could creatively support each other. Decidedly against coercive leadership, Greenleaf advocated using communication to build consensus in groups.

Greenleaf credits his formulation of servant leadership to Hermann Hesse's (1956) novel *The Journey to the East*. It tells the story of a group of travelers on a mythical journey who are accompanied by a servant who does menial chores for the travelers but also sustains them with his spirits and song. The servant's presence has an extraordinary impact on the group. When the servant becomes lost and disappears from the group, the travelers fall into disarray and abandon the journey. Without the servant, they are unable to carry on. It was the servant who was ultimately leading the group, emerging as a leader through his selfless care of the travelers.

In addition to serving, Greenleaf states that a servant leader has a social responsibility to be concerned about the "have-nots" and those less privileged. If inequalities and social injustices exist, a servant leader tries to remove them (Graham, 1991). In becoming a servant leader, a leader uses less institutional power and control while shifting authority to those who are being led. Servant leadership values community because it provides a face-to-face opportunity for individuals to experience interdependence, respect, trust, and individual growth (Greenleaf, 1970).

Ten Characteristics of a Servant Leader

In an attempt to clarify servant leadership for practitioners, Spears (2002) identified 10 characteristics in Greenleaf's writings that are central to the development of servant leadership. Together, these characteristics comprise the first model or conceptualization of servant leadership.

1. *Listening.* Communication between leaders and followers is an interactive process that includes sending and receiving messages (i.e., talking and listening). Servant leaders communicate by listening first. They recognize that listening is a learned discipline that involves hearing and being receptive to what others have to say. Through listening, servant leaders acknowledge the viewpoint of followers and validate these perspectives.

2. *Empathy.* Empathy is "standing in the shoes" of another person and attempting to see the world from that person's point of view. Empathetic servant leaders demonstrate that they truly understand what followers are thinking and feeling. When a servant leader shows empathy, it is confirming and validating for the follower. It makes the follower feel unique.

 Unexpected Servant Leaders

3. *Healing.* To heal means to make whole. Servant leaders care about the personal well-being of their followers. They support followers by helping them overcome personal problems. Greenleaf argues that the process of healing is a two-way street—in helping followers become whole, servant leaders themselves are healed.

4. *Awareness.* For Greenleaf, awareness is a quality within servant leaders that makes them acutely attuned and receptive to their physical, social, and political environments. It includes understanding oneself and the impact one has on others. With awareness, servant leaders are able to step aside and view themselves and their own perspectives in the greater context of the situation.

5. *Persuasion.* Persuasion is clear and persistent communication that convinces others to change. As opposed to coercion, which utilizes positional authority to force compliance, persuasion creates change through the use of gentle nonjudgmental argument. According to Spears (2002), Greenleaf's emphasis on persuasion over coercion is perhaps related to his denominational affiliation with the Religious Society of Friends (Quakers).

6. *Conceptualization.* Conceptualization refers to an individual's ability to be a visionary for an organization, providing a clear sense of its goals and direction. This characteristic goes beyond day-to-day operational thinking to focus on the "big picture." Conceptualization also equips servant leaders to respond to complex organizational problems in creative ways, enabling them to deal with the intricacies of the organization in relationship to its long-term goals.

7. *Foresight.* Foresight encompasses a servant leader's ability to know the future. It is an ability to predict what is coming based on what is occurring in the present and what has happened in the past. For Greenleaf, foresight has an ethical dimension because he believes leaders should be held accountable for any failures to anticipate what reasonably could be foreseen and to act on that understanding.

8. *Stewardship.* Stewardship is about taking responsibility for the leadership role entrusted to the leader. Servant leaders accept the responsibility to carefully manage the people and organization they have been given to lead. In addition, they hold the organization in trust for the greater good of society.

9. *Commitment to the growth of people.* Greenleaf's conceptualization of servant leadership places a premium on treating each follower as a unique person with intrinsic value that goes beyond his or her tangible contributions to the organization. Servant leaders are committed to helping each person in the organization grow personally and professionally. Commitment

 Stewardship

can take many forms, including providing followers with opportunities for career development, helping them develop new work skills, taking a personal interest in the their ideas, and involving them in decision making (Spears, 2002).

10. *Building community.* Servant leadership fosters the development of community. A community is a collection of individuals who have shared interests and pursuits and feel a sense of unity and relatedness. Community allows followers to identify with something greater than themselves that they value. Servant leaders build community to provide a place where people can feel safe and connected with others, but are still allowed to express their own individuality.

These 10 characteristics of servant leadership represent Greenleaf's seminal work on the servant as leader. They provide a creative lens from which to view the complexities of servant leadership.

Building a Theory About Servant Leadership

For more than three decades after Greenleaf's original writings, servant leadership remained a set of loosely defined characteristics and normative principles. In this form it was widely accepted as a leadership approach, rather than a theory, that has strong heuristic and practical value. Praise for servant leadership came from a wide range of well-known leadership writers, including Bennis (2002), Blanchard and Hodges (2003), Covey (2002), DePree (2002), Senge (2002), and Wheatley (2002). At the same time, servant leadership was adopted as a guiding philosophy in many well-known organizations such as The Toro Company, Herman Miller, Synovus Financial Corporation, ServiceMaster, Men's Wearhouse, Southwest Airlines, and TDIndustries (Spears, 2002). Although novel and paradoxical, the basic ideas and prescriptions of servant leadership resonated with many as an ideal way to run an organization.

More recently, researchers have begun to examine the conceptual underpinnings of servant leadership in an effort to build a theory about it. These studies have resulted in a wide array of models that describe servant leadership using a multitude of variables. For example, Russell and Stone (2002) developed a practical model of servant leadership that contained 20 attributes, nine functional characteristics (distinctive behaviors observed in the workplace), and 11 accompanying characteristics that augment these behaviors. Similarly, Patterson (2003) created a value-based model of servant leadership that distinguished seven constructs that characterize the virtues and shape the behaviors of servant leaders.

 Dave Ramsey   Servant Leadership Framework

Table 10.1 Key Characteristics of Servant Leadership

Laub (1999)	Wong & Davey (2007)	Barbuto & Wheeler (2006)	Dennis & Bocarnea (2005)	Sendjaya, Sarros, & Santora (2008)	van Dierendonck & Nuijten (2011)
• Developing people • Sharing leadership • Displaying authenticity • Valuing people • Providing leadership • Building community	• Serving and developing others • Consulting and involving others • Humility and selflessness • Modeling integrity and authenticity • Inspiring and influencing others	• Altruistic calling • Emotional healing • Persuasive mapping • Organizational stewardship • Wisdom	• Empowerment • Trust • Humility • Agapao love • Vision	• Transforming influence • Voluntary subordination • Authentic self • Transcendental spirituality • Covenantal relationship • Responsible morality	• Empowerment • Humility • Standing back • Authenticity • Forgiveness • Courage • Accountability • Stewardship

SOURCE: Adapted from van Dierendonck, D. (2011). Servant leadership: A review and syntheses. *Journal of Management, 37*(4), 1228–1261.

230

Other conceptualizations of servant leadership have emerged from researchers' efforts to develop and validate instruments to measure the core dimensions of the servant leadership process. Table 10.1 provides a summary of some of these studies, illustrating clearly the extensiveness of characteristics related to servant leadership. This table also exhibits the lack of agreement among researchers on what specific characteristics define servant leadership. While some of the studies include common characteristics, such as humility or empowerment, none of the studies conceptualize servant leadership in exactly the same way. In addition, Table 10.1 demonstrates how servant leadership is treated as a trait phenomenon (e.g., courage, humility) in some studies while other researchers regard it as a behavioral process (e.g., serving and developing others). Although scholars are not in agreement regarding the primary attributes of servant leadership, these studies provide the groundwork necessary for the development of a refined model of servant leadership.

MODEL OF SERVANT LEADERSHIP

This chapter presents a servant leadership model based on Liden, Wayne, Zhao, and Henderson (2008) and Liden, Panaccio, Hu, and Meuser (2014) that has three main components: *antecedent conditions, servant leader behaviors,* and *leadership outcomes* (Figure 10.1). The model is intended to clarify the phenomenon of servant leadership and provide a framework for understanding its complexities.

Antecedent Conditions

As shown on the left side of Figure 10.1, three antecedent, or existing, conditions have an impact on servant leadership: *context and culture, leader attributes,* and *follower receptivity.* These conditions are not inclusive of all the conditions that affect servant leadership, but do represent some factors likely to influence the leadership process.

Context and Culture. Servant leadership does not occur in a vacuum but occurs within a given organizational context and a particular culture. The nature of each of these affects the way servant leadership is carried out. For example, in health care and nonprofit settings, the norm of caring is more prevalent, while for Wall Street corporations it is more common to have competition as an operative norm. Because the norms differ, the ways servant leadership is performed may vary.

Dimensions of culture (see Chapter 16, "Culture and Leadership") will also influence servant leadership. For example, in cultures where power distance

Figure 10.1 Model of Servant Leadership

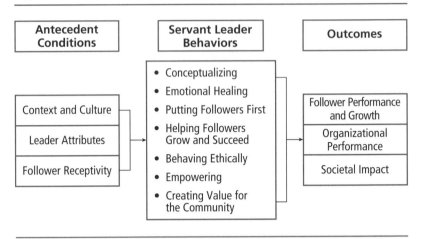

SOURCE: Adapted from Liden, R. C., Panaccio, A., Hu, J., & Meuser, J. D. (2014). Servant leadership: Antecedents, consequences, and contextual moderators. In D. V. Day (Ed.), *The Oxford handbook of leadership and organizations.* Oxford, England: Oxford University Press; and van Dierendonck, D. (2011). Servant leadership: A review and syntheses. *Journal of Management, 37*(4), 1228–1261.

is low (e.g., Nordic Europe) and power is shared equally among people at all levels of society, servant leadership may be more common. In cultures with low humane orientation (e.g., Germanic Europe), servant leadership may present more of a challenge. The point is that cultures influence the way servant leadership is able to be achieved.

Leader Attributes. As in any leadership situation, the qualities and disposition of the leader influence the servant leadership process. Individuals bring their own traits and ideas about leading to leadership situations. Some may feel a deep desire to serve or are strongly motivated to lead. Others may be driven by a sense of higher calling (Sendjaya, Sarros, & Santora, 2008). These dispositions shape how individuals demonstrate servant leadership. In addition, people differ in areas such as moral development, emotional intelligence, and self-determinedness, and these traits interact with their ability to engage in servant leadership.

Follower Receptivity. The receptivity of followers is a factor that appears to influence the impact of servant leadership on outcomes such as personal and organizational job performance. Follower receptivity concerns the

N The Ripple Effect   **in** Antecedents of Servant Leadership question "Do all followers show a desire for servant leadership?" Research suggests the answer may be no. Some followers do not want to work with servant leaders. They equate servant leadership with micromanagement, and report that they do not want their leader to get to know them or try to help, develop, or guide them (Liden, Wayne, et al., 2008). Similarly, Meuser, Liden, Wayne, and Henderson (2011) found empirical evidence showing that when servant leadership was matched with followers who desired it, this type of leadership had a positive impact on performance and organizational citizenship behavior. The opposite was seen when there was no match between servant leadership and the desire of followers for it. It appears that, for some followers, servant leadership has a positive impact and, for others, servant leadership is not effective.

Servant Leader Behaviors

The middle component of Figure 10.1 identifies seven *servant leader behaviors* that are the core of the servant leadership process. These behaviors emerged from Liden, Wayne, et al.'s (2008) vigorous efforts to develop and validate a measure of servant leadership. The findings from their research provide evidence for the soundness of viewing servant leadership as a multidimensional process. Collectively, these behaviors are the central focus of servant leadership. Individually, each behavior makes a unique contribution.

Conceptualizing. Conceptualizing refers to the servant leader's thorough understanding of the organization—its purposes, complexities, and mission. This capacity allows servant leaders to think through multifaceted problems, to know if something is going wrong, and to address problems creatively in accordance with the overall goals of the organization.

For example, Kate Simpson, a senior nursing supervisor in an emergency room of a large hospital, uses conceptualizing to lead her department. She fully understands the mission of the hospital and, at the same time, knows how to effectively manage staff on a day-to-day basis. Her staff members say Kate has a sixth sense about what is best for people. She is known for her wisdom in dealing with difficult patients and helping staff diagnose complex medical problems. Her abilities, competency, and value as a servant leader earned her the hospital's Caregiver of the Year Award.

Emotional Healing. Emotional healing involves being sensitive to the personal concerns and well-being of others. It includes recognizing others'

Servant Leader Beginnings

problems and being willing to take the time to address them. Servant leaders who exhibit emotional healing make themselves available to others, stand by them, and provide them with support.

Emotional healing is apparent in the work of Father John, a much sought-after hospice priest on Chicago's South Side. Father John has a unique approach to hospice patients: He doesn't encourage, give advice, or read Scripture. Instead he simply listens to them. "When you face death, the only important thing in life is relationships," he says. "I practice the art of standing by. I think it is more important to come just to be there than to do anything else."

Putting Followers First. Putting others first is the sine qua non of servant leadership—the defining characteristic. It means using actions and words that clearly demonstrate to followers that their concerns are a priority, including placing followers' interests and success ahead of those of the leader. It may mean a leader breaks from his or her own tasks to assist followers with theirs.

Dr. Autumn Klein, a widely published health education professor at a major research university, is responsible for several ongoing large interdisciplinary public health studies. Although she is the principal investigator on these studies, when multiauthored articles are submitted for publication, Dr. Klein puts the names of other researchers before her own. She chooses to let others be recognized because she knows it will benefit them in their annual performance reviews. She puts the success of her colleagues ahead of her own interests.

Helping Followers Grow and Succeed. This behavior refers to knowing followers' professional or personal goals and helping them to accomplish those aspirations. Servant leaders make followers' career development a priority, including mentoring followers and providing them with support. At its core, helping followers grow and succeed is about aiding these individuals to become self-actualized, reaching their fullest human potential.

An example of how a leader helps others grow and succeed is Mr. Yon Kim, a high school orchestra teacher who consistently receives praise from parents for his outstanding work with students. Mr. Kim is a skilled violinist with high musical standards, but he does not let that get in the way of helping each student, from the most highly accomplished to the least capable. Students like Mr. Kim because he listens to them and treats them as adults.

He gives feedback without being judgmental. Many of his former students have gone on to become music majors. They often visit Mr. Kim to let him know how important he was to them. Yon Kim is a servant leader who helps students grow through his teaching and guidance.

Behaving Ethically. Behaving ethically is doing the right thing in the right way. It is holding to strong ethical standards, including being open, honest, and fair with followers. Servant leaders do not compromise their ethical principles in order to achieve success.

An example of ethical behavior is how CEO Elizabeth Angliss responded when one of her employees brought her a copy of a leaked document from their company's chief competitor, outlining its plans to go after some of Angliss's largest customers. Although she knew the document undoubtedly had valuable information, she shredded it instead of reading it. She then called the rival CEO and told him she had received the document and wanted him to be aware that he might have a security issue within his company. "I didn't know if what I received was real or not," she explains. "But it didn't matter. If it was the real thing, someone on his end did something wrong, and my company wasn't going to capitalize on that."

Empowering. Empowering refers to allowing followers the freedom to be independent, make decisions on their own, and be self-sufficient. It is a way for leaders to share power with followers by allowing them to have control. Empowerment builds followers' confidence in their own capacities to think and act on their own because they are given the freedom to handle difficult situations in the way they feel is best.

For example, a college professor teaching a large lecture class empowers two teaching assistants assigned to him by letting them set their own office hours, independently grade student papers, and practice teaching by giving one of the weekly class lectures. They become confident in their teaching abilities and bring new ideas to the professor to try in the classroom.

Creating Value for the Community. Servant leaders create value for the community by consciously and intentionally giving back to the community. They are involved in local activities and encourage followers to also volunteer for community service. Creating value for the community is one way for leaders to link the purposes and goals of an organization with the broader purposes of the community.

 Community Building

An example of creating value for the community can be seen in the leadership of Mercedes Urbanez, principal of Alger High School. Alger is an alternative high school in a midsize community with three other high schools. Mercedes's care and concern for students at Alger is remarkable. Ten percent of Alger's students have children, so the school provides on-site day care. Fifteen percent of the students are on probation, and Alger is often their last stop before dropping out entirely and resuming criminal activities. While the other schools in town foster competition and push advanced placement courses, Alger focuses on removing the barriers that keep its students from excelling and offers courses that provide what its students need including multimedia skills, reading remediation, and parenting.

Under Mercedes, Alger High School is a model alternative school appreciated at every level in the community. Students, who have failed in other schools, find they have a safe place to go where they are accepted and adults try to help them solve their problems. Law enforcement supports the school's efforts to help these students get back into the mainstream of society and away from crime. The other high schools in the community know that Alger provides services they find difficult to provide. Mercedes Urbanez serves the have-nots in the community, and the whole community reaps the benefits.

Outcomes

Although servant leadership focuses primarily on leader behaviors, it is also important to examine the potential outcomes of servant leadership. The outcomes of servant leadership are *follower performance and growth, organizational performance*, and *societal impact* (see Figure 10.1). As Greenleaf highlighted in his original work (1970), the central goal of servant leadership is to create healthy organizations that nurture individual growth, strengthen organizational performance, and, in the end, produce a positive impact on society.

Follower Performance and Growth. In the model of servant leadership, most of the servant leader behaviors focus directly on recognizing followers' contributions and helping them realize their human potential. The expected outcome for followers is greater self-actualization. That is, followers will realize their full capabilities when leaders nurture them, help them with their personal goals, and give them control.

Another outcome of servant leadership, suggested by Meuser et al. (2011), is that it will have a favorable impact on follower in-role performance—the way followers do their assigned work. When servant leaders were matched with followers who were open to this type of leadership, the results were positive. Followers became more effective at accomplishing their jobs and fulfilling their job descriptions.

Finally, another expected result of servant leadership is that followers themselves may become servant leaders. Greenleaf's conceptualization of servant leadership hypothesizes that when followers receive caring and empowerment from ethical leaders they, in turn, will likely begin treating others in this way. Servant leadership would produce a ripple effect in which servant leaders create more servant leaders. Further research is needed, however, to test this hypothesis.

Organizational Performance. In addition to positively affecting followers and their performance, initial research has shown that servant leadership has an influence on organizational performance. Several studies have found a positive relationship between servant leadership and organizational citizenship behaviors (OCBs), which are follower behaviors that go beyond the basic requirements of their duties and help the overall functioning of the organization (Ehrhart, 2004; Liden, Wayne, et al., 2008; Neubert, Kacmar, Carlson, Chonko, & Roberts, 2008; Walumbwa et al., 2010).

Servant leadership also affects the way organizational teams function. Hu and Liden (2011) found that servant leadership enhanced team effectiveness by increasing the members' shared confidence that they could be effective as a work group. Furthermore, their results showed that servant leadership contributed positively to team potency by enhancing group process and clarity. However, when servant leadership was absent, team potency decreased, despite clearer goals. In essence, it frustrates people to know exactly what the goal is, but not get the support needed to accomplish the goal.

Current research on organizational outcomes is in its initial stages. Further study is needed to substantiate the direct and indirect ways that servant leadership is related to organizational performance.

Societal Impact. Another outcome expected of servant leadership is that it is likely to have a positive impact on society. Although societal impact is not commonly measured in studies of servant leadership, there are examples of servant leadership's impact that are highly visible. One example we are all familiar with is the work of Mother Teresa whose years of service for the

 Cultural Servant Leadership

hungry, homeless, and unwanted resulted in the creation of a new religious order, the Missionaries of Charity. This order now has more than 1 million workers in over 40 countries that operate hospitals, schools, and hospices for the poor. Mother Teresa's servant leadership has had an extraordinary impact on society throughout the world.

In the business world, an example of the societal impact of servant leadership can be observed at Southwest Airlines (see Case 10.3). Leaders at Southwest instituted an "others first" organizational philosophy in the management of the company, which starts with how it treats its employees. This philosophy is adhered to by those employees who themselves become servant leaders in regards to the airline's customers. Because the company thrives, it impacts society by providing jobs in the communities it serves and, to a lesser extent, by providing the customers who rely on it with transportation.

In his conceptualization of servant leadership, Greenleaf did not frame the process as one that was intended to directly change society. Rather, he visualizes leaders who become servants first and listen to others and help them grow. As a result, their organizations are healthier, ultimately benefiting society. In this way, the long-term outcomes of putting others first include positive social change and helping society flourish.

Summary of the Model of Servant Leadership

In summary, the model of servant leadership consists of three components: antecedent conditions, servant leader behaviors, and outcomes. The central focus of the model is the seven behaviors of leaders that foster servant leadership: conceptualizing, emotional healing, putting followers first, helping followers grow and succeed, behaving ethically, empowering, and creating value for the community. These behaviors are influenced by context and culture, the leader's attributes, and the followers' receptivity to this kind of leadership. When individuals engage in servant leadership, it is likely to improve outcomes at the individual, organizational, and societal levels.

HOW DOES SERVANT LEADERSHIP WORK? ────

The servant leadership approach works differently than many of the prior theories we have discussed in this book. For example, it is unlike the trait approach (Chapter 2), which emphasizes that leaders should have certain specific traits. It is also unlike path–goal theory (Chapter 6), which lays out principles regarding what style of leadership is needed in various situations.

N Servant Leaders   ▶ Iron Man Helps the Homeless

Instead, servant leadership focuses on the behaviors leaders should exhibit to put followers first and to support followers' personal development. It is concerned with how leaders treat followers and the outcomes that are likely to emerge.

So what is the mechanism that explains how servant leadership works? It begins when leaders commit themselves to putting their followers first, being honest with them, and treating them fairly. Servant leaders make it a priority to listen to their followers and develop strong long-term relationships with them. This allows leaders to understand the abilities, needs, and goals of followers, which, in turn, allows these followers to achieve their full potential. When many leaders in an organization adopt a servant leadership orientation, a culture of serving others within and outside the organization is created (Liden, Wayne, et al., 2008).

Servant leadership works best when leaders are altruistic and have a strong motivation and deep-seated interest in helping others. In addition, for successful servant leadership to occur, it is important that followers are open and receptive to servant leaders who want to empower them and help them grow.

It should be noted that in much of the writing on servant leadership there is an underlying philosophical position, originally set forth by Greenleaf (1970), that leaders should be altruistic and humanistic. Rather than using their power to dominate others, leaders should make every attempt to share their power and enable others to grow and become autonomous. Leadership framed from this perspective downplays competition in the organization and promotes egalitarianism.

Finally, in an ideal world, servant leadership results in community and societal change. Individuals within an organization who care for each other become committed to developing an organization that cares for the community. Organizations that adopt a servant leadership culture are committed to helping those in need who operate outside of the organization. Servant leadership extends to serving the "have-nots" in society (Graham, 1991). Case 10.2 in this chapter provides a striking example of how one servant leader's work led to positive outcomes for many throughout the world.

STRENGTHS

In its current stage of development, research on servant leadership has made several positive contributions to the field of leadership. First, while there are other leadership approaches such as transformational and

 Service Leadership

authentic leadership that include an ethical dimension, servant leadership is unique in the way it makes altruism the central component of the leadership process. Servant leadership argues unabashedly that leaders should put followers first, share control with followers, and embrace their growth. It is the only leadership approach that frames the leadership process around the principle of caring for others.

Second, servant leadership provides a counterintuitive and provocative approach to the use of influence, or power, in leadership. Nearly all other theories of leadership treat influence as a positive factor in the leadership process, but servant leadership does just the opposite. It argues that leaders should not dominate, direct, or control; but rather, leaders should share control and influence. To give up control rather than seek control is the goal of servant leadership. Servant leadership is an influence process that does not incorporate influence in a traditional way.

Third, rather than imply that servant leadership is a panacea, research on servant leadership has shown there are conditions under which servant leadership is not a preferred kind of leadership. Findings indicate that servant leadership may not be effective in contexts where followers are not open to being guided, supported, and empowered. Followers' readiness to receive servant leadership moderates the potential usefulness of leading from this approach (Liden, Wayne, et al., 2008).

Fourth, recent research has resulted in a sound measure of servant leadership. Using a rigorous methodology, Liden, Wayne, et al. (2008) developed and validated the Servant Leadership Questionnaire (SLQ), which appears at the end of the chapter. It comprises 28 items that identify seven distinct dimensions of servant leadership. Studies show that the SLQ is unique and measures aspects of leadership that are different from those measured by the transformational and leader–member exchange theories (Liden, Wayne, et al., 2008; Schaubroeck, Lam, & Peng, 2011). The SLQ has proved to be a suitable instrument for use in future research on servant leadership.

CRITICISMS

In addition to the positive features of servant leadership, this approach has several limitations. First, the paradoxical nature of the title "servant leadership" creates semantic noise that diminishes the potential value of the approach. Because the name appears contradictory, servant leadership is prone to be perceived as fanciful or whimsical. In addition, being a servant leader implies following, and following is viewed as the opposite of leading. Although servant leadership incorporates influence, the mechanism of how influence functions as a part of servant leadership is not fully explicated in the approach.

Second, there is debate among servant leadership scholars regarding the core dimensions of the process. As illustrated in Table 10.1, servant leadership is hypothesized to include a multitude of abilities, traits, and behaviors. To date, researchers have been unable to reach consensus on a common definition or theoretical framework for servant leadership (van Dierendonck, 2011). Until a larger body of findings is published on servant leadership, the robustness of theoretical formulations about it will remain limited.

Third, a large segment of the writing on servant leadership has a prescriptive overtone that implies that good leaders "put others first." While advocating an altruistic approach to leadership is commendable, it has a utopian ring because it conflicts with individual autonomy and other principles of leadership such as directing, concern for production, goal setting, and creating a vision (Gergen, 2006). Furthermore, along with the "value-push" prescriptive quality, there is an almost moralistic nature that seems to surround servant leadership. As a result, many practitioners of servant leadership are not necessarily researchers who want to conduct studies to test the validity of servant leadership theory.

Finally, it is unclear why "conceptualizing" is included as one of the servant leadership behaviors in the model of servant leadership (see Figure 10.1). Is conceptualizing actually a behavior, or is it a cognitive ability? Furthermore, what is the rationale for identifying conceptualizing as a determinant of servant leadership? Being able to conceptualize is undoubtedly an important cognitive capacity in all kinds of leadership, but why is it a defining characteristic of servant leadership? A clearer explanation for its central role in servant leadership needs to be addressed in future research.

APPLICATION

Servant leadership can be applied at all levels of management and in all types of organizations. Within a philosophical framework of caring for others, servant leadership sets forth a list of behaviors that individuals can engage in if they want to be servant leaders. The prescribed behaviors of servant leadership are not esoteric; they are easily understood and generally applicable to a variety of leadership situations.

Unlike leader–member exchange theory (Chapter 7) or authentic leadership (Chapter 9), which are not widely used in training and development, servant leadership has been used extensively in a variety of organizations for more than 30 years. Many organizations in the Fortune 500 (e.g., Starbucks, AT&T, Southwest Airlines, and Vanguard Group) employ ideas from servant leadership. Training in servant leadership typically involves self-assessment exercises, educational sessions, and goal setting. The content of servant leadership is straightforward and accessible to followers at every level within the organization.

Liden, Wayne, et al. (2008) suggest that organizations that want to build a culture of servant leadership should be careful to select people who are interested in and capable of building long-term relationships with followers. Furthermore, because "behaving ethically" is positively related to job performance, organizations should focus on selecting people who have high integrity and strong ethics. In addition, organizations should develop training programs that spend time helping leaders develop their emotional intelligence, ethical decision making, and skills for empowering others. Behaviors such as these will help leaders nurture followers to their full potential.

Servant leadership is taught at many colleges and universities around the world and is the focus of numerous independent coaches, trainers, and consultants. In the United States, Gonzaga University and Regent University are recognized as prominent leaders in this area because of the academic attention they have given to servant leadership. Overall, the most recognized and comprehensive center for training in servant leadership is the Greenleaf Center for Servant Leadership (www.greenleaf.org).

In summary, servant leadership provides a philosophy and set of behaviors that individuals in the organizational setting can learn and develop. The following section features cases illustrating how servant leadership has been manifested in different ways.

CASE STUDIES

This section provides three case studies (Cases 10.1, 10.2, and 10.3) that illustrate different facets of servant leadership. The first case describes the servant leadership of a high school secretary. The second case is about Dr. Paul Farmer and his efforts to stop disease in Haiti and other parts of the world. The third case is about the leaders of Southwest Airlines who created a servant leadership culture that permeates the company. At the end

Emotional Intelligence in Servant Leaders

of each case, several questions are provided to help you analyze the case from the perspective of servant leadership.

CASE 10.1

Everyone Loves Mrs. Noble

Sharon Noble is in charge of the main office at Essex High School, a position she has held for nearly 30 years. She does not have a college degree, but that does not seem to hinder her work as "secretary" for the school. She is an extravert, and people say her jokes are corny, but she runs the office efficiently and well, getting along with teachers and students and dealing with the rules and procedures that govern day-to-day Essex school life.

When people describe Sharon, they say that she is wise and seems to know just about everything there is to know about the school. She understands the core curriculum, testing, dress code, skip policy, after-school programs, helicopter parents, and much more. If students want to have a bake sale, she tells them the best way to do it. If they want to take Advanced Placement courses, she tells them which ones to take. The list of what she knows is endless. For years parents have told one another, "If you want to know anything about the school, go to Mrs. Noble—she *is* Essex High School."

There is nothing pretentious about Mrs. Noble. She drives an old car and wears simple clothes. Students say they've never seen her wear makeup. But nevertheless, she is still "with it" when it comes to student fads and eccentricities. When students had long hair and fringed vests in the 1970s, Sharon was cool with it. She never mocks students who are "way out" and seems to even enjoy these students. When students wear clothes to get attention because they feel ostracized, Sharon is accepting and even acknowledges the "uniqueness" of their act, unless it violates the dress code. In those cases, she talks nonjudgmentally with students about their clothing, guiding them to make different choices to stay out of trouble.

Even though it isn't technically in her job description, Mrs. Noble excels at helping juniors prepare applications for college. She knows all the requirements and deadlines and the materials required by the different universities. She spends hours pushing, nudging, and convincing students to stay on task and get their applications submitted. She doesn't care if students go to Ivy League schools, state schools, or community colleges; but she does care if they go on to school. Mrs. Noble regrets not having been able to attend college, so it is important to her that "her" students do everything they can to go.

(Continued)

(Continued)

At times her job is challenging. For example, the principal made teaching assignments that the faculty did not like, and Sharon was the one they shared their concerns with. She was a great listener and helped them see the differing perspectives of the situation. One year, when a student was in a car accident and unable to come to school for several months, Sharon personally worked with each one of the student's teachers to get her assignments, delivered them to the student's home, and picked them up when they were complete. When the seniors held a dance marathon to raise money for cancer research, it was Sharon who pledged the most, even though she didn't make very much as the school's secretary. She wanted to make sure each senior participating had at least one pledge on his or her roster; in most cases it was Sharon's.

In 2010, the class of 1989 had its 25-year reunion, and of all the memories shared, the most were about Sharon Noble. Essex High School had a wonderful principal, many good teachers, and great coaches, but when alumni were asked, who runs the school? The answer was always "Mrs. Noble."

Questions

1. What servant leader behaviors would you say Mrs. Noble demonstrates?

2. Who are Mrs. Noble's followers?

3. Based on the model of servant leadership (Figure 10.1), what outcomes has Mrs. Noble's servant leadership attained?

4. Can you think of someone at a school or organization you were part of who acted like Mrs. Noble? Describe what this person did and how it affected you and the school or organization.

CASE 10.2

Doctor to the Poor

"Education wasn't what he wanted to perform on the world . . . He was after transformation."

—Kidder (2003, p. 44)

When Paul Farmer graduated from Duke University at 22, he was unsure whether he wanted to be an anthropologist or a doctor. So he went to Haiti. As a student, Paul had become obsessed with the island nation after meeting many Haitians at local migrant camps. Paul was used to the grittier side of life; he had grown up in a family of eight that lived in a converted school bus and later on a houseboat moored in a bayou. But what he observed at the migrant camps and learned from his discussions with Haitian immigrants made his childhood seem idyllic.

In Haiti, he volunteered for a small charity called Eye Care Haiti, which conducted outreach clinics in rural areas. He was drawn in by the deplorable conditions and lives of the Haitian people and determined to use his time there to learn everything he could about illness and disease afflicting the poor. Before long, Paul realized that he had found his life's purpose: He'd be a doctor to poor people, and he'd start in Haiti.

Paul entered Harvard University in 1984 and, for the first two years, traveled back and forth to Haiti where he conducted a health census in the village of Cange. During that time he conceived of a plan to fight disease in Haiti by developing a public health system that included vaccination programs and clean water and sanitation. The heart of this program, however, would be a cadre of people from the villages who were trained to administer medicines, teach health classes, treat minor ailments, and recognize the symptoms of grave illnesses such as HIV, tuberculosis, and malaria.

His vision became reality in 1987, thanks to a wealthy donor who gave $1 million to help Paul create Partners In Health (PIH). At first it wasn't much of an organization—no staff, a small advisory board, and three committed volunteers. But its work was impressive: PIH began building schools and clinics in and around Cange. Soon PIH established a training program for health outreach workers and organized a mobile unit to screen residents of area villages for preventable diseases.

In 1990, Paul finished his medical studies and became a fellow in infectious diseases at Brigham and Women's Hospital in Boston. He was able to remain in Haiti for most of each year, returning to Boston to work at Brigham for a few months at a time, sleeping in the basement of PIH headquarters.

It wasn't long before PIH's successes started gaining attention outside of Haiti. Because of its success treating the disease in Haiti, the World Health Organization appointed Paul and PIH staffer Jim Yong Kim to spearhead pilot treatment programs for multiple-drug-resistant tuberculosis (MDR-TB). Paul's attention was now diverted to the slums of Peru and Russia where cases of MDR-TB were on the rise. In Peru, Paul and PIH

(Continued)

(Continued)

encountered barriers in treating MDR-TB that had nothing to do with the disease. They ran headlong into governmental resistance and had to battle to obtain expensive medications. Paul learned to gently navigate governmental obstacles, while the Bill & Melinda Gates Foundation stepped in with a $44.7 million grant to help fund the program.

In 2005, PIH turned its attention to another part of the world: Africa, the epicenter of the global AIDS pandemic. Beginning its efforts in Rwanda, where few people had been tested or were receiving treatment, PIH tested 30,000 people in 8 months and enrolled nearly 700 in drug therapy to treat the disease. Soon, the organization expanded its efforts to the African nations of Lesotho and Malawi (Partners In Health, 2011).

But Paul's efforts weren't just in far-flung reaches of the world. From his work with patients at Brigham, Paul observed the needs of the impoverished in Boston. The Prevention and Access to Care and Treatment (PACT) project was created to offer drug therapy for HIV and diabetes for the poor residents of the Roxbury and Dorchester districts. PIH has since sent PACT project teams across the United States to provide support to other community health programs.

By 2009, Partners in Health had grown to 13,600 employees working in health centers and hospitals in 8 countries (Partners In Health, 2013), including the Dominican Republic, Peru, Mexico, Rwanda, Lesotho, Malawi, Navajo Nation (U.S.), and Russia. Each year the organization increases the number of facilities and personnel that provide health care to the residents of some of the most impoverished and diseased places in the world. Paul continues to travel around the world, monitoring programs and raising funds for PIH in addition to leading the Department of Global Health and Social Medicine at Harvard Medical School.

Questions

1. Would you characterize Paul Farmer as a servant leader? Explain your answer.

2. Putting others first is the essence of servant leadership. In what way does Paul Farmer put others first?

3. Another characteristic of a servant leader is getting followers to serve. Who are Paul's followers, and how did they become servants to his vision?

4. What role do you think Paul's childhood had in his development as a servant leader?

CASE 10.3

Servant Leadership Takes Flight

A young mother traveling with a toddler on a long cross-country flight approached the flight attendant looking rather frantic. Because of weather and an hour-and-a-half wait on the runway to take off, the plane would arrive at its destination several hours late. The plane had made an intermediate stop in Denver to pick up passengers but not long enough for travelers to disembark. The mother told the attendant that with the delays and the long flight, her child had already eaten all the food she brought and if she didn't feed him soon he was bound to have a total meltdown. "Can I get off for five minutes just to run and get something for him to eat?" she pleaded.

"I have to recommend strongly that you stay on the plane," the attendant said, sternly. But then, with a smile, she added, "But I can get off. The plane won't leave without me. What can I get your son to eat?"

Turns out that flight attendant not only got the little boy a meal, but brought four other children on board meals as well. Anyone who has traveled in a plane with screaming children knows that this flight attendant not only took care of some hungry children and frantic parents, but also indirectly saw to the comfort of a planeload of other passengers.

This story doesn't surprise anyone familiar with Southwest Airlines. The airline's mission statement is posted every 3 feet at all Southwest locations: Follow the Golden Rule—treat people the way you want to be treated.

It's a philosophy that the company takes to heart and begins with how it treats employees. Colleen Barrett, the former president of Southwest Airlines, says the company's cofounder and her mentor, Herb Kelleher, was adamant that "a happy and motivated workforce will essentially extend that goodwill to Southwest's customers" (Knowledge@ Wharton, 2008). If the airline took care of its employees, the employees would take care of the customers, and the shareholders would win, too.

From the first days of Southwest Airlines, Herb resisted establishing traditional hierarchies within the company. He focused on finding employees with substance, willing to say what they thought and committed to doing things differently. Described as "an egalitarian spirit," he employed a collaborative approach to management that involved his associates at every step.

(Continued)

(Continued)

Colleen, who went from working as Herb's legal secretary to being the president of the airline, is living proof of his philosophy. A poor girl from rural Vermont who got the opportunity of a lifetime to work for Herb when he was still just a lawyer, she rose from his aide to become vice president of administration, then executive vice president of customers, and then president and chief operating officer in 2001 (which she stepped down from in 2008). She had no formal training in aviation, but that didn't matter. Herb "always treated me as a complete equal to him," she says.

It was Colleen who instituted the Golden Rule as the company motto and developed a model that focuses on employee satisfaction and issues first, followed by the needs of the passengers. The company hired employees for their touchy-feely attitudes and trained them for skill. Southwest Airlines developed a culture that celebrated and encouraged humor. The example of being themselves on the job started at the top with Herb and Colleen.

This attitude has paid off. Southwest Airlines posted a profit for 35 consecutive years and continues to make money while other airlines' profits are crashing. Colleen says the most important numbers on the balance sheet, however, are those that indicate how many millions of people have become frequent flyers of the airline, a number that grows every year.

Questions

1. What type of servant leader behaviors did Herb Kelleher exhibit in starting the airline? What about Colleen Barrett?

2. How do the leaders of Southwest Airlines serve others? What others are they serving?

3. Southwest Airlines emphasizes the Golden Rule. What role does the Golden Rule play in servant leadership? Is it always a part of servant leadership? Discuss.

4. Based on Figure 10.1, describe the outcomes of servant leadership at Southwest Airlines, and how follower receptivity may have influenced those outcomes.

LEADERSHIP INSTRUMENT

Many questionnaires have been used to measure servant leadership (see Table 10.1). Because of its relevance to the content, the Servant Leadership Questionnaire (SLQ) by Liden, Wayne, et al. (2008) was chosen for inclusion in this chapter. It is a 28-item scale that measures seven major dimensions of servant leadership: conceptualizing, emotional healing, putting followers first, helping followers grow and succeed, behaving ethically, empowering, and creating value for the community. Using exploratory and confirmatory factor analysis, Liden, Wayne, et al. established the multiple dimensions of this scale and described how it is uniquely different from other leadership measures.

By completing the SLQ you will gain an understanding of how servant leadership is measured and explore where you stand on the different dimensions of servant leadership. Servant leadership is a complex process, and taking the SLQ is one way to discover the dynamics of how it works.

Servant Leadership Questionnaire

Instructions: Select two people who know you in a leadership capacity such as a coworker, fellow group member, or follower. Make two copies of this questionnaire and give a copy to each individual you have chosen. Using the following 7-point scale, ask them to indicate the extent to which they agree or disagree with the following statements as they pertain to your leadership. In these statements, "He/She" is referring to you in a leadership capacity.

Key: 1 = Strongly disagree 2 = Disagree 3 = Disagree somewhat
       4 = Undecided 5 = Agree Somewhat 6 = Agree 7 = Strongly agree

1. Others would seek help from him/her if they had a personal problem. 1 2 3 4 5 6 7

2. He/She emphasizes the importance of giving back to the community. 1 2 3 4 5 6 7

3. He/She can tell if something work related is going wrong. 1 2 3 4 5 6 7

4. He/She gives others the responsibility to make important decisions about their own jobs. 1 2 3 4 5 6 7

5. He/She makes others' career development a priority. 1 2 3 4 5 6 7

6. He/She cares more about others' success than his/her own. 1 2 3 4 5 6 7

7. He/She holds high ethical standards. 1 2 3 4 5 6 7

8. He/She cares about others' personal well-being. 1 2 3 4 5 6 7

9. He/She is always interested in helping people in the community. 1 2 3 4 5 6 7

10. He/She is able to think through complex problems. 1 2 3 4 5 6 7

11. He/She encourages others to handle important work decisions on their own. 1 2 3 4 5 6 7

12. He/She is interested in making sure others reach their career goals. 1 2 3 4 5 6 7

13. He/She puts others' best interests above his/her own. 1 2 3 4 5 6 7

14. He/She is always honest. 1 2 3 4 5 6 7

15. He/She takes time to talk to others on a personal level. 1 2 3 4 5 6 7

16. He/She is involved in community activities. 1 2 3 4 5 6 7

17. He/She has a thorough understanding of the organization and its goals. 1 2 3 4 5 6 7

18. He/She gives others the freedom to handle difficult situations in the way they feel is best. 1 2 3 4 5 6 7

19. He/She provides others with work experiences that enable them to develop new skills. 1 2 3 4 5 6 7

20. He/She sacrifices his/her own interests to meet others' needs. 1 2 3 4 5 6 7

21. He/She would not compromise ethical principles in order to meet success. 1 2 3 4 5 6 7

22. He/She can recognize when others are feeling down without asking them. 1 2 3 4 5 6 7

23. He/She encourages others to volunteer in the community. 1 2 3 4 5 6 7

24. He/She can solve work problems with new or creative ideas. 1 2 3 4 5 6 7

25. If others need to make important decisions at work, they do not need to consult him/her. 1 2 3 4 5 6 7

26. He/She wants to know about others' career goals. 1 2 3 4 5 6 7

27. He/She does what he/she can to make others' jobs easier. 1 2 3 4 5 6 7

28. He/She values honesty more than profits. 1 2 3 4 5 6 7

SOURCE: Reprinted (adapted version) from "Servant Leadership: Development of a Multidimensional Measure and Multi-Level Assessment," by R. C. Liden, S. J. Wayne, H. Zhao, and D. Henderson, 2008, *The Leadership Quarterly, 19,* 161–177. Copyright © Reprinted with permission from Elsevier Science.

Scoring

Using the questionnaires on which others assessed your leadership, take the separate scores for each item, add them together, and divide that sum by two. This will give you the average score for that item. For example, if Person A assessed you at 4 for Item 2, and Person B marked you as a 6, your score for Item 2 would be 5.

Once you have averaged each item's scores, use the following steps to complete the scoring of the questionnaire:

1. Add up the scores on 1, 8, 15, and 22. This is your score for emotional healing.

2. Add up the scores for 2, 9, 16, and 23. This is your score for creating value for the community.

3. Add up the scores for 3, 10, 17, and 24. This is your score for conceptual skills.

4. Add up the scores for 4, 11, 18, and 25. This is your score for empowering.

5. Add up the scores for 5, 12, 19, and 26. This is your score for helping followers grow and succeed.

6. Add up the scores for 6, 13, 20, and 27. This is your score for putting followers first.

7. Add up the scores for 7, 14, 21, and 28. This is your score for behaving ethically.

Scoring Interpretation

- *High range:* A score between 23 and 28 means you strongly exhibit this servant leadership behavior.

- *Moderate range:* A score between 14 and 22 means you tend to exhibit this behavior in an average way.

- *Low range:* A score between 8 and 13 means you exhibit this leadership below the average or expected degree.

- *Extremely low range:* A score between 0 and 7 means you are not inclined to exhibit this leadership behavior at all.

The scores you received on the Servant Leadership Questionnaire indicate the degree to which you exhibit the seven behaviors characteristic of a servant leader. You can use the results to assess areas in which you have strong servant leadership behaviors and areas in which you may strive to improve.

SUMMARY

Originating in the seminal work of Greenleaf (1970), servant leadership is a paradoxical approach to leadership that challenges our traditional beliefs about leadership and influence. Servant leadership emphasizes that leaders should be attentive to the needs of followers, empower them, and help them develop their full human capacities.

Servant leaders make a conscious choice to *serve first*—to place the good of followers over the leaders' self-interests. They build strong relationships with others, are empathic and ethical, and lead in ways that serve the greater good of followers, the organization, the community, and society at large.

Based on an idea from Hermann Hesse's (1956) novel *The Journey to the East,* Greenleaf argued that the selfless servant in a group has an extraordinary impact on the other members. Servant leaders attend fully to the needs of followers, are concerned with the less privileged, and aim to remove inequalities and social injustices. Because servant leaders shift authority to those who are being led, they exercise less institutional power and control.

Scholars have conceptualized servant leadership in multiple ways. According to Spears (2002), there are 10 major characteristics of servant leadership: listening, empathy, healing, awareness, persuasion, conceptualization, foresight, stewardship, commitment to the growth of people, and building community. Additional efforts by social science researchers to develop and validate measures of servant leadership have resulted in an extensive list of other servant leadership attributes.

Liden, Panaccio, et al. (2014) have created a promising model of servant leadership that has three main components: antecedent conditions, servant leader behaviors, and leadership outcomes. *Antecedent conditions* that are likely to impact servant leaders include context and culture, leader attributes, and follower receptivity. Central to the servant leader process are the seven *servant leader behaviors:* conceptualizing, emotional healing, putting followers first, helping followers grow and succeed, behaving ethically, empowering, and creating value for the community. The *outcomes* of servant leadership are follower performance and growth, organizational performance, and societal impact.

Research on servant leadership has several strengths. First, it is unique because it makes altruism the main component of the leadership process. Second, servant leadership provides a counterintuitive and provocative approach to the use of influence wherein leaders give up control rather than seek control. Third, rather than a panacea, research has shown that there are conditions under which servant leadership is not a preferred kind of leadership. Last, recent research has resulted in a sound measure of servant leadership (Servant Leadership Questionnaire) that identifies seven distinct dimensions of the process.

The servant leadership approach also has limitations. First, the paradoxical nature of the title "servant leadership" creates semantic noise that diminishes the potential value of the approach. Second, no consensus exists on a common theoretical framework for servant leadership. Third, servant leadership has a utopian ring that conflicts with traditional approaches to leadership. Last, it is not clear why "conceptualizing" is a defining characteristic of servant leadership.

Despite the limitations, servant leadership continues to be an engaging approach to leadership that holds much promise. As more research is done to test the substance and assumptions of servant leadership, a better understanding of the complexities of the process will emerge.

Sharpen your skills with SAGE edge at **edge.sagepub.com/northouse7e**

REFERENCES

Barbuto, J. E., Jr., & Wheeler, D. W. (2006). Scale development and construct clarification of servant leadership. *Group and Organizational Management, 31,* 300–326.

Bennis, W. (2002). Become a tomorrow leader. In L. C. Spears & M. Lawrence (Eds.), *Focus on leadership: Servant-leadership for the twenty-first century* (pp. 101–110). New York: Wiley.

Blanchard, K., & Hodges, P. (2003). *The servant leader: Transforming your hearts, heads, hands, and habits.* Nashville, TN: Thomas Nelson.

Covey, S. R. (2002). Foreword. In R. K. Greenleaf (Ed.), *Servant leadership: A journey into the nature of legitimate power and greatness* (pp. 1–14). New York: Paulist Press.

Dennis, R. S., & Bocarnea, M. (2005). Development of the servant leadership assessment instrument. *Leadership & Organization Development Journal, 26,* 600–615.

DePree, M. (2002). Servant-leadership: Three things necessary. In L. C. Spears & M. Lawrence (Eds.), *Focus on leadership: Servant-leadership for the twenty-first century* (pp. 27–34). New York: Wiley.

Ehrhart, M. G. (2004). Leadership and procedural justice climate as antecedents of unit-level organizational citizenship behavior. *Personnel Psychology, 57,* 61–94.

Gergen, D. (2006, June 11). Bad news for bullies. *U.S. News and World Report, 140,* 54.

Graham, J. W. (1991). Servant leadership in organizations: Inspirational and moral. *Leadership Quarterly, 2,* 105–119.

Greenleaf, R. K. (1970). *The servant as leader.* Westfield, IN: Greenleaf Center for Servant Leadership.

Greenleaf, R. K. (1972). *The institution as servant.* Westfield, IN: Greenleaf Center for Servant Leadership.

Greenleaf, R. K. (1977). *Servant leadership: A journey into the nature of legitimate power and greatness.* New York: Paulist Press.

Hale, J. R., & Fields, D. L. (2007). Exploring servant leadership across cultures: A study of followers in Ghana and the USA. *Leadership, 3,* 397–417.

Hesse, H. (1956). *The journey to the East.* London: P. Owen.

Hu, J., & Liden, R. C. (2011). Antecedents of team potency and team effectiveness: An examination of goal and process clarity and servant leadership. *Journal of Applied Psychology, 96*(4), 851–862.

Kidder, T. (2003). *Mountains beyond mountains: The quest of Dr. Paul Farmer, a man who would cure the world.* New York: Random House.

Knowledge@Wharton. (2008, July 9). *Southwest Airlines' Colleen Barrett flies high on fuel hedging and "servant leadership."* Retrieved November 13, 2011, from http://knowledge.wharton.upenn.edu/article.cfm?articleid=2006

Laub, J. A. (1999). Assessing the servant organization: Development of the servant organizational leadership assessment (SOLA) instrument. *Dissertation Abstracts International, 60*(2), 308. (UMI No. 9921922)

Liden, R. C., Panaccio, A., Hu, J., & Meuser, J. D. (2014). Servant leadership: Antecedents, consequences, and contextual moderators. In D. V. Day (Ed.), *The Oxford handbook of leadership and organizations.* Oxford: Oxford University Press.

Liden, R. C., Wayne, S. J., Zhao, H., & Henderson, D. (2008). Servant leadership: Development of a multidimensional measure and multi-level assessment. *Leadership Quarterly, 19,* 161–177.

Meuser, J. D., Liden, R. C., Wayne, S. J., & Henderson, D. J. (2011, August). *Is servant leadership always a good thing? The moderating influence of servant leadership prototype.* Paper presented at the meeting of the Academy of Management, San Antonio, TX.

Neubert, M. J., Kacmar, K. M., Carlson, D. S., Chonko, L. B., & Roberts, J. A. (2008). Regulatory focus as a mediator of the influence of initiating structure and servant leadership on employee behavior. *Journal of Applied Psychology, 93,* 1220–1233.

Partners In Health. (2011). *History.* Retrieved September 27, 2011, from http://www.pih.org/pages/partners-in-health-history.html

Partners In Health. (2013) *2013 annual report.* Retrieved August 15, 2014, from http://www.pih.org/pages/2013-annual-report

Patterson, K. A. (2003). *Servant leadership: A theoretical model* (Doctoral dissertation, Regent University, ATT 30882719).

Russell, R. F., & Stone, A. G. (2002). A review of servant-leadership attributes: Developing a practical model. *Leadership & Organization Development Journal, 23,* 145–157.

Schaubroeck, J., Lam, S. S. K., & Peng, A. C. (2011). Cognition-based and affect-based trust as mediators of leader behavior influences on team performance. *Journal of Applied Psychology, 96*(4), 863–871.

Sendjaya, S., Sarros, J. C., & Santora, J. C. (2008). Defining and measuring servant leadership behaviour in organizations. *Journal of Management Studies, 45*(2), 402–424.

Senge, P. M. (2002). Afterword. In R. K. Greenleaf (Ed.), *Servant leadership: A journey into the nature of legitimate power and greatness* (pp. 343–360). New York: Paulist Press.

Spears, L. C. (2002). Tracing the past, present, and future of servant-leadership. In L. C. Spears & M. Lawrence (Eds.), *Focus on leadership: Servant-leadership for the 21st century* (pp. 1–16). New York: Wiley.

Spears, L. C. (2010). Servant leadership and Robert K. Greenleaf's legacy. In D. van Dierendonck & K. Patterson (Eds.), *Servant leadership: Developments in theory and research* (pp. 11–24). New York: Palgrave Macmillan.

van Dierendonck, D. (2011). Servant leadership: A review and synthesis. *Journal of Management, 37*(4), 1228–1261.

van Dierendonck, D., & Nuijten, I. (2011). The servant leadership survey: Development and validation of a multidimensional measure. *Journal of Business and Psychology, 26*, 249–267.

Walumbwa, F. O., Hartnell, C. A., & Oke, A. (2010). Servant leadership, procedural justice climate, service climate, employee attitudes, and organizational citizenship behavior: A cross-level investigation. *Journal of Applied Psychology, 95*, 517–529.

Wheatley, M. (2002). The work of the servant leader. In L. C. Spears & M. Lawrence (Eds.), *Focus on leadership: Servant-leadership for the twenty-first century* (pp. 349–362). New York: Wiley.

Wong, P. T. P., & Davey, D. (2007). *Best practices in servant leadership*. Paper presented at the Servant Leadership Research Roundtable, Regent University, Virginia Beach, VA.

11

Adaptive Leadership

DESCRIPTION

As the name of the approach implies, adaptive leadership is about how leaders encourage people to adapt—to face and deal with problems, challenges, and changes. Adaptive leadership focuses on the *adaptations* required of people in response to changing environments. Simply stated, adaptive leaders prepare and encourage people to deal with change. Unlike the trait approach (Chapter 2) or authentic leadership (Chapter 9), which focus predominantly on the characteristics of the leader, adaptive leadership stresses the *activities of the leader* in relation to the *work of followers* in the *contexts* in which they find themselves.

Since Heifetz first published *Leadership Without Easy Answers* (1994), the seminal book on adaptive leadership, this approach has occupied a unique place in the leadership literature. Adaptive leadership has been used effectively to explain how leaders encourage effective change across multiple levels, including self, organizational, community, and societal. However, most of the writing about adaptive leadership has been prescriptive and based on anecdotal and observational data rather than data derived from rigorous scientific inquiry. Scholars and practitioners have recognized the merits of the approach, but the theoretical underpinnings of adaptive leadership remain in the formative stages.

Development of the adaptive leadership framework emerged largely from the work of Heifetz and his associates (Heifetz, 1994; Heifetz & Sinder, 1988; Heifetz, Grashow, & Linsky, 2009; Heifetz & Laurie, 1997; Heifetz & Linsky, 2002). From the beginning, they set out to create a different approach to leadership. Rather than seeing the leader as a savior who solves

 Adaptive Leadership

 Ronald Heifetz on Adaptive Leadership

problems for people, they conceptualized the leader as one who plays the role of mobilizing people to tackle tough problems (e.g., drug abuse or sexism in the workplace). An adaptive leader challenges others to face difficult challenges, providing them with the space or opportunity they need to learn new ways of dealing with the inevitable changes in assumptions, perceptions, beliefs, attitudes, and behaviors that they are likely to encounter in addressing real problems.

Adaptive Leadership Defined

Although people often think of adaptive leadership as being leader centered, it is actually more follower centered. It focuses primarily on how leaders help others do the work they need to do, in order to adapt to the challenges they face. Generally, adaptive leadership is concerned with how people change and adjust to new circumstances. In this chapter, we emphasize the process leaders use to encourage others to grapple with difficult problems.

In the leadership literature, Heifetz and his colleagues suggest that "adaptive leadership is the practice of mobilizing people to tackle tough challenges and thrive" (Heifetz et al., 2009, p. 14). In contrast to emphasizing the position or characteristics of the leader, this definition suggests that leadership is concerned with the *behaviors* of leaders. This approach also makes a distinction between leadership and authority (Heifetz and Sinder, 1988). Leadership revolves around work and how people are mobilized to do work. It is not defined by position, so anyone can exhibit leadership. In contrast, authority revolves around power and how it is formally (e.g., position) and informally (e.g., admiration) conferred to leaders by followers. Authority allows leaders to do what followers expect them to do and is a primary tool for exercising leadership and giving followers a sense of security and protection.

Adaptive leaders engage in activities that *mobilize, motivate, organize, orient, and focus the attention of others* (Heifetz, 1994). In addition, this approach to leadership is about helping others to explore and change their values. The goal of adaptive leadership is to encourage people to change and learn new ways of living so that they may do well and grow. In short, adaptive leadership is the behavior of leaders and the actions they take to encourage others to address and resolve changes that are central in their lives. To better understand how adaptive leadership works, Table 11.1 provides some examples of "real world" situations in which adaptive leadership would be ideal.

Conceptually, the process of adaptive leadership incorporates ideas from four different viewpoints: the systems, biological, service orientation, and psychotherapy perspectives (Heifetz, 1994). First, adaptive leadership takes a *systems*

▶ Nature of Adaptive Leadership

Table 11.1 Adaptive Leadership in Practice

Adaptive leaders mobilize, motivate, organize, orient, and focus the attention of others to address and resolve changes that are central in their lives. The first step will be to help followers address the challenges they are experiencing. These are some examples of cases where adaptive leadership would be beneficial:

Church Membership

Over the past decade, the membership of a large traditional denomination of churches in the United States has shrunken by 200,000 members, which many attribute to the denomination's stand against same-sex marriage. If the church wants to reverse the trend and begin to grow, the church leadership and its membership need to confront the social implications of their doctrinal stand on marriage and members of the LGBT community.

Company Merger

A midsize family-owned paper company merges with another similar paper company. The merger creates tensions between the employees regarding job titles and duties, different wage schedules, overtime, and vacation pay. The new owners must bring these disparate groups of employees together to have their company function successfully. They will have to identify their adaptive challenges and then decide what work needs to be done (e.g., learning new ways of performing, shedding old ways that no longer work, and reevaluating their beliefs and values).

Merit Pay

In an established engineering company, a small group of young high-achieving engineers wants to change the way merit pay is given by removing seniority and years of service as part of the criteria. Longtime employees are resisting the change. The management must find a way to address this issue without alienating either group.

Condominium Rules

You are president of a small condo association, and two groups in the association are at odds about an association rule requiring condo owners to be 55 years old or older. Some think it is important to have young people around while others do not. In addition, in this area, young, new homeowners are buying condos at higher rates than empty nesters. The president must guide the association to reach consensus in a way that will benefit the association.

---

perspective, in that this approach assumes that many problems people face are actually embedded in complicated interactive systems. Problems are viewed as complex with many facets, dynamic in that they can evolve and change, and connected to others in a web of relationships. Second, the *biological perspective* to adaptive leadership recognizes that people develop and evolve as a result of having to adapt to both their internal cues/state and external environments. The ability to adapt allows people to thrive in new circumstances. Third, adaptive leadership assumes a *service orientation*. Similar to a physician, an adaptive leader uses his or her expertise or authority *to serve* the people by diagnosing their problems and prescribing possible solutions. Fourth, this approach incorporates the *psychotherapy perspective* to explain how people accomplish adaptive work. Adaptive leaders understand that people need a supportive environment and adapt more successfully when they face difficult problems directly, learn to distinguish between fantasy and reality, resolve internal conflicts, and learn new attitudes and behaviors. Taken together, these four viewpoints help explain and characterize the nature of adaptive leadership.

In addition to the way Heifetz and his colleagues defined adaptive leadership, it has been conceptualized as an element or subset of Complexity Leadership Theory, a framework designed to explain leadership for organizations of the 21st century that concentrate on knowledge or information as a core commodity rather than the production of goods that was prevalent in the industrial era (Uhl-Bien, Marion, & McKelvey, 2007). Complexity Leadership Theory (which includes administrative, adaptive, and enabling leadership) focuses on the strategies and behaviors that encourage learning, creativity, and adaptation in complex organizational systems. Within this framework, adaptive leadership is described as a complex process that emerges to produce adaptive change in a social system. It originates in struggles or tensions among people over conflicting needs, ideas, and preferences. It is conceptualized not as a person or a specific act (Uhl-Bien et al., 2007), but rather as a dynamic process.

Adaptive leadership is a unique kind of leadership that focuses on the dynamics of mobilizing people to address change. In the next section, we will describe the various components of adaptive leadership and discuss how each component contributes to the overall process of adaptive leadership.

A MODEL OF ADAPTIVE LEADERSHIP

Although adaptive leadership is in the early stages of theoretical development, the initial writings about this approach provide a basis for formulating a model of the adaptive leadership process. Based on the work of Heifetz and his associates (Heifetz, 1994; Heifetz & Sinder, 1988; Heifetz et al., 2009; Heifetz & Laurie, 1997; Heifetz & Linsky, 2002), Figure 11.1 offers a visual representation of the major components of adaptive leadership and how they fit together, including situational challenges, leader behaviors, and adaptive work. Heuristically, this model provides a basis for clarifying the process of adaptive leadership as well as generating empirical research to validate and refine the concepts and principles described by the model.

▶ Adaptive Leader Behaviors

Situational Challenges

As illustrated on the left side of Figure 11.1, the practice of leadership requires that leaders address three kinds of situational challenges. There are challenges or problems that are primarily *technical* in nature, challenges that have both *a technical and an adaptive dimension*, and challenges that are primarily *adaptive* in nature. Not all situational challenges are adaptive challenges. While addressing technical challenges is important, adaptive leadership is concerned with helping people address adaptive challenges.

Figure 11.1   Model of Adaptive Leadership

Situational Challenges	Leader Behaviors	Adaptive Work
Technical Challenges	1. Get on the Balcony 2. Identify the Adaptive Challenge 3. Regulate Distress 4. Maintain Disciplined Attention 5. Give the Work Back to the People 6. Protect Leadership Voices from Below	Holding Environment Leader ⟷ Followers Interaction
Technical and Adaptive Challenges		
Adaptive Challenges		

Technical Challenges

Technical challenges are problems in the workplace or community that are clearly defined with known solutions that can be implemented through existing organizational rules and procedures. They are problems that can be solved by experts. For technical challenges, people look to the leader for a solution, and they accept the leader's authority to resolve the problem. For example, if employees at a tax accounting firm are frustrated about a newly adopted tax software program, the manager at the firm could assess the software issues, identify the weaknesses and problems with the software, contact the company that provided the software, and have the programs modified in accordance with the accountants' needs at the tax firm. In this example, the problem is identifiable, it has an achievable solution, and the manager at the tax firm has the authority to address it through the accepted

 Peace Corps Challenges

structures and procedures of the organization. The employees look to the manager to solve the technical problem and accept her or his authority to do so.

Technical and Adaptive Challenges

Some challenges have both a technical and an adaptive dimension. In this case, the challenges are clearly defined but do not have distinct straightforward solutions within the existing organizational system. The responsibility of tackling this type of challenge is shared between the leader and the people. The leader may act as a resource for others and provide support, but the people need to do the work—they need to learn to change and adapt. For example, if an urban hospital with a traditional approach to care (i.e., providers are the experts, and patients are the visitors) wanted to establish a patient-centered culture, the goal could be clearly laid out. To reach the goal, the hospital leadership, through its hierarchical authority, could provide in-service training on how to involve patients in their own care. New rules could be designed to preserve patients' personal routines, to give them access to their own records, and to give them more control of their own treatment. However, the staff, doctors, patients, and family members would need to accept the proposed change and learn how to implement it. Making the hospital a model of patient-centered care would require a lot of work and adaptation on the part of many different people.

Adaptive Challenges

Central to the process of adaptive leadership are adaptive challenges. Adaptive challenges are problems that are not clear-cut or easy to identify. They cannot be solved by the leader's authority or expertise or through the normal ways of doing things in the organization. Adaptive challenges require that leaders encourage others, with their support, to define challenging situations and implement solutions. Not easy to tackle and often resisted, adaptive challenges are difficult because they usually require changes in people's assumptions, perceptions, beliefs, attitudes, and behaviors. An example of adaptive challenges would be the problems and concerns a family confronts when placing a parent in hospice care. In a hospice, there is a great deal of uncertainty for patients and families about how and when the patient will die and how to best comfort the patient during this time. While hospice workers can give support and informal feedback about the dying process, the patient and his or her family have to come to grips with how they want to approach the patient's final days. What does the impending loss mean? How can they

▶ Technical or Adaptive Challenge

prepare for it? How will they cope with the loss going forward? In this context, adaptive leadership is about mobilizing the patient and family members to address the many questions and concerns that surround the death of the family member. Hospice nurses, social workers, and staff all play an important role in helping families cope, but at the same time, it is the families that have to confront the complexities and concerns of the impending loss.

Leader Behaviors

As shown in the middle of Figure 11.1, six leader behaviors, or activities, play a pivotal role in the process of adaptive leadership. Based on the work of Heifetz and his colleagues (Heifetz, 1994; Heifetz & Laurie, 1997), these behaviors are general prescriptions for leaders when helping others confront difficult challenges and the inevitable changes that accompany them. Although there is a general order as to which leader behavior comes first in the adaptive leadership process, many of these behaviors overlap with each other and should be demonstrated by leaders at the same time. Taken together, these leader behaviors suggest a kind of recipe for being an adaptive leader.

1. Get on the Balcony

A prerequisite for the other adaptive leader behaviors, "getting on the balcony" is a metaphor for stepping out of the fray and finding perspective in the midst of a challenging situation. It is an allusion to a dance floor and that one needs to be above the dancing to understand what's going on below. Being on the balcony enables the leader to see the big picture—what is really happening. On the balcony, the leader is momentarily away from the noise, activity, and chaos of a situation, allowing him or her to gain a clearer view of reality. It allows the leader to identify value and power conflicts among people, ways they may be avoiding work, and other dysfunctional reactions to change (Heifetz & Laurie, 1997). Getting on the balcony can include such things as taking some quiet time, forming a group of unofficial advisers for alternative discussions about organizational issues, or simply attending meetings as an observer. In the model, the adaptive leader is urged to step away from the conflict in order to see it fully, but never to dissociate entirely from the conflict. Effective leaders are able to move back and forth as a participant and observer between the struggles of their people and the intentions of the group, organization, or community.

To understand what it means to stand on the balcony, imagine yourself as the principal of an elementary school. From the balcony, you see all the pieces that go into educating your students: federal and state requirements, teachers and staff, budgets, teacher evaluations, parents and discipline, not to mention the children themselves. From above, you can see how these issues relate to and affect one another, and who is dancing with which partners, all while working toward the common goal of educating children.

Another example would be a chief union negotiator, who in the midst of difficult labor talks steps away from the table for a moment to separate from the emotion and intensity and reflect on the goals of the talks. Once this leader feels she again has a grasp of the issues at hand, she dives directly back into negotiations. In both of these examples, the leader takes time to see the "big" picture as an observer but also stays engaged as a participant with the challenges his or her people are confronting.

2. Identify Adaptive Challenges

In addition to getting on the balcony and observing the dynamics of the complex situations people face, leaders must analyze and diagnose these challenges. Central to this process is differentiating between technical and adaptive challenges. Failures in leadership often occur because leaders fail to diagnose challenges correctly. The adaptive leadership process suggests that leaders are most effective using adaptive leadership behaviors for adaptive challenges and technical leadership for technical challenges. Treating challenges with the wrong kind of leadership is maladaptive.

If challenges are technical in nature, leaders can fix the problem with their own expertise. For example, in a manufacturing environment, problems that arise in scheduling, product sales quotas, facility expansion, or raising the minimum wage are all problems the leader can use his or her authority to resolve. However, it is essential that a leader also know when his or her authority is not sufficient or appropriate to address a particular challenge. When people's beliefs, attitudes, and values are affected by a problem, leaders need to take an adaptive approach. How a leader decides if he or she faces an adaptive challenge is to determine whether or not the challenge strikes at the core feelings and thoughts of others. Adaptive challenges are usually value laden and stir up people's emotions. Furthermore, if challenges require that people learn new ways of coping, they are adaptive. Take the manufacturing environment that was discussed earlier. If another company buys that manufacturing facility and the new owners implement production procedures and standards that the facility's workers are unfamiliar with, these changes would create adaptive challenges for the workers. Identifying adaptive challenges means leaders need to focus their attention on problems

Member Expertise

they cannot solve themselves and that demand collaboration between the leader and followers. For adaptive challenges, leaders do what is necessary (e.g., give support, challenge, or even take themselves out of the picture) to mobilize others to do the work they need to do.

To more easily identify complex adaptive challenges and also distinguish them from technical challenges, there are four archetypes or basic patterns of adaptive change to consider (Heifetz et al., 2009).

Archetype 1: Gap Between Espoused Values and Behavior. This archetype is present when an organization espouses, or claims, to adhere to values that it doesn't in reality support by its actions. For example, a company that promotes itself as a family-friendly place to work but does not have a flexible-hour work policy, an extended maternity leave policy, or in-house child care doesn't have behaviors that match the family-friendly image it promotes itself as having.

Archetype 2: Competing Commitments. When an organization has numerous commitments and some come into conflict with each other, this archetype is in play. For example, a health and fitness center wants to grow and expand its services but at the same time sees the best way to reduce costs is by trimming the number of trainers and staff it employs.

Archetype 3: Speaking the Unspeakable. The phrases "sacred cow" and "elephant in the room" are examples of this archetype—when there are radical ideas, unpopular issues, or conflicting perspectives that people don't dare address because of their sensitive or controversial nature. Speaking out about these is seen as "risky." Consider an organization with a well-liked, established owner who is perceived by the employees as "over the hill" and not in touch with the current business climate, but no one is willing to discuss the matter. It is easier to suffer the consequences of the owner's dated leadership than confront the man and risk hurting him.

Archetype 4: Work Avoidance. This archetype represents a situation where people avoid addressing difficult issues by staying within their "comfort zone" or by using diversionary methods. For example, coworkers at a company refuse to confront or discuss a very skilled employee who is not participating in organizational planning because he feels the company suffers from institutional racism. It is easier to continue to do the same things and avoid the concerns of the disgruntled employee. Another example would be an ad agency that has a graphic designer who is not able to produce the quality of creative work needed, so, rather than address the problem directly, that designer is assigned menial jobs that are essentially busy work. The agency then hires a second graphic designer to do the more creative work despite the cost and the fact that the agency doesn't have enough work to justify two designers.

These four archetypes are representative of some of the common challenges that require adaptive change. Although they do not describe every possible type of adaptive change, they are useful as frames of reference when trying to identify adaptive challenges in a particular organizational setting.

3. Regulate Distress

A third behavior, or activity, important for adaptive leaders is to regulate distress (Figure 11.1). Psychologically, we all have a need for consistency—to keep our beliefs, attitudes, and values the same. In fact, it is quite natural for individuals to be more comfortable when things are predictable and their way of doing things stays the same. But adaptive challenges create the need to change, and the process of change creates uncertainty and distress for people. Feeling a certain level of distress during change is inevitable and even useful for most, but feeling too much distress is counterproductive and can be debilitating. The challenge for a leader is to help others recognize the need for change but not become overwhelmed by the need for the change itself. The adaptive leader needs to monitor the stress people are experiencing and keep it within a productive range. This is what it means to regulate distress. The model suggests three ways that leaders can maintain productive levels of stress: *(1) create a holding environment; (2) provide direction, protection, orientation, conflict management, and productive norms; and (3) regulate personal distress.*

Creating a holding environment. This refers to establishing an atmosphere in which people can feel safe tackling difficult problems, but not so much so that they can avoid the problem. You can think of a holding environment in terms of a child learning to swim—the instructor is within a watchful distance, but allows the child to do the hard work of overcoming his or her fears and learning to kick, breathe, and stroke in sync. A holding environment is a structural, procedural, or virtual space formed by cohesive relationships between people. It can be physical space, a shared language, common history, a deep trust in an institution and its authority, or a clear set of rules and processes that allow groups to function with safety. As illustrated in Figure 11.1, the holding environment represents the space where the work of adaptive leadership gets played out. The idea of a holding environment has its roots in the field of psychotherapy where the counselor creates a therapeutic setting and uses effective communication and empathy to provide a sense of safety and protection for the client (Heifetz & Linsky, 2002;

Modell, 1976). Within the holding environment, adaptive leaders use authority to help people attend to the issues, to act as a reality test regarding information, to orchestrate conflicting perspectives, and to facilitate decision making (Heifetz, 1994, p. 113).

Creating a holding environment also allows a leader to regulate the pressures people face when confronting adaptive challenges. It can be described as analogous to a pressure cooker because initially a leader turns up the heat on the issues. This gets dialogue started and also allows some of the pressures from the issues to escape. If too much tension concerning issues is expressed, the holding environment can become too intense and ineffective for addressing problems. However, without the leader's initial catalyst of the issues, little dialogue would transpire.

Similar to labor negotiations in organizations, the holding environment is the place where all parties gather to begin talking to each other, define issues, and clarify competing interests and needs. If this discussion is too heated, negotiations reach a quick impasse. However, as negotiation develops, newer issues can be addressed. Over time the holding environment provides the place where new contractual relationships can be agreed upon and enacted.

Providing direction, protection, orientation, conflict management, and productive norms. These are specific ways leaders can use their formal and informal authority to help people manage the uncertainty and distress that accompany adaptive work. They are prescribed behaviors for adaptive leaders.

- *Providing direction* involves helping identify the adaptive challenges that others face and then framing these so they can be addressed. In difficult situations it is not uncommon for people to be unclear or confused about their goals. Sometimes the goal is unknown, sometimes it is obscure, and at other times it is entangled with competing goals. By providing direction, the leader helps people feel a sense of clarity, order, and certainty, reducing the stress people feel in uncertain situations.

- *Protection* refers to a leader's responsibility to manage the rate of adaptive change. It includes monitoring whether the change is too much or too fast for people. Furthermore, it requires monitoring external pressures people are experiencing and keeping these within a range they can tolerate.

- *Orientation* is the responsibility a leader has to orient people to new roles and responsibilities that may accompany adaptive change. When a change requires adopting new values and acting in accordance with those values, people may need to adopt entirely new roles

Adaptive Work

within the organization. Orientation is the process of helping people to find their identity within a changing system.

- *Conflict management* refers to the leader's responsibility to handle conflict effectively. Conflict is inevitable in groups and organizations during adaptive challenges and presents an opportunity for people to learn and grow. Although conflict can be uncomfortable, it is not unhealthy, nor is it necessarily bad. The question is not "How can people avoid conflict and eliminate change?" but rather "How can people manage conflict and produce positive change?"

- Establishing *productive norms* is a responsibility of the adaptive leader. Norms are the rules of behavior that are established and shared by group members and are not easily changed. When norms are constructive, they have a positive influence on the progress of the group. However, when norms are unproductive and debilitating, they can impede the group. A leader should pay close attention to norms and challenge those that need to be changed and reinforce those that maximize the group's effectiveness and ability to adapt to change.

Collectively, the five prescribed behaviors above provide a general blueprint for how adaptive leaders can mitigate the frustrations people feel during adaptive change. While not inclusive, they highlight some of the many important ways leaders can help people during the change process.

Regulating personal distress. This is a third way leaders can maintain a productive level of stress during adaptive change. As we discussed previously, change and growth within an organization do not occur without uncertainty and stress. Because stress is inherent in change, adaptive leaders need to withstand the pressures from those who want to avoid change and keep things the same. While moderate amounts of tension are normal and necessary during change, too much or too little tension is unproductive. Leaders need to keep people focused on the hard work they need to do and the tension that accompanies that, while at the same time being sensitive to the very real frustrations and pain that people feel when doing adaptive work.

To help others through the adaptive process, adaptive leaders need to make sure they have their own act together. They must be strong and steady because people look to and depend on them for support in situations that can be very trying and painful. Adaptive leaders need to be role models and exhibit confidence and the emotional capacity to handle conflict. This is not a stress-free role. Adaptive leaders need to be willing to experience the frustrations and pain that people feel during change but not to the extent that they lose their own sense of who they are as leaders.

An example of the demands of regulating personal distress can be seen in the leadership of a therapist who runs a support group for high school students recovering from substance abuse. In her role as a group facilitator, the therapist faces many challenges. She has to listen to students' stories and the challenges they face as they try to stay clean. She also has to push people to be honest about their successes and failures regarding drug use. She cannot push so hard, however, that group members feel threatened, stop communicating, or stop attending the group sessions. In the holding environment, she has to be able to show nurturance and support, but not enable destructive behavior. The pain and frustrations recovering addicts feel are tremendous, and the therapist has to be in touch with this pain without losing her role as therapist. Hearing stories of recovery and failed recovery can be heartbreaking, while hearing success stories can be uplifting. Throughout all of this, the therapist needs to monitor herself closely and control her own anxieties regarding recovery. Group members look to the therapist for direction and support. They want the therapist to be strong, confident, and empathic. Regulating her own stress is essential in order to make herself fully available to students who are recovering from substance abuse.

4. Maintain Disciplined Attention

As illustrated in Figure 11.1, the fourth leader behavior described by the adaptive leadership process is to *maintain disciplined attention*. This means that the leader needs to encourage people to *focus* on the tough work they need to do. This does not come easily; people naturally do not want to confront change, particularly when it is related to changing their beliefs, values, or behaviors. It is common for all of us to resist change and strive for a sense of balance and equilibrium in our day-to-day experiences. People do not like things "out of sync," so when their sense of balance is disrupted by the need to change, it is natural for them to engage in avoidance behavior. Maintaining disciplined attention is about the leader helping people address change and not avoid it.

Avoidance behaviors can take many forms. People can ignore the problem, blame the problem on the authority, blame coworkers for the problem, attack those who want to address the problem, pretend the problem does not exist, or work hard in areas unrelated to the problem. No matter the form of avoidance, the leader's task is to mobilize and encourage people to drop their defenses and openly confront their problems. Adaptive leaders help people focus on issues. If some topics are deemed to "hot" in the organization, the leader should support people in getting these topics on the agenda for discussion. If some issues create deep divisions between people, the leadership

📖 Wicked and Tame Problems

should provide a vessel of safety where competing sides can address the issues without feeling as if the organization will explode. If there is an "elephant in the room"—an issue no one wants to address but that is pivotal in making change—the leader needs to nudge people to talk about it. Whatever the situation, the adaptive leader gets people to focus—to show disciplined attention to the work at hand.

An example of disciplined attention can be seen in how the director of an assisted care facility responds to the members of a family who are struggling with their decision to move their 80-year-old mother into nursing care. The mother has early signs of dementia, but has successfully lived alone since her husband died 10 years earlier and prides herself on being able to cook, drive, and live independently. Although her forgetfulness and physical problems have her two adult children very concerned about their mother's health and safety, they just cannot bring themselves to make their mother move from her home. They say things like "Mom just doesn't need it yet. She is so much better than those people at the care facility. She won't survive in a new environment. She just won't be herself if she's not at her own home." The director of the assisted care facility's challenge is to help them make the decision—a decision they are afraid of making, and avoiding. He always gives a listening ear and sets up multiple appointments for the children to visit the care facility. In addition, he arranges for the children to talk to staff members and other families who have a parent at the facility. In all of these sessions, the director emphasizes the importance of the children communicating their concerns while letting them know that the children's concerns and hesitations are normal because accepting the failing health of a parent is very difficult. He continues to tell them gently, without sounding like he's selling something, the benefits of going into the assisted care facility: The parent will be safer, receive good care, and learn to thrive in her new home. In this example, the director is sensitive to the adaptive challenges the children face, and he makes a point of "standing by" and giving guidance and support. The director helps the children stay focused on the changes they need to make and mobilizes them to confront their decisions.

5. Give the Work Back to the People

A fifth leader behavior important for adaptive leaders is to *give the work back to the people* (Figure 11.1). People want leaders to provide some direction and structure to their work and want to feel secure in what they are doing, but too much leadership and authority can be debilitating, decrease people's confidence to solve problems on their own, and suppress their creative capacities. Overly directive leadership can result in people being dependent on their leaders and inhibit them from doing adaptive work. Even though it makes people feel comfortable and secure to have leaders tell them what to do, leaders need to learn ways to curtail their influence and shift problem solving back to the people involved.

Leaders need to be aware of and monitor the impact they have on others. Giving work back to the people requires a leader to be attentive to when he or she should drop back and let the people do the work that they need to do. This can be a fine line; leaders have to provide direction, but they also have to say, "This is your work—how do you think you want to handle it?" For adaptive leaders, giving work back to the people means empowering people to decide what to do in circumstances where they feel uncertain, expressing belief in their ability to solve their own problems, and encouraging them to think for themselves rather than thinking for them.

The famous boarding school Summerhill, on the east coast of England, provides a good example of where giving the work back to the people takes center stage. Summerhill is a self-governing, democratic school where adults and students have equal status. Summerhill's philosophy stresses that students have the freedom to take their own path in life and develop their own interests so long as it does not harm others. Classes are optional for students who have the freedom to choose what they do with their time. The schedules and rules of the school are established in weekly group meetings at which all participants have an equal vote. Summerhill's leaders give the work of learning back to the students. Instead of the teachers telling students what to study and learn, the students themselves make those decisions within a supportive environment. It is an unusual model of education and not without its problems, but it clearly demonstrates recognition of the need for students, and not their teachers, to identify and define their goals and take responsibility for meeting those goals.

6. Protect Leadership Voices from Below

A final leader behavior that is important to the adaptive leadership process is *protecting leadership voices from below* (Figure 11.1). This means that adaptive leaders have to be cautious to listen and be open to the ideas of people who may be at the fringe, marginalized, or even deviant in the group or organization. This is a challenge because when the leader gives voice to an out-group member, it is upsetting to the social equilibrium of the group. To be open to the ideas of low-status individuals, who often may express themselves ineffectively, is also challenging because it is disruptive to the "normal" way of doing things. Too often, leaders find it convenient

Learning and Adaptive Leadership

to ignore the dissident, nonconforming voices in an effort to maintain things as they are and keep things moving. Adaptive leaders should try to resist the tendency to minimize or shut down minority voices for the sake of the majority. To give voice to others requires that a leader relinquish some control, giving other individual members more control. This is why it is a challenging process.

Protecting voices from below is important because it puts low-status individuals on equal footing with other members of the group. It means the leader and the other people of the group give credence to the out-group members' ideas and actions. When out-group members have a voice, they know their interests are being recognized and that they can have an impact on the leader and the group. Giving them voice allows low-status members to be more involved, independent, and responsible for their actions. It allows them to become more fully engaged in the adaptive work of the group, and they can feel like full members in the planning and decision making of the group.

Consider a college social work class in which students are required to do a service-learning project. For this project, one group chose to build a wheelchair ramp for an elderly woman in the community. In the initial stages of the project, morale in the group was down because one group member (Alissa) chose not to participate. Alissa said she was not comfortable using hand tools, and she chose not to do manual labor. The other team members, who had been doing a lot of planning for the project, wanted to proceed without her help. Alissa felt rejected and began to criticize the purpose of the project and the personalities of the other team members. At that point, one of the group's leaders decided to start listening to Alissa's concerns. He learned that while Alissa could not work with her hands, she had two other talents: She was good with music, and she made wonderful lunches. As a result, Alissa was asked to use her strengths for the group. During the construction of the ramp, Alissa kept up morale by playing each group member's and the elderly woman's favorite music while they worked on the ramp. In addition, Alissa made sandwiches and provided drinks that accommodated each of the group members' unique dietary interests. By the last day, Alissa felt so included by the group, and was praised so frequently for providing great food, that she joined in the manual labor and began raking up trash around the ramp site. Although Alissa's talents didn't tie in directly with constructing a ramp, she still contributed to building a successful team, which would not have happened if the leader had not given voice to Alissa's concerns and talents.

Wicked Problems and Public Policy

Adaptive Work

As represented on the right side of the model of adaptive leadership (Figure 11.1), *adaptive work* is the process toward which adaptive leaders direct their work. It is the focus and intended goal of adaptive leadership. Adaptive work develops from the communication process that occurs between the leader and followers but is primarily the work of followers. It occurs within a holding environment where people can feel safe as they confront possible changes in their roles, priorities, and values.

The model illustrates that the *holding environment* is the place where adaptive work is conducted. It is a real or virtual space where people can address the adaptive challenges that confront them. Because the holding environment plays a critical role in the adaptive process, leaders direct considerable energy toward establishing and maintaining it.

While the term *followers* is used in the holding environment portion of the model to depict individuals who are not the leader, it is important to note that throughout most of the writing on adaptive leadership, the term *follower* is not used because it implies a submissive role in relationship to the leader. In adaptive leadership, leaders do not use their authority to control others; rather, leaders *interact* with people to help them do adaptive work. The term *followers* is used in the model simply to distinguish the specific individuals who are doing adaptive work.

An example of adaptive work can be seen at a fitness center where a fitness instructor is running a class for a group of individuals who have had heart problems and struggle with being overweight. The goal of the instructor is to provide a safe place where people can challenge themselves to do training exercises that will help them to lose weight and reduce their risk for health problems. Because the people must change their lifestyles to live more healthfully, they must engage in adaptive work with the support of the fitness instructor.

Another example where adaptive work can be observed is in a public elementary school where the principal is asking the teachers to adopt the Common Core State Standards but the teachers, who have a proven record of success using their own student-centered curriculum, are resisting. To help the teachers with the intended change, the principal sets up a series of 10 open faculty meetings where teachers are invited to discuss freely their concerns about the new policies. The meetings provide a holding environment where teachers can confront their deeply held positions regarding the usefulness and efficacy of standardized testing and what it will mean for them to

Creative Holding Environment

have to shift to the Common Core. The principal's role is to communicate in ways that support the teachers in their adaptive work.

HOW DOES ADAPTIVE LEADERSHIP WORK?

Adaptive leadership is a complex process comprising multiple dimensions, including situational challenges, leader behaviors, and adaptive work. The overriding focus of the process is to engage individuals in doing adaptive work. This unique emphasis, on mobilizing individuals (followers) to confront adaptive challenges, makes adaptive leadership very different from other traditional leadership approaches that focus on leader traits (Chapter 2), skills (Chapter 3), behaviors (Chapter 4), and authenticity (Chapter 9). Adaptive leadership centers on the adaptations required of people in response to changing environments and how leaders can support them during these changes.

The process of adaptive leadership works like this: First, the leader takes time to step back from a challenging situation to understand the complexities of the situation and obtain a fuller picture of the interpersonal dynamics occurring among the participants. Second, in any situation or context where people are experiencing change, the leader first makes an assessment to determine if the change creates challenges that are technical or adaptive in nature. If the challenges are technical, the leader addresses the problems with his or her authority and expertise or through the rules and procedures of the organization. If the challenges are adaptive, the leader engages in several specific leader behaviors to move the adaptive process forward.

While the recipe for adaptive leadership is composed of many leader behaviors and activities, there is no particular order to the prescribed behaviors. Adaptive leadership incorporates many of these behaviors simultaneously, and interdependently, with some of them more important at the beginning of the process and others at the end. Some important adaptive leader behaviors are regulating distress, creating a holding environment, providing direction, keeping people focused on important issues, empowering people, and giving voice to those who feel unrecognized or marginalized.

Overall, it is safe to say that adaptive leadership works because leaders are willing to engage in all of these behaviors with the intention of helping followers do adaptive work.

N Using Adaptive Leadership

STRENGTHS

In its present stage of development, adaptive leadership has multiple strengths. First, in contrast to many other leadership theories, adaptive leadership takes a *process* approach to the study of leadership. Consistent with the process definition of leadership discussed in Chapter 1, adaptive leadership underscores that leadership is not a trait or characteristic of the leader, but rather a complex interactional event that occurs between leaders and followers in different situations. The process perspective highlights that leaders and followers mutually affect each other, making leadership an interactive activity that is not restricted to only a formal, designated leader. This approach emphasizes that the phenomenon of leadership is a complex interactive process comprising multiple dimensions and activities.

Second, adaptive leadership stands out because it is *follower centered.* Adaptive leaders mobilize people to engage in adaptive work. The adaptive approach to leadership is other directed, stressing follower involvement and follower growth. The raison d'être of adaptive leaders is to provide a holding environment where others can learn, grow, and work on the changes that are needed. This approach encapsulates leadership as those behaviors and actions leaders need to engage in to give followers the greatest opportunity to do adaptive work.

Third, adaptive leadership is unique in how it directs attention to the use of leadership to help followers *deal with conflicting values* that emerge in changing work environments and social contexts. Change and learning are inherent in organizational life, and adaptive leadership focuses specifically on helping followers to confront change and examine the emergence of new values that may accompany change. No other leadership approach's central purpose is to help followers confront their personal values and adjust these as needed in order for change and adaptation to occur.

Another strength of adaptive leadership is that it provides a *prescriptive approach* to leadership that is useful and practical. In their writings, Heifetz and his colleagues (Heifetz, 1994; Heifetz & Sinder, 1988; Heifetz et al., 2009; Heifetz & Laurie, 1997; Heifetz & Linsky, 2002) identify many things leaders can do to facilitate adaptive leadership. The leader behaviors in Figure 11.1 are prescriptions for what an adaptive leader should do. For example, "get on the balcony," "regulate distress," and "give work back to the people" are all prescriptive behaviors leaders can use to mobilize followers to do the work they need to do to adapt or change. In a general sense, even the model is prescriptive. It suggests that followers should learn to adapt and leaders should set up a context where this is most likely to occur. In short, adaptive leadership provides a

▶ Adaptive Transformational Leadership

recipe for what leaders and followers should do to facilitate adaptive change. It describes the kind of work that followers should address and then the behaviors leaders should employ to help them accomplish this work.

Finally, adaptive leadership makes a unique contribution to the field of leadership studies by identifying the concept of *a holding environment* as an integral part of the leadership process. Few leadership theories discuss how leaders are responsible for creating a safe environment for followers to address difficult issues. The holding environment can be physical, virtual, or relational, but most importantly, it is an atmosphere where people should feel safe tackling difficult issues. It is a place where leaders get a dialogue started but do not let it become too heated or explosive. Although abstract, the concept of a holding environment can be easily visualized and is useful for anyone wanting to demonstrate adaptive leadership.

CRITICISMS

In addition to its strengths, adaptive leadership has several weaknesses. First, very little empirical research has been conducted to test the claims of adaptive leadership theory even though the conceptual framework for this approach was set forth more than 20 years ago in Heifetz's *Leadership Without Easy Answers* (1994). Originally intended as a practical framework for theory building, adaptive leadership is based on ideas and assumptions, but not on established research. Without evidence-based support for the tenets of the model, the ideas and principles set forth on adaptive leadership should be viewed cautiously.

Second, conceptualization of the process of adaptive leadership needs further refinement. Adaptive leadership was designed intentionally as a practical approach to leadership and is composed of a series of prescriptions about what leaders should do to help people engage in adaptive work. However, the major factors in the adaptive process and the way these factors relate to one another to facilitate adaptive work is not clearly delineated. Figure 11.1 provides a "first attempt" at modeling the phenomenon of adaptive leadership, but much more needs to be done to clarify the essential factors in the model, the empirical relationships among these factors, and the process through which these factors lead to adaptive change within groups and organizations.

Third, adaptive leadership can be criticized for being too wide ranging and abstract. For example, the approach suggests that leaders should "identify your loyalties," "protect leadership voices from below," "mobilize the system," "name the default," "hold steady," "act politically," "anchor yourself," and many more that were not discussed in this chapter. Interpreting what these prescriptions mean and their relationship to being an adaptive leader can become overwhelming because of the breadth and wide-ranging nature of these prescriptions. In addition, the recommended leader behaviors such as "give the work back to the people" often lack specificity and conceptual clarity. Without clear conceptualizations of recommended behaviors, it is difficult to know how to analyze them in research or implement them in practice. As a result, leaders may infer their own conceptualizations of these prescriptions, which may vary widely from what Heifetz and his colleagues (Heifetz, 1994; Heifetz & Sinder, 1988; Heifetz et al., 2009; Heifetz & Laurie, 1997; Heifetz & Linsky, 2002) intended.

Finally, from a theoretical perspective, adaptive leadership hints at but does not directly explain how adaptive leadership incorporates a moral dimension. Adaptive leadership focuses on how people evolve and grow through change. It implies that the evolution of one's values leads to a greater common good, but the way the evolution of values leads to a greater common good is not fully explicated. It advocates mobilizing people to do adaptive work but does not elaborate or explain how doing adaptive work leads to socially useful outcomes. The model acknowledges the importance of promoting values such as equality, justice, and community, but the link between adaptive work and achieving those social values is not clear.

APPLICATION

How can adaptive leadership be applied to real-life situations? There are several ways. On an individual level, adaptive leadership provides a conceptual framework made up of a unique set of constructs that help us determine what type of challenges we face (e.g., *technical vs. adaptive*) and strategies for managing them (e.g., *establishing a holding environment*). Individuals can easily integrate these constructs into their own practice of leadership. Furthermore, it is an approach to leadership that people can apply in a wide variety of settings, including family, school, work, community, and societal.

On the organizational level, adaptive leadership can be used as a model to explain and address a variety of challenges that are ever present during change and growth. It has been studied as a model to train urban school superintendants (Chace, 2013) and to enhance the leadership education of aspiring school principals (Guilleux, 2010). Consultants have applied adaptive leadership at all levels in many different kinds of organizations. In

 Technical Leadership

particular, it has been an approach to leadership of special interest to people in nonprofits, faith-based organizations, and health care.

At this point in the development of adaptive leadership, the context in which most of the research has been conducted is health care. For example, one group of researchers suggests that adaptive leadership can improve the practice of medicine (Thygeson, Morrissey, & Ulstad, 2010). They contend that health professionals who practice from an adaptive leadership perspective view patients as complex adaptive systems who face both technical and adaptive challenges (Figure 11.2). Overall, they claim the adaptive leadership approach has promise to make health care more efficient, patient centered, and sustainable.

Figure 11.2   Adaptive Leadership Framework Developed by Heifetz & Linsky

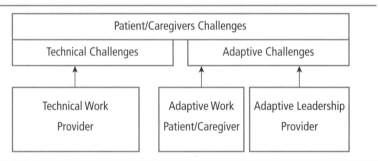

SOURCE: Adapted from Adams, J. A., Bailey, D. E., Jr., Anderson, R. A., & Thygeson, M. (2013). Finding your way through EOL challenges in the ICU using Adaptive Leadership behaviours: A qualitative descriptive case study. *Intensive and Critical Care Nursing, 29,* 329–336 and Thygeson, M., Morrissey, L., & Ulstad, V. (2010). Adaptive leadership and the practice of medicine: A complexity-based approach to reframing the doctor-patient relationship. *Journal of Evaluation in Clinical Practice, 16,* 1009–1015.

Eubank, Geffken, Orzano, and Ricci (2012) used adaptive leadership as the overarching framework to guide the curriculum they developed for a family medicine residency program. They argue that if physicians practice the behaviors promoted in adaptive leadership (e.g., *get on the balcony, identify adaptive challenges,* or *regulate distress*), they can acquire the process skills that are necessary to implement and sustain true patient-centered care and healing relationships. Furthermore, to assist patients who are suffering, Eubank et al. contend that physicians need more than technical problem-solving competencies. Physicians also need adaptive skills that will enable them to help patients process and learn to live with the challenges resulting from changes in their health and well-being.

In two separate case studies, researchers found adaptive leadership could be used to help patients and family members confront health care challenges.

Using the adaptive leadership framework, Adams, Bailey, Anderson, and Thygeson (2013) identified nurse and physician behaviors that can facilitate the transition from curative to palliative care by helping family members do the adaptive work of letting go. Similarly, Adams, Bailey, Anderson, and Galanos (2013) found adaptive leadership principles were useful in helping family members of patients in intensive care units to come to terms with loss and change, and to make decisions consistent with the patient's goals.

In summary, there are many applications for adaptive leadership, both on the personal and on the organizational level, as well as in the research environment. While further research needs to be done to support the tenets of adaptive leadership, it is clearly a leadership approach that can be utilized in many settings.

CASE STUDIES

This section provides three case studies (Cases 11.1, 11.2, and 11.3) from very different contexts where adaptive leadership is present to a degree. The first case describes the challenges faced by two editors of a high school newspaper who wanted to lessen the stigma of mental illness by sharing other students' stories. The second case is about how two co-captains tried to change the culture of their college ultimate disc team. The third case describes the challenges faced by people in a small town when trying to change the name of a high school mascot. At the end of each case, questions are provided to help you explore dimensions of adaptive leadership and how it can be utilized in addressing "real" problems.

CASE 11.1

Silence, Stigma, and Mental Illness

Madeline Halpert and Eva Rosenfeld had three things in common: Both were on the high school newspaper staff, both suffered from depression, and until they shared their experiences with each other, both felt the isolation of the stigma that comes with suffering from mental illness.

The two student editors knew they were far from the only ones in their high school who experienced these challenges, and in a concerted effort

(Continued)

(Continued)

to support others and lessen the stigma of mental illness, they decided to do an in-depth feature on the topic for their student newspaper. Recent cases of school shootings had brought mental illness in teens to the forefront, and evidence shows that depression is a major cause of suicide in young people (Halpert & Rosenfeld, 2014). Yet, the strong stigma that surrounds depression and mental illness often isolates those who suffer from it. The purpose of Eva and Madeline's feature was to open the dialogue and end the stigma. They interviewed a number of teens from schools in the surrounding area who agreed to use their real names and share their personal stories about mental illness including depression, eating disorders, and homelessness. The student editors even obtained waivers from the subjects' parents giving them permission to use the stories. However, their stories never made it to print.

While they were putting the story together, their school's principal called them into her office and told them about a former college football player from the area who struggled with depression and would be willing to be interviewed. The editors declined, not wanting to replace the deeply personal articles about their peers with one from someone removed from the students. The principal then told them she wouldn't support printing the stories. She objected to the use of students' real names, saying she feared potential personal repercussions such as bullying or further mental health problems that publishing such an article could have on those students. District officials stood by the principal's decision to halt printing of the piece, saying it was the right one to protect the students featured in the article.

This move surprised the two student editors because they felt that their school had a very tolerant atmosphere, which included offering a depression awareness group. "We were surprised that the administration and the adults who advocated for mental health awareness were the ones standing in the way of it," they wrote. "By telling us that students could not talk openly about their struggles, they reinforced the very stigma we were trying to eliminate."

Instead, the two editors penned an op-ed piece, "Depressed, but Not Ashamed," which was published in *The New York Times*. The article discussed their dismay with having the student articles halted by school administrators, an act that they believe further stigmatized those with mental illnesses.

"By interviewing these teenagers for our newspaper, we tried—and failed—to start small in the fight against stigma. Unfortunately, we've learned this won't be easy. It seems that those who are charged with advocating for our well-being aren't ready yet to let us have an open and honest dialogue about depression," they wrote.

The op-ed piece generated a response—and, interestingly, a dialogue—about the topic.

The two student editors were subsequently interviewed on the National Public Radio show *Weekend Edition.* In that interview, the editors acknowledged that they had experienced mostly positive reactions to their piece, with more than 200 comments after the initial publishing of their article. Many of those comments said the article resonated with readers and gave them the courage to talk to someone about their struggles with mental illness in a way they hadn't before.

"And I think, most importantly, it's opening a dialogue," said one of the editors in the interview. "There were negative comments. There were positive comments. But the most important thing is that it's so amazing to see people discussing this and finally opening up about it."

Questions

1. How do you define the problem the editors were trying to address? Was this a *technical* or an *adaptive* challenge?

2. What is your reaction to what the principal did in this situation? How do you think what she did fits in with *providing direction, protection, orientation, conflict management,* and *productive norms*?

3. Describe the *holding environment* in this case. Was the holding environment sufficient to meet the adaptive challenges in this situation? How would you improve it?

4. Based on Figure 11.1, discuss who were the adaptive leaders in this case. Which of the leader behaviors (*get on the balcony, identify adaptive challenges, regulate distress,* etc.) did these leaders exhibit?

CASE 11.2

Taming Bacchus

Kyle Barrett is a serious ultimate disc player. He became involved in the sport—which is a bit like soccer only with a flying disc—in middle school and played competitively in high school. When he went to college at a small liberal arts school in the Pacific Northwest, he was excited to find the school had an ultimate disc team. His excitement quickly turned to dismay when he found the team members were more interested in partying than playing.

(Continued)

(Continued)

Kyle remembers this about his first year on the team: "The team really had this sort of fraternity culture in that there was light hazing, drinking was a priority, and tournaments were about parties, not competition. The team threw a lot of parties and had this reputation for exclusivity." Even the team's name, Bacchus (the Roman god of wine and drunkenness), reflected this culture.

Kyle found a like-minded soul in his teammate Harrison, and together they sought to turn the club team into a program that operated on a more competitive level. The pair was chosen as team co-captains and began to share their deeper knowledge of the sport with the team. They also communicated their aspirations for success. This flew in the face of some team members who were there for the parties. As one player put it, "You were either down with it, or you decided it was too intense and you left the club."

The two captains knew that the team's culture wasn't going to change just because they wanted it to. They also knew that they couldn't be captains, coach the team, and be players at the same time. So they began taking a number of steps to help the team change its own culture.

First, they brought in Mario O'Brien, a well-known ultimate disc coach, to help guide the team and teach the players skills and strategy. The team had had other coaches in the past, but none of those had the knowledge, experience, or reputation that O'Brien did.

"That really took some forethought," says a player, "to be able to step back and say, 'What does this team really need to become a strong program?' And then making a move to bring in someone of O'Brien's stature."

After a few weeks of practice with O'Brien, the captains and coach organized a team dinner. Before the dinner they asked each player to anonymously submit in writing what he thought of the team and what he wanted to see the team be. "There were no rules—just say what you need to say," says a player. Each submission was read aloud and discussed by team members.

"No one was put in the position of having to publically speak out and be embarrassed in front of the others," says a player. "We came out of that meeting more together, more bonded as a team. We hashed out a lot of issues, and came to the realization that we were looking for the same goals. The process helped filter out those who weren't as committed to those goals, but not in a confrontational way."

The goals agreed to at that dinner meeting were for the team to do well enough at the sectional competition to obtain a berth at the national collegiate competition. But the team was young with a number of inexperienced players, which sometimes caused stress, frustration, and friction. The captains, however, continued to have multiple meetings to talk about concerns, discussed the team's goals before and after each practice, and organized social events (with a minimum of drinking) where team members engaged in activities together other than playing ultimate disc. Older, more experienced players began mentoring the younger, newer players to help them improve their skills. Even Harrison, who was an exceptional offensive player, put himself on the defensive line to help improve those players' skills. While it wasn't optimal for his own enjoyment and playing abilities, he felt it was needed to help improve the team.

Bacchus reached its goals two years later; it came in second at sectionals and earned a spot in the national competition. After the team completed its last game at nationals, Kyle and Harrison gathered the team members together in a circle. "We accomplished something more than being here today," Kyle said. "We've become a family with goals, and with respect for one another and for our game. And that's a better victory than any other."

Questions

1. What changes were Kyle and Harrison trying to make? How did these changes affect the beliefs, attitudes, or values of the players?

2. Were the challenges the team faced technical, technical and adaptive, or adaptive? What examples can you give to explain your answer?

3. Citing examples, explain how the captains engaged in each of these adaptive leader behaviors: (1) *get on the balcony,* (2) *identify adaptive challenges,* (3) *regulate distress,* (4) *maintain disciplined attention,* (5) *give the work back to people,* and (6) *protect leadership voices from below.*

4. Describe the holding environment that the co-captains created for the team. Do you think it was successful? Why or why not?

CASE 11.3

Redskins No More

When there became a vacancy on the school board for Gooding Public Schools, Scott Rogers decided to throw his hat into the ring for consideration. A former college professor who had retired with his wife to the

(Continued)

(Continued)

small Midwestern town, Scott was hoping to help the board, which had for years been a "good old boy" network, focus more on educational pursuits than its traditional emphasis on high school athletics.

Shortly after Scott was appointed to the board, a local family with Native American ancestry came before the board to ask that the name of Gooding High School's athletic teams be changed from the Redskins. The family found the use of the name Redskins to be offensive. "The use of the word *Redskins* is essentially a racial slur," says Scott, "and as a racial slur, it needed to be changed."

The request set off a firestorm in the small town of 7,000. The school's athletic teams had competed as Redskins for 50 years, and many felt the name was an integral part of the community. People personally identified with the Redskins, and the team and the team's name were ingrained in the small town's culture.

"We went through months of folks coming to the school board meetings to speak on the issue and it got totally out of control," Scott says. "Locals would say, 'I was born a Redskin, and I'll die a Redskin.' They argued that the name was never intended to be offensive and that it honored the area's relatively strong Native American presence. The local family that raised the issue was getting all sorts of national support, and speakers came in from as far away as Oklahoma to discuss the negative ramifications of Native American mascots. Local groups argued back that these speakers weren't from Gooding and shouldn't even be allowed to be at the board meetings."

Scott felt strongly that the name needed to be changed. In meeting after meeting, he tried to explain to both his fellow board members and those in the audience that if the name was offensive to someone and recognized as a racial slur, then the intent of its original choosing was irrelevant. If someone was offended by the name, then it was wrong to maintain it.

Finally, Scott put forward a motion to change the name. That motion included a process for the students at Gooding High School to choose a new name for their athletic teams. The board approved the motion 5–2. The students immediately embraced the opportunity to choose a new name, developing designs and logos for their proposed choices. In the end, the student body voted to become the Redhawks.

There was still an angry community contingent, however, that was festering over the change. They began circulating petitions to recall the school board members and received enough signatures for the recall to be put up for an election.

"While the kids are going about the business of changing the name and the emblem, the community holds an election and proceeds to recall five of the seven members of the board," Scott says. The five recalled members included Scott and the other board members who voted in favor of the name change.

The remaining two board members, both of whom were ardent members of the athletic booster organization, held a special meeting of the board (all two of them) and voted to change the name back to the Redskins.

That's when the state Department of Civil Rights and the state's Commission for High School Athletics stepped in. They told the Gooding School Board there could not be a reversal of the name change and that Gooding High School's teams would have to go for four years without one, competing only as Gooding.

Over the course of those four years, new school board members were elected, and the issue quieted down. At the end of that period, the students again voted to become the Gooding Redhawks.

"You know, the kids were fine with it," says Scott. "It's been 10 years, and there's an entire generation of kids who don't have a clue that it was ever different. They are Redhawks and have always been Redhawks.

"It was the adults who had the problem. There's still a small contingent today that can't get over it. A local hardware store still sells Gooding Redskins T-shirts and other gear. There is just this group of folks who believe there was nothing disrespectful in the Redskins name. Once that group is gone, it will be a nonissue."

Questions

1. What change were the people in Gooding trying to avoid? Why do you think they wanted to avoid this change? What tactics did they use to resist change?

2. Would you describe the efforts of Scott Rogers or the school board as adaptive leadership? Why or why not?

3. How would you describe the holding environment created by the school board? Do you think it was successful? Why or why not?

4. Citing examples, describe how the school board engaged or didn't engage in each of these adaptive leader behaviors: (1) *get on the balcony,* (2) *maintain disciplined attention,* and (3) *give the work back to people.*

5. What group would you describe as the "low-status group"? How did the school board seek to give voice to this group?

LEADERSHIP INSTRUMENT ————————————

To assist you in understanding the process of adaptive leadership and what your own style might be, the adaptive leadership questionnaire is included in this section. This questionnaire provides 360-degree, or multirater, feedback about your leadership. The adaptive leadership questionnaire is composed of 30 items that assess six dimensions of adaptive leadership discussed earlier in this chapter: *get on the balcony, identify the adaptive challenge, regulate distress, maintain disciplined attention, give the work back to people,* and *protect leadership voices from below.* The results you obtain on this questionnaire will provide you with information on how you view yourself and how others view you on these six dimensions of adaptive leadership. This questionnaire is intended for practical applications. It is not designed for research purposes. For research purposes, the psychometric properties of the questionnaire (i.e., reliability and validity) would need to be established.

Adaptive leadership is a complex process, and taking this questionnaire will help you understand the theory of adaptive leadership as well as your own style of adaptive leadership.

ADAPTIVE LEADERSHIP QUESTIONNAIRE

Instructions: This questionnaire contains items that assess different dimensions of adaptive leadership and will be completed by you and others who know you (coworkers, friends, members of a group you belong to).

1. Make five copies of this questionnaire.

2. Fill out the assessment about yourself; where you see the phrase "this leader," replace it with "I" or "me."

3. Have each of five individuals indicate the degree to which they agree with each of the 30 statements below regarding your leadership by circling the number from the scale that they believe most accurately characterizes their response to the statement. There are no right or wrong responses.

Key: 1 = Strongly   2 = Disagree   3 = Neutral   4 = Agree   5 = Strongly
             disagree   agree

1. When difficulties emerge in our organization, this leader is good at stepping back and assessing the dynamics of the people involved.   1 2 3 4 5

2. When events trigger strong emotional responses among employees, this leader uses his/her authority as a leader to resolve the problem.   1 2 3 4 5

3. When people feel uncertain about organizational change, they trust that this leader will help them work through the difficulties.   1 2 3 4 5

4. In complex situations, this leader gets people to focus on the issues they are trying to avoid.   1 2 3 4 5

5. When employees are struggling with a decision, this leader tells them what he/she thinks they should do.   1 2 3 4 5

6. During times of difficult change, this leader welcomes the thoughts of group members with low status.   1 2 3 4 5

7. In difficult situations, this leader sometimes loses sight of the "big picture."   1 2 3 4 5

8. When people are struggling with a value conflict, this leader uses his or her expertise to tell them what to do.   1 2 3 4 5

9. When people begin to be disturbed by unresolved conflicts, this leader encourages them to address the issues.   1 2 3 4 5

10. During organizational change, this leader challenges people to concentrate on the "hot" topics.   1 2 3 4 5

11. When employees look to this leader for answers, he/she encourages them to think for themselves.   1 2 3 4 5

12. Listening to group members with radical ideas is valuable to this leader.   1 2 3 4 5

13. When this leader disagrees with someone, he/she has difficulty listening to what the other person is really saying.   1 2 3 4 5

14. When others are struggling with intense conflicts, this leader steps in to resolve their differences for them.   1 2 3 4 5

15. This leader has the emotional capacity to comfort others as they work through intense issues.   1 2 3 4 5

16. When people try to avoid controversial organizational issues, this leader brings these conflicts into the open.   1 2 3 4 5

17. This leader encourages his/her employees to take initiative in defining and solving problems.   1 2 3 4 5

18. This leader is open to people who bring up unusual ideas that seem to hinder the progress of the group.   1 2 3 4 5

19. In challenging situations, this leader likes to observe the parties involved and assess what's really going on.   1 2 3 4 5

20. This leader encourages people to discuss the "elephant in the room."   1 2 3 4 5

21. People recognize that this leader has confidence to tackle challenging problems.   1 2 3 4 5

22. This leader thinks it is reasonable to let people avoid confronting difficult issues.   1 2 3 4 5

23. When people look to this leader to solve problems, he/she enjoys providing solutions.   1 2 3 4 5

24. This leader has an open ear for people who don't seem to fit in with the rest of the group.   1 2 3 4 5

25. In a difficult situation, this leader will step out of the dispute to gain perspective on it.   1 2 3 4 5

26. This leader thrives on helping people find new ways of coping with organizational problems.   1 2 3 4 5

27. People see this leader as someone who holds steady in the storm.   1 2 3 4 5

28. In an effort to keep things moving forward, this leader lets people avoid issues that are troublesome.   1 2 3 4 5

29. When people are uncertain about what to do, this leader empowers them to decide for themselves.   1 2 3 4 5

30. To restore equilibrium in the organization, this leader tries to neutralize comments of out-group members.   1 2 3 4 5

Scoring

Get on the Balcony—This score represents the degree to which you are able to step back and see the complexities and interrelated dimensions of a situation.

To arrive at this score:

Sum items 1, 19, and 25 and the reversed (R) score values for 7 and 13 (i.e., change 1 to 5, 2 to 4, 4 to 2, and 5 to 1, with 3 remaining unchanged).

_____ 1 _____ 7(R) _____ 13(R) _____ 19 _____ 25 _____ Total

Identify the Adaptive Challenge—This score represents the degree to which you recognize adaptive challenges and do not respond to these challenges with technical leadership.

To arrive at this score:

Sum items 16 and 20 and the reversed (R) score values for 2, 8 and 14 (i.e., change 1 to 5, 2 to 4, 4 to 2, and 5 to 1, with 3 remaining unchanged).

_____ 2(R) _____ 8(R) _____ 14(R) _____ 16 _____ 20 _____ Total

Regulate Distress—This score represents the degree to which you provide a safe environment in which others can tackle difficult problems and to which you are seen as confident and calm in conflict situations.

To arrive at this score:

Sum items 3, 9, 15, 21, and 27.

_____ 3 _____ 9 _____ 15 _____ 21 _____ 27 _____ Total

Maintain Disciplined Attention—This score represents the degree to which you get others to face challenging issues and not let them avoid difficult problems.

To arrive at this score:

Sum items 4, 10, and 26 and the reversed (R) score values for 22 and 28 (i.e., change 1 to 5, 2 to 4, 4 to 2, and 5 to 1, with 3 remaining unchanged).

_____ 4 _____ 10 _____ 26 _____ 22(R) _____ 28(R) _____ Total

Give the Work Back to People—This score is the degree to which you empower others to think for themselves and solve their own problems.

To arrive at this score:

Sum items 11, 17, and 29 and the reversed (R) score values for 5 and 23 (i.e., change 1 to 5, 2 to 4, 4 to 2, and 5 to 1, with 3 remaining unchanged).

_____ 5(R) _____ 11 _____ 17 _____ 23(R) _____ 29 _____ Total

Protect Leadership Voices From Below—This score represents the degree to which you are open and accepting of unusual or radical contributions from low-status group members.

To arrive at this score:

Sum items 6, 12, 18, and 24 and the reversed (R) score value for 30 (i.e., change 1 to 5, 2 to 4, 4 to 2, and 5 to 1, with 3 remaining unchanged).

_____ 6 _____ 12 _____ 18 _____ 24 _____ 30(R) _____ Total

Scoring Chart

To complete the scoring chart, enter the raters' scores and your own scores in the appropriate column on the scoring sheet below. Find the average score from your five raters, and then calculate the difference between the average and your self-rating.

	Rater 1	Rater 2	Rater 3	Rater 4	Rater 5	Average Rating	Self-Rating	Difference
Get on the Balcony								
Identify the Adaptive Challenge								
Regulate Distress								
Maintain Disciplined Attention								
Give the Work Back to the People								
Protect Leadership Voices From Below								

Scoring Interpretation

- *High range:* A score between 21 and 25 means you are strongly inclined to exhibit this adaptive leadership behavior.

- *Moderately high range:* A score between 16 and 20 means you moderately exhibit this adaptive leadership behavior.

- *Moderate low range:* A score between 11 and 15 means you at times exhibit this adaptive leadership behavior.

- *Low range:* A score between 5 and 10 means you are seldom inclined to exhibit this adaptive leadership behavior.

This questionnaire measures adaptive leadership by assessing six components of the process: *get on the balcony, identify the adaptive challenge, regulate distress, maintain disciplined attention, give the work back to people,* and *protect leadership voices from below.* By comparing your scores on each of these components, you can determine which are your stronger and which are your weaker components. The scoring chart allows you to see where your perceptions are the same as those of others and where they differ. There are no "perfect" scores for this questionnaire. While it is confirming when others see you in the same way as you see yourself, it is also beneficial to know when they see you differently. This assessment can help you understand those dimensions of your adaptive leadership that are strong and dimensions of your adaptive leadership you may seek to improve.

SUMMARY

Adaptive leadership is about helping people change and adjust to new situations. Originally formulated by Heifetz (1994), adaptive leadership conceptualizes the leader not as one who solves problems for people, but rather as one who encourages others to do the problem solving. Adaptive leadership occupies a unique place in the leadership literature. While the merits of the approach are well recognized, the theoretical conceptualizations of adaptive leadership remain in the formative stages.

While the name of this approach, adaptive leadership, makes one think it is concerned with how leaders adapt, it is actually more about the adaptations of followers. Adaptive leadership is defined as "the practice of mobilizing people to tackle tough challenges and thrive" (Heifetz et al., 2009, p. 14). Consistent with complexity theory, adaptive leadership is about leader behaviors that encourage learning, creativity, and adaptation by followers in complex situations.

This chapter offers a model of the major components of adaptive leadership and how they fit together, including *situational challenges, leader behaviors,* and *adaptive work* (Figure 11.1). Leaders confront three kinds of *situational challenges* (technical, technical and adaptive, and adaptive); adaptive leadership is concerned with helping people address adaptive challenges. The six *leader behaviors* that play a major role in the process are (1) *get on the balcony,* (2) *identify adaptive challenges,* (3) *regulate distress,* (4) *maintain disciplined attention,* (5) *give the work back to people,* and (6) *protect leadership voices from below.* These six behaviors form a kind of recipe for being an adaptive leader. *Adaptive work* is the focus and goal of adaptive leadership. Central to adaptive work is creating *a holding environment,* a space created and maintained by adaptive leaders where people can feel secure as they confront and resolve difficult life challenges.

Adaptive leadership has several strengths. First, adaptive leadership takes a unique approach that emphasizes that leadership is a complex interactive process composed of multiple dimensions and activities. Second, unlike most other leadership theories, adaptive leadership clearly describes leadership as actions the leaders undertake to afford followers the best opportunity to do adaptive work. Third, adaptive leadership is unique in describing how leaders can help people confront and adjust their values in order to adapt and thrive. Fourth, adaptive leadership provides a useful and practical set of prescriptions for what leaders and followers should do to facilitate adaptive change. Last, adaptive leadership highlights the important role a holding environment plays in the leadership process.

The adaptive leadership process also has certain weaknesses. Foremost, there is very little empirical research to support the claims and tenets of adaptive leadership. Second, the conceptualizations of the process of adaptive leadership need further refinement. The major factors and how they fit together are not clearly delineated. Third, interpreting the prescriptions of adaptive leadership can become overwhelming because of the breadth and wide-ranging nature of these prescriptions. In addition, the abstract nature of the recommended leadership behaviors makes these behaviors difficult to analyze in research or implement in practice. Finally, on a theoretical level, adaptive leadership acknowledges the moral dimension of leadership and the importance of change for the common good, but does not show how doing adaptive work leads to such socially useful outcomes.

Overall, adaptive leadership offers a unique prescriptive approach to leadership that is applicable in many situations. Going forward, more research is needed to clarify the conceptualizations of adaptive leadership and validate the assumptions and propositions regarding how it works.

Sharpen your skills with SAGE edge at **edge.sagepub.com/northouse7e**

REFERENCES

Adams, J. A., Bailey, D. E., Jr., Anderson, R. A., & Galanos, A. N. (2013). Adaptive leadership: A novel approach for family decision making. *Journal of Palliative Medicine, 16*(3), 326–329.

Adams, J. A., Bailey, D. E., Jr., Anderson, R. A., & Thygeson, M. (2013). Finding your way through EOL challenges in the ICU using Adaptive Leadership behaviours: A qualitative descriptive case study. *Intensive and Critical Care Nursing, 29,* 329–336.

Chace, S. (2013). *Learning leadership: A case study on influences of a leadership training program on the practices of one group of urban school superintendents* (Unpublished doctoral dissertation). Teachers College Columbia University, New York, NY.

Eubank, D., Geffken, D., Orzano, J., & Ricci, R. (2012, September). Teaching adaptive leadership to family medicine residents: What? Why? How? *Families, Systems & Health, 30*(3), 241–252.

Guilleux, F. (2010). A *developmental perspective on leadership education of aspiring principals* (Unpublished doctoral dissertation). University of Pittsburgh, Pittsburgh, PN.

Halpert, M., & Rosenfeld, E. (2014, May 21). Depressed, but not ashamed. *The New York Times.* Retrieved from http://www.nytimes.com/2014/05/22/opinion/depressed-but-not-ashamed.html

Heifetz, R. A. (1994). *Leadership without easy answers.* Cambridge, MA: Belknap Press.

Heifetz, R. A., Grashow, A., & Linsky, M. (2009). *The practice of adaptive leadership: Tools and tactics for changing your organization and the world.* Boston, MA: Harvard Business School Press.

Heifetz, R. A., & Laurie, D. L. (1997). The work of leadership. *Harvard Business Review, 7*(1), 124–134.

Heifetz, R. A., & Linsky, M. (2002). *Leadership on the line: Staying alive through the dangers of leading.* Boston, MA: Harvard Business School Press.

Heifetz, R.A., & Sinder, R. M. (1988). Political leadership: Managing the public's problem solving. In R. B. Reich (Ed.), The power of public ideas (pp. 179-204). Boston, MA: Harvard University Press.

Modell, A. H. (1976). The "holding environment" and the therapeutic action of psychoanalysis. *Journal of the American Psychological Association 24,* 285–307.

National Public Radio. (2014, May 24). Students struggle with depression—and with telling the story [S. Simon, interviewer]. *Weekend Edition.* Retrieved from http://www.npr.org/2014/05/24/315445104/students-struggle-with-depression-and-with-telling-the-story

Thygeson, M., Morrissey, L., & Ulstad, V. (2010). Adaptive leadership and the practice of medicine: A complexity-based approach to reframing the doctor-patient relationship. *Journal of Evaluation in Clinical Practice, 16,* 1009–1015.

Uhl-Bien, M., Marion, R., & McKelvey, B. (2007). Complexity Leadership Theory: Shifting leadership from the industrial age to the knowledge era. *Leadership Quarterly, 18,* 298–318.

12

Psychodynamic Approach

Manfred F. R. Kets de Vries and Alicia Cheak

DESCRIPTION

The interpretation of dreams is the royal road to a knowledge of the unconscious activities of the mind.

—Sigmund Freud

Kafka truly illustrates the way the environment oppresses the individual. He shows how the unconscious controls our lives.

—Manuel Puig

At its heart, leadership is about human behavior—what we do, how we do it, and why we do it. Leadership is about the way people behave in organizations, and effective leaders are those who meet the needs of their followers, pay careful attention to group processes, calm anxieties and arouse hopes and aspirations, and know how to liberate human energy and inspire people to positive action. In short, leadership involves harnessing and leveraging the different and complex forces and dynamics at play in organizational functioning.

Our everyday lives consist of webs of constantly shifting and irrational forces that underlie seemingly "rational" behaviors and choices—and life in organizations is no exception. However, most definitions of leadership,

 The Psychodynamic Approach

methodologies for studying leadership, and recommendations for leadership development address observable, conscious, and rational phenomena. Moreover, historically, many organizational practitioners and researchers have tended to avoid treading in the emotional and psychological realm of organizational life, fearing the messy but real-life complexities and the relationships within (Kets de Vries, 1980, 2006b; Kets de Vries & Miller, 1984; Volkan, 1988). The result is that too many organizational phenomena remain unresolved and unexplained. Any meaningful explanation of human behaviors therefore requires both a rational and an irrational lens of investigation.

The psychodynamic approach to leadership study and development focuses on the dynamics of human behavior, which are often the most difficult to understand. It acknowledges that people are complex, unique, and paradoxical beings with rich and myriad motivational drivers and decision-making and interaction patterns. Applying psychodynamic concepts to the ebb and flow of life in organizations contributes to our understanding of the vicissitudes of life and leadership. Only through accepting and exploring the hidden undercurrents that affect human behavior can we begin to understand organizational life in all its complexities.

THE CLINICAL PARADIGM

The Clinical Paradigm is the framework through which we apply a psychodynamic lens to the study of behavior in organizations. By making sense out of leaders' deeper wishes and fantasies, and showing how these fantasies influence behavior in the organizational world, this paradigm offers a practical way of discovering how leaders and organizations *really* function (Kets de Vries & Miller, 1984).

The Clinical Paradigm consists of four basic premises:

- First, it argues that there is a *rationale behind every human act*—a logical explanation—even for actions that seem irrational. This point of view stipulates that all behavior has an explanation. Because that explanation may be elusive—inextricably interwoven with unconscious needs and desires—one has to do "detective work" to tease out hints and clues underlying perplexing behavior.

- The second premise is that a great deal of *mental life—feelings, fears, and motives—lies outside of conscious awareness*, but still affects conscious reality and even physical well-being. We all have blind spots. People aren't always aware of what they are doing much less

▶ Emotional Intelligence　　　🌐 Effect of Early IQ Testing

why they are doing it. Though hidden from rational thought, the human unconscious affects (and in some cases even dictates) conscious reality. Even the most "rational" people have blind spots, and even the "best" people have a shadow side—a side that they don't know, and don't *want* to know.

- The third premise states that nothing is more central to whom a person is than the way he or she *regulates and expresses emotions*. Emotions color experiences with positive and negative connotations, creating preference in the choices we make and the way we deal with the world. Emotions also form the basis for the internalization of mental representations of the self and others that guide relationships throughout one's life. The way a person perceives and expresses emotions may change as the years go by, influenced by life experiences (Darwin, 1920; Plutchick, 1980; Tomkins, 1995).

- The fourth premise underlying the Clinical Paradigm is that human development is an inter- and intrapersonal process; we are all *products of our past experiences,* and those experiences, including the developmental experiences provided by our early caregivers, continue to influence us throughout life (Emde, 1980; Erikson, 1950; Kagan, 1994; Kohlberg, 1981; Oglensky, 1995; Piaget, 1952; Pine, 1985).

The Clinical Paradigm unlocks and reveals the subconscious forces underlying human behavior. It illuminates the human mind—a dark sea filled with strange life-forms, most of them unconscious. And unless we can understand the motives and reasonings for this obscurity, we can hardly hope to foresee or control them. Unless we recognize the role that psychodynamic processes play in organizational life, we will never truly understand why leaders, and followers, act the way they do.

HISTORY OF THE PSYCHODYNAMIC APPROACH

The psychodynamic paradigm has its origins in Freud's psychoanalytic theories of human behavior. Specifically, this approach draws attention to the sources of energy and motivational forces that drive human actions by considering what is "within"—the inner world of individuals, including their emotions—and relationships between individuals—the "reality" created by the dynamics of groups (Neumann & Hirschhorn, 1999).

Freud also believed that neurotic symptoms or dysfunctional behavior were manifestations of a person's inner drivers and that these types of acting-out behaviors can be seen as "the royal road to an understanding

 Sigmund Freud

of the unconscious" (Freud, 1900/1953, p. 608). This perspective implies that every neurotic symptom or act has an underlying reason. The repetition of certain dysfunctional patterns suggests the existence of specific motivational undercurrents underlying decision making and behavior.

Freud himself didn't make any direct observations about the application of his ideas to the working world, but the psychoanalytic paradigm was taken up by many of his contemporaries and became a critical element of analyses of modern society. Many scholars, influenced by Freud's contributions, applied aspects of the psychodynamic paradigm to the workplace by claiming that the inner world of the leader—his or her early childhood experiences, and related hopes, fears, and desires—was extremely influential, even at a systemic level in organizations, and should not be ignored (Erikson, 1950).

Most noticeably, in the aftermath of World War II, four streams of research from the London Tavistock Institute, the Menninger Clinic in Topeka, Kansas, Harvard Business School, and Weill Cornell Medical College significantly advanced the application of the psychodynamic approach to the study of organizations by being among the first to argue that applying psychoanalytic concepts to organizational life could help in illuminating the irrational processes that underlie leader and follower behavior and decision making.

Founded in 1946, London-based Tavistock brought together an illustrious group of psychoanalysts such as Elliott Jaques, Wilfred Bion, John Bowlby, Eric Trist, Melanie Klein, and R. D. Laing. Elaborating on Bion's work on the unconscious functioning of the group as a whole, rather than as an aggregate of individuals (Bion, 1961; Bion & Rickman, 1943), the Tavistock group contributed a great deal to our understanding of the hidden dynamics within organizations that may directly influence leadership through *sociotechnical systems* (Trist & Bamforth, 1951); *industrial democracy* (Jaques, 1951); *social systems as a defense against anxiety* (Jaques, 1955, 1970; Menzies Lyth, 1959); the interpretation of *social dreaming* as a way to define meaning for a group (Lawrence, 1998); and *organizational role analysis* (Newton, Long & Sievers, 2006). However, members of the Tavistock Institute focused primarily on group processes in public organizations such as hospitals and schools, and not specifically in business organizations, with the notable exception of Elliott Jaques, who in partnership with businessman Wilfred Brown conducted a 17-year study, "the Glacier project," that explored the underlying motives and drivers of authority, role clarity, accountability, and power of both leaders and workers in a Scottish factory, Glacier Metal, of which Brown was the CEO.

 Psychoanalytic Approach

The Menninger Clinic, founded in 1942 to promote the training of psychoanalysts, also began to apply a psychodynamic approach to the world of work, notably through the work of Will Menninger and Harry Levinson with the Menninger Foundation Division of Industrial Mental Health. In the mid-1950s, an extensive national survey of mental health problems in industries was conducted, including recommendations on how to solve or alleviate them. In response to the findings of the survey, Menninger offered weeklong seminars for executives from all parts of the country in order to give these business leaders an understanding of why human beings act as they do. At Harvard Business School, Levinson continued to apply psychoanalytic theory to management and leadership and linked the failure of managers to effectively contain the anxieties of workers to employee depression and low productivity. He proposed the concept of a "psychological contract" between leaders and followers, arguing in *Men, Management and Mental Health* (1962) that if management did not pay attention to the conscious and subconscious needs of their employees, organizational performance would be adversely affected. His seminal book, *Organizational Diagnosis,* outlined a new, clinical contribution to the diagnosis of systemic organizational problems (1972).

Around the same time, Abraham Zaleznik (while in training as a psychoanalyst at the Boston Psychoanalytic Society & Institute) started to influence a group of young scholars, including Manfred Kets de Vries, Sudhir Kakar, Pierre Laurin, Anne Jardim, Roland Reitter, Georges Trepo, and Michael Hofmann, who were interested in marrying the world of work and the world of psychoanalysis. Zaleznik (1989) argued that businesspeople focused too much on process and structure, and not enough on ideas and emotions, and suggested that leaders should relate to followers in more empathetic and intuitive ways. To emphasize this point, in *Power and the Corporate Mind,* Zaleznik and Kets de Vries (1975) applied concepts from psychoanalysis, political science, and management theory to examine the effect that the conscious and unconscious motivations of the chief executive have upon his or her organization. In the seminal study, *The Neurotic Organization,* Kets de Vries and Miller (1984) integrated psychiatric and psychological findings and insights with organizational behavior theories to create a new framework for analysis of organizations, proposing that the neuroses of a top leader can be re-created throughout the organization.

The early work of Zaleznik and his group of young scholars also provided the stimulus for the first International Symposium on Applied Psychoanalysis and Organizations in 1980, organized by Michael Hofmann of the Wirtschaftsuniversität of Vienna (in collaboration with the Vienna

Psychoanalytic Society). A further impetus came from Leopold Gruenfeld, who organized a number of conferences under the auspices of Cornell University. Eventually, in 1983, these various symposia led to the founding of the International Society for the Psychoanalytic Study of Organizations (ISPSO); by the early 2000s, ISPSO had a worldwide reach, whose vision was to provide "a forum for academics, clinicians, consultants and others interested in working in and with organizations utilizing psychoanalytic concepts and insights" (www.ispso.org).

Larry Hirschhorn, another influential scholar in the study of organizational dynamics, used the term *applied clinical practice* to describe organizational consulting interventions that included diagnostic methods and actions based on a clinical, applied approach: exploring the organization systemically, and drawing on personality theory and group and organizational processes. His study *The Workplace Within: Psychodynamics of Organizational Life* (1988) opened the door to a better understanding of the irrational and emotional character of organizations. With the goal of creating healthier organizational cultures, Hirschhorn proposed a systemic, psychodynamic model of work that entailed working with real clients on practical outcomes, by addressing the hidden, and unconscious mechanisms underlying patterns of organizational behavior.

In Germany, psychoanalyst Alexander Mitscherlich applied the principles of psychoanalysis to postwar society, and his books *Society Without the Father* (1963) and *The Inability to Mourn* (with Margarete Mitscherlich, 1975) became extremely influential works that not only shaped Germany's analyses of the causes of its war, but also opened the field of social psychology to a much broader audience. In France, a sociopsychoanalytic movement emerged that included scholars such as Gérard Mendel (1968), Didier Anzieu (1972, 1999), René Kaës (1993), Eugène Enriquez (1992), Gilles Amado and Leopold Vansina (2005), and Jean Benjamin Stora (2007), who used psychoanalytic conceptualizations to better understand the fantasies, projections, and identifications that play themselves out in groups, as well as the processes of repression, suppression, and idealization that are manifest in organizational life.

As this brief history of the psychodynamic approach shows, the field has come a long way from the early roots in Freud's psychoanalytic concepts and techniques with clinical patients to its application on a larger scale to the dynamics and functioning of leaders and organizations. Through the work of researchers and practitioners working at the interface of psychoanalysis and organizational studies, psychoanalytic theory and techniques have become increasingly sophisticated, incorporating the findings from domains such as dynamic psychiatry, developmental psychology, ethology, anthropology,

Psychological Development

neuroscience, cognitive theory, family systems theory, and individual and group psychotherapy. The clinical lens addresses practical problems and opportunities in social systems from a simultaneously deep (psychodynamic) and broad (organizational theory) perspective. Although quite a few aspects of Freud's theories are no longer valid in light of new information about the workings of the mind, fundamental components of psychoanalytic theory and technique have been scientifically and empirically tested and verified, specifically as they relate to cognitive and emotional processes (Barron & Eagle, 1992; Westen, 1998). Hence, many of Freud's ideas have retained their relevance and have contributed to our understanding of organizations, the practice of management, and the hidden dynamics in the world of work (Czander, 1993; DeBoard, 1978; Gabriel, 1999; Kets de Vries, 1984, 1989, 1991, 2004, 2005, 2006a, 2006b, 2009, 2011a, 2011b, 2014; Kets de Vries & Korotof, 2011; Kets de Vries & Miller, 1984; Kets de Vries, Vrignaud, Agrawal, & Florent-Treacy, 2010; Levinson, 1972; Zaleznik, 1966, 1989; Zaleznik & Kets de Vries, 1975). The psychodynamic approach has greatly advanced the understanding of the vicissitudes of organizational behavior and the people working in such systems.

KEY CONCEPTS AND DYNAMICS WITHIN THE PSYCHODYNAMIC APPROACH

This section describes the key concepts and ideas that have emerged from the psychodynamic field as it relates to leadership and organization study. Each perspective or lens provides a way of looking at the hidden dynamics and undercurrents of organizational behavior in order to decipher the motives for why people behave the way they do.

1. Focus on the Inner Theatre

One of the core concepts of the psychodynamic paradigm is the "inner theatre" (McDougall, 1985). It is the stage filled with people who have influenced, for better or worse, our experiences in life. Early experiences with key individuals (such as early caregivers) contribute to the creation of response patterns that have a tendency to repeat themselves in other contexts with different people.

Within the inner theatre, certain relationship themes develop over time—themes rooted in our deepest wishes, needs, and goals, which contribute to our unique personality style. These "core conflictual relationship themes"

(CCRTs; Luborsky & Crits-Christoph, 1998) become recurring relationship patterns that we take into adulthood. In the context of the workplace, replete with superior and subordinate relationships, we act out these themes onto others and, based on those wishes, rightly or wrongly anticipate how others will react to us; then we react to their *perceived* reactions, and not to their *actual* reactions. Unfortunately, these scripts drawn up in childhood on the basis of our CCRTs can become psychic prisons—ineffectual and even dysfunctional in adult situations.

Attending to the CCRT of an individual allows us to understand the motivation behind human behavior, identify key relationship conflicts affecting one's ability to live and work productively, and in doing so work to align these deep wishes to more productive and mutually enhancing interpersonal relationships.

2. Focus on the Leader-Follower Relationships

A study of leader-follower relationships necessarily addresses the psychology of groups. The psychiatrist Wilfred Bion (1961) identified three basic assumptions in groups—dependency, fight-flight, and pairing—that may result in pathological regressive processes, deflecting people from the principal tasks to be performed.

People often assume, at an unconscious level, that the leader or organization can and should offer protection and guidance similar to that offered by parents in earlier years. Groups subject to the *dependency assumption* are united by feelings of helplessness, inadequacy, neediness, and fear of the outside world. They perceive the leader as omnipotent, and as a result, readily give up their autonomy. This contributes to goal-directedness and cohesiveness, but impairs followers' critical judgment and leaves them unwilling to take initiative.

Another common unconscious assumption is that the organizational world is dangerous and participants must use fight or flight as a defense mechanism. In groups subject to the *fight-flight assumption,* there is a tendency to split the world into camps of friend or foe. Fight reactions manifest themselves in aggression against the self, peers, or authority and include avoidance, absenteeism, and resignation. Subscribing to a rigid, bipolar view of the world, these groups possess a strong desire for protection from and conquest of "the enemy." Some leaders even encourage the fight-flight assumption, inflaming their followers against real and/or imagined enemies, using the in-group/out-group division to motivate people and to channel anxiety outward. This enforces the group's identity and creates meaning for followers who feel lost. The resulting sense of unity is highly reassuring but makes the group increasingly dependent on their leader.

▶ Michael McCoby

Bion's third assumption is that pairing up with a person or subgroup perceived as powerful will help a person cope with anxiety, alienation, and loneliness. People experiencing the *pairing assumption* fantasize that strength will take place in pairs. Unfortunately, pairing also implies splitting, which may result in intra- and intergroup conflict and building of smaller systems within the group. It also manifests itself in ganging up against the leader perceived as an aggressor or authority figure.

Social Defense Mechanisms

Organizational life is filled with angst and unpredictability, and leaders need to know how to deal adequately with the emerging anxiety of working in a social setting (Diamond, 1993; Gilmore & Krantz, 1985; Gould, Stapley & Stein, 2001; Hirschhorn, 1988; Jaques, 1951; Kets de Vries, 2011a; Menzies Lyth, 1959). When organizational anxieties are not properly managed, people may act out and engage in regressive social defenses to transform and neutralize strong tensions. These defenses include splitting (seeing everything as black or white); projection (seeing one's own shortcomings in others); displacement (expressing negative emotions by focusing on a less threatening target); and denial (refusal to accept facts).

Typically, executives rely on existing structures and processes to "contain" anxiety. When these ways of dealing with organizational anxieties become the dominant mode of operation (rather than an occasional stopgap measure), they become dysfunctional for the organization as a whole by creating bureaucratic obstacles. Task forces, administrative procedures, rationalization, intellectualization, and other structures and processes are used to keep people emotionally uninvolved and to help them feel safe and in control. However, these bureaucratic routines and pseudorational activities can also obscure personal and organizational realities, allowing people to detach themselves by replacing creativity, empathy, awareness, openness to change, and meaning with control and impersonality.

Mirroring and Idealizing

Mirroring and idealizing are two types of transferential processes that are especially common in the workplace. It is said that the first mirror for a baby is the mother's face. From that point on, the process of mirroring—that is, taking our cues about being and behaving from those around

 Leaders and Followers

us—becomes an ongoing aspect of our daily life and of our relationships with others (Kets de Vries, 2011a; Kohut, 1971, 1985). In organizations, this mirroring dynamic between leader and follower can become collusive. Followers are eager to use their leaders to reflect what they would like to see. Leaders, on the other hand, find the affirmation of followers hard to resist. The result is often a mutual admiration society that encourages leaders to take actions that shore up their image rather than serve the needs of the organization. When these transferential patterns persist, however, leader and followers gradually stop responding to the reality of the situation, allowing their past hopes and fantasies instead to govern their interactions.

Identification With the Aggressor

To overcome the anxiety prompted by a leader's aggressive behavior, some followers may resort to the defensive process known as "identification with the aggressor." Confronted with a superior force, people sometimes feel a strong incentive to become like that superior force, to protect against possible aggression (Freud, 1966; Kets de Vries, 2009). In full-fledged identification with the aggressor, individuals impersonate the aggressor, transforming themselves from those threatened to those making threats. In this climate of dependency, the world becomes starkly black and white. In other words, the leader sees people as being either for or against him or her. When a leader has this kind of mind-set, independent thinkers are "removed"; those who hesitate to collaborate become fresh targets for the leader's anger or become scapegoats, designated victims on whom the group assigns blame whenever things go wrong.

Folie à Deux

Some leader-follower collusions can be described as "*folie à deux*," or shared madness (Kets de Vries, 1979, 2001). In such collusions, there is usually a dominant person whose delusions become adopted by other members of the organization. Leaders whose capacity for reality testing has become impaired may transfer their delusions to their followers, who in order to minimize conflict and disagreement and risk opportunities for self-enhancement will sacrifice truth and honest criticism to maintain a connection with the leader even though he or she has lost touch with reality. In extreme cases, a *folie à deux* can lead to the self-destruction of the leader, professionally speaking, and to the collective demise of followers.

 Archetypes

3. Focus on the Shadow Side of Leadership

Narcissism

At the heart of leadership lies narcissism (Freud, 1914/1957; Kernberg, 1975; Kets de Vries, 1989; Kets de Vries & Miller, 1985; Kohut, 1971, 1985; Maccoby, 1976). Narcissism—which Freud (1914/1957) summarized as behaviors that range from a normal self-interest to a pathological self-absorption—offers leaders the conviction about the righteousness of their cause, which in turn inspires loyalty and group identification. Narcissism can be either constructive or reactive (Kets de Vries, 2004; Kets de Vries & Miller, 1985). Constructive, or healthy, narcissists have been fortunate enough to have caretakers who provided a supportive environment that led to basic trust and to a sense of control over one's actions. In leadership roles, constructive narcissists tend to be relatively well balanced and have vitality and a sense of self-esteem, capacity for intro-spection, and empathy. They inspire others not only to be better at what they do, but also to entirely change what they do. Reactive, or excessive, narcissistic leaders, on the other hand, were not as fortunate in childhood. Instead, they were the recipients of over- or understimulation, or inconsistent stimulation. Typically, such leaders are fixated on issues of power, status, prestige, and supe-riority. They are often driven toward achievement and attainment by the need to get even for perceived slights experienced in childhood. Unwilling to tolerate disagreement and criticism, such leaders rarely consult with others. The result is that reactive narcissists operate in their own reality, and without any measures of control or reality testing, this can wreak havoc in the organization.

HOW DOES THE PSYCHODYNAMIC APPROACH WORK?

As mentioned, the essence of leadership is about human behavior and effec-tive leadership is rooted in the underlying motives that govern such behavior. Contrary to the writings of various management theorists who attribute organizational effectiveness to environmental constraints, the psychodynamic approach defends the idea that psychological, social and emotional processes between leaders and followers have a great influence and need to be taken into consideration. That is not to minimize the context in which leaders oper-ate. But a company can have all the "environmental" advantages in the world—strong financial resources, enviable market position, and state-of-the-art technology—and still fail in the absence of leadership.

Anyone wanting to create or manage an effective organization needs to understand the complexity of why leaders act the way they do. What the psychodynamic study of leadership effectiveness demonstrates more clearly

 Narcissistic Personality

 Narcissism

than other conceptual frameworks is that leaders need to recognize that *people differ in their motivational patterns* (Kets de Vries, 2006). This approach also acknowledges that leaders and followers are not one-dimensional entities, but rather *complex and paradoxical* people who radiate a combination of soaring idealism and gloomy pessimism, stubborn short-sightedness and courageous vision, narrow-minded suspicion and open-handed trust, irrational envy and greed and unbelievable unselfishness. Taking the emotional pulse of followers, both individually and as a group, is essential, but that alone does not comprise effective leadership. The essence of leadership is *the ability to use motivational patterns to influence others*—in other words, to get people to voluntarily do things that they would not otherwise do.

Scholars and leaders who adopt a psychodynamic approach to organizational studies look at the *dark side of leadership* as well as the *atypical successes* (Czander, 1993; DeBoard, 1978; Eisold, 2010; Gabriel, 1999; Hirschhorn, 1988; Kets de Vries, 1989; Kets de Vries & Miller, 1985; Krantz, 2010; Levinson, 1962; Obholzer & Zagier Roberts, 1994; Zaleznik, 1966; Zaleznik & Kets de Vries, 1975). They realize that only by accepting the fact that leaders, like the rest of us, are not paragons of rationality can we begin to understand why many well-laid plans and strategies derail or, conversely, why great leaders sometimes come from very unexpected places.

However, the application of psychodynamics into leadership or organizational phenomena is not without challenges. Neumann and Hirschhorn (in a special issue of *Human Relations)* identified this challenge as the "limited degree to which those working with psychodynamic theories have managed to also relate to organizational theories, and vice versa" (1999, p. 683). They also identified a delicate balance that needs to be maintained in the psychodynamic approach to organizational study. A too narrowly focused psychodynamic approach could limit the scope of interventions to the unconscious motivation of individuals and groups. Conversely, a broader organizational theory perspective that focuses on large systems or environments might overlook major sources of motivation and energy that are imperceptible at the organizational level, but influential at the individual level. However, both authors agreed that despite this challenge, integrating psychodynamic and organizational theory would promote better analyses of the "motivational forces in individuals, groups and their leaders in the context of structures and processes within major subsystems, organizations, and their environments—and vice versa" (1999, p. 685).

STRENGTHS

The psychodynamic approach provides another lens to the study of organizational dynamics beyond a purely rational, structural approach. Specifically,

 Mood Matters

it addresses the undercurrents of organizational life through issues such as interpersonal communication, group processes, social defenses, and organization-wide neurosis. A clinically informed approach aims to instill in the organization's leaders an interest in and understanding of their own behavior—why they do what they do—as well as the behavior of others in order to best influence and leverage the potential of their followers. In short, the psychodynamic approach focuses on personal and collective insight on the part of the leader and follower—it strives to create reflective practitioners.

Another strength is that the psychodynamic approach involves an in-depth and systemic investigation of a single person, group, event, or community. It consists not only of an analysis of the self but also of the self in relation to others and to the context in which he or she exists. To this end, life case studies, coaching, and 360° feedback assessments gathered from a variety of sources may be used to provide rich and detailed insight into a person's behavior.

Another strength is that the psychodynamic approach emphasizes the relationship between leader and follower by focusing on the underlying drivers of each and what accounts for the type of relationship between them. Ideally, leaders will eventually internalize the ability to learn, work, and reflect with the psychological realm in mind, and in doing so improve their organizational relationships and team performance.

CRITICISMS

The most prevalent criticism of the psychodynamics approach comes from the fact that much of the early work was based on clinical observation of the treatment of individuals with serious mental issues. This approach focuses on dysfunction and is premised on atypical or abnormal rather than the typical behavior. Many of the concepts central to Freud's theories are subjective and difficult to prove scientifically.

Another criticism is that the psychodynamic approach does not lend itself to training in a conventional sense. This is because the focus is to increase an individual's self-awareness in order to find better ways to behave and relate personally. The route to change therefore varies from individual to individual, with no standard solution that can be applied broadly. This makes it difficult to provide specific guidelines for systematic change. A third criticism, related to the second, is that it situates the intervention at the individual level, focusing on the leader's personality and leadership style, and hence, more structural and systemic organizational issues, while important, remain in the background. Team dynamics can be addressed through psychodynamic team coaching, although the focus again is on the interpersonal relationships and issues within the group. Structural issues may, however, arise through team discussions, but they are not the focal point of discussion. Just as the structural approach to leadership studies and development may fail to address people issues, the psychodynamic approach likewise may fail to capture key structural issues. Hence the best intervention is a holistic one, which adopts both a structural and a psychodynamic lens.

APPLICATION

As mentioned, the psychodynamic approach to organizational study has evolved visibly during the last 25 years or so, rooted in the Clinical Paradigm of psychoanalysis and in particular the psychoanalytic study of organizations (Czander, 1993; Diamond, 1993; Gabriel, 1999). Kets de Vries (2005) argued that to be more effective in developing reflective leaders, leadership development programs should integrate a clinical or psychodynamic orientation, because this paradigm provides a solid framework for designing executive programs in which participants learn to become "organizational detectives," uncovering the nonrational patterns—the intrapsychic and interpersonal undercurrents—that influence the behavior of individuals, dyads, and groups.

One of the objectives of a psychodynamic leadership development program is to create an opportunity for participants that provokes an exploration of hidden or unconscious rationale—often related in some way to sexuality, financial issues, a search for happiness and meaning, or fears of mortality—for what may appear to be irrational career choices and leadership decisions. Leadership coaches and organizational consultants work with their clients to explore undercurrents that drive behavior so that executives can better manage defenses, learn how to express emotions in a situation-appropriate manner, and cultivate a perception of self and others that is in accord with reality (Kets de Vries, 2006; McCullough Vaillant, 1997).

In such programs, a *peer group coaching* methodology plays a vital role wherein group dynamic effects such as social reciprocity, peer pressure, and network contagion are harnessed. Participants work together to uncover blind spots, challenge one another, identify behavior for change, and experiment with new behavior in their workplace that will help them advance in their career trajectory and future goals (Dubouloy, 2004; Kets de Vries, 2005, 2011a, 2011b; Kets de Vries & Korotov, 2011).

Mirvis (2008) suggested that executive programs may be, under some circumstances, a "consciousness-raising" experience that cultivates participants'

 Team Coaching

self-awareness, deepens their understanding of others, and helps them to relate to society. Some of these programs may even be described by the participants themselves as "a transformative experience through which an individual comes to a new or altered sense of identity" (Bennis & Thomas, 2002, p. 40). By paying attention to behavioral patterns that may have their origin in their clients' earlier life experiences, consultants and coaches look for thematic unity (Kets de Vries, 2011a) to create meaning at multiple levels to determine the individual and organizational roots and consequences of actions and decisions. When the link between present and distant past relationships is made meaningful, leaders are more likely to arrive at *tipping points for change.* Indeed, one of the most powerful and effective experiences in leadership programs is creating such turning points in which participants make a connection between their current choices in life, see the discrepancies in their lives, and work to realign them.

Moreover the clinical intervention can have team and organizational benefits beyond just individual change. By making conscious what had been unconscious and then working to address dysfunctional behavior patterns at the team and organizational level, the consultant and the client can work together to address social defenses with the aim of healing organizational neurosis.

Group Coaching

A group coaching intervention is one very effective methodology for applying the psychodynamic principles to leadership development. Guided by an experienced external group facilitator, group coaching brings a group of leaders together to reflect on their interpersonal relationships, work practices, leadership styles, decision-making practices, and organizational culture. An always-present agenda, however, is to create alignment and become more effective in implementing the organizational strategy.

Prior to the actual intervention, the group facilitator/coach interviews the participants to get a better idea of individual and team issues and identify the major themes preoccupying the group. Participants are also asked to answer a number of 360° feedback surveys on various dimensions such as leadership behaviors, personality, inner drivers, and leadership roles. The purpose of these surveys is to draw from multiple sources of feedback, from the individual's private and public/work life to provide a more well-rounded view of the individual and the system within which he or she operates. The day prior to the actual intervention, participants are given a copy of their assessment results to reflect on.

Identity and Self-Concept

On the day of the group intervention, the group coach gives a short lecture about high-performance organizations and effective leadership. Subsequently, using an approach popularized at INSEAD, a top business school with campuses in France, Singapore, and Abu Dhabi, the coach asks all members of the leaders' committee to draw a self-portrait of how they see themselves as it relates to their head, heart, stomach, past, present, work, and leisure. When all the self-portraits are complete and displayed on the wall, the group coach begins the session by asking a first participant to kick off the process by telling the group about his or her drawing. Through the narrative of one's self-portrait, the group is able to learn intimate facts about the individual in question. Next, the group coach focuses on the 360° survey feedback reports, which were handed out to the group the night before. The coach then asks the participant about his or her own and observers' feedback, and if there was anything in the report that was not new or surprising to the participant. Specifically, the coach draws attention to the discrepancies between self and observers' perceptions in order to examine blind spots, or areas of a person's personality not known to the self but perceived to be poignant by others. Through further exploration of the feedback report and personal narrative and history of the individual, the participant continues to reveal aspects of his or her life underlying major life decisions and current behaviors. The coach then asks other members of the team to provide feedback to the participant. This begins a two-way dialogue between the individual and the group, with the purpose of arriving at mutual understanding—and making the person in the "hot seat" more effective. The participant, working with the coach and other team members, identifies a number of specific behaviors to focus on to facilitate communication and collaboration with the other team members. These priorities are aimed at drawing out one's strengths while minimizing less effective behavior. The participant then confirms publically his or her commitments to change. In response, others voice their understanding and support of this change process. Subsequently, each member of the executive team goes through the same process. Each takes the "hot seat" in turn to tell his or her story and is given constructive feedback by the group. Each individual session is concluded with an action plan to identify ways in which the team member could improve his or her leadership behaviors and personally contribute to team alignment and performance.

Group coaching has several advantages. Compared to one-on-one coaching, group coaching has proven to be a highly intensive and effective intervention to prepare leaders for individual and organizational change. Although individual interventions can be valuable, they don't create the same intensity and focus in a single session that group coaching does. Group coaching ensures that, after the intervention, the team will assume a constructively challenging follow-up role supporting one another. By contrast, in one-on-one coaching, follow-up is conducted by executive coaches who are often available irregularly, leaving individual leaders very much on their own to get things done. In group coaching, individuals also benefit from the peer group; they become mutually invested in encouraging the new behaviors that each one has identified, and they are committed to working together to achieve their goals. Group members get the opportunity to know each other much better—even though some of them may have worked together for many years. Furthermore, it encourages them to really have courageous conversations—and to be more open with one another. This kind of "group contagion" is a powerful way to bring about tipping points for change. A final benefit is the opportunity for peer coaching, in which members of the group learn to give and receive feedback. When continued beyond the intervention and into the workplace, this peer coaching relationship is a powerful means for supporting one another through the change process.

The following are a number of complex (conscious and unconscious) psychological processes at play that bring about the much desired tipping points for change:

1. To start, a group intervention provides a context for *cathartic experiences*. The group setting allows executives to get things off their chest—a forum, at least figuratively, for "emotional cleansing." The group becomes an enabler of bringing repressed feelings, fears, and covert conflicts to the surface. Putting out into the open the things that trouble them can be an extremely powerful emotional experience. Under the right circumstances, using the narrative technique provides an opportunity to reexperience and transform deeply troubling incidents, helping executives better understand why they do what they do.

2. Furthermore, while listening to the other leaders' life stories and challenges, the members of the group come to realize that they are not alone in their confusion. They are not the only ones who, at times, feel like impostors working in the organization. Others, too, struggle with similar fears. This realization can bring a great sense of relief. *Mutual identification* with specific problems brings the team together and offers opportunities to jointly discuss more effective ways of dealing with knotty issues at work.

3. A *psychodynamic lens* into the discussion can set into motion a whole process of associations of why a leader has been doing things in a particular way. It contributes to reflections whether there are other, better ways to solve problems they may be struggling with. Is a particular behavioral repertoire that was extremely appropriate at one point in time still effective in the present? Should other ways be explored to deal with specific issues? While these reflections take place, a major tool in the intervention

methodology will be transferential interpretations—the realization that we tend to act toward people in the present based on models of the past. Understanding these old patterns of interaction can help us unpack dysfunctional behavior. Through recognizing long-standing and maladaptive past patterns, the link between present relationships and distant past is made meaningful, thereby improving the chances for change.

4. In addition (very much encouraged by the other members of the group), such reflections can lead to a *willingness to experiment* in doing things differently—and by doing so, create new scenarios for the future. Leaders may come to realize that they can free themselves from what may resemble psychic prisons. In many instances, such self-understanding and insight moves people a long way along the road to personal and organizational change.

5. What also should be kept in mind is that every presentation—not just one's own—offers the opportunity for *vicarious learning*. Leaders soon come to realize that learning does not only occur through direct participation in dialogue (being in the "hot seat"), but that much of the learning takes place vicariously through observing and listening to other people's stories. This kind of learning implies retaining and replicating effective behavior observed in others. Furthermore, as there are always leaders in the group who are admired because of the way they deal with life's adversities, they may turn into role models, the kind of people the others would like to emulate. Imitative, mirroring behavior—or identification with the other—is an important part of the interpersonal learning process and a very powerful force for change.

6. During the group coaching process (if done well), the leaders going through it become a *real community*, members of a "tribe" that have gone through the same emotional experience. Tribe people draw on a great deal of mutual support whenever one of them embarks on a new challenge. This feeling of social belonging also becomes a very powerful catalyst for change.

7. A group setting is also an opportunity for *collective learning*. Occasionally, didactic instruction by the group coach can be beneficial, although (in my experience) it should be given sparingly. Explanation, clarification, and even direct advice about how to do things better within the group can reduce anxiety and establish control when there is a troublesome issue. However, it should not only be the leadership coach who offers suggestions, as leaders themselves are vast troves of expertise. And here again, the process of vicarious experience can be extremely powerful. Leaders can draw from their own rich experiences to share information about work issues and recommend different approaches and ways of doing things. And

by giving advice to others, they are practicing the supportive and challenging behaviors that can help the team function better.

8. Finally, a further positive force for change can be the *altruistic motive*, or the desire to put the needs of others above our own. While helping for helping's sake—the genuine desire to make things better for others—may seem selfless, ironically, it can have some selfish side effects. The act of giving to others can have numerous personal benefits. Helping others—offering support, reassurance, suggestions, and insights—can have a therapeutic effect, contributing to each leader's level of positive emotion, sense of self-respect, and well-being.

CASE STUDIES

In this section, we present three cases (12.1, 12.2, and 12.3) onto which you can apply the psychodynamic lens to decipher why the leader behaves the way he or she does and to think about ways a coach can help address the underlying dynamics and help the individual change his or her behavior.

CASE 12.1

Dealing With Passive-Aggressives

Robert wondered why he was always so stressed out when he was dealing with Lucas, the latest addition to his team. On the face of it, the new hire seemed very agreeable and supportive, but whatever interactions Robert had with Lucas left him wondering about Lucas's true intentions. Lucas made lots of promises but never really seemed to deliver on them. What troubled him especially was that Lucas didn't respect deadlines. Whenever he pointed this out, Lucas always had a good excuse: The instructions hadn't been clear, perhaps, or he had misunderstood, or he had been relying on someone else for some key task and that person hadn't come through. To make matters even worse (according to some colleagues), Lucas also had the habit of constantly complaining about Robert behind his back. It is not difficult to ascertain that Lucas's behavior is passive-aggressive: continuously expressing negative feelings, resentment, and aggression in an unassertive, passive manner. All the while, people like Lucas show all the signs of agreeable compliance, which makes them difficult to pin down and hold to account. As a coach, what can you do to help Robert and Lucas work more effectively together?

(Continued)

314 LEADERSHIP | THEORY AND PRACTICE

(Continued)

Questions

1. Should Robert confront Lucas directly?

2. What can the coach do to get Lucas to express his negative feelings openly?

3. What subjects or issues should be explored with Lucas?

4. What exercises can Lucas do to practice direct confrontation with Robert?

5. What can Robert do to improve his relationship with Lucas?

CASE 12.2

The Fear of Success

Tim had been on the fast track. An Ivy League graduate, he had joined one of the premier consulting firms as an associate. He went on to earn an MBA, graduating at the top of his class. Recruited by a pharmaceutical firm, he rose quickly through the ranks, joining the executive team in record time. Just eight years after joining the company, he was appointed its CEO. That was when things started to fall apart. Colleagues soon noticed that Tim seemed oddly reluctant to make important decisions. He would put off big projects and spend an inordinate amount of time on minor problems. As a result, the company missed out on some big opportunities. His behavior became increasingly worrisome. He would even turn up visibly drunk for important meetings. Although the board cut Tim some slack at first, his shortcomings quickly became too obvious to be ignored, and within two years of his appointment the board dismissed him. What went wrong?

Tim appears to have functioned extremely well as long as he wasn't in the number-one position. But the moment he was placed in the spotlight, he was in uncharted territory and could no longer hide behind someone else. In that extremely visible role, he became highly vulnerable, and his effectiveness diminished as he succumbed to self-destructive behaviors. At times, he even felt like an impostor. He also feared that the higher he climbed, the further he would fall when he made a mistake.

Tim seemed to have unconscious feelings of guilt about his success. He was consumed by the idea that his being too successful would upset his father, who had repeatedly failed in his business endeavors and had become embittered by it. He had taken out these emotions on Tim, constantly telling him that he didn't have what it took to be successful. As the years went by, Tim had internalized these criticisms. But this debasing sense of self remained dormant until Tim finally became CEO.

Questions

1. Should the executive board have fired Tim for failing to live up to expectations? What alternatives are there?

2. What could the board have done to help Tim address these disruptive behaviors?

3. What areas should be explored with Tim in trying to decode his negative associations with success?

4. What can Tim do to develop an alternative, more constructive internal narrative of success?

5. As a coach, how would you work with Tim to confront his fear of success?

CASE 12.3

Helping a Bipolar Leader

John is a talented executive with extraordinary drive and charisma. The people reporting to him all agreed that he provided outstanding leadership in the company's last crisis; his refusal to bow to adversity and his ability to rally people behind him had been truly remarkable. But they also agreed he could go over the top. He sent emails at 2 a.m., and it was sometimes hard to follow exactly what he was saying. He would jump suddenly from one idea to another, and some of his plans seemed unrealistic, even grandiose. And whenever anyone tried to slow him down, John wouldn't hear of it. His sense of invincibility made him feel that he could do anything. Once he had made up his mind, it was almost impossible to change it. His inability to listen coupled with his lack of judgment eventually resulted in his making a number of seriously bad decisions, plunging his unit into the red. The board was considering firing him.

John suffers from a mood disorder called bipolar dysfunction, previously known as manic depression, a condition that haunts approximately 4% of the population. People suffering from this condition report they

(Continued)

(Continued)

periodically experience an overactive mind and often seem to get by on little or no sleep. They often feel a heightening of the senses, which may trigger increased sexual activity, and are highly prone to bouts of extravagant behavior. Their moods swing wildly from this state of exuberance to the polar opposite, when they suddenly become withdrawn and inert, shunning the company of others. Bipolar dysfunction is a condition often associated with highly creative people (e.g., William Blake, Friedrich Nietzsche, and Ludwig van Beethoven, as well as many famous leaders such as Theodore Roosevelt, Winston Churchill, and General George Patton).

As history shows, manic-depressive leaders are great in a crisis, refusing to bow to adversity. They rush in where others fear to tread and can inspire others to follow. The downside is that due to their extreme sense of empowerment, energy, and optimism, their thinking and judgment can be flawed. Caught up in their grandiosity, they overestimate their capabilities and try to do more than they can handle. The problems are often aggravated by an inability to recognize that their behavior is dysfunctional. While "high," they rarely have insight into their condition. They like the sense of invulnerability that comes with the "high," and are reluctant to give that up.

When the inevitable setbacks and disasters happen, they fall into a tailspin of depression. This had just happened to John, who had gone so far as to check himself into a hospital psychiatric ward for a brief stay. Adding to his woes, his wife asked for a trial separation. Apparently John had been reckless with his personal finances and had been involved in numerous affairs. John is a clearly talented executive, but his behavior is self-destructive.

Questions

1. What should the board members do with regard to John's poor decisions? Should they fire him? What alternative routes are available?

2. How can John be made aware of his disruptive behaviors?

3. What role can his wife/family play to help John address his bipolarity?

4. Within the workplace, what can be done to leverage John's strengths (creativity) and minimize his disruptive behavior? What type of structure will be a best fit for John in the organization?

5. As a coach, how can you help John to rebalance his life?

LEADERSHIP INSTRUMENT

Effective leaders have two roles—a charismatic one and an architectural one. In the charismatic role, leaders envision a better future and empower and energize their followers to work toward this vision. In the architectural role, leaders address issues related to organizational design processes and control and reward systems. Both roles are necessary for effective leadership, but it is a rare leader who can fulfill both roles seamlessly. Usually, alignment is only achieved within a leadership role constellation that enables members to take different but complementary roles. A diverse group of carefully selected individuals can be structured to become a highly effective team that delivers much more than the sum of its parts. The first step is to identify each individual's personality makeup and leadership style, and then match his or her strengths and competencies to particular roles and challenges. This sort of creative team configuration can energize and enhance the workplace.

The Leadership Archetype Questionnaire (Kets de Vries, 2006b) is a psychometrically validated 360° feedback instrument designed to identify individuals' dominant leadership behaviors and what steps are needed to create a well-balanced team. Leadership archetypes are prototypes of leadership styles in today's complex organizational environment. Successful organizations are characterized by a distributive, collective, complementary form of leadership, wherein a group of carefully selected individuals can become a highly effective team that delivers much more than the sum of its parts. Although individuals may "drift" toward one particular archetype, it is more common for a person to possess the characteristics of a number of archetypes. It is also important to keep in mind that each of these leadership archetypes will prove more or less effective, depending on the situation. Therefore, the ideal leadership team should include people with diverse dominant leadership characteristics. A team in which multiple archetypes are represented should be able to cover most of the leadership needs that are required, whatever the context.

From a psychodynamic point of view, leadership archetypes represent different leadership styles and different ways of behaving in the organizational environment. These behaviors in turn are rooted in different personalities, inner drivers, and strengths. Some of these styles can come in conflict with others, while others are more complementary. In becoming aware of these different ways of being and behaving, leaders can better understand their own strengths and weaknesses, as well as the strengths and weaknesses of others. This awareness can then be used to help them better influence their people, through leveraging their strengths and managing weaknesses, and in doing so create balanced, symbiotic, and mutually enhancing teams.

The Leadership Archetype Questionnaire
(Abridged Version)

To assist you in understanding the process of what your own dominant leadership behaviors might be, this questionnaire provides 360°, or multi-rater, feedback about your leadership. The Leadership Archetype Questionnaire (LAQ), Abridged Version, comprises 8 items that assess 8 archetypes: the strategist, the change catalyst, the transactor, the builder, the innovator, the processor, the coach, and the communicator. The results you obtain on this questionnaire will provide you with information on what your own leadership archetype may be.

Note: Another recommendation is to get other members of your team to complete the questionnaire for themselves so that you can map out your team constellation to see how balanced your team is, or if there are areas that are lacking.

Instructions: This questionnaire contains items that assess different dimensions of your leadership and will be completed by you and others who know you (coworkers, friends, members of a group you belong to).

1. Make five copies of this questionnaire.

2. Self-assessment: Fill out the assessment about yourself.

3. For the 360° feedback, have each individual answer the same questions about you. It is insightful to see how other people perceive you; their perceptions also influence the way they deal and interact with you.

Study the following statements and mark the ones that you think are true for you. Select more than one if appropriate.

1. I have great strategic sense.

2. I take on the role of deal maker, always prepared to make propositions about new business deals.

3. I am highly experienced at turning around difficult situations.

4. I suggest entrepreneurial ways of developing the business.

5. I come up with a number of new product or process innovations.

6. I promote and monitor structures, systems, and tasks.

7. I am very interested in devising creative ways to develop people.

8. I take on the role of communicator in my organizations.

Scoring Interpretation

Each statement corresponds to one of the following leadership archetypes:

1. **The Strategist**—Leadership as a game of chess
2. **The Change Catalyst**—Leadership as a turnaround activity
3. **The Transactor**—Leadership as deal making
4. **The Builder**—Leadership as entrepreneurial activity
5. **The Innovator**—Leadership as creative idea generation
6. **The Processor**—Leadership as an exercise in efficiency
7. **The Coach**—Leadership as people development
8. **The Communicator**—Leadership as stage management

1. The Strategist

Strategists are good at dealing with developments in the organization's environment. They provide vision, strategic direction, and outside-the-box thinking to create new organizational forms and generate future growth. They can see the big picture, anticipate future developments, and respond quickly to change. Although strategists have a talent for aligning vision with strategy, they are not always good at taking the next step—aligning strategy with values and behavior. They prefer to ignore "soft" issues and avoid conflict, focusing instead on facts, figures, and abstract scenarios. To compensate for this deficiency, strategists often join forces with coaches. Strategists are often not good communicators. Their followers may not always fully understand what they are trying to do or what message they are trying to get across. Because they are preoccupied with the big picture, strategists may ignore some of the "micro" issues that warrant attention to keep organizational processes on track. In these instances, processors and communicators can be very helpful to them.

2. The Change Catalyst

Change catalysts function best in the integration of organizational cultures after a merger or acquisition or when spearheading reengineering or turnaround projects. They are also excellent at managing rapidly growing organizational units and recognizing opportunities for organizational transformation. Change catalysts are implementation driven and very good at selecting talent to get the task done. Unlike strategists, they have the talent to align vision, strategy, and behavior. They are both outcome and process oriented. The flip side is that change catalysts can quickly become bored in stable situations and are not suited to participating in small, incremental change efforts. Many operate on a short-term timeline, and need to see immediate results. If no challenging assignment is available, these leaders may try to create one (sometimes for the wrong reasons). Although many change catalysts have a talent for people management, there will be times when their sense of urgency may override their sensitivity to people and make them poor communicators. Change catalysts also tend to have a starkly black-and-white view of what is right or wrong. Thus, they are not always politically sensitive enough to handle complex organizational problems. What they see as innocent actions can have disastrous consequences. Some of these problems can be avoided, however, if they team up with coaches.

3. The Transactor

Transactors like making acquisitions or other deals. Extremely dynamic and enthusiastic, they thrive on new challenges and negotiations. They like novelty, adventure, and exploration, and have high risk tolerance.

Proactive in welcoming change and instinctive networkers, transactors know how to lobby inside and outside the organization to get their point of view across. They are outcome oriented but not as effective at processes. Like change catalysts, transactors can become very restless if they do not have enough stimulation. As a result, they can be seduced by the excitement of mergers and takeovers. Once they get going, there is no holding them back, and they can take other people on a very risky journey. After they pull off a deal, however, transactors lose interest in taking the project to the next phase. Their impatience with structures, processes, and systems means that they are poor at organization building. Their sometimes mercurial temperaments can also create very stressful situations. Being good deal makers and negotiators, they are frequently hard to read—an asset in negotiation, which can confuse collaborators. They need others, such as strategists, processors, and coaches, to compensate for their limitations.

4. The Builder

Builders enjoy starting and building their own organizations or setting up "skunkworks" and other entrepreneurial ventures inside a large organization. They have a powerful need for independence and to be in control. They also have the talent to make their dreams come true: They possess an enormous amount of energy, drive, dynamism, and enterprise. Builders are creative, decisive, focused, single-minded, and persevering, and have a great capacity to deal with setbacks. They also have a high, but calculated, propensity to take risks, and they are quick to adapt when they see opportunities. They know how to get other people to produce results. Builders have to be at the center of things, however. They tend to have little regard for authority and great difficulties with delegation. Although a builder's leadership can be inspirational, poor communication and a culture of domination and control can contribute to dysfunctional decision making. Builders need others, such as processors and coaches, to be their sparring partners.

5. The Innovator

Extremely curious, innovators want to learn more about anything and everything that grabs their attention. Their passion for learning new things and their insatiable search for knowledge can be a source of inspiration to others. Innovators are the most reluctant of all the leadership archetypes to do things in a particular way simply because that is how things have always been done. Because of this innovative mind-set, they can bring fresh, new approaches to their organizations. More politically astute innovators can be good at managing innovative projects, if not hampered by routine. Starting in childhood, innovators tend to be introverts, stimulated by thoughts and ideas rather than people and things. Adept at logic and reason, they typically lack the usual social graces and may not always express their feelings appropriately. They are poor social sensors, unskilled at decoding body language, sensing others' feelings, or recognizing hidden agendas, thus making a rather "nerdy" impression. Moreover, innovators' driven way of working means that they have trouble conforming to organizational norms and may be treated as outsiders. In going their own way, they may lose sight of the financial realities and limitations, thus endangering the viability of the organization.

6. The Processor

Processors like to create order out of disorder and are adept at helping organizations make an effective transition from an entrepreneurial to a more professionally managed stage. Talented at setting boundaries and at creating the structures and systems necessary to support the organization's objectives, they have a systemic, practical outlook and dislike unstructured situations. They are good at time management, very conscientious, reliable, and efficient, able to keep a cool head in stressful situations. As team players, they have a very positive attitude toward authority and are committed corporate citizens. Because they tend to be adaptable and collaborative, processors complement most other leadership styles and thus play an important role in any executive role constellation. Sometimes, however, a processor's need for order, systems, and rules can shade into stubbornness and inflexibility, so these leaders can be slow to respond to new opportunities or even hinder them. They tend to lack imagination, flexibility, and spontaneity. Their inflexibility can create people-management problems. Not only will it be helpful for processors to be paired up with coaches, but strategists or innovators can also help to bring in an element of out-of-the-box thinking.

7. The Coach

Coaches are very good at instituting culture change projects to address organizational alienation and loss of trust. They are exceptional people developers who possess empathy, are extremely good listeners, and have high emotional intelligence. With their positive, constructive outlook on life, they inspire confidence and trust. Great communicators and motivators, coaches are excellent at handling difficult interpersonal and group situations and at giving constructive feedback. They create high-performance teams and high-performance cultures. They are great believers in participatory management and know how to delegate. The downside is that their sensitivity to others' feelings can make them overly careful when giving feedback: They may find it hard to be tough when needed, and they may shy away from dealing with difficult underperformance and personal issues. In crisis situations, some coaches may be slow to act or may procrastinate about important issues, a danger when speed is a competitive advantage. Given the organizational context, teaming coaches with executives who possess other archetypes can be highly effective.

8. The Communicator

With their ability to express a vision strongly and powerfully, communicators can inspire people at all levels. They are good at projecting optimism in times of adversity or crisis and are strongly influential with the various constituencies in the organization. Possessing impressive theatrical skills and great presence, communicators are very effective in building alliances and enlisting the support of other people. However, a communicator's preference for looking at the big picture, rather than dealing with details, means that these leaders need others, such as strategists and processors, to make their dreams become reality. Communicators can also appear to operate on the surface: When it's time to deliver, very little happens, and everything they have been saying can seem like empty rhetoric. Expert in looking out for number one, they are not averse to obtaining excessive perks and other benefits for themselves. They sometimes latch on to others for support and even take credit for other people's achievements, a self-serving style that can contribute to organizational disintegration. In their drive to acquire the symbols of power, they will tolerate warfare between internal fiefdoms in the organization. As in the case of coaches, when balanced with other archetypes, communicators can play an essential role in many role constellations.

When interpreting the Leadership Archetype Questionnaire results, keep this in mind:

- The results are based on your own (and your observers') perceptions at a single point in time. Though the responses certainly reflect long-standing behavioral characteristics, situational factors can have considerable influence.
- Most of us—and most effective leaders—can be slotted into more than one archetype. Archetype identifications change as our life changes. Assessing where and what we are is not a static, one-off, operation.
- Furthermore, it is a rare leader who can fulfill all the roles seamlessly. Successful organizations are characterized by a distributive, collective, complementary form of leadership.
- Finally, people are much more complex than the scores shown on the LAQ (or any other instrument). What the LAQ attempts to do is capture some of that complexity and illuminate basic elements of your behavior. The results are jumping-off points for self-examination and discussion.

For more information on the development and validation of the Leadership Archetype Questionnaire, please refer to Kets de Vries et al. (2010). Development and application of the Leadership Archetype Questionnaire. *International Journal of Human Resource Management, 21*(15), 2846–2861.

SUMMARY

This chapter proposes an approach to leadership that goes beyond the traditional, more conventional "rational" approach. The psychodynamic approach is the flip side of the coin, and looks at the underlying irrational processes and dynamics governing human behavior. Indeed, much of what we do, whether we want to admit it or not, is guided by deep-seated experiences and patterns that are first mapped out in early infancy, through our experiences with early caregivers. We carry these patterns subconsciously into our adult and working lives, and they color our interactions with those we work with—superiors, peers, and followers alike. Any understanding of leadership behavior needs to consider these undercurrents. Only in understanding ourselves and our drivers, and in turn turning our analytic gaze to deciphering the motivations and behaviors of others around us, can we truly understand the complexity of the system in which we live and work. The psychodynamic approach not only provides us with better self-knowledge, but this knowledge can also be used in our interface with other organizational actors in a way that allows us to shape, influence, and leverage organizational dynamics.

Sharpen your skills with SAGE edge at **edge.sagepub.com/northouse7e**

REFERENCES

Amado, G., & Vansina, L. (2005). *The transitional approach in action.* London: Karnac Books.

Anzieu, D. (1972). *Le travail psychanalytique dans les groupes.* Paris: Dunod.

Anzieu, D. (1999). *Le groupe et l'inconscient. L'imaginaire groupal.* Paris: Dunod.

Barron, J. W., & Eagle, M. N. (Eds.). (1992). *The interface of psychoanalysis and psychology.* Washington, DC: American Psychological Association.

Bennis, W. G., & Thomas, R. J. (2002, September). Crucibles of leadership. *Harvard Business Review, 80*(9), pp. 39–45.

Bion, W. R. (1961). *Experiences in groups.* London: Tavistock.

Bion, W. R., & Rickman, J. (1943). Intra-group tensions in therapy. *Lancet, 242,* 678–682.

Czander, W. M. (1993). *The psychodynamics of work and organizations.* New York: Guilford Press.

Darwin, C. (1920). *The expression of emotion in man and animals.* New York: Appleton-Century-Crofts.

DeBoard, R. (1978). *The psychoanalysis of organisations.* London: Routledge.

Diamond, M. A. (1993). *The unconscious life of organizations: Interpreting organizational identity.* Westport, CT: Quorum Books.

Dubouloy, M. (2004). The transitional space and self-recovery: A psychoanalytical approach to high-potential managers' training. *Human Relations, 57*(4), 467–496.

Eisold, K. (2010). *What you don't know you know.* New York: Other Press.

Emde, R. N. (1980). Toward a psychoanalytic theory of affect: II. Emerging models of emotional development in infancy. In S. Greenspan & G. Pollock (Eds.), *The course of life: Psychoanalytic contributions toward understanding personality development. Vol. I: Infancy and early childhood* (pp. 85–112). Washington, DC: U.S. Government Printing Office.

Enriquez, E. (1992). *L'Organisation en analyse.* Paris: Presses Universitaires de France.

Erikson, E. H. (1950). *Childhood and society.* New York: Norton.

Freud, S. (1953). The interpretation of dreams (first part). In J. Strachey (Ed., Trans.), *The standard edition of the complete psychological works of Sigmund Freud* (Vol. IV). London: The Hogarth Press and the Institute of Psychoanalysis. (Original work published 1900)

Freud, S. (1957). On narcissism. In J. Strachey (Ed., Trans.), *The standard edition of the complete psychological works of Sigmund Freud* (Vol. XIV). London: The Hogarth Press and the Institute of Psychoanalysis. (Original work published 1914)

Freud, A. (1966). *The ego and the mechanisms of defense.* Madison, CT: International Universities Press.

Gabriel, Y. (1999). *Organizations in depth.* London: SAGE.

Gilmore, T., & Krantz, J. (1985). Projective identification in the consulting relationship: Exploring the unconscious dimensions of a client system. *Human Relations 38*(12), 1159–1177.

Gould, L., Stapley, L., & Stein, M. (Eds.). (2001). *The systems psychodynamics of organizations: Integrating the group relations, psychoanalytic, and open systems perspectives.* London: Karnac Books.

Hirschhorn, L. (1988). *The workplace within: Psychodynamics of organizational life.* Cambridge, MA: The MIT Press.

Jaques, E. (1951). *The changing culture of a factory.* London: Routledge.

Jaques, E. (1955). Social systems as a defense against persecutory and depressive anxiety. In M. Klein, P. Heimann, & R. E. Money-Kyrle (Eds.), *New directions in psychoanalysis.* London: Tavistock.

Jaques, E. (1970). *Work, creativity, and social justice.* New York: International Universities Press.

Kaës, R. (1993). *Le groupe et le sujet du groupe.* Paris: Dunod.

Kagan, J. (1994). *Nature of the child.* New York: Basic Books.

Kernberg, O. (1975). *Borderline conditions and pathological narcissism.* New York: Aronson.

Kets de Vries, M. F. R. (1979, July/August). Managers can drive their subordinates mad. *Harvard Business Review,* pp. 125–134.

Kets de Vries, M. F. R. (1980). *Organizational paradoxes: Clinical approaches to management.* London: Tavistock.

Kets de Vries, M. F. R. (Ed.). (1984). *The irrational executive: Psychoanalytic explorations in management.* New York: International Universities Press.

Kets de Vries, M. F. R. (1989). Leaders who self-destruct: The causes and cures. *Organizational Dynamics 17*(4), 4–17.

Kets de Vries, M. F. R. (Ed.). (1991). *Organizations on the couch.* San Francisco: Jossey-Bass.

Kets de Vries, M. F. R. (2001). *Struggling with the demon: Perspectives on individual and organizational irrationality.* Madison, WI: Psychosocial Press.

Kets de Vries, M. F. R. (2004). *Lessons on leadership by terror: Finding Shaka Zulu in the attic.* London: Edgar Allen.

Kets de Vries, M. F. R. (2005). Leadership group coaching in action: The zen of creating high performance teams. *Academy of Management Executive, 19*(1), 61–76.

Kets de Vries, M. F. R. (2006a). Decoding the team conundrum: The eight roles executives play. *Organisational Dynamics,* Fall.

Kets de Vries, M. F. R. (2006b). *The leader on the couch: A clinical approach to changing people and organizations.* San Francisco: Jossey-Bass.

Kets de Vries, M. F. R. (2009). *Reflections on leadership and character.* London: Wiley.

Kets de Vries, M. F. R. (2011a). *Reflections on groups and organizations: On the couch with Manfred Kets de Vries.* London: Wiley.

Kets de Vries, M. F. R. (2011b). *The hedgehog effect: The secrets of building high performance teams.* London: Wiley.

Kets de Vries, M. F. R. (2014). Vision without action is a hallucination: Making strategy implementation a reality. *INSEAD Working Paper Series.*

Kets de Vries, M. F. R., & Korotov, K. (2011). Transformational leadership development programs: Creating long-term sustainable change. In S. Snook, N. Nohria, & R. Khurana (Eds.), *The handbook for teaching leadership: Knowing, being, and doing.* Thousand Oaks, CA: SAGE.

Kets de Vries, M. F. R., & Miller, D. (1984). *The neurotic organization.* San Francisco: Jossey-Bass.

Kets de Vries, M. F. R., & Miller, D. (1985). Narcissism and leadership: An object relations perspective. *Human Relations, 36*(6), 583–601.

Kets de Vries, M. F. R., Vrignaud, P., Agrawal, A., & Florent-Treacy, E. (2010). Development and application of the Leadership Archetype Questionnaire. *International Journal of Human Resource Management, 21*(15), 2846–2861.

Kohlberg, L. (1981). *The philosophy of moral development.* New York: Harper & Row.

Kohut, H. (1971). *The analysis of the self.* New York: International Universities Press.

Kohut, H. (1985). *Self psychology and the humanities.* New York: Norton.

Krantz, J. (2010). *The myth that binds: Psychoanalytic perspectives on a turbulent world.* London: Karnac Books.

Lawrence, W. G. (1998). *Social dreaming @ work.* London: Karnac Books.

Levinson, H. (1962). *Men, management, and mental health.* Cambridge, MA: Harvard University Press.

Levinson, H. (1972). *Organizational diagnosis.* Cambridge, MA: Harvard University Press.

Luborsky, L., & Crits-Christoph, P. (1998). *Understanding transference: The core conflictual relationship theme method.* Washington, DC: American Psychological Organization.

Maccoby, M. (1976). *The gamesman: The new corporate leaders.* New York: Simon & Schuster.

McCullough Vaillant, L. (1997). *Changing character.* New York: Basic Books.

McDougall, J. (1985). *Theaters of the mind.* New York: Basic Books.

Mendel, G. (1968). *La révolte contre le père.* Paris: Payot.

Menzies Lyth, I. (1959). The functions of social systems as a defence against anxiety: A report on a study of the nursing service of a general hospital. *Human Relations, 13,* 95–121; reprinted in *Containing anxiety in institutions: Selected essays* (Vol. 1, pp. 43–88). Free Association Books, 1988.

Mirvis, P. (2008). Executive development through consciousness-raising experiences. *Academy of Management Learning and Education, 7*(2).

Mitscherlich, A. (1963). *Society without the father: A contribution to social psychology.* New York: Harper.

Mitscherlich, A., & Mitscherlich, M. (1975). *The inability to mourn: Principles of collective behavior.* New York: Grove Press.

Neumann, J. E., & Hirschhorn, L. (1999). The challenge of integrating psychodynamic and organizational theory. *Human Relations, 52*(6).

Newton, J., Long, S., & Sievers, B. (2006). *Coaching in depth: The organizational role analysis approach.* London: Karnac Books.

Obholzer, A., & Zagier Roberts, V. (Eds.). (1994). *The unconscious at work.* London: Routledge.

Oglensky, B. (1995). Socio-psychoanalytic perspectives on the subordinate. *Human Relations 48*(9), 1029–1054.

Piaget, J. (1952). *The origins of intelligence in children.* New York: International Universities Press.

Pine, F. (1985). *Developmental theory and clinical process.* New Haven, CT: Yale University Press.

Plutchick, R. (1980). *Emotions: A psycho-evolutionary synthesis.* New York: HarperCollins.

Stora, J. B. (2007). *When the body displaces the mind: Stress, trauma and somatic disease.* London: Karnac Books.

Tomkins, S. S. (1995). Script theory: Differential magnification of affect. *Exploring affect: Selections from the writings of Silvan S. Tomkins* (pp. 312–410). New York: Cambridge University Press.

Trist, E., & Bamforth, K. (1951). Some social and psychological consequences of the longwall method of coal getting. *Human Relations, 4,* 3–38.

Volkan, V. D. (1988). *The need to have enemies and allies: From clinical practice to international relationships.* Northvale, NJ: Jason Aronson.

Westen, D. (1998). The scientific legacy of Sigmund Freud: Toward a psychodynamically informed psychological science. *Psychological Bulletin, 124*(3), 333–371.

Zaleznik, A. (1966). *Human dilemmas of leadership.* New York: Harper & Row.

Zaleznik, A. (1989). *The managerial mystique: Restoring leadership in business.* New York: Harper & Row.

Zaleznik, A., & Kets de Vries, M. F. R. (1975). *Power and the corporate mind.* Oxford: Houghton Mifflin.

13

Leadership Ethics

DESCRIPTION

This chapter is different from many of the other chapters in this book. Most of the other chapters focus on one unified leadership theory or approach (e.g., trait approach, path–goal theory, or transformational leadership), whereas this chapter is multifaceted and presents a broad set of ethical viewpoints. The chapter is intended not as an "ethical leadership theory," but rather as a guide to some of the ethical issues that arise in leadership situations.

Probably since our cave-dwelling days, human beings have been concerned with the ethics of our leaders. Our history books are replete with descriptions of good kings and bad kings, great empires and evil empires, and strong presidents and weak presidents. But despite a wealth of biographical accounts of great leaders and their morals, very little research has been published on the theoretical foundations of leadership ethics. There have been many studies on business ethics in general since the early 1970s, but these studies have been only tangentially related to leadership ethics. Even in the literature of management, written primarily for practitioners, there are very few books on leadership ethics. This suggests that theoretical formulations in this area are still in their infancy.

One of the earliest writings that specifically focused on leadership ethics appeared as recently as 1996. It was a set of working papers generated from a small group of leadership scholars, brought together by the W. K. Kellogg Foundation. These scholars examined how leadership theory and practice could be used to build a more caring and just society. The ideas of the Kellogg group are now published in a volume titled *Ethics, the Heart of Leadership* (Ciulla, 1998).

N Ethical Leadership

Interest in the nature of ethical leadership has continued to grow, particularly because of the many recent scandals in corporate America and the political realm. On the academic front, there has also been a strong interest in exploring the nature of ethical leadership (see Aronson, 2001; Ciulla, 2001, 2003; Johnson, 2011; Kanungo, 2001; Price, 2008; Trevino, Brown, & Hartman, 2003).

Ethics Defined

From the perspective of Western tradition, the development of ethical theory dates back to Plato (427–347 B.C.) and Aristotle (384–322 B.C.). The word *ethics* has its roots in the Greek word *ethos*, which translates to "customs," "conduct," or "character." Ethics is concerned with the kinds of values and morals an individual or a society finds desirable or appropriate. Furthermore, ethics is concerned with the virtuousness of individuals and their motives. Ethical theory provides a system of rules or principles that guide us in making decisions about what is right or wrong and good or bad in a particular situation. It provides a basis for understanding what it means to be a morally decent human being.

In regard to leadership, ethics is concerned with what leaders do and who leaders are. It has to do with the nature of leaders' behavior, and with their virtuousness. In any decision-making situation, ethical issues are either implicitly or explicitly involved. The choices leaders make and how they respond in a given circumstance are informed and directed by their ethics.

A leader's choices are also influenced by their moral development. The most widely recognized theory advanced to explain how people think about moral issues is *Kohlberg's stages of moral development*. Kohlberg (1984) presented a series of dilemmas (the most famous of which is "the Heinz dilemma") to groups of young children who he then interviewed about the reasoning behind their choices regarding the dilemmas. From these data he created a classification system of moral reasoning that was divided into six stages: *Stage 1—Obedience and Punishment, Stage 2—Individualism and Exchange, Stage 3—Interpersonal Accord and Conformity, Stage 4—Maintaining the Social Order, Stage 5—Social Contract and Individual Rights,* and *Stage 6—Universal Principles* (see Table 13.1). Kohlberg further classified the first two stages as preconventional morality, the second two as conventional morality, and the last two as postconventional morality.

 Ethics Introduction

Table 13.1   Kohlberg's Stages of Moral Development

LEVEL 1: PRECONVENTIONAL MORALITY	
Reasoning based on self-interest, avoiding punishment, and rewards	
STAGE 1	STAGE 2
Obedience and Punishment	Individualism and Exchange
"I follow the rules so I don't get hurt"	"I will do a favor for you, if you do one for me"

LEVEL 2: CONVENTIONAL MORALITY	
Reasoning based on society's views and expectations	
STAGE 3	STAGE 4
Interpersonal Accord and Conformity	Maintaining the Social Order
"I try to be good and do what others expect of me"	"I follow the rules and support the laws of society"

LEVEL 3: POSTCONVENTIONAL MORALITY	
Reasoning based on conscience and creating a just society	
STAGE 5	STAGE 6
Social Contract and Individual Rights	Universal Principles
"I work with others to do what is best for all of us"	"I act out of my internalized and universal principle of justice"

Level 1. Preconventional Morality

When an individual is at the preconventional morality level, he or she tends to judge the morality of an action by its direct consequences. There are two stages that fall within preconventional morality:

Stage 1—Obedience and Punishment. At this stage, the individual is egocentric and sees morality as external to self. Rules are fixed and handed down by authority. Obeying rules is important because it means avoiding punishment. For example, a child reasons it is bad to steal because the consequence will be to go to jail.

Stage 2—Individualism and Exchange. At this stage, the individual makes moral decisions based on self-interest. An action is right if it serves the individual. Everything is relative, so each person is free to do his or her own thing. People do not identify with the values of the community (Crain,

1985) but are willing to exchange favors. For example, an individual might say, "I'll do a favor for you, if you do a favor for me."

Level 2. Conventional Morality

Those who are at this level judge the morality of actions by comparing them to society's views and expectations. Authority is internalized but not questioned, and reasoning is based on the norms of the group to which the person belongs. Kohlberg identified two stages at the conventional morality level:

Stage 3—Interpersonal Accord and Conformity. At this stage, the individual makes moral choices based on conforming to the expectations of others and trying to behave like a "good" person. It is important to be "nice" and live up to the community standard of niceness. For example, a student says, "I am not going to cheat because that is not what a good student does."

Stage 4—Maintaining the Social Order. At this stage, the individual makes moral decisions in ways that show concern for society as a whole. In order for society to function, it is important that people obey the laws, respect authority, and support the rules of the community. For example, a person does not run a red light in the middle of the night when no other cars are around because it is important to maintain and support the traffic laws of the community.

Level 3. Postconventional Morality

At this level of morality, also known as the principled level, individuals have developed their own personal set of ethics and morals that guide their behavior. Postconventional moralists live by their own ethical principles—principles that typically include such basic human rights as life, liberty, and justice. There are two stages that Kohlberg identified as part of the postconventional morality level:

Stage 5—Social Contract and Individual Rights. At this stage, the individual makes moral decisions based on a social contract and his or her views on what a good society should be like. A good society supports values such as liberty and life, and fair procedures for changing laws (Crain, 1985), but recognizes that groups have different opinions and values. Societal laws are important, but people need to agree on them. For example, if a boy is dying of cancer and his parents do not have money to pay for his treatment, the state should step in and pay for it.

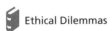 Ethical Dilemmas

Stage 6—Universal Principles. At this stage, the individual's moral reasoning is based on internalized universal principles of justice that apply to everyone. Decisions that are made need to respect the viewpoints of all parties involved. People follow their internal rules of fairness, even if they conflict with laws. An example of this stage would be a civil rights activist who believes a commitment to justice requires a willingness to disobey unjust laws.

Kohlberg's model of moral development has been criticized for focusing exclusively on justice values, for being sex-biased since it is derived from an all-male sample, for being culturally biased since it is based on a sample from an individualist culture, and for advocating a postconventional morality where people place their own principles above those of the law or society (Crain, 1985). Regardless of these criticisms, this model is seminal to developing an understanding of what forms the basis for individuals' ethical leadership.

Ethical Theories

For the purposes of studying ethics and leadership, ethical theories can be thought of as falling within two broad domains: theories about leaders' *conduct* and theories about leaders' *character* (Table 13.2). Stated another way, ethical theories when applied to leadership are about both the actions of leaders and who they are as people. Throughout the chapter, our discussions about ethics and leadership will always fall within one of these two domains: conduct or character.

Ethical theories that deal with the conduct of leaders are in turn divided into two kinds: theories that stress the *consequences* of leaders' actions and those that emphasize the *duty* or *rules* governing leaders' actions (see Table 13.2). Teleological theories, from the Greek word *telos,* meaning "ends" or "purposes," try to answer questions about right and wrong by focusing on whether a person's conduct will produce desirable consequences. From the

Table 13.2   Domains of Ethical Theories

Conduct	Character
Consequences (teleological theories)	Virtue-based theories
• Ethical egoism	
• Utilitarianism	
Duty (deontological theories)	

 Consequences

teleological perspective, the question "What is right?" is answered by looking at results or outcomes. In effect, the consequences of an individual's actions determine the goodness or badness of a particular behavior.

In assessing consequences, there are three different approaches to making decisions regarding moral conduct (Figure 13.1): *ethical egoism, utilitarianism,* and *altruism. Ethical egoism* states that a person should act so as to create the greatest good for her- or himself. A leader with this orientation would take a job or career that she or he selfishly enjoys (Avolio & Locke, 2002). Self-interest is an ethical stance closely related to transactional leadership theories (Bass & Steidlmeier, 1999). Ethical egoism is common in some business contexts in which a company and its employees make decisions to achieve its goal of maximizing profits. For example, a midlevel, upward-aspiring manager who wants her team to be the best in the company could be described as acting out of ethical egoism.

Figure 13.1 Ethical Theories Based on Self-Interest Versus Interest for Others

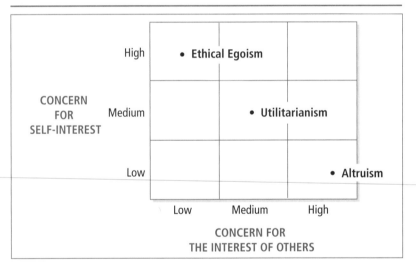

A second teleological approach, *utilitarianism,* states that we should behave so as to create the greatest good for the greatest number. From this viewpoint, the morally correct action is the action that maximizes social benefits while minimizing social costs (Schumann, 2001). When the U.S. government allocates a large part of the federal budget for preventive health care rather than for catastrophic illnesses, it is acting from a utilitarian perspective, putting money where it will have the best result for the largest number of citizens.

Closely related to utilitarianism, and opposite of ethical egoism, is a third teleological approach, *altruism*. Altruism is an approach that suggests that actions are moral if their primary purpose is to promote the best interests of others. From this perspective, a leader may be called on to act in the interests of others, even when it runs contrary to his or her own self-interests (Bowie, 1991). Authentic transformational leadership (Chapter 8) is based on altruistic principles (Bass & Steidlmeier, 1999; Kanungo & Mendonca, 1996) and altruism is pivotal to exhibiting servant leadership (Chapter 10). The strongest example of altruist ethics can be found in the work of Mother Teresa, who devoted her life to helping the poor.

Quite different from looking at which actions will produce which outcomes, deontological theory is derived from the Greek word *deos*, which means "duty." Whether a given action is ethical rests not only with its consequences (teleological), but also with whether the action itself is good. Telling the truth, keeping promises, being fair, and respecting others are all examples of actions that are inherently good, independent of the consequences. The deontological perspective focuses on the actions of the leader and his or her moral obligations and responsibilities to do the right thing. A leader's actions are moral if the leader has a moral right to do them, if the actions do not infringe on others' rights, and if the actions further the moral rights of others (Schumann, 2001).

In the late 1990s, the president of the United States, Bill Clinton, was brought before Congress for misrepresenting under oath an affair he had maintained with a White House intern. For his actions, he was impeached by the U.S. House of Representatives, but then was acquitted by the U.S. Senate. At one point during the long ordeal, the president appeared on national television and, in what is now a famous speech, declared his innocence. Because subsequent hearings provided information that suggested that he may have lied during this television speech, many Americans felt President Clinton had violated his duty and responsibility (as a person, leader, and president) to tell the truth. From a deontological perspective, it could be said that he failed his ethical responsibility to do the right thing—to tell the truth.

Whereas teleological and deontological theories approach ethics by looking at the behavior or conduct of a leader, a second set of theories approaches ethics from the viewpoint of a leader's character (see Table 13.2). These theories are called virtue-based theories; they focus on who leaders are as people. In this perspective, virtues are rooted in the heart of the individual and in the individual's disposition (Pojman, 1995). Furthermore, it is believed that virtues and moral abilities are not innate but can be acquired and learned through practice. People can be taught by their families and communities to be morally appropriate human beings.

N Approaches to Ethical Leadership

With their origin traced back in the Western tradition to the ancient Greeks and the works of Plato and Aristotle, virtue theories are experiencing a resurgence in popularity. The Greek term associated with these theories is *aretaic*, which means "excellence" or "virtue." Consistent with Aristotle, current advocates of virtue-based theory stress that more attention should be given to the development and training of moral values (Velasquez, 1992). Rather than telling people what to *do*, attention should be directed toward telling people what to *be*, or helping them to become more virtuous.

What, then, are the virtues of an ethical person? There are many, all of which seem to be important. Based on the writings of Aristotle, a moral person demonstrates the virtues of courage, temperance, generosity, self-control, honesty, sociability, modesty, fairness, and justice (Velasquez, 1992). For Aristotle, virtues allowed people to live well in communities. Applying ethics to leadership and management, Velasquez has suggested that managers should develop virtues such as perseverance, public-spiritedness, integrity, truthfulness, fidelity, benevolence, and humility.

In essence, virtue-based ethics is about being and becoming a good, worthy human being. Although people can learn and develop good values, this theory maintains that virtues are present in one's disposition. When practiced over time, from youth to adulthood, good values become habitual, and part of the people themselves. By telling the truth, people become truthful; by giving to the poor, people become benevolent; by being fair to others, people become just. Our virtues are derived from our actions, and our actions manifest our virtues (Frankena, 1973; Pojman, 1995).

Centrality of Ethics to Leadership

As discussed in Chapter 1, leadership is a process whereby the leader influences others to reach a common goal. The *influence* dimension of leadership requires the leader to have an impact on the lives of those being led. To make a change in other people carries with it an enormous ethical burden and responsibility. Because leaders usually have more power and control than followers, they also have more responsibility to be sensitive to how their leadership affects followers' lives.

Whether in group work, organizational pursuits, or community projects, leaders engage followers and utilize them in their efforts to reach common goals. In all these situations, leaders have the ethical responsibility to treat followers with dignity and respect—as human beings with unique identities. This "respect for people" demands that leaders be sensitive to followers' own

▶ Integrity Drives Growth

interests, needs, and conscientious concerns (Beauchamp & Bowie, 1988). Although all of us have an ethical responsibility to treat other people as unique human beings, leaders have a special responsibility, because the nature of their leadership puts them in a special position in which they have a greater opportunity to influence others in significant ways.

Ethics is central to leadership, and leaders help to establish and reinforce organizational values. Every leader has a distinct philosophy and point of view. "All leaders have an agenda, a series of beliefs, proposals, values, ideas, and issues that they wish to 'put on the table'" (Gini, 1998, p. 36). The values promoted by the leader have a significant impact on the values exhibited by the organization (see Carlson & Perrewe, 1995; Schminke, Ambrose, & Noel, 1997; Trevino, 1986). Again, because of their influence, leaders play a major role in establishing the ethical climate of their organizations.

In short, ethics is central to leadership because of the nature of the process of influence, the need to engage followers in accomplishing mutual goals, and the impact leaders have on the organization's values.

The following section provides a discussion of some of the work of prominent leadership scholars who have addressed issues related to ethics and leadership. Although many additional viewpoints exist, those presented are representative of the predominant thinking in the area of ethics and leadership today.

Heifetz's Perspective on Ethical Leadership

Based on his work as a psychiatrist and his observations and analysis of many world leaders (e.g., President Lyndon Johnson, Mohandas Gandhi, and Margaret Sanger), Ronald Heifetz (1994) has formulated a unique approach to ethical leadership. His approach emphasizes how leaders help followers to confront conflict and to address conflict by effecting changes. Heifetz's perspective is related to ethical leadership because it deals with values: the values of workers and the values of the organizations and communities in which they work. According to Heifetz, leadership involves the use of authority to help followers deal with the conflicting values that emerge in rapidly changing work environments and social cultures. It is an ethical perspective because it speaks directly to the values of workers.

For Heifetz (1994), leaders must use authority to mobilize people to face tough issues. As was discussed in the chapter on adaptive leadership (Chapter 11), it is up to the leader to provide a "holding environment" in

 Ethical Norms

which there is trust, nurturance, and empathy. In a supportive context, followers can feel safe to confront hard problems. Specifically, leaders use authority to get people to pay attention to the issues, to act as a reality test regarding information, to manage and frame issues, to orchestrate conflicting perspectives, and to facilitate decision making (Heifetz, 1994, p. 113). The leader's duties are to assist the follower in struggling with change and personal growth.

Burns's Perspective on Ethical Leadership

As discussed in Chapter 8, Burns's theory of transformational leadership places a strong emphasis on followers' needs, values, and morals. Transformational leadership involves attempts by leaders to move followers to higher standards of moral responsibility. This emphasis sets transformational leadership apart from most other approaches to leadership because it clearly states that leadership has a moral dimension (see Bass & Steidlmeier, 1999).

Similar to that of Heifetz, Burns's (1978) perspective argues that it is important for leaders to engage themselves with followers and help them in their personal struggles regarding conflicting values. The resulting connection raises the level of morality in both the leader and the follower.

The origins of Burns's position on leadership ethics are rooted in the works of such writers as Abraham Maslow, Milton Rokeach, and Lawrence Kohlberg (Ciulla, 1998). The influence of these writers can be seen in how Burns emphasizes the leader's role in attending to the personal motivations and moral development of the follower. For Burns, it is the responsibility of the leader to help followers assess their own values and needs in order to raise them to a higher level of functioning, to a level that will stress values such as liberty, justice, and equality (Ciulla, 1998).

Burns's position on leadership as a morally uplifting process has not been without its critics. It has raised many questions: How do you choose what a better set of moral values is? Who is to say that some decisions represent higher moral ground than others? If leadership, by definition, entails raising individual moral functioning, does this mean that the leadership of corrupt leaders is not actually leadership? Notwithstanding these very legitimate questions, Burns's perspective is unique in that it makes ethics the central characteristic of the leadership process. His writing has placed ethics at the forefront of scholarly discussions of what leadership means and how leadership should be carried out.

Teaching Ethical Leadership

The Dark Side of Leadership

Although Burns (1978) placed ethics at the core of leadership, there still exists a dark side of leadership that exemplifies leadership that is unethical and destructive. It is what we defined in Chapter 8 ("Transformational Leadership") as *pseudotransformational leadership*. The dark side of leadership is the destructive and toxic side of leadership in that a leader uses leadership for personal ends. Lipman-Blumen (2005) suggests that toxic leaders are characterized by destructive behaviors such as leaving their followers worse off than they found them, violating the basic human rights of others, and playing to their basest fears. Furthermore, Lipman-Blumen identifies many dysfunctional personal characteristics destructive leaders demonstrate including lack of integrity, insatiable ambition, arrogance, and reckless disregard for their actions. The same characteristics and behaviors that distinguish leaders as special can also be used by leaders to produce disastrous outcomes (Conger, 1990). Because researchers have been focused on the positive attributes and outcomes of effective leadership, until recently, there has been little attention paid to the dark side of leadership. Nevertheless, it is important to understand that it exists.

In a meta-analysis of 57 studies of destructive leadership and its outcomes, Schyns and Schilling (2013) found a strong relationship between destructive leadership and negative attitudes in followers toward the leader. Destructive leadership is also negatively related to followers' attitudes toward their jobs and toward their organization as a whole. Furthermore, Schyns and Schilling found it closely related to negative affectivity and to the experience of occupational stress.

In an attempt to more clearly define destructive leadership, Padilla, Hogan, and Kaiser (2007) developed the concept of a toxic triangle that focuses on the influences of destructive leaders, susceptible followers, and conducive environments (see Figure 13.2). As shown in the model, *destructive leaders* are characterized by having charisma and a need to use power and coercion for personal gains. They are also narcissistic and often attention-getting and self-absorbed. Destructive leaders often have negative life stories that can be traced to traumatic childhood events. Perhaps from self-hatred, they often express an ideology of hate in their rhetoric and worldview.

As illustrated in Figure 13.2, destructive leadership also incorporates *susceptible followers* who have been characterized as *conformers* and *colluders*. *Conformers* go along with destructive leaders to satisfy unmet needs such as emptiness, alienation, or need for community. These followers have low self-esteem and identify with charismatic leaders in an attempt to become more

 The Dark Side of Leadership

Figure 13.2 The Toxic Triangle

SOURCE: Padilla, A., Hogan, R., & Kaiser, R. B. (2007). The toxic triangle: Destructive leaders, susceptible followers, and conducive environments. *The Leadership Quarterly, 18,* 180.

desirable. Because they are psychologically immature, conformers more easily go along with authority and engage in destructive activity. On the other hand, *colluders* may respond to destructive leaders because they are ambitious, desire status, or see an opportunity to profit. Colluders may also go along because they identify with the leader's beliefs and values, which may be unsocialized such as greed and selfishness.

Finally, the toxic triangle illustrates that destructive leadership includes a *conducive environment.* When the environment is unstable, the leader is often granted more authority to assert radical change. When there is a perceived threat, followers often accept assertive leadership. People are attracted to leaders who will stand up to the threats they feel in the environment. Destructive leaders who express compatible cultural values with followers are more likely to succeed. For example, cultures high on collectiveness would prefer a leader who promotes community and group identity. Destructive

 Opportunism and Ethics

leadership will also thrive when the checks and balances of the organization are weak and the rules of the institution are ineffective.

Although research on the dark side of leadership has been limited, it is an area critical to our understanding of leadership that is unethical. Clearly, there is a need for the development of models, theories, and assessment instruments about the process of destructive leadership.

Principles of Ethical Leadership

In this section, we turn to a discussion of five principles of ethical leadership, the origins of which can be traced back to Aristotle. The importance of these principles has been discussed in a variety of disciplines, including biomedical ethics (Beauchamp & Childress, 1994), business ethics (Beauchamp & Bowie, 1988), counseling psychology (Kitchener, 1984), and leadership education (Komives, Lucas, & McMahon, 1998), to name a few. Although not inclusive, these principles provide a foundation for the development of sound ethical leadership: *respect, service, justice, honesty,* and *community* (Figure 13.3).

Figure 13.3   Principles of Ethical Leadership

Ethical Leaders Respect Others

Philosopher Immanuel Kant (1724–1804) argued that it is our duty to treat others with respect. To do so means always to treat others as ends in

 Practical Ethical Theory

themselves and never as means to ends. As Beauchamp and Bowie (1988, p. 37) pointed out, "Persons must be treated as having their own autonomously established goals and must never be treated purely as the means to another's personal goals." These writers then suggested that treating others as ends rather than as means requires that we treat other people's decisions and values with respect: Failing to do so would signify that we were treating them as a means to our own ends.

Leaders who respect others also allow them to be themselves, with creative wants and desires. They approach other people with a sense of their unconditional worth and valuable individual differences (Kitchener, 1984). Respect includes giving credence to others' ideas and confirming them as human beings. At times, it may require that leaders defer to others. As Burns (1978) suggested, leaders should nurture followers in becoming aware of their own needs, values, and purposes, and assist followers in integrating these with the leader's needs, values, and purposes.

Respect for others is a complex ethic that is similar to but goes deeper than the kind of respect that parents teach little children. Respect means that a leader listens closely to followers, is empathic, and is tolerant of opposing points of view. It means treating followers in ways that confirm their beliefs, attitudes, and values. When a leader exhibits respect to followers, followers can feel competent about their work. In short, leaders who show respect treat others as worthy human beings.

Ethical Leaders Serve Others

Earlier in this chapter, we contrasted two ethical theories, one based on a concern for self (ethical egoism) and another based on the interests of others (ethical altruism). The service principle clearly is an example of altruism. Leaders who serve are altruistic: They place their followers' welfare foremost in their plans. In the workplace, altruistic service behavior can be observed in activities such as mentoring, empowerment behaviors, team building, and citizenship behaviors, to name a few (Kanungo & Mendonca, 1996).

The leader's ethical responsibility to serve others is very similar to the ethical principle in health care of beneficence. Beneficence is derived from the Hippocratic tradition, which holds that health professionals ought to make choices that benefit patients. In a general way, beneficence asserts that providers have a duty to help others pursue their own legitimate interests and goals (Beauchamp & Childress, 1994). Like health professionals, ethical

Ethical School Leadership

leaders have a responsibility to attend to others, be of service to them, and make decisions pertaining to them that are beneficial and not harmful to their welfare.

In the past decade, the service principle has received a great deal of emphasis in the leadership literature. It is clearly evident in the writings of Block (1993), Covey (1990), De Pree (1989), Gilligan (1982), and Kouzes and Posner (1995), all of whom maintained that attending to others is the primary building block of moral leadership. Further emphasis on service can be observed in the work of Senge (1990) in his well-recognized writing on learning organizations. Senge contended that one of the important tasks of leaders in learning organizations is to be the steward (servant) of the vision within the organization. Being a steward means clarifying and nurturing a vision that is greater than oneself. This means not being self-centered, but rather integrating one's self or vision with that of others in the organization. Effective leaders see their own personal vision as an important part of something larger than themselves—a part of the organization and the community at large.

The idea of leaders serving others was more deeply explored by Robert Greenleaf (1970, 1977), who developed the *servant leadership* approach. Servant leadership, which is explored in depth in Chapter 10, has strong altruistic ethical overtones in how it emphasizes that leaders should be attentive to the concerns of their followers and should take care of them and nurture them. In addition, Greenleaf argues that the servant leader has a social responsibility to be concerned with the have-nots and should strive to remove inequalities and social injustices. Greenleaf places a great deal of emphasis on listening, empathy, and unconditional acceptance of others.

In short, whether it is Greenleaf's notion of waiting on the have-nots or Senge's notion of giving oneself to a larger purpose, the idea behind service is contributing to the greater good of others. Recently, the idea of serving the "greater good" has found an unusual following in the business world. In 2009, 20% of the graduating class of the Harvard Business School, considered to be one of the premier schools producing today's business leaders, took an oath pledging that they will act responsibly and ethically, and refrain from advancing their own ambitions at the expense of others. Similarly, Columbia Business School requires all students to pledge to an honor code requiring they adhere to truth, integrity, and respect (Wayne, 2009). In practicing the principle of service, these and other ethical leaders must be willing to be follower centered, must place others' interests foremost in their work, and must act in ways that will benefit others.

Ethical Leaders Are Just

Ethical leaders are concerned about issues of fairness and justice. They make it a top priority to treat all of their followers in an equal manner. Justice demands that leaders place issues of fairness at the center of their decision making. As a rule, no one should receive special treatment or special consideration except when his or her particular situation demands it. When individuals are treated differently, the grounds for different treatment must be clear and reasonable, and must be based on moral values.

For example, many of us can remember being involved with some type of athletic team when we were growing up. The coaches we liked were those we thought were fair with us. No matter what, we did not want the coach to treat anyone differently from the rest. When someone came late to practice with a poor excuse, we wanted that person disciplined just as we would have been disciplined. If a player had a personal problem and needed a break, we wanted the coach to give it, just as we would have been given a break. Without question, the good coaches were those who never had favorites and who made a point of playing everyone on the team. In essence, what we wanted was that our coach be fair and just.

When resources and rewards or punishments are distributed to employees, the leader plays a major role. The rules that are used and how they are applied say a great deal about whether the leader is concerned about justice and how he or she approaches issues of fairness.

Rawls (1971) stated that a concern with issues of fairness is necessary for all people who are cooperating together to promote their common interests. It is similar to the ethic of reciprocity, otherwise known as the Golden Rule—"Do unto others as you would have them do unto you"—variations of which have appeared in many different cultures throughout the ages. If we expect fairness from others in how they treat us, then we should treat others fairly in our dealings with them. Issues of fairness become problematic because there is always a limit on goods and resources, and there is often competition for the limited things available. Because of the real or perceived scarcity of resources, conflicts often occur between individuals about fair methods of distribution. It is important for leaders to clearly establish the rules for distributing rewards. The nature of these rules says a lot about the ethical underpinnings of the leader and the organization.

Beauchamp and Bowie (1988) outlined several of the common principles that serve as guides for leaders in distributing the benefits and burdens fairly in an organization (Table 13.3). Although not inclusive, these principles point to the reasoning behind why leaders choose to distribute things as they

 Ethics in Management   Ethics in Nursing

do in organizations. In a given situation, a leader may use a single principle or a combination of several principles in treating followers.

To illustrate the principles described in Table 13.3, consider the following hypothetical example: You are the owner of a small trucking company that employs 50 drivers. You have just opened a new route, and it promises to be one that pays well and has an ideal schedule. Only one driver can be assigned to the route, but seven drivers have applied for it. Each driver wants an *equal opportunity* to get the route. One of the drivers recently lost his wife to breast cancer and is struggling to care for three young children (*individual need*). Two of the drivers are minorities, and one of them feels strongly that he has a *right* to the job. One of the drivers has logged more driving hours for three consecutive years, and she feels her *effort* makes her the logical candidate for the new route. One of the drivers serves on the National Transportation Safety Board and has a 20-year accident-free driving record (*societal contribution*). Two drivers have been with the company since its inception, and their *performance* has been meritorious year after year.

As the owner of the company, your challenge is to assign the new route in a fair way. Although many other factors could influence your decision (e.g., seniority, wage rate, or employee health), the principles described in Table 13.3 provide guidelines for deciding who is to get the new route.

Table 13.3   Principles of Distributive Justice

These principles are applied in different situations.

To each person

- An equal share or opportunity
- According to individual need
- According to that person's rights
- According to individual effort
- According to societal contribution
- According to merit or performance

Ethical Leaders Are Honest

When we were children, grown-ups often told us we must "never tell a lie." To be good meant we must be truthful. For leaders the lesson is the same: To be a good leader, one must be honest.

The importance of being honest can be understood more clearly when we consider the opposite of honesty: dishonesty (see Jaksa & Pritchard, 1988). Dishonesty is a form of lying, a way of misrepresenting reality. Dishonesty may bring with it many objectionable outcomes; foremost among those outcomes

 Developing Leadership Character

is the distrust it creates. When leaders are not honest, others come to see them as undependable and unreliable. People lose faith in what leaders say and stand for, and their respect for leaders is diminished. As a result, the leader's impact is compromised because others no longer trust and believe in the leader.

When we relate to others, dishonesty also has a negative impact. It puts a strain on how people are connected to each other. When we lie to others, we are in essence saying that we are willing to manipulate the relationship on our own terms. We are saying that we do not trust the other person in the relationship to be able to deal with information we have. In reality, we are putting ourselves ahead of the relationship by saying that we know what is best for the relationship. The long-term effect of this type of behavior is that it weakens relationships. Even when used with good intentions, dishonesty contributes to the breakdown of relationships.

But being honest is not just about telling the truth. It has to do with being open with others and representing reality as fully and completely as possible. This is not an easy task, however, because there are times when telling the complete truth can be destructive or counterproductive. The challenge for leaders is to strike a balance between being open and candid while monitoring what is appropriate to disclose in a particular situation. Many times, there are organizational constraints that prevent leaders from disclosing information to followers. It is important for leaders to be authentic, but it is also essential that they be sensitive to the attitudes and feelings of others. Honest leadership involves a wide set of behaviors.

Dalla Costa (1998) made the point clearly in his book, *The Ethical Imperative*, that being honest means more than not deceiving. For leaders in organizations, being honest means, "Do not promise what you can't deliver, do not misrepresent, do not hide behind spin-doctored evasions, do not suppress obligations, do not evade accountability, do not accept that the 'survival of the fittest' pressures of business release any of us from the responsibility to respect another's dignity and humanity" (p. 164). In addition, Dalla Costa suggested that it is imperative that organizations recognize and acknowledge the necessity of honesty and reward honest behavior within the organization.

Ethical Leaders Build Community

In Chapter 1, we defined leadership as a process whereby an individual influences a group of individuals to achieve a common goal. This definition has a clear ethical dimension because it refers to a *common* goal. A common goal requires that the leader and followers agree on the direction to be taken by

Group Ethical Voice

the group. Leaders need to take into account their own and followers' purposes while working toward goals that are suitable for both of them. This factor, concern for others, is the distinctive feature that delineates *authentic* transformational leaders from *pseudo*transformational leaders (Bass & Steidlmeier, 1999) (for more on pseudotransformational leadership see page 163 in Chapter 8). Concern for the common good means that leaders cannot impose their will on others. They need to search for goals that are compatible with everyone.

Burns (1978) placed this idea at the center of his theory on transformational leadership. A transformational leader tries to move the group toward a common good that is beneficial for both the leaders and the followers. In moving toward mutual goals, both the leader and the followers are changed. It is this feature that makes Burns's theory unique. For Burns, leadership has to be grounded in the leader–follower relationship. It cannot be controlled by the leader, such as Hitler's influence in Germany. Hitler coerced people to meet his own agenda and followed goals that did not advance the goodness of humankind.

An ethical leader takes into account the purposes of everyone involved in the group and is attentive to the interests of the community and the culture. Such a leader demonstrates an ethic of caring toward others (Gilligan, 1982) and does not force others or ignore the intentions of others (Bass & Steidlmeier, 1999).

Rost (1991) went a step farther and suggested that ethical leadership demands attention to a civic virtue. By this, he meant that leaders and followers need to attend to more than their own mutually determined goals. They need to attend to the *community's* goals and purpose. As Burns (1978, p. 429) wrote, transformational leaders and followers begin to reach out to wider social collectivities and seek to establish higher and broader moral purposes. Similarly, Greenleaf (1970) argued that building community was a main characteristic of servant leadership. All of our individual and group goals are bound up in the common good and public interest. We need to pay attention to how the changes proposed by a leader and followers will affect the larger organization, the community, and society. An ethical leader is concerned with the common good, in the broadest sense.

STRENGTHS

This chapter discusses a broad set of ideas regarding ethics and leadership. This general field of study has several strengths. First, it provides a body

 Ethical Role of Management

of timely research on ethical issues. There is a high demand for moral leadership in our society today. Beginning with the Nixon administration in the 1970s and continuing through Barack Obama's administration, people have been insisting on higher levels of moral responsibility from their leaders. At a time when there seems to be a vacuum in ethical leadership, this research offers us some direction on how to think about and practice ethical leadership.

Second, this body of research suggests that ethics ought to be considered as an integral part of the broader domain of leadership. Except for servant, transformational, and authentic leadership, none of the other leadership theories discussed in this book includes ethics as a dimension of the leadership process. This chapter suggests that leadership is not an amoral phenomenon. Leadership is a process of influencing others; it has a moral dimension that distinguishes it from other types of influence, such as coercion or despotic control. Leadership involves values, including showing respect for followers, being fair to others, and building community. It is not a process that we can demonstrate without showing our values. When we influence, we have an effect on others, which means we need to pay attention to our values and our ethics.

Third, this body of research highlights several principles that are important to the development of ethical leadership. The virtues discussed in this research have been around for more than 2,000 years. They are reviewed in this chapter because of their significance for today's leaders.

CRITICISMS

Although the area of ethics and leadership has many strengths, it also has some weaknesses. First, it is an area of research in its early stage of development, and therefore lacks a strong body of traditional research findings to substantiate it. As was pointed out at the beginning of the chapter, very little research has been published on the theoretical foundations of leadership ethics. Although many studies have been published on business ethics, these studies have not been directly related to ethical leadership. The dearth of research on leadership ethics makes speculation about the nature of ethical leadership difficult. Until more research studies have been conducted that deal directly with the ethical dimensions of leadership, theoretical formulations about the process will remain tentative.

Another criticism is that leadership ethics today relies primarily on the writings of just a few people who have written essays and texts that are

 Ethical Issues in Nursing

strongly influenced by their personal opinions about the nature of leadership ethics and their view of the world. Although these writings, such as Heifetz's and Burns's, have stood the test of time, they have not been tested using traditional quantitative or qualitative research methods. They are primarily descriptive and anecdotal. Therefore, leadership ethics lacks the traditional kind of empirical support that usually accompanies accepted theories of human behavior.

APPLICATION

Although issues of morality and leadership are discussed more often in society today, these discussions have not resulted in a large number of programs in training and development designed to teach ethical leadership. Many new programs are oriented toward helping managers become more effective at work and in life in general, but these programs do not directly target the area of ethics and leadership.

Yet the ethics and leadership research in this chapter can be applied to people at all levels of organizations and in all walks of life. At a very minimum, it is crucial to state that *leadership involves values,* and one cannot be a leader without being aware of and concerned about one's own values. Because leadership has a moral dimension, being a leader demands awareness on our part of the way our ethics defines our leadership.

Managers and leaders can use the information in this research to better understand themselves and strengthen their own leadership. Ethical theories can remind leaders to ask themselves, "What is the right and fair thing to do?" or "What would a good person do?" Leaders can use the ethical principles described in this research as benchmarks for their own behavior. Do I show respect to others? Do I act with a generous spirit? Do I show honesty and faithfulness to others? Do I serve the community? Finally, we can learn from the overriding theme in this research that the leader–follower relationship is central to ethical leadership. To be an ethical leader, we must be sensitive to the needs of others, treat others in ways that are just, and care for others.

CASE STUDIES

The following section contains three case studies (Cases 13.1, 13.2, and 13.3) in which ethical leadership is needed. Case 13.1 describes a department chair

 Ethical Case Study

who must choose which student will get a special assignment. Case 13.2 is concerned with one manufacturing company's unique approach to safety standards. Case 13.3 deals with the ethical issues surrounding how a human resource service company established the pricing for its services. At the end of each case, there are questions that point to the intricacies and complexities of practicing ethical leadership.

CASE 13.1

Choosing a Research Assistant

Dr. Angi Dirks is the chair of the state university's organizational psychology department, which has four teaching assistants (TAs). Angi has just found out that she has received a grant for research work over the summer and that it includes money to fund one of the TAs as her research assistant. In Angi's mind, the top two candidates are Roberto and Michelle, who are both available to work over the summer. Roberto, a foreign student from Venezuela, has gotten very high teaching evaluations and is well liked by the faculty. Roberto needs a summer job to help pay for school since it is too expensive for him to return home for the summer to work. Michelle is also an exceptional graduate student; she is married and doesn't necessarily need the extra income, but she is going to pursue a PhD, so the extra experience would be beneficial to her future endeavors.

A third teaching assistant, Carson, commutes to school from a town an hour away, where he is helping to take care of his aging grandparents. Carson manages to juggle school, teaching, and his home responsibilities well, carrying a 4.0 GPA in his classwork. Angi knows Carson could use the money, but she is afraid that he has too many other responsibilities to take on the research project over the summer.

As Angi weighs which TA to offer the position, a faculty member approaches her about considering the fourth TA, Analisa. It's been a tough year with Analisa as a TA. She has complained numerous times to her faculty mentor and to Angi that the other TAs treat her differently, and she thinks it's because of her race. The student newspaper printed a column she wrote about "being a speck of brown in a campus of white," in which she expressed her frustration with the predominantly white faculty's inability to understand the unique perspectives and experiences of minority students. After the column came out, the faculty in the department became wary of working with Analisa, fearing becoming part of the controversy. Their lack of interaction with her made Analisa feel further alienated.

Angi knows that Analisa is a very good researcher and writer, and her skills would be an asset to the project. Analisa's faculty mentor says that giving the position to her would go a long way to "smooth things over" between faculty and Analisa and make Analisa feel included in the department. Analisa knows about the open position and has expressed interest in it to her faculty mentor, but hasn't directly talked to Angi. Angi is afraid that by not giving it to Analisa, she may stir up more accusations of ill treatment while at the same time facing accusations from others that she is giving Analisa preferential treatment.

1. Of the four options available to Angi, which is the most ethical?

2. Using the principles of distributive justice, who would Angi choose to become the research assistant?

3. From Heifetz's perspective, can Angi use this decision to help her department and faculty face a difficult situation? Should she?

4. Do you agree with Burns's perspective that it is Angi's responsibility to help followers assess their own values and needs in order to raise them to a higher level that will stress values such as liberty, justice, and equality? If so, how can Angi do that through this situation?

CASE 13.2

How Safe Is Safe?

Perfect Plastics Incorporated (PPI) is a small injection molding plastics company that employs 50 people. The company is 10 years old, has a healthy balance sheet, and does about $4 million a year in sales. The company has a good safety record, and the insurance company that has PPI's liability policy has not had to pay any claims to employees for several years. There have been no major injuries of any kind since the company began.

Tom Griffin, the owner, takes great pride in the interior design and working conditions at PPI. He describes the interior of the plant as being like a hospital compared with his competitors. Order, efficiency, and cleanliness are top priorities at PPI. It is a remarkably well-organized manufacturing company.

PPI has a unique approach to guaranteeing safe working conditions. Each year, management brings in outside consultants from the insurance industry and the Occupational Safety and Health Administration (OSHA) to audit

(Continued)

(Continued)

the plant for unsafe conditions. Each year, the inspections reveal a variety of concerns, which are then addressed through new equipment, repairs, and changed work-flow designs. Although the inspectors continue to find opportunities for improvement, the overall safety improves each year.

The attorneys for PPI are very opposed to the company's approach to safety. The lawyers are vehemently against the procedure of having outside auditors. If a lawsuit were to be brought against PPI, the attorneys argue that any previous issues could be used as evidence of a historical pattern and knowledge of unsafe conditions. In effect, the audits that PPI conducts voluntarily could be used by plaintiffs to strengthen a case against the company.

The president and management recognize the potential downside of outside audits, but they point out that the periodic reviews are critical to the ongoing improvement of the safety of everyone in the plant. The purpose of the audits is to make the shop a secure place, and that is what has occurred. Management also points out that PPI employees have responded positively to the audits and to the changes that result.

Questions

1. As a company, would you describe PPI as having an identifiable philosophy of moral values? How do its policies contribute to this philosophy?

2. Which ethical perspective best describes PPI's approach to safety issues? Would you say PPI takes a utilitarian-, duty-, or virtue-based approach?

3. Regarding safety issues, how does management see its responsibilities toward its employees? How do the attorneys see their responsibilities toward PPI?

4. Why does it appear that the ethics of PPI and its attorneys are in conflict?

CASE 13.3

Reexamining a Proposal

After working 10 years as the only minority manager in a large printing company, David Jones decided he wanted to set out on his own. Because of his experience and prior connections, David was confident he could survive in the printing business, but he wondered whether he should buy an existing business or start a new one. As part of his planning, David contacted a professional employer organization (PEO), which had a sterling reputation, to obtain an estimate for human resource services for a startup company. The estimate was to include costs for payroll, benefits, workers' compensation, and other traditional human resource services. Because David had not yet started his business, the PEO generated a generic quote applicable to a small company in the printing industry. In addition, because the PEO had nothing tangible to quote, it gave David a quote for human resource services that was unusually high.

In the meantime, David found an existing small company that he liked, and he bought it. Then he contacted the PEO to sign a contract for human resource services at the previously quoted price. David was ready to take ownership and begin his new venture. He signed the original contract as presented.

After David signed the contract, the PEO reviewed the earlier proposal in light of the actual figures of the company he had purchased. This review raised many concerns for management. Although the goals of the PEO were to provide high-quality service, be competitive in the marketplace, and make a reasonable profit, the quote it had provided David appeared to be much too high. It was not comparable in any way with the other service contracts the PEO had with other companies of similar size and function.

During the review, it became apparent that several concerns had to be addressed. First, the original estimate made the PEO appear as if it was gouging the client. Although the client had signed the original contract, was it fair to charge such a high price for the proposed services? Would charging such high fees mean that the PEO would lose this client or similar clients in the future? Another concern was related to the PEO's support of minority businesses. For years, the PEO had prided itself on having strong values about affirmative action and fairness in the workplace, but this contract appeared to actually hurt and to be somewhat unfair to a minority client. Finally, the PEO was concerned with the implications of the contract for the salesperson who drew up the proposal for David. Changing the estimated costs in the proposal would have a significant impact on the salesperson's commission, which would negatively affect the morale of others in the PEO's sales area.

After a reexamination of the original proposal, a new contract was drawn up for David's company with lower estimated costs. Though lower than the original proposal, the new contract remained much higher than the average contract in the printing industry. David willingly signed the new contract.

(Continued)

(Continued)

Questions

1. What role should ethics play in the writing of a proposal such as this? Did the PEO do the ethical thing for David? How much money should the PEO have tried to make? What would you have done if you were part of management at the PEO?

2. From a deontological (duty) perspective and a teleological (consequences) perspective, how would you describe the ethics of the PEO?

3. Based on what the PEO did for David, how would you evaluate the PEO on the ethical principles of respect, service, justice, honesty, and community?

4. How would you assess the ethics of the PEO if you were David? If you were among the PEO management? If you were the salesperson? If you were a member of the printing community?

LEADERSHIP INSTRUMENT

Ethics and morals often are regarded as very personal, and we resist having others judge us about them. We also resist judging others. Perhaps for this reason, very few questionnaires have been designed to measure ethical leadership. To address this problem, Craig and Gustafson (1998) developed the Perceived Leader Integrity Scale (PLIS), which is based on utilitarian ethical theory. The PLIS attempts to evaluate leaders' ethics by measuring the degree to which coworkers see them as acting in accordance with rules that would produce the greatest good for the greatest number of people. Craig and Gustafson found PLIS ratings to be strongly and positively related to subordinates' job satisfaction, and negatively related to their desire to quit their jobs.

Parry and Proctor-Thomson (2002) used the PLIS in a study of 1,354 managers and found that perceived integrity was positively related to transformational leadership. Leaders who were seen as transformational were also seen as having more integrity. In addition, the researchers found that perceived integrity was positively correlated with leader and organizational effectiveness.

By taking the PLIS, you can try to assess the ethical integrity of a leader you know, such as a supervisor or leader of a group or organization of which you are a member. At the same time, the PLIS will allow you to apply the ideas we discussed in the chapter to a real-world setting. By focusing on observers' impressions, the PLIS represents one way to assess the principle of ethical leadership.

In addition, the PLIS can be used for feedback to employees in organizations and as a part of leadership training and development. Finally, if used as part of an organizational climate survey, the PLIS could be useful as a way of identifying areas in an organization that may need an ethics intervention (Craig & Gustafson, 1998).

Perceived Leader Integrity Scale (PLIS)

Instructions: The following items concern your perceptions of another person's behavior. Circle responses to indicate how well each item describes the person you are rating.

Key: 1 = Not at all   2 = Barely   3 = Somewhat   4 = Well

1. Puts his or her personal interests ahead of the organization — 1 2 3 4
2. Would risk other people to protect himself or herself in work matters — 1 2 3 4
3. Enjoys turning down requests — 1 2 3 4
4. Deliberately fuels conflict between other people — 1 2 3 4
5. Would blackmail an employee if she or he thought she or he could get away with it — 1 2 3 4
6. Would deliberately exaggerate people's mistakes to make them look bad to others — 1 2 3 4
7. Would treat some people better if they were of the other sex or belonged to a different ethnic group — 1 2 3 4
8. Ridicules people for their mistakes — 1 2 3 4
9. Can be trusted with confidential information — 1 2 3 4
10. Would lie to me — 1 2 3 4
11. Is evil — 1 2 3 4
12. Is not interested in tasks that don't bring personal glory or recognition — 1 2 3 4
13. Would do things that violate organizational policy and then expect others to cover for him or her — 1 2 3 4
14. Would allow someone else to be blamed for his or her mistake — 1 2 3 4
15. Would deliberately avoid responding to email, telephone, or other messages to cause problems for someone else — 1 2 3 4
16. Would make trouble for someone who got on his or her bad side — 1 2 3 4
17. Would engage in sabotage against the organization — 1 2 3 4

18.	Would deliberately distort what other people say	1	2	3	4
19.	Is a hypocrite	1	2	3	4
20.	Is vindictive	1	2	3	4
21.	Would try to take credit for other people's ideas	1	2	3	4
22.	Likes to bend the rules	1	2	3	4
23.	Would withhold information or constructive feedback because he or she wants someone to fail	1	2	3	4
24.	Would spread rumors or gossip to try to hurt people or the organization	1	2	3	4
25.	Is rude or uncivil to coworkers	1	2	3	4
26.	Would try to hurt someone's career because of a grudge	1	2	3	4
27.	Shows unfair favoritism toward some people	1	2	3	4
28.	Would steal from the organization	1	2	3	4
29.	Would falsify records if it would help his or her work situation	1	2	3	4
30.	Has high moral standards	1	2	3	4

SOURCE: Adapted from a version of the PLIS that appeared in *Leadership Quarterly*, 9(2), S. B. Craig and S. B. Gustafson, "Perceived Leader Integrity Scale: An Instrument for Assessing Employee Perceptions of Leader Integrity," pp. 143–144, 1998. Used with permission of the authors.

Scoring

The PLIS measures your perceptions of another person's integrity in an organizational setting. Your responses on the PLIS indicate the degree to which you see that person's behavior as ethical.

Score the questionnaire by doing the following. First, reverse the scores on items 9 and 30 (i.e., 1 becomes 4, 2 becomes 3, 3 becomes 2, and 4 becomes 1). Next, sum the responses on all 30 items. A low score on the questionnaire indicates that you perceive the person you evaluated to be highly ethical. A high score indicates that you perceive that person to be very unethical. The interpretation of what the score represents follows.

Scoring Interpretation

Your score is a measure of your perceptions of another person's ethical integrity. Based on previous findings (Craig & Gustafson, 1998), the following interpretations can be made about your total score:

- 30–32 High ethical: If your score is in this range, it means that you see the person you evaluated as highly ethical. Your impression is that the person is very trustworthy and principled.

- 33–45 Moderate ethical: Scores in this range mean that you see the person as moderately ethical. Your impression is that the person might engage in some unethical behaviors under certain conditions.

- 46–120 Low ethical: Scores in this range describe people who are seen as very unethical. Your impression is that the person you evaluated does things that are dishonest, unfair, and unprincipled almost any time he or she has the opportunity.

SUMMARY

Although there has been an interest in ethics for thousands of years, very little theoretical research exists on the nature of leadership ethics. This chapter has presented an overview of ethical theories as they apply to the leadership process.

Ethical theory provides a set of principles that guide leaders in making decisions about how to act and how to be morally decent. In the Western tradition, ethical theories typically are divided into two kinds: theories about *conduct* and theories about *character*. Theories about conduct emphasize the consequences of leader behavior (teleological approach) or the rules that govern their behavior (deontological approach). Virtue-based theories focus on the character of leaders, and they stress qualities such as courage, honesty, fairness, and fidelity.

Ethics plays a central role in the leadership process. Because leadership involves influence and leaders often have more power than followers, they have an enormous ethical responsibility for how they affect other people. Leaders need to engage followers to accomplish mutual goals; therefore, it is imperative that they treat followers and their ideas with respect and dignity. Leaders also play a major role in establishing the ethical climate in their organization; that role requires leaders to be particularly sensitive to the values and ideals they promote.

Several prominent leadership scholars, including Heifetz, Burns, and Greenleaf, have made unique contributions to our understanding of ethical leadership. The theme common to these authors is an ethic of caring, which pays attention to followers' needs and the importance of leader–follower relationships.

This chapter suggests that sound ethical leadership is rooted in respect, service, justice, honesty, and community. It is the duty of leaders to treat others with *respect*—to listen to them closely and be tolerant of opposing points of view. Ethical leaders *serve* others by being altruistic, placing others' welfare ahead of their own in an effort to contribute to the common good. *Justice* requires that leaders place fairness at the center of their decision making, including the challenging task of being fair to the individual while simultaneously being fair to the common interests of the community. Good leaders are *honest*. They do not lie, nor do they present truth to others in ways that are destructive or counterproductive. Finally, ethical leaders are committed to building *community*, which includes searching for goals that are compatible with the goals of followers and with society as a whole.

Research on ethics and leadership has several strengths. At a time when the public is demanding higher levels of moral responsibility from its leaders, this research provides some direction in how to think about ethical leadership and how to practice it. In addition, this research reminds us that leadership is a moral process. Scholars should include ethics as an integral part of the leadership studies and research. Third, this area of research describes basic principles that we can use in developing real-world ethical leadership.

On the negative side, this research area of ethical leadership is still in an early stage of development. Few studies have been done that directly address the nature of ethical leadership. As a result, the theoretical formulations about the process remain tentative. Second, this area of research relies on the writings of a few individuals whose work has been primarily descriptive and anecdotal. As a result, the development of theory on leadership ethics lacks the traditional empirical support that usually accompanies theories of human behavior. Despite these weaknesses, the field of ethical leadership is wide open for future research. There remains a strong need for research that can advance our understanding of the role of ethics in the leadership process.

Sharpen your skills with SAGE edge at **edge.sagepub.com/northouse7e**

REFERENCES

Aronson, E. (2001). Integrating leadership styles and ethical perspectives. *Canadian Journal of Administrative Sciences, 18*(4), 244–256.

Avolio, B. J., & Locke, E. E. (2002). Contrasting different philosophies of leader motivation: Altruism versus egoism. *Leadership Quarterly, 13,* 169–191.

Bass, B. M., & Steidlmeier, P. (1999). Ethics, character, and authentic transformational leadership behavior. *Leadership Quarterly, 10*(2), 181–217.

Beauchamp, T. L., & Bowie, N. E. (1988). *Ethical theory and business* (3rd ed.). Englewood Cliffs, NJ: Prentice Hall.

Beauchamp, T. L., & Childress, J. F. (1994). *Principles of biomedical ethics* (4th ed.). New York: Oxford University Press.

Block, P. (1993). *Stewardship: Choosing service over self-interest.* San Francisco: Berrett-Koehler.

Bowie, N. E. (1991). Challenging the egoistic paradigm. *Business Ethics Quarterly, 1*(1), 1–21.

Burns, J. M. (1978). *Leadership.* New York: Harper & Row.

Carlson, D. S., & Perrewe, P. L. (1995). Institutionalization of organizational ethics through transformational leadership. *Journal of Business Ethics, 14*(10), 829–838.

Ciulla, J. B. (1998). *Ethics, the heart of leadership.* Westport, CT: Greenwood.

Ciulla, J. B. (2001). Carving leaders from the warped wood of humanity. *Canadian Journal of Administrative Sciences, 18*(4), 313–319.

Ciulla, J. B. (2003). *The ethics of leadership.* Belmont, CA: Wadsworth/Thomson Learning.

Conger, J. (1990). The dark side of leadership. *Organizational Dynamics, 19,* 44–55.

Covey, S. R. (1990). *Principle-centered leadership.* New York: Fireside.

Craig, S. B., & Gustafson, S. B. (1998). Perceived Leader Integrity Scale: An instrument for assessing employee perceptions of leader integrity. *Leadership Quarterly, 9*(2), 127–145.

Crain, W. C. (1985). Kohlberg's stages of moral development. In W. C. Crain (Ed.), *Theories of development: Concepts and applications* (pp. 118–136). New York: Prentice-Hall.

Dalla Costa, J. (1998). *The ethical imperative: Why moral leadership is good business.* Reading, MA: Addison-Wesley.

De Pree, M. (1989). *Leadership is an art.* New York: Doubleday.

Frankena, W. (1973). *Ethics* (2nd ed.). Englewood Cliffs, NJ: Prentice Hall.

Gilligan, C. (1982). *In a different voice: Psychological theory and women's development.* Cambridge, MA: Harvard University Press.

Gini, A. (1998). Moral leadership and business ethics. In J. B. Ciulla (Ed.), *Ethics, the heart of leadership* (pp. 27–46). Westport, CT: Greenwood.

Greenleaf, R. K. (1970). *The servant as leader.* Newton Centre, MA: Robert K. Greenleaf Center.

Greenleaf, R. K. (1977). *Servant leadership: A journey into the nature of legitimate power and greatness.* New York: Paulist.

Heifetz, R. A. (1994). *Leadership without easy answers.* Cambridge, MA: Harvard University Press.

Jaksa, J. A., & Pritchard, M. S. (1988). *Communication ethics: Methods of analysis.* Belmont, CA: Wadsworth.

Johnson, C. R. (2011). *Meeting the ethical challenges of leadership* (4th ed.). Thousand Oaks, CA: SAGE.

Kanungo, R. N. (2001). Ethical values of transactional and transformational leaders. *Canadian Journal of Administrative Sciences, 18*(4), 257–265.

Kanungo, R. N., & Mendonca, M. (1996). *Ethical dimensions of leadership.* Thousand Oaks, CA: SAGE.

Kitchener, K. S. (1984). Intuition, critical evaluation, and ethical principles: The foundation for ethical decisions in counseling psychology. *Counseling Psychologist, 12*(3), 43–55.

Kohlberg, L. (1984). *Essays on moral development, Vol. 2: The psychology of moral development.* New York: Harper & Row.

Komives, S. R., Lucas, N., & McMahon, T. R. (1998). *Exploring leadership: For college students who want to make a difference.* San Francisco: Jossey-Bass.

Kouzes, J. M., & Posner, B. Z. (1995). *The leadership challenge: How to keep getting extraordinary things done in organizations* (2nd ed.). San Francisco: Jossey-Bass.

Lipman-Blumen, J. (2005). *The allure of toxic leaders.* New York: Oxford University Press.

Padilla, A., Hogan, R., & Kaiser, R. B. (2007). The toxic triangle: Destructive leaders, susceptible followers, and conducive environments. *The Leadership Quarterly, 18,* 176–194.

Parry, K. W., & Proctor-Thomson, S. B. (2002). Perceived integrity of transformational leaders in organisational settings. *Journal of Business Ethics, 35,* 75–96.

Pojman, L. P. (1995). *Ethical theory: Classical and contemporary readings* (2nd ed.). Belmont, CA: Wadsworth.

Price, T. (2008). *Leadership ethics: An introduction.* New York: Cambridge University Press.

Rawls, J. (1971). *A theory of justice.* Boston: Harvard University Press.

Rost, J. C. (1991). *Leadership for the twenty-first century.* New York: Praeger.

Schminke, M., Ambrose, M. L., & Noel, T. W. (1997). The effect of ethical frameworks on perceptions of organizational justice. *Academy of Management Journal, 40*(5), 1190–1207.

Schumann, P. L. (2001). A moral principles framework for human resource management ethics. *Human Resource Management Review, 11,* 93–111.

Schyns, B., & Schilling, J. (2013). How bad are the effects of bad leaders? A meta-analysis of destructive leadership and its outcomes. *The Leadership Quarterly, 24,* 138–158.

Senge, P. M. (1990). *The fifth discipline: The art and practice of the learning organization.* New York: Doubleday.

Trevino, L. K. (1986). Ethical decision making in organizations: A person–situation interactionist model. *Academy of Management Review, 11*(3), 601–617.

Trevino, L. K., Brown, M., & Hartman, L. P. (2003). A qualitative investigation of perceived executive ethical leadership: Perceptions from inside and outside the executive suite. *Human Relations, 56*(1), 5–37.

Velasquez, M. G. (1992). *Business ethics: Concepts and cases* (3rd ed.). Englewood Cliffs, NJ: Prentice Hall.

Wayne, L. (2009, May 30). A promise to be ethical in an era of immorality. *The New York Times.* Retrieved June 15, 2009, from http://www.nytimes.com/2009/05/30/business

14

Team Leadership

Susan E. Kogler Hill

DESCRIPTION

Work teams are very prevalent in today's organizations. The reliance on teams is due partially to increasingly complex tasks, more globalization, and the flattening of organizational structures. A team is a type of organizational group that is composed of members who are interdependent, who share common goals, and who must coordinate their activities to accomplish these goals. Team members must work collectively to achieve their goals. Examples of organizational teams include senior executive teams, project management teams, task forces, work units, standing committees, quality teams, and improvement teams. Teams can be located in the same place meeting face-to-face, or they can be geographically dispersed "virtual" teams meeting via various forms of communication technology. The exact definition of which organizational group is a team or not is constantly evolving as organizations confront the many new forms of contemporary collaboration (Wageman, Gardner, & Mortensen, 2012).

The study of organizational teams has focused on strategies for maintaining a competitive advantage. Team-based organizations have faster response capability because of their flatter organizational structures, which rely on teams and new technology to enable communication across time and space (Porter & Beyerlein, 2000). These newer organizational structures have been referred to as "team-based and technology-enabled" (Mankin, Cohen, &

Bikson, 1996). Increasingly, companies are depending on virtual teams, or teams that are geographically dispersed and rely on technology to interact and collaborate (Muethel, Gehrlein, & Hoegl, 2012).

The organizational team-based structure is an important way for organizations to remain competitive by responding quickly and adapting to constant, rapid changes. Studies of both face-to-face and virtual teams have increasingly become focused on team processes and team outcomes (Ilgen, Hollenbeck, Johnson, & Jundt, 2005; Thomas, Martin, & Riggio, 2013). Also, researchers focused on the problems work teams confront as well as how to make these work teams more effective (Ilgen, Major, Hollenbeck, & Sego, 1993). Effective organizational teams lead to many desirable outcomes, such as

- greater productivity,
- more effective use of resources,
- better decisions and problem solving,
- better-quality products and services, and
- greater innovation and creativity (Parker, 1990).

However, for teams to be successful, the organizational culture needs to support member involvement. The traditional authority structure of many organizations does not support decision making at lower levels, and this can lead to the failure of many teams. Teamwork is an example of lateral decision making as opposed to the traditional vertical decision making that occurs in the organizational hierarchy based on rank or position in the organization. The dynamic and fluid power shifting in teams has been referred to as *heterarchy* (Aime, Humphrey, DeRue, & Paul, 2014). Such power shifting within teams can lead to positive outcomes as long as team members see these shifting sources of power as legitimate. Teams will have great difficulty in organizational cultures that are not supportive of such collaborative work and decision making. Changing an organizational culture to one that is more supportive of teams is possible, but it takes time and effort (Levi, 2011).

Leadership of teams has also become an important area of study. The ideas of "team leadership" are quite different from leadership within the organizational vertical structure. Many theories of leadership, such as situational (discussed in Chapter 5) and transformational (discussed in Chapter 8), can be applied in the team setting. However, team leadership is a unique setting for leadership, and it is very process oriented. How do teams develop their

▶ Traits of Healthy Teams

"critical capabilities"? How do team leaders shift their actions over time to deal with contingencies as they arise? How do leader actions promote task and interpersonal development (Kozlowski, Watola, Jensen, Kim, & Botero, 2009)? Effective team leadership facilitates team success and helps teams to avoid team failure (Stagl, Salas, & Burke, 2007; Stewart & Manz, 1995). Effective leadership processes are the most critical factor in team success (Zaccaro, Rittman, & Marks, 2001, p. 452).

Shared or Distributed Leadership: The complexities of team processes demand the attention and focus of all members of the team. Some teams are autonomous and self-directed with no formal leader. But even those with a formal leader will benefit from shared leadership among team members. Team leadership functions can be performed by the formal team leader *and/or* shared by team members. Shared team leadership occurs when members of the team take on leadership behaviors to influence the team and to maximize team effectiveness (Bergman, Rentsch, Small, Davenport, & Bergman, 2012). Shared leadership has been referred to as *team leadership capacity,* encompassing the leadership repertoire of the entire team (Day, Gronn, & Salas, 2004). Such distributed leadership involves the sharing of influence by team members. Team members step forward when situations warrant, providing the leadership necessary, and then step back to allow others to lead. Such shared leadership has become more and more important in today's organizations to allow faster responses to more complex issues (Morgeson, DeRue, & Karam, 2010; Pearce, Manz, & Sims, 2009; Solansky, 2008).

Shared leadership, while very important, does involve risk and takes some courage for the member who steps forward to provide leadership outside the formal role of team leader (Amos & Klimoski, 2014). Risks aside, teams with shared leadership have less conflict, more consensus, more trust, and more cohesion than teams that do not have shared leadership (Bergman et al., 2012). Shared leadership is even more important for virtual teams. Virtual teams are more effective when there is shared team leadership (Hoch & Kozlowski, 2014; Muethel et al., 2012). Virtual teams especially benefit from shared leadership when the task is complex (Wang, Waldman, & Zhang, 2014).

How leaders and members can share the leadership of teams so that these teams can truly become effective and achieve excellence will be discussed in this chapter. It will introduce a model that provides a mental road map to help the leader or any team member providing leadership diagnose team problems and take appropriate action to correct those problems.

 Self-Managed Teams   Shared Leadership

Team Leadership Model

The Hill Model for Team Leadership (Figure 14.1) is based on the functional leadership claim that the leader's job is to monitor the team and then take whatever action is necessary to ensure team effectiveness. The model provides a tool for understanding the very complex phenomenon of team leadership, starting at the top with its initial leadership decisions, moving to leader actions, and finally focusing on the indicators of team effectiveness. In addition, the model suggests specific actions that leaders can perform to improve team effectiveness. Effective team leaders need a wide repertoire of communication skills to monitor and take appropriate action. The model is designed to simplify and clarify the complex nature of team leadership and to provide an easy tool to aid leadership decision making for team leaders and members alike.

Effective team performance begins with how the leader sees the situation that the team is experiencing (the leader's *mental model*). This mental model reflects not only the components of the problem confronting the team, but also the environmental and organizational contingencies that define the larger context of team action. The leader develops a mental conception of what the team problem is and what solutions are possible in this context, given the environmental and organizational constraints and resources (Zaccaro et al., 2001).

To respond appropriately to the problem envisioned in the mental model, a good team leader needs to be behaviorally flexible and have a wide repertoire of actions or skills to meet the team's diverse needs (Barge, 1996). When the leader's behavior matches the complexity of the situation, he or she is behaving with "requisite variety," or the set of behaviors necessary to meet the team's needs (Drecksel, 1991). Effective team leaders are able to construct accurate mental models of the team's problems by observing team functioning, and can take requisite action to solve these problems. Effective team leaders can diagnose correctly and choose the right action.

The leader has special responsibility for functioning in a manner that will help the team achieve effectiveness. Within this perspective, leadership behavior is seen as team-based problem solving, in which the leader attempts to achieve team goals by analyzing the internal and external situation and then selecting and implementing the appropriate behaviors to ensure team effectiveness (Fleishman et al., 1991). Leaders must use discretion about which problems need intervention, and make choices about which solutions are the most appropriate (Zaccaro et al., 2001). The appropriate solution varies by circumstance and focuses on what should be done to make the team

 Team Effectiveness

more effective. Effective leaders have the ability to determine what leadership interventions are needed, if any, to solve team problems. When leadership is shared throughout the team, various members are diagnosing problems and intervening with appropriate behaviors. The monitoring and selection of behaviors is shared throughout the team membership. Given the complexity of team functioning, such shared leadership can—and, in fact, does—lead to greater team effectiveness.

Figure 14.1   The Hill Model for Team Leadership

Leadership Decisions

- Monitor or Take Action
- Task or Relational
- Internal or External

Internal Leadership Actions

External Leadership Actions

Task	Relational	Environmental
Goal Focusing	Coaching	Networking
Structuring for Results	Collaborating	Advocating
Facilitating Decisions	Managing Conflict	Negotiating Support
Training	Building Commitment	Buffering
Maintaining Standards	Satisfying Needs	Assessing
	Modeling Principles	Sharing Information

Team Effectiveness

Performance
Development

Team Effectiveness

At the bottom of the Hill Model for Team Leadership (Figure 14.1) is "Team Effectiveness," which focuses on team excellence or the desired outcomes of teamwork. Two critical functions of team effectiveness are

 Goals

performance (task accomplishment) and *development* (team maintenance). *Performance* refers to the quality of the outcomes of the team's work. Did the team accomplish its goals and objectives in a quality manner? *Development* refers to the cohesiveness of the team and the ability of team members to satisfy their own needs while working effectively with other team members (Nadler, 1998). Excellent teams accomplish both of these objectives: getting the job done and maintaining a cohesive team.

Scholars have systematically studied organizational work teams and developed standards of effectiveness or criteria of excellence that can be used to assess a team's health (Hackman, 1990, 2002, 2012; Hughes, Ginnett, & Curphey, 1993; LaFasto & Larson, 2001; Larson & LaFasto, 1989; Zaccaro et al., 2001). Hackman (2012) has posited six enabling conditions that lead to effective team functioning: (1) Is it a real team? (2) Does it have a compelling purpose? (3) Does it have the right people? (4) Are the norms of conduct clear? (5) Is there support from the organizational context? (6) Is there team-focused coaching? Larson and LaFasto (1989) studied successful teams and found that, regardless of the type of team, eight characteristics were consistently associated with team excellence. Table 14.1 demonstrates the similarity of these excellence characteristics to the enabling conditions suggested by Hackman (2012).

It is helpful if team leaders understand the conditions that contribute to or enable team excellence. Such understanding will allow the leader to benchmark or compare his or her team's performance to these standards and to determine possible areas of team weakness or ineffectiveness. Assessing how well the team compares to these established indicators of team success provides a valuable source of information to guide the leader to take appropriate actions to improve team success.

1. *Clear, Elevating Goal.* "A compelling purpose energizes team members, orients them toward their collective objective, and fully engages their talents" (Hackman, 2012, p. 437). Team goals must be very clear so that one can tell whether the performance objective has been realized. Teams sometimes fail because they are given a vague task and then asked to work out the details (Hackman, 1990). In addition, the team goal must be involving or motivating so that the members believe it to be worthwhile and important. Teams often fail because they let something else replace their goal, such as personal agendas or power issues (Larson & LaFasto, 1989). Research data from numerous teams show that effective leaders keep the team focused on the goal (LaFasto & Larson, 2001).

Future Team Effectiveness

Table 14.1 Comparison of Theory and Research Criteria of Team Effectiveness

Enabling Conditions of Group Effectiveness (Hackman, 2012)	Characteristics of Team Excellence (Larson & LaFasto, 1989)
Compelling purpose	Clear, elevating goal
	Results-driven structure
Right people	Competent team members
Real team	Unified commitment
	Collaborative climate
Clear norms of conduct	Standards of excellence
Supportive organizational context	External support and recognition
Team-focused coaching	Principled leadership

2. *Results-Driven Structure.* Teams need to find the best structure for accomplishing their goals. Structural features that lead to effective team-work include task design, team composition, and core norms of conduct (Wageman, Fisher, & Hackman, 2009). Top management teams typically deal with power and influence, task forces deal with ideas and plans, customer service teams deal with clients, and production teams deal with technology (Hackman, 1990). Problem resolution teams such as task forces need a structure that emphasizes trust so that all will be willing and able to contribute. Creative teams such as advertising teams need to emphasize autonomy so that all can take risks and be free from undue censorship. Tactical teams such as emergency room teams need to emphasize clarity so that everyone knows what to do and when. In addition, all teams need clear roles for team members, a good communication system, methods of assessing individual performance, and an emphasis on fact-based judgments (Larson & LaFasto, 1989). Appropriate structures enable teams to meet their needs while still accomplishing team goals.

3. *Competent Team Members.* Teams should be composed of the right number and mix of members to accomplish all the tasks of the team. In addition, members need sufficient information, education, and training to

 Coaching and Goals

become or remain competent team members (Hackman & Walton, 1986). As a whole, the individual team members need to possess the requisite technical competence to accomplish the team's goals. Members also need to be personally competent in interpersonal and teamwork skills. A common mistake in forming teams is to assume that people who have all the technical skills necessary to solve a problem also have the interpersonal skills necessary to collaborate effectively (Hackman, 1990). Just because someone is a good engineer or doctor does not mean he or she has the interpersonal skills to function on a team. Team members need certain core competencies that include the ability to do the job and the ability to solve problems. In addition, members need certain teamwork factors such as openness, supportiveness, action orientation, and a positive personal style (LaFasto & Larson, 2001).

4. *Unified Commitment.* A common mistake is to call a work group a *team* but treat it as a collection of individuals (Hackman, 1990). Teams do not just happen: They are carefully designed and developed. Excellent teams are those that have developed a sense of unity or identification. Such *team spirit* often can be developed by involving members in all aspects of the process (Larson & LaFasto, 1989).

5. *Collaborative Climate.* The ability of a team to collaborate or work well together is essential to team effectiveness. A collaborative climate is one in which members can stay problem focused, listen to and understand one another, feel free to take risks, and be willing to compensate for one another. To build an atmosphere that fosters collaboration, we need to develop trusting relationships based on honesty, openness, consistency, and respect (Larson & LaFasto, 1989). Integration of individual actions is one of the fundamental characteristics of effective teams. Team members each have their own unique roles that they typically perform to contribute to the team's success. Team failure may result from the members' "collective failure to coordinate and synchronize their individual contributions" (Zaccaro et al., 2001, p. 451). Effective team leaders can facilitate a collaborative climate by managing their own needs to control, by making communication safe, by demanding and rewarding collaborative behavior, and by guiding the team's problem-solving efforts (LaFasto & Larson, 2001).

6. *Standards of Excellence.* Clear norms of conduct (how we should behave) are important for team functioning (Hackman, 2012). Team members' performance should be regulated so that actions can be coordinated and tasks completed (Hackman & Walton, 1986). It is especially important that the organizational context or the team itself set up standards of excellence so

Ⓝ Cohesiveness in Teams

that members will feel pressure to perform at their highest levels. The standards must be clear and concrete, and all team members must be required to perform to standard (Larson & LaFasto, 1989). A team leader can facilitate this process by requiring results—making expectations clear and reviewing results—providing feedback to resolve performance issues, and rewarding results by acknowledging superior performance (LaFasto & Larson, 2001). With such standards in place and monitored, members will be encouraged to perform at their highest levels.

7. *External Support and Recognition.* A supportive organizational context includes material resources, rewards for excellent performance, an educational system to develop necessary team skills, and an information system to provide data needed to accomplish the task (Wageman et al., 2009). A common mistake is to give organizational teams challenging assignments but fail to give them organizational support to accomplish these assignments (Hackman, 1990). The leader must identify which type of support is needed and intervene as needed to secure this support (Hackman, 2002). The best goals, team members, and commitment will not mean much if there is no money, equipment, or supplies for accomplishing the goals. Also, organizations often ask employees to work on a difficult team assignment and then do not reward them with raises or bonuses for that performance. Hyatt and Ruddy (1997) found that having systems in place to support teams (clear direction, information, data, resources, rewards, and training) enables the team to become more effective and achieve performance goals. Teams can achieve excellence if they are given the resources needed to do their jobs, are recognized for team accomplishments, and are rewarded for team performance rather than for individual performances (Larson & LaFasto, 1989).

8. *Principled Leadership.* Effective team leadership has been found to consistently relate to team effectiveness (Zaccaro, Heinen, & Shuffler, 2009). Leadership has been described as the central driver of team effectiveness, influencing the team through four sets of processes: cognitive, motivational, affective, and coordination (Zaccaro et al., 2001). Cognitively, the leader helps the team understand the problems confronting the team. Motivationally, the leader helps the team become cohesive and capable by setting high performance standards and helping the team to achieve them. Affectively, the leader helps the team handle stressful circumstances by providing clear goals, assignments, and strategies. Coordinately, the leader helps integrate the team's activities by matching members' skills to roles, providing clear performance strategies, monitoring feedback, and adapting to environmental changes.

Nursing Team Leaders

Effective team leaders are committed to the team's goals and give members autonomy to unleash their talents when possible. Leaders can reduce the effectiveness of their team by being unwilling to confront inadequate performance, diluting the team's ability to perform by having too many priorities, and overestimating the positive aspects of team performance. Leaders can enhance the effectiveness of their team by keeping the team focused on its goals, maintaining a collaborative climate, building confidence among members, demonstrating technical competence, setting priorities, and managing performance (Larson & LaFasto, 1989). It is essential that the leadership of the team be assessed along with the other criteria of team excellence. Such feedback is essential to the health and effectiveness of the team.

The leadership of the team can use these eight characteristics of team excellence (Table 14.1) in a normative fashion to assess the health of the team and to take appropriate action to address any weaknesses. If the team leader assesses that one or more of the eight characteristics of team success are not being achieved, then he or she needs to address these weaknesses. Continually assessing the standards of team effectiveness can also provide feedback, enabling leaders to determine whether past actions and interventions had the desired results. To assess team effectiveness, team leaders need to use whatever tools are at their disposal, such as direct observation, surveys, feedback, and performance indicators. The information gained from the analysis of team effectiveness can provide feedback to the leader and guide future leadership decisions. The line on the Hill Model of Team Leadership (Figure 14.1) that connects the "Team Effectiveness" box at the bottom to the "Leadership Decisions" box at the top reflects the ongoing learning process of data gathering, analysis, and decision making. Such feedback loops demonstrate the dynamic and evolving nature of teams (Ilgen et al., 2005). Past leadership decisions and actions are reflected in the team's performance and relational outcomes. In turn, these indicators of team effectiveness shape the future analysis and decisions of the team leadership.

Leadership Decisions

At the top of the Hill Model for Team Leadership (Figure 14.1) are "Leadership Decisions," which include the major decisions the team's leadership needs to make when determining whether and how to intervene to improve team functioning. The first of these decisions is whether it is most appropriate to continue to observe and monitor the team or to intervene in the team's activities and take action. The second decision is to choose whether a task or a relational intervention is needed (i.e., does the team need help in accomplishing its tasks, or does it need help in

Assessing Fit in Teams

maintaining relationships?). The final decision is whether to intervene at the internal level (within the team itself) or at the external level (in the team's environment).

Figure 14.2 McGrath's Critical Leadership Functions

	MONITOR	EXECUTIVE ACTION
INTERNAL	Diagnosing Group Deficiencies 1	Taking Remedial Action 2
EXTERNAL	Forecasting Environmental Changes 3	Preventing Deleterious Changes 4

SOURCE: McGrath's critical leadership functions as cited in "Leading Groups in Organizations," by J. R. Hackman and R. E. Walton, 1986, in P. S. Goodman & Associates (Eds.), *Designing Effective Work Groups* (p. 76). San Francisco: Jossey-Bass.

Leadership Decision 1: Should I monitor the team or take action? The first decision confronting the team's leadership is whether to keep observing the team or to take action to help the team. McGrath (as cited in Hackman & Walton, 1986) outlined the critical leadership functions of group effectiveness, taking into account the analysis of the situation both internally and externally and whether this analysis indicates that the leader should take an immediate action. Figure 14.2, "McGrath's Critical Leadership Functions," demonstrates these two dimensions of leadership behavior: *monitoring versus taking action* and *internal group issues versus external group issues.* As leaders, we can diagnose, analyze, or forecast problems (monitoring), or we can take immediate action to solve a problem. We can also focus on the problems within the group (internal) or problems outside the group (external). These two dimensions result in the four types of team leadership functions shown in Figure 14.2.

Quadrants 1 and 2 in Figure 14.2 focus on the internal operations of the team. In Quadrant 1, the leader is diagnosing group deficiencies, and in Quadrant 2, the leader is acting to repair or remedy the observed problems. Quadrants 3 and 4 focus on the external operations of the team. In the third quadrant, the leader is scanning the environment to determine and forecast any external changes that will affect the group. In the fourth quadrant, the leader acts to prevent any negative changes in the environment from hurting the team.

Therefore, the first decision confronting the team's leadership is "Should I continue monitoring these factors, or should I take action based on the information I have already gathered and structured?" To develop an accurate mental model of team functioning, leaders need to monitor both the internal and external environments to gather information, reduce equivocality, provide structure, and overcome barriers. Fleishman et al. (1991) described two phases in this initial process: information search and structuring. A leader must first seek out information to understand the current state of the team's functioning (information search), and then this information must be analyzed, organized, and interpreted so the leader can decide how to act (information structuring). Leaders can also help their information search process by obtaining feedback from team members, networking with others outside the team, conducting team assessment surveys, and evaluating team outcomes. Once information on the team is gathered, the leader needs to structure or interpret this information so that he or she can make action plans. Virtual teams operate under the same group dynamics principles and also need to monitor and intervene as appropriate (Berry, 2011).

All members of the team can engage in monitoring (information search and structuring) and collectively provide distributed or shared leadership to help the team adapt to changing conditions. In fast-paced, rapidly changing situations, the team leader and members might have to work in concert to assess the situation accurately. The official leader of the team might be too busy processing information from the environment to process information internal to the team. The team members can help the leader by staying on top of internal problems. Together, they can form an accurate picture of the team's effectiveness.

In addition to gathering and interpreting information, team leaders must take the right action based on this information. Determining the right action to take is at the very heart of team leadership. It involves selecting from among competing courses of action to facilitate the team's work (Barge, 1996). Leaders differ in their tendencies to take action quickly (hasty to act) or their tendencies to delay taking action by analyzing the situation at length (slow to act). "Hasty to act" leaders might prevent problems from getting out of control; however, they might not make the right intervention because they do not have all the information, and such fast action might undermine the development of shared leadership. "Slow to act" leaders might encourage other team members to emerge as leaders (shared leadership), but the action-taking delay might cause the team's problem to become unmanageable.

High-Risk Environments

The exact timing of a leadership intervention is as important as the specific type of intervention (Wageman et al., 2009). It has been proposed that groups go through developmental stages of forming, storming, norming, performing, and adjourning (Tuckman & Jensen, 2010). Certain behaviors are common and even expected at each of these stages. If, for example, conflict was occurring during the storming stage of team life, the leadership might not intervene at that time but just continue monitoring. Or, the leadership might choose an intervention that advances the team to the next phase of norming. Others have described three phases of group life and the leadership needed during each: (1) motivational coaching (at start), (2) consultative coaching (at midpoint), and (3) educational coaching (at end). The important aspect of timing is that the leader should understand where the team is in its life cycle and provide the type of leadership needed at that time (Hackman, 2012).

Leadership Decision 2: Should I intervene to meet task or relational needs? Returning to the top box in Figure 14.1 ("Leadership Decisions"), the second decision confronting the leader is whether the team needs help in dealing with relational issues or task issues. Since the early study of small groups, the focus has been on two critical leadership functions: task and maintenance. Task leadership functions include getting the job done, making decisions, solving problems, adapting to changes, making plans, and achieving goals. Maintenance functions include developing a positive climate, solving interpersonal problems, satisfying members' needs, and developing cohesion. These two functions have also been referred to in terms of performance and development (i.e., how well the team has accomplished its task and how well the team has developed effective relationships).

Superior team leadership focuses constantly on both task and maintenance functions (Kinlaw, 1998); both types of leadership behaviors (task-focused and person-focused) have been found to be related to perceived team effectiveness (Burke et al., 2006).

Task functions are closely intertwined with relational functions. If the team is well maintained and has good interpersonal relationships, then the members will be able to work together effectively and get their job done. If not, they will spend all of their time infighting, sniping, and working at cross-purposes. Similarly, if the team is productive and successful in accomplishing its task, it will be easier to maintain a positive climate and good relations. Conversely, failing teams often take their lack of performance out on each other, and fighting teams often accomplish little.

In virtual teams connected across time and space by electronic media, focusing on building team relationships is even more critical than in traditional co-located teams. Virtual team leaders must be able to "read" all the personal and contextual nuances in a world of electronic communications. They must be able to understand the possible causes of silence, misunderstanding, and slights without any of the usual signs to guide them. Leaders must be sensitive to the team process and must pay attention to even small matters that could interfere with the team's success (Pauleen, 2004). Virtual teams place even greater demands on team leaders—50% more time investment—than the more traditional co-located team (Dyer, Dyer, & Dyer, 2007). As the prevalence of virtual teams expands, specific leadership issues and interventions related to these virtual teams are increasingly the focus of study (Berry, 2011; Cordery, Soo, Kirkman, Rosen, & Mathieu, 2009; Zaccaro, Ardison, & Orvis, 2004).

Leadership Decision 3: Should I intervene internally or externally? If a decision was made to take action or intervene, the leader must make the third strategic leadership decision in Figure 14.1 and determine what *level of the team process* needs leadership attention: internal leadership actions or external leadership actions. Do I need to intervene inside of the team, or is the problem external to the team? Effective team leaders analyze and balance the internal and external demands of the team and react appropriately (Barge, 1996).

Is there internal conflict between members of the team? Then perhaps taking an *internal relational action* to maintain the team and improve interpersonal relationships would be most appropriate. Are the team goals unclear? Then perhaps an *internal task intervention* is needed to focus on goals. Is the organizational environment not providing proper support to the team to do its job? Then perhaps an *external environmental intervention* focusing on obtaining external support for the team might be the most appropriate intervention.

The current focus of research is on real-life organizational work teams that exist within a larger organizational environment. In addition to balancing the internal task and relational needs of the team, the leader has to help the team adapt to and function effectively in its environment. Most teams focus on the internal problems of the team. But it is increasingly important for teams to also be externally oriented to "reach across boundaries to forge dense networks of connection, both inside and outside the organization" so that they can deal effectively with the fast changing environment (Ancona, Bresman, & Caldwell, 2009).

 Relational Actions

Leadership Actions

The middle section of the Hill Model for Team Leadership (Figure 14.1) lists a number of specific leadership actions that can be performed internally ("Task" and "Relational") or externally ("Environmental"). These lists are not exhaustive but are compiled from research on team excellence and team performance discussed earlier in this chapter. For example, teams that have clear goals, standards, effective structure, and decision making will have higher task performance. Teams that can manage conflict, collaborate well together, and build commitment will have good relationships. Teams that are well connected to and protected from their environment will also be more productive.

It is up to the leader to assess what action, if any, is needed and then intervene with the specific leadership function to meet the demands of the situation. The leader needs the ability to perform these skills and to make a strategic choice as to the most *appropriate function or skill* for the intervention. For example, if the leader decided that team members were arguing, he or she might decide to initiate conflict management. *To be an effective leader, one needs to respond with the action that is required of the situation.* Thus, it is the job of the leader to analyze and mediate the situation to make the best decisions for the good of the team. A detailed knowledge of group dynamics and interpersonal processes is key to effective team leadership.

A team leader also needs to recognize and interpret what is getting in the way of the team's goal accomplishment and then make a strategic choice and respond with the appropriate action (Gouran & Hirokawa, 1996). If a problem is diagnosed as a team performance problem, then the leader needs to determine the appropriate action to solve this task problem (e.g., goal focusing, standard setting, or training). If a problem is diagnosed as a team development problem, then the leader needs to determine the appropriate action to solve this relational problem (e.g., managing conflict or building commitment). If a problem is diagnosed as an environmental problem, then the leader needs to determine the appropriate action to solve this context problem (e.g., networking, advocating, or sharing information).

Internal Task Leadership Actions. The "Task" box in the Hill Model for Team Leadership (Figure 14.1) lists the set of skills or actions that the leader might perform to improve task performance. After monitoring the team's performance, the leader might choose to intervene in one of the following task areas:

- *Goal focusing* (clarifying, gaining agreement)

  For example, if team members seem to be going off in different directions, the leader might intervene to clarify the team's goals or work with members to obtain agreement on goals.

 Resourcing

- *Structuring for results* (planning, visioning, organizing, clarifying roles, delegating)

  For example, if the leader determines that the team is stuck in day-to-day affairs and not looking to or building for the future, then he or she might intervene by helping the team vision and plan for the future.

- *Facilitating decision making* (informing, controlling, coordinating, mediating, synthesizing, focusing on issues)

  For example, if the leader determines that members are not adequately sharing information with each other, he or she might ask questions to seek out the information that is not being shared.

- *Training team members in task skills* (educating, developing)

  For example, if the leader observes that the team members do not have the skills necessary to make well-reasoned decisions, the leader might provide a training seminar in decision making.

- *Maintaining standards of excellence* (assessing team and individual performance, confronting inadequate performance)

  For example, if the leader observes that some team members are coming late to meetings or not attending meetings, the leader might have to take direct action and confront these members to address this inadequate performance.

Internal Relational Leadership Actions. The second set of internal leadership actions in Figure 14.1 reflects those that the leader needs to implement to improve team relationships. After monitoring the team's performance, the leader might choose to intervene in one of the following interpersonal areas:

- *Coaching team members in interpersonal skills*

  For example, if the team leader observes that team members do not seem to be listening to one another, then he or she might intervene by leading team members in a listening exercise.

- *Collaborating* (including, involving)

  For example, if the leader observes that some team members are not taking others' opinions into account, then the leader might intervene to encourage compromise.

- *Managing conflict and power issues* (fighting or avoiding confrontation, questioning ideas, avoiding groupthink)

 Decision-Making

For example, if the leader observes that the members are not questioning ideas and are just agreeing with each other in order to move quickly to a decision, then the leader might intervene by providing a discussion on the negative aspects of groupthink (Neck & Manz, 1994).

- *Building commitment and esprit de corps* (being optimistic, innovating, envisioning, socializing, rewarding, recognizing)

  For example, if the team seems to have low morale, the leader could intervene to build commitment and unity by recognizing past team successes.

- *Satisfying individual member needs* (trusting, supporting, advocating)

  For example, if a team member seems stressed due to disrespect from other members, the leader might provide support to the upset member and advocate to the team on his or her behalf.

- *Modeling ethical and principled practices* (fair, consistent, normative)

  For example, if a team leader monitors the team and observes that he or she is inconsistent vis-à-vis the members sometimes treating in-group members differently from out-group members, then the leader might intervene and change his or her own behavior to be fair and consistent to all members.

External Environmental Leadership Actions. The "External Leadership Actions" (Figure 14.1) reflect those actions the leader might implement to improve the environmental interface with the team. Real-life teams do not exist in a laboratory—they are subsystems of the larger organizational and societal context. To stay viable, the team needs to monitor this environment closely and determine what actions should be taken to enhance team effectiveness (Barge, 1996; Hyatt & Ruddy, 1997; Zaccaro et al., 2001). If environmental monitoring suggests a leadership intervention, then the leader needs to select from the following functions:

- *Networking and forming alliances in environment* (gathering information, increasing influence)

  For example, if the leader observes that the team's members are not well known or are not well connected throughout the organization, then the leader might intervene by interacting and forming relationships with powerful and respected individuals in the organization.

 Flat Office Structures

- *Advocating and representing team to environment*

  For example, if the leader learns that organizational superiors are unaware of the team's successes, the leader might initiate an "FYI" policy, sending information about all successes upward as they happen. The leader can also initiate a team newsletter that chronicles team efforts to accomplish the same function but to a broader context.

- *Negotiating upward to secure necessary resources, support, and recognition for team*

  For example, a leader might determine that the team does not have enough clerical support to accomplish its goals. The leader then negotiates with upper management to provide the needed support or, if failing in this, to persuade upper management to alter the team's goals accordingly.

- *Buffering team members from environmental distractions*

  For example, if the leader observes that the team is overloaded with tasks, then he or she might intervene by keeping unnecessary demands and distractions away from the team members so that they can concentrate on their goals.

- *Assessing environmental indicators of team's effectiveness* (surveys, evaluations, performance indicators)

  For example, if the leader observes that the members of the team have no way of knowing how well they are doing, the leader can provide data from the environment as to how their performance stacks up with other teams.

- *Sharing relevant environmental information with team*

  For example, if the team leader reviews the environment and finds that the organization's business is going in a new direction, he or she can share this information with the team to keep them in line with these new directions.

Team leadership is complex; there are no simple recipes for team success. Team leaders must learn to be open and objective in understanding and diagnosing team problems and skillful in selecting the most appropriate actions (or inactions) to help achieve the team's goals. It is important to reemphasize that these critical functions need not be carried out only by the leader. Experienced members in a mature team might share these leadership behaviors. As long as the team's critical needs have been met, the leadership behavior, whether enacted by the leader or team members, has been effective. *The key assertion of the functional perspective is that the leader is to do whatever*

Team Leadership and Performance

is necessary to take care of unmet needs of the team. If the team members are taking care of most of the needs, then the leader has to do very little.

HOW DOES THE TEAM LEADERSHIP MODEL WORK?

Team leaders and team members can use the model to help them make decisions about the current state of their team and the specific actions they need to take, if any, to improve the team's functioning. The model portrays leadership as a team oversight function in which the leader's role is to do whatever is necessary to help the team achieve effectiveness. The model provides the leader with a cognitive map for identifying team needs, and offers suggestions about how to take appropriate corrective actions. The model helps the leader make sense of the complexity of teams and offers practical suggestions based on theory and research.

In using the model, the team leadership engages in the leader mediation process by deciding which option is most appropriate for the team: monitoring or taking action. If the monitoring reveals that all aspects of the team's functioning are satisfactory, then the leadership should not take any direct actions but continue to monitor the internal and external environments in terms of team performance and development. If monitoring reveals that action is needed, then the leadership decides whether to take an internal-level action or an external-level action or both. Finally, the leadership decides which action is appropriate to meet the needs of the team.

Determining the exact intervention is not as easy as it sounds, however, and it clearly reflects the skills necessary for team leadership. For example, a leader monitoring the internal functioning of the team notices there is infighting for control and power. The leader might see this as an *internal relationship problem* because of the authoritarian and autocratic behavior of one team member. Or perhaps the leader might see it as an *internal task problem* because the structure of the team is not appropriate and the roles and responsibilities of some members are unclear. The leader might also see the problem as an *external environmental problem* because the team is not given sufficient autonomy from the organization; consequently, the members are fighting over what little power and control exist. Or perhaps the leader sees the conflict as temporary given the stage of group development (e.g., storming).

In any case, the leader can decide to keep monitoring the situation and not take any immediate action because of the group's phase of development.

Or the leader can decide at which level to intervene and then decide to enact the most appropriate leadership function at that level. The leader might decide to intervene at all three levels, addressing the authoritarian individual (internal, relational), clarifying team roles (internal, task), and negotiating more team autonomy with those higher up in the organization (external).

The team leadership model aids in team analysis and improvement, much like that of sports teams. In sports, the coach does not stop working just because the team is winning. The coach keeps working to build commitment, develop young players, share expertise, create new methods and strategies, and generally improve team functioning. The effective coach never rests on past successes, but works to improve the team's functioning for the future. After a win or a loss, a football coach will have the team review videos of the game to determine areas of success and failure. Organizational team leaders could learn a great deal from sports team coaches. By comparing their own teams with established standards or criteria of team excellence, leaders can determine the areas of greatest weakness that might need critical intervention.

STRENGTHS

One of the strengths of this model is that it is designed to focus on the real-life organizational work group and the leadership needed therein. The model places the ongoing work group or team in an environmental context within the organization, industry, or society. In addition, the real-life focus on performance and team effectiveness enables leaders and members to diagnose and correct team problems. A team leader can present the model to his or her team as a teaching tool. By learning what constitutes excellent teams and applying these criteria to team performance, leaders and members can learn how to better lead teams to the highest levels of excellence.

A second strength of the model is that it provides a cognitive guide that helps leaders to design and maintain effective teams, especially when performance is below standards. Such an approach is consistent with the emerging theoretical notions of the leader as a medium whose job it is to process the complex information inherent in teamwork (Fisher, 1985). Any model or theory that tries to simplify such a complex process would be inappropriate and inadequate. The team leadership model is not simplistic, and it integrates in a manageable and practical form many complex factors that can help a leader be a good medium or processor of information.

Another strength of the model is that it takes into account the changing role of leaders and followers in organizations (shared leadership). The model does not focus on the position of power of a leader, but instead focuses on the critical functions of leadership as diagnosis and action taking. Any team member can perform the critical leadership functions to assess the current effectiveness of the team and then take appropriate action. This approach is consistent with the current movement in organizations to rethink leadership responsibilities in work teams. The responsibilities or functions of team leadership—such as setting goals, coaching, and rewarding—historically have rested with the team's formal leader, but now, with organizational restructuring, these duties and responsibilities often are distributed across the team.

In addition, this approach to team leadership can help in selection of team leaders and team members. If a leader must be chosen for the team, it might be best to select one who is perceptive, open, objective, analytical, and a good listener who has good diagnostic skills. In addition, it would be wise to select a leader who has a wide repertoire of action-taking skills and is comfortable intervening in the team's processes in many ways, such as with negotiation, conflict resolution, problem solving, goal focusing, and influencing upward. Good leaders not only can diagnose the team's problems, but also can reach into their bag of tricks and pull out the appropriate action or actions. For example, if a leader determines that two members of a team are in conflict with one another, he or she needs to be able to determine the root cause of that conflict and select the most appropriate action (or select nonaction).

CRITICISMS

The Hill Model for Team Leadership (Figure 14.1) is a conceptual framework to assist team-based leadership in its decision making. As such, it lists only some of the many skills that leadership might need to employ in making such decisions. Depending on the type of team or situation, additional skills might be needed that focus more on the environment (Cobb, 2012), coaching and training (Zaccaro, Heinen, & Shuffler, 2009), or preplanning and timing (Wageman et al., 2009). A team might need to modify the model to include skills that are particularly relevant to its effectiveness.

Even though the model does not include all possible leadership skills, it is still quite complex. Team leaders need to spend time adjusting to the framework so that it comes naturally to them when decisions are needed. This framework also does not provide on-the-spot answers to specific problems facing the team leader, such as "When is the best time to intervene?" "What do you say to a member who is upset and crying?" or "What specific action do you take to deal with an organizational culture that is not supporting teamwork?" The model only points the leader in the right direction and suggests skills needed to solve these complex problems. The model assumes that the leader is skilled in group process, decision making, interpersonal communication, conflict resolution, and other abilities.

To make matters worse, many teams have shared leadership necessitating that everyone who provides team leadership has a wide range of team-oriented skills. In addition, the roles of leaders and followers can change over time, making it very important for the team leader and team members to possess the requisite leadership skills. In immature teams leaders might need to take on more of the leadership roles, whereas in a mature team the leader might be able to sit back and let the team lead itself. Increasingly, scholars are providing instruction in diagnosing weaknesses in team leadership skills and offering methods for development and improvement (Cobb, 2012; Levi, 2011; Morgeson et al., 2010; Salas, Burke, & Stagl, 2004). Instruction in teamwork and team leadership needs to focus on team diagnosing and action taking so that team leadership skills can be developed throughout the team and be more easily implemented.

APPLICATION

There are many ways to apply the team leadership model to increase the effectiveness of organizational teams. The model is useful in helping the leader make decisions: Should I act? If so, how should I do so? For example, if the team is not performing effectively (*team effectiveness*), then the leader can make the first strategic choice by monitoring the situation or acting to improve team functioning. If an action seems warranted, then the leader needs to decide whether the action should be directed inward toward team functioning, outward toward the environment, or both. Once the context for the action is determined, then the leader needs to choose the most appropriate skill for the situation from his or her behavioral repertoire. It is important to continue monitoring the results of the intervention and adapting accordingly, depending on these results.

The leader might choose to use an assessment tool such as the Team Excellence and Collaborative Team Leader Questionnaire included in this chapter to help conduct the team's diagnosis and set the steps needed for taking action. Team members are asked to fill out the questionnaire, as is the

Team Pep Talk

team leader. The results are fed back to the team members and team leader, allowing them to see the areas of greatest strength and weakness. It is particularly important that both team leaders and team members fill out the questionnaire. Research suggests that team leaders overestimate their effectiveness on these dimensions and often score themselves much higher than do team members (LaFasto & Larson, 2001). By comparing the scores by leaders and by members, the leader along with team members can determine which dimensions of team or leadership effectiveness need improvement. The team and leader can then prepare action plans to correct the highest-priority problems. Such a team assessment approach is very helpful in monitoring and diagnosing team problems. It aids in determining the complex factors affecting team excellence to build a committed team involved in action planning.

--- **CASE STUDIES** ---

To improve your understanding of the team leadership model, refer to the following case studies (Cases 14.1, 14.2, and 14.3). For each case, you will be asked to put yourself in the role of team leader and apply the team leadership model in analyzing and offering solutions to the team problems.

CASE 14.1

Can This Virtual Team Work?

Jim Towne heads a newly formed information technology team for a major international corporation. The team is composed of 20 professionals who live and work in Canada, the United States, Europe, South America, Africa, and Australia. All members of the team report to Jim. The team is a virtual team connected primarily via videoconference, group decision-support software, e-mail, text, and telephone. The team has met twice in a face-to-face setting to set goals and plan. All of the team members are quite competent in their respective technical areas. Some team members have a long and valued history with the company; others have recently joined the company through a corporate merger. The team members have never worked together on any projects.

The task of the team is to develop and implement technology innovations for all global business units. The team members are excited about the importance and the innovative nature of their assignment. They

(Continued)

(Continued)

respect each other and enjoy being part of this team. However, the team is having difficulty getting off the ground, and the members report being extremely overloaded. Most team members travel to business sites at least 2 weeks each month. The travel is important, but it causes team members to get farther behind.

The team has one half-time secretary, located in New York. Her primary responsibility is to organize travel and meetings of team members. Team members are working on several projects at once and have great difficulty finishing any of the projects. One team member has 500 unread e-mail messages because each team member sends copies of all messages to everyone on the team. Jim is under great pressure to prove that this team can work and provide a valuable function to the organization.

Questions

1. Which of the eight characteristics (Table 14.1) of team excellence are lacking in this team?

2. Based on this analysis of team effectiveness, should Jim intervene at this time, or should he just keep monitoring the team? If you think he should take action, at what level should he intervene (internal or external)? If internal, should his action be task or relational?

3. What specific leadership functions should Jim implement to improve the team? Why?

CASE 14.2

They Dominated the Conversation

The local cancer center has a health team designed to coordinate the care of children with cancer. The team is composed of a physician, Dr. Sherif Hidyat (a clinical oncologist); a radiologist, Dr. Wayne Linett; a nurse practitioner, Sharon Whittling; a social worker, Cathy Ing; a physical therapist, Nancy Crosby; and a child life worker, Janet Lewis. The team members meet on a weekly basis to discuss the 18 children under their care and agree on the best course of treatment for each child. Cathy Ing, the social worker, is the head of the team and is responsible for the case management of each child. However, when the team meets, Drs. Hidyat and Linett dominate the conversation. They feel that their medical background gives them greater knowledge and skill in treating cancer in children. They welcome input from the women on the team. When it comes to making a decision, however, they insist on doing it their way for the good of the patient. Cathy Ing (the social worker), Janet Lewis (the child life worker), Nancy Crosby (the physical therapist), and Sharon Whittling (the nurse practitioner) resent this behavior because they are the health care workers who spend the most time with the children and feel that they know best how to handle their long-term care. As a result, the patients feel as if no one cares or understands them. The team is also having trouble working together, and no one on the team is satisfied with the outcome.

Questions

1. How would you assess the effectiveness of this team?

2. In monitoring this team, at what level and function do you see the most serious problems? Internal task? Internal relational? External?

3. Would you take action to improve team functioning? If so, how would you intervene? Why?

4. What specific leadership skill or skills would you use to improve team functioning?

CASE 14.3

Starts With a Bang, Ends With a Whimper

A faculty member, Kim Green from the Management Department, was asked to chair a major university committee to plan the mission of the university for the next 20 years. Three other senior faculty and seven administrators from across the campus were also asked to serve on this committee. The president of the university, Dr. Sulgrave, gave the committee its charge: What should Northcoast University be like in the year 2020? Dr. Sulgrave told the committee that the work of this task force was of utmost importance to the future of the university, and the charge of this committee should take precedence over all other matters. The task force was allowed to meet in the president's conference room and use the president's secretary. The report of the committee was due in 2 months.

(Continued)

(Continued)

The task force members felt very good about being selected for such an important team. The team met on a weekly basis for about 2 hours each time. At first, the members were very interested in the task and participated enthusiastically. They were required to do a great deal of outside research. They came back to the meetings proud to share their research and knowledge. However, after a while the meetings did not go well. The members could not seem to agree on what the charge to the team meant. They argued about what they were supposed to accomplish and resented the time the committee was taking from their regular jobs. Week after week the team met but accomplished nothing. Attendance became a problem, with people skipping several meetings, showing up late, or leaving early. Team members stopped working on their committee assignments. Kim didn't want to admit to the university president that the team didn't know what it was doing; instead, she just got more and more frustrated. Meetings became sporadic and eventually stopped altogether. The president was involved in a crisis in the university and seemed to lose interest in the committee. The president never called for the report from the committee, and the report was never completed.

Questions

1. Which characteristics of excellence were lacking in this task force?

2. Which characteristics of excellence were evident in this task force?

3. How would you assess Kim as a leader?

4. What actions would you take (internally or externally) if you were the leader of this task force?

LEADERSHIP INSTRUMENT

Larson and LaFasto developed an assessment tool to gauge team effectiveness (a team's health) based on their study of many different types of excellent organizational teams (see Larson & LaFasto, 1989). Their research demonstrated eight criteria or factors that are consistently associated with team excellence and high performance that were discussed earlier in the chapter. The complete Team Excellence Survey contains more than 40 questions across the eight factors that are used to determine a team's performance level and suggest areas that might need corrective action. The eighth factor on this instrument is *principled leadership.* Subsequent research by LaFasto and Larson led to the development of a 42-item questionnaire focusing on this criterion of leadership. The full Collaborative Team Leader Instrument and a discussion of its reliability and validity can be found in their latest text (LaFasto & Larson, 2001). The questionnaire included here provides a sample of questions from these two surveys so that the reader can see how team and team leadership effectiveness can be evaluated. (Readers who want to assess their own organizational teams are advised to use the complete versions of both surveys.)

The team members are given the questionnaire, and their scores are combined and averaged to obtain a team view; the leader fills out the same questionnaire. The responses from the team leader are then compared with the team members' responses to determine the areas of greatest weakness, if any. Based on these comparisons, the team and its leader can plan the action steps needed to correct and improve the weak areas of team functioning. The action planning is done collaboratively with leader and team members working together.

The Team Excellence and Collaborative Team Leader assessments are designed as diagnostic tools to help teams sort through any problems and to pinpoint areas for action taking. The Team Excellence and Collaborative Team Leader Questionnaire provided in this chapter combines sample questions from the two instruments developed by LaFasto and Larson. The first seven questions are taken from the Team Excellence Survey, developed by LaFasto and Larson in 1987 (cited in Larson & LaFasto, 1989) to measure a team's health in terms of the criteria of team excellence (goal, structure, team members, commitment, climate, standards, and external support). Leadership is measured by the next six questions, taken from the Collaborative Team Leader Instrument developed by LaFasto and Larson in 1996 (LaFasto & Larson, 2001, pp. 151–154). These six questions assess the effectiveness of the leader in goal focusing, ensuring a collaborative climate, building confidence, demonstrating know-how, setting priorities, and managing performance. All of these team and leadership factors have been found to relate to team effectiveness.

As you fill out the sample questionnaire, think about a team to which you belong or have belonged as a member or as the leader. The items that you score as 1 or 2 (*False* or *More false than true*) are the areas of team weakness from your perspective. To obtain a team assessment, you would compare your scores on this instrument with the scores of the other team members. For example, if almost everyone on the team responds with a 1 or 2 to Item 3 ("Team members possess the essential skills and abilities to accomplish the team's objectives"), then the team leader might need to provide training to increase the competence of team members. Such an instrument that assesses team effectiveness is particularly helpful to the team leader in identifying areas of team or leadership weakness and suggesting solutions for improving team effectiveness.

Team Excellence and Collaborative
Team Leader Questionnaire

Instructions: This questionnaire contains questions about your team and the leadership within this team. Indicate whether you feel each statement is true or not true of your team. Use the following scale:

Key: 1 = False   2 = More false than true   3 = More true than false   4 = True

1. There is a clearly defined need—a goal to be achieved   1 2 3 4
    or a purpose to be served—that justifies the existence
    of our team. (team: clear, elevating goal)

2. We have an established method for monitoring   1 2 3 4
    individual performance and providing feedback.
    (team: results-driven structure)

3. Team members possess the essential skills and abilities   1 2 3 4
    to accomplish the team's objectives.
    (team: competent team members)

4. Achieving our team goal is a higher priority than any   1 2 3 4
    individual objective. (team: unified commitment)

5. We trust each other sufficiently to accurately share   1 2 3 4
    information, perceptions, and feedback.
    (team: collaborative climate)

6. Our team exerts pressure on itself to improve performance.   1 2 3 4
    (team: standards of excellence)

7. Our team is given the resources it needs to get the job done.   1 2 3 4
    (team: external support and recognition)

8. If it's necessary to adjust the team's goal, our team leader   1 2 3 4
    makes sure we understand why. (leadership: focus
    on the goal)

9. Our team leader creates a safe climate for team members   1 2 3 4
    to openly and supportively discuss any issue related to
    the team's success. (leadership: ensure collaborative climate)

10. Our team leader looks for and acknowledges contributions   1 2 3 4
    by team members. (leadership: build confidence)

11. Our team leader understands the technical issues we must   1 2 3 4
    face in achieving our goal. (leadership: demonstrate sufficient
    technical know-how)

12. Our team leader does not dilute our team's effort with too   1 2 3 4
    many priorities. (leadership: set priorities)

13. Our team leader is willing to confront and resolve issues   1 2 3 4
associated with inadequate performance by team members.
(leadership: manage performance)

SOURCES: Questions 1–7: Adapted from the Team Excellence Survey (copyright 1987
LaFasto and Larson; portions reprinted with permission of Profact). Questions 8–13:
Adapted from the Collaborative Team Leader Instrument (copyright 1996 LaFasto and
Larson; portions reprinted with permission).

Scoring Interpretation

In addition to such targeted questions on each of the criteria of excellence,
the complete surveys also ask open-ended questions to allow team members to comment on issues that might not be specifically covered in the
directed questions, such as strengths and weaknesses of the team and its
leadership, necessary changes, problematic norms, or issues that need to be
addressed. The complete version of the survey is given to team members
and the team leader, and all are involved in the diagnosis and the resulting
action planning. Such a method is clearly consistent with the empowerment
movement in organizational teams and helps address the enormous complexity involved in making teams effective.

SUMMARY

The increased importance of organizational teams and the leadership needed for them has produced a growing interest in team leadership theory. The team leadership model provides a framework in which to study the systematic factors that contribute to a team's outcomes or general effectiveness. Within this approach, the critical function of leadership is to help the team accomplish its goals by monitoring and diagnosing the team and taking the requisite action.

A strategic decision model has been developed to reveal the various decisions team leaders must make to improve their team's effectiveness. The model describes the decisions: What type of intervention should be used (monitoring or action taking)? At what level should the intervention be targeted (internal or external)? What leadership function should be implemented to improve team functioning?

Questionnaires filled out by team members and the team leader can aid in diagnosing specific areas of team problems and suggest action steps to be taken by the team.

The strength of this approach is its practical focus on real-life organizational teams and their effectiveness. The model also emphasizes the functions of leadership that can be shared and distributed within the work team. The model offers guidance in selecting leaders and team members with the appropriate diagnostic and action-taking skills. Furthermore, the model is appropriately complex, providing a cognitive model for understanding and improving organizational teams.

Sharpen your skills with SAGE edge at **edge.sagepub.com/northouse7e**

REFERENCES

Aime, F., Humphrey, S., DeRue, D. S., & Paul, J. B. (2014). The riddle of heterarchy: Power transitions in cross-functional teams. *Academy of Management Journal, 57*(2), 327–352.

Amos, B., & Klimoski, R. J. (2014). Courage: Making teamwork work well. *Group & Organizational Management, 39*(1), 110–128.

Ancona, D., Bresman, H., & Caldwell, D. (2009). The x-factor: Six steps to leading high-performing x-teams. *Organizational Dynamics, 38*(3), 217–224.

Barge, J. K. (1996). Leadership skills and the dialectics of leadership in group decision making. In R. Y. Hirokawa & M. S. Poole (Eds.), *Communication and group decision making* (2nd ed., pp. 301–342). Thousand Oaks, CA: SAGE.

Bergman, J. Z, Rentsch, J. R., Small, E. E., Davenport, S. W., & Bergman, S. M. (2012). The shared leadership process in decision-making teams. *The Journal of Social Psychology, 152*(1), 17–42.

Berry, G. R. (2011). Enhancing effectiveness on virtual teams: Understanding why traditional team skills are insufficient. *Journal of Business Communication, 48*(2), 186–206.

Burke, C. S., Stagl, K. C., Klein, C., Goodwin, G. F., Salas, E., & Halpin, S. M. (2006). What type of leadership behaviors are functional in teams? A meta-analysis. *Leadership Quarterly, 17,* 288–307.

Cobb, A. T. (2012). *Leading project teams: The basics of project management and team leadership* (2nd ed.). Thousand Oaks, CA: SAGE.

Cordery, J., Soo, C., Kirkman, B., Rosen, B., & Mathieu, J. (2009). Leading parallel global virtual teams: Lessons from Alcoa. *Organizational Dynamics, 38*(3), 204–216.

Day, D. V., Gronn, P., & Salas, E. (2004). Leadership capacity in teams. *Leadership Quarterly, 15,* 857–880.

Drecksel, G. L. (1991). Leadership research: Some issues. *Communication Yearbook, 14,* 535–546.

Dyer, W. G., Dyer, W. G., Jr., & Dyer, J. H. (2007). *Team building: Proven strategies for improving team performance* (4th ed.). San Francisco: Jossey-Bass.

Fisher, B. A. (1985, May). Leadership as medium: Treating complexity in group communication research. *Small Group Behavior, 16*(2), 167–196.

Fleishman, E. A., Mumford, M. D., Zaccaro, S. J., Levin, K. Y., Korotkin, A. L., & Hein, M. B. (1991). Taxonomic efforts in the description of leader behavior: A synthesis and functional interpretation. *Leadership Quarterly, 2*(4), 245–287.

Gouran, D. S., & Hirokawa, R. Y. (1996). Functional theory and communication in decision-making and problem-solving groups: An expanded view. In R. Y. Hirokawa & M. D. Poole (Eds.), *Communication and group decision making* (2nd ed., pp. 55–80). Thousand Oaks, CA: SAGE.

Hackman, J. R. (1990). Work teams in organizations: An orienting framework. In J. R. Hackman (Ed.), *Groups that work (and those that don't): Creating conditions for effective teamwork* (pp. 1–14). San Francisco: Jossey-Bass.

Hackman, J. R. (2002). *Leading teams: Setting the stage for great performances.* Boston: Harvard Business School Press.

Hackman, J. R. (2012). From causes to conditions in group research. *Journal of Organizational Behavior, 33,* 428–444.

Hackman, J. R., & Walton, R. E. (1986). Leading groups in organizations. In P. S. Goodman & Associates (Eds.), *Designing effective work groups* (pp. 72–119). San Francisco: Jossey-Bass.

Hoch, J. E., & Kozlowski, W. J. (2014). Leading virtual teams: Hierarchical leadership, structural supports, and shared team leadership. *Journal of Applied Psychology, 99*(3), 390–403.

Hughes, R. L., Ginnett, R. C., & Curphey, G. J. (1993). *Leadership: Enhancing the lessons of experience.* Homewood, IL: Irwin.

Hyatt, D. E., & Ruddy, T. M. (1997). An examination of the relationship between work group characteristics and performance: Once more into the breach. *Personnel Psychology, 50,* 553–585.

Ilgen, D. R., Hollenbeck, J. R., Johnson, M., & Jundt, D. (2005). Teams in organizations: From input–process–output models to IMOI models. *Annual Review of Psychology, 56,* 517–543.

Ilgen, D. R., Major, D. A., Hollenbeck, J. R., & Sego, D. J. (1993). Team research in the 1990s. In M. M. Chemers & R. Ayman (Eds.), *Leadership theory and research: Perspectives and directions* (pp. 245–270). San Diego, CA: Academic Press.

Kinlaw, D. C. (1998). *Superior teams: What they are and how to develop them.* Hampshire, UK: Grove.

Kozlowski, S. W. J., Watola, D. J., Jensen, J. M., Kim, B. H., & Botero, I. C. (2009). Developing adaptive teams: A theory of dynamic team leadership. In E. Salas, G. F. Goodwin, & C. S. Burke (Eds.), *Team effectiveness in complex organizations: Cross–disciplinary perspectives and approaches* (pp. 113–155). New York: Taylor & Francis Group.

LaFasto, F. M. J., & Larson, C. E. (1987). *Team excellence survey.* Denver, CO: Author.

LaFasto, F. M. J., & Larson, C. E. (1996). *Collaborative team leader survey.* Denver, CO: Author.

LaFasto, F. M. J., & Larson, C. E. (2001). *When teams work best: 6,000 team members and leaders tell what it takes to succeed.* Thousand Oaks, CA: SAGE.

Larson, C. E., & LaFasto, F. M. J. (1989). *Teamwork: What must go right/what can go wrong.* Newbury Park, CA: SAGE.

Levi, D. (2011). *Group dynamics for teams.* Thousand Oaks, CA: SAGE.

Mankin, D., Cohen, S. G., & Bikson, T. K. (1996). *Teams and technology.* Boston: Harvard Business School Press.

Morgeson, F. P., DeRue, D. S., & Karam, E. P. (2010). Leadership in teams: A functional approach to understanding leadership structures and processes. *Journal of Management, 36*(1), 5–39.

Muethel, M., Gehrlein, S., Hoegl, M. (2012). Socio-demographic factors and shared leadership behaviors in dispersed teams: Implications for human resource management. *Human Resource Management, 51*(4), 525–548.

Nadler, D. A. (1998). Executive team effectiveness: Teamwork at the top. In D. A. Nadler & J. L. Spencer (Eds.), *Executive teams* (pp. 21–39). San Francisco: Jossey-Bass.

Neck, C. P., & Manz, C. C. (1994). From groupthink to teamthink: Toward the creation of constructive thought patterns in self-managing work teams. *Human Relations, 47*(8), 929–952.

Parker, G. M. (1990). *Team players and teamwork.* San Francisco: Jossey-Bass.

Pauleen, D. J. (2004). An inductively derived model of leader-initiated relationship building with virtual team members. *Journal of Management Information Systems, 20*(3), 227–256.

Pearce, C. L., Manz, C. C., & Sims, H. P. (2009). Where do we go from here? Is shared leadership the key to team success? *Organizational Dynamics, 38*(3), 234–238.

Porter, G., & Beyerlein, M. (2000). Historic roots of team theory and practice. In M. M. Beyerlein (Ed.), *Work teams: Past, present and future* (pp. 3–24). Dordrecht, Netherlands: Kluwer.

Salas, E., Burke, C. S., & Stagl, D. C. (2004). Developing teams and team leaders: Strategies and principles. In D. V. Day, S. J. Zaccaro, & S. M. Halpin (Eds.), *Leader development for transforming organizations: Growing leaders for tomorrow* (pp. 325–355). Mahwah, NJ: Lawrence Erlbaum.

Solansky, S. T. (2008). Leadership style and team processes in self-managed teams. *Journal of Leadership and Organizational Studies, 14*(4), 332–341.

Stagl, K. C., Salas, E., & Burke, C. S. (2007). Best practices in team leadership: What team leaders do to facilitate team effectiveness. In J. A. Conger & R. E. Riggio (Eds.), *The practice of leadership: Developing the next generation of leaders* (pp. 172–197). San Francisco: Jossey-Bass.

Stewart, G. L., & Manz, C. C. (1995). Leadership for self-managing work teams: A typology and integrative model. *Human Relations, 48*(7), 747–770.

Thomas, G., Martin, R., & Riggio, R. E. (2013). Leading groups: Leadership as a group process. *Group Processes and Intergroup Relations, 16*(1), 3–16.

Tuckman, B. W., & Jensen, M. A. C. (2010). Stages of small-group development revisited. *Group Facilitation: A Research and Applications Journal, 10*, 43–48.

Wageman, R., Fisher, C. M., & Hackman, J. R. (2009). Leading teams when the time is right: Finding the best moments to act. *Organizational Dynamics, 38*(3), 192–203.

Wageman, R., Gardner, H., & Mortensen, M. (2012). The changing ecology of teams: New directions for teams research. *Journal of Organizational Behavior, 33*, 301–315.

Wang, D., Waldman, D. A., & Zhang, Z. (2014). A meta-analysis of shared leadership and team effectiveness. *Journal of Applied Psychology, 99*(2), 181–198.

Zaccaro, S. J., Ardison, S. D., & Orvis, K. L. (2004). Leadership in virtual teams. In D. V. Day, S. J. Zaccaro, & S. M. Halpin (Eds.), *Leader development for transforming organizations: Growing leaders for tomorrow* (pp. 267–292). Mahwah, NJ: Lawrence Erlbaum.

Zaccaro, S. J., Heinen, B., & Shuffler, M. (2009). Team leadership and team effectiveness. In E. Salas, G. F. Goodwin, & C. S. Burke (Eds.), *Team effectiveness in complex organizations: Cross-disciplinary perspectives and approaches* (pp. 83–111). New York: Taylor & Francis Group.

Zaccaro, S. J., Rittman, A. L., & Marks, M. A. (2001). Team leadership. *Leadership Quarterly, 12*, 451–483.

15

Gender and Leadership

Crystal L. Hoyt and Stefanie Simon

DESCRIPTION

> *When you meet a human being, the first distinction you make is "male or female?" and you are accustomed to make the distinction with unhesitating certainty.*

—Sigmund Freud (1965, p. 141)

While academic researchers ignored issues related to gender and leadership until the 1970s (Chemers, 1997), the increasing number of women in leadership positions and women in academia brought about by dramatic changes in American society have fueled the now robust scholarly interest in the study of leadership and gender.

Scholars started out asking, "Can women lead?"—a question that is now moot. In addition to the increasing presence of women in corporate and political leadership roles, we can point to highly effective female leaders including former prime ministers such as Benazir Bhutto (Pakistan), Margaret Thatcher (UK), Gro Harlem Brundtland (Norway), and Indira Gandhi (India), and current world leaders such as Chancellor Angela Merkel of Germany and President Dilma Rousseff of Brazil. Beyond politics, there are many examples of highly effective female leaders including PepsiCo's CEO Indra Nooyi, Xerox's CEO Ursula Burns, retired Four-Star General Ann E. Dunwoody, and retired U.S. Supreme Court Justice Sandra Day O'Connor. The primary research questions now are "Do men and women lead differently?" and "Are men more effective leaders than women?" which are often subsumed under a larger question: "Why are women underrepresented in elite leadership roles?" This chapter explores empirical evidence related to these issues of gender and leadership by discussing the gender gap in leadership and prominent explanations for it, and addressing approaches to promoting women in leadership.

The Glass Ceiling Turned Labyrinth

We still think of a powerful man as a born leader and a powerful woman as an anomaly.

—Margaret Atwood (Hengen & Thomson, 2007, p. 336)

Evidence of the Leadership Labyrinth

Although the predicament of female leaders has improved significantly in recent decades, there is still a long way to go. Women earn 57% of the bachelor's degrees, 60% of the master's degrees, and more than half of the doctoral degrees (National Center for Education Statistics, 2011), and they make up nearly half of the U.S. labor force (46.8%; Catalyst, 2014c). However, women are still underrepresented in the upper echelons of America's corporations and political system. Women are among the leadership ranks in American organizations, occupying more than half of all management and professional positions (51.4%; Catalyst, 2014c) and a quarter of all CEO positions (26.8%; U.S. Bureau of Labor Statistics, 2013). However, more elite leadership positions show a different story; women represent only 4% of Fortune 500 CEOs (Catalyst, 2014a), and hold only 16.9% of the Fortune 500 board seats and a mere 14.6% of the Fortune 500 executive officer positions (Catalyst, 2014c).

On the political front, women currently occupy 100 of the 535 seats in the U.S. Congress (18.7%; 20% in the Senate and 18.4% in the House of Representatives); women of color occupy just 31 seats (Center for American Women and Politics, 2014a, 2014b). Indeed, as of April 2014, the world average of women's representation in national legislatures or parliaments was 21.9%, with the United States ranked 84th out of 189

▶ "Glass Ceiling" Misleading

countries (Inter-Parliamentary Union, 2014). Moreover, women represent just 6.9% of military officers at the level of brigadier general and rear admiral or higher (U.S. Department of Defense, 2014).

The invisible barrier preventing women from ascending into elite leadership positions was initially dubbed the *glass ceiling,* a term introduced into the American vernacular by two *Wall Street Journal* reporters in 1986 (Hymowitz & Schellhardt, 1986). Even in female-dominated occupations, women face the glass ceiling, whereas White men appear to ride a *glass escalator* to the top leadership positions (Maume, 1999; Williams, 1992, 1995). Eagly and Carli (2007) identified limitations with the glass ceiling metaphor, including that it implies that everyone has equal access to lower positions until all women hit this single, invisible, and impassable barrier. They put forward an alternative image of a leadership labyrinth conveying the impression of a journey riddled with challenges all along the way—not just near the top—that can and has been successfully navigated by women. Related, Facebook CEO Sheryl Sandberg recently proffered the metaphor of a jungle gym in her book *Lean In* (2013).

Understanding the Labyrinth

The gender gap in leadership is a global phenomenon whereby women are disproportionately concentrated in lower-level and lower-authority leadership positions compared to men (Powell & Graves, 2003). Discussions of women's underrepresentation in high-level leadership positions generally revolve around three types of explanations (Figure 15.1). The first set of explanations highlights differences in women's and men's investments in human capital. The next category of explanations considers gender differences between women and men. The final type of explanation focuses on prejudice and discrimination against female leaders.

Human Capital Differences. One prominent set of explanations for the labyrinth is that women have less human capital investment in education, training, and work experience than men (Eagly & Carli, 2004, 2007). This supposed lack of human capital is said to result in a dearth of qualified women, sometimes called a "pipeline problem." However, a closer look at the numbers reveals that women are indeed in the pipeline but that the pipeline is leaking. As already discussed, women are obtaining undergraduate degrees at a far higher rate than men, and women are earning professional and doctoral degrees at a rate greater than or nearly equal to that of men, but women are still vastly underrepresented in top leadership positions. In the domain of law, although women earn 47.3%

 Women in Politics

 Glass Ceiling

Figure 15.1 Understanding the Leadership Labyrinth

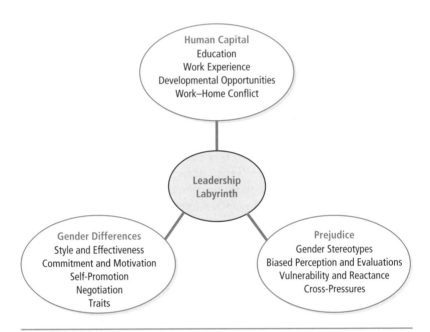

of all law degrees and make up 45% of associates, they make up only 19.9% of partners (American Bar Association, 2013). And even though women represent about one third of those graduating with MBAs from the top 10 business schools (Catalyst, 2014b), their representation in the upper echelons of American business pales in comparison to men.

Women do have somewhat less work experience and employment continuity than men, driven largely by the disproportionate responsibility women assume for child rearing and domestic duties (Bowles & McGinn, 2005; Eagly & Carli, 2007). Although men's participation in domestic labor has increased in recent years (Galinsky, Aumann, & Bond, 2008), women continue to do the majority of the child care responsibilities and household chores (Belkin, 2008; Craig, 2006; Pailhe & Solaz, 2006). Women respond to these work–home conflicts in a variety of ways (Bowles & McGinn, 2005). Some women choose not to marry or have children, others choose to become "superwomen" and attempt to excel in every role, and others take leaves of absence, take sick days, or choose part-time employment to juggle these work–home conflicts (Hewlett, 2002; Nieva & Gutek, 1981). Antiquated workplace norms make it difficult for women to rise in the leadership ranks:

 Gender Differences   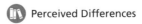 Perceived Differences

Those who take advantage of workplace leave and flexibility programs are often marginalized, and those who take time off from their careers often find reentry difficult, returning at a lower level than the level they left (Williams, 2010). A related explanation for the leadership gap is that this culturally prescribed division of labor leads women to self-select to take themselves out of leadership tracks by choosing "mommy track" positions that do not funnel into leadership positions (Belkin, 2003); however, research does not support this argument (Eagly & Carli, 2004; Williams, 2010).

Although women occupy more than half of all management and professional positions (Catalyst, 2014c), they have fewer developmental opportunities at work than do men. Many of these gender differences in developmental opportunities may be driven in part by the prejudice women experience in the domain of leadership. In addition to having fewer responsibilities in the same jobs as men, women are less likely to receive encouragement, be included in key networks, and receive formal job training than their male counterparts (Knoke & Ishio, 1998; Morrison & Von Glinow, 1990; Ohlott, Ruderman, & McCauley, 1994; Powell & Graves, 2003). One important developmental experience that affects career success is effective mentor relationships (Ensher & Murphy, 2005), and women confront greater barriers to establishing informal mentor relationships than men do (Powell & Graves, 2003). Additionally, women are disproportionately represented in business positions that are less visible, have less responsibility, and do not lead to top leadership positions (Bowles & McGinn, 2005). Relatedly, when women are promoted to leadership positions, they are more likely than men are to be placed on a "glass cliff," appointed to precarious leadership situations associated with greater risk and criticism (Ryan, Haslam, Hersby, & Bongiorno, 2011).

In sum, there is scant support for the notions that women receive less education than men, that they quit their jobs more often than men do, or that they opt out of the leadership track for the mommy track. There is support for the notion that women have less work experience and more career interruptions than men, largely because women assume significantly more domestic responsibility. Finally, women receive less formal training and have fewer developmental opportunities at work than men, both of which likely are related to prejudice against female leaders.

GENDER DIFFERENCES IN LEADERSHIP STYLES AND EFFECTIVENESS

Other arguments attempting to explain the leadership gap revolve around the notion that women are just different from men. One argument in this

 Effectiveness   Barriers

vein is that women's underrepresentation in elite leadership positions is a result of differences in leadership style and effectiveness.

Increasingly, writers in the mainstream press are asserting that there are indeed gender differences in leadership styles, and that women's leadership is more effective in contemporary society (Book, 2000; Helgesen, 1990; Rosener, 1995). Rather than explaining the leadership gap, these assertions make the gap that much more perplexing. However, academic researchers have a greater diversity in their views; indeed, many argue that gender has little or no relationship to leadership style and effectiveness (Dobbins & Platz, 1986; van Engen, Leeden, & Willemsen, 2001; Powell, 1990).

Meta-analyses of research examining style differences between women and men found that, contrary to stereotypic expectations, women were not found to lead in a more interpersonally oriented and less task-oriented manner than men in organizational studies. One robust gender difference found across settings is that women led in a more democratic, or participative, manner than men (Eagly & Johnson, 1990; van Engen & Willemsen, 2004). It is important to consider these results in conjunction with findings from a large-scale meta-analysis of the literature on evaluations of female and male leaders showing that women were devalued compared to men when they led in a masculine manner, when they occupied a typically masculine leadership role, and when the evaluators were male (Eagly, Makhijani, & Klonsky, 1992). These findings indicate that women's greater use of democratic style appears to be adaptive in that they are using the style that produces the most favorable evaluations.

More recent research has examined gender differences in transformational leadership (Bass, 1985; Burns, 1978; see Chapter 8). A meta-analysis by Eagly, Johannesen-Schmidt, and van Engen (2003) found small but robust differences between female and male leaders on these styles such that women's styles tend to be more transformational than men's, and women tend to engage in more contingent reward behaviors than men. Although these styles predict effectiveness, recent findings suggest that the devaluation of female leaders by male subordinates has been shown to extend to female transformational leaders (Ayman, Korabik, & Morris, 2009).

In addition to leadership style, the relative effectiveness of male and female leaders has been assessed in a number of studies (Jacobson & Effertz, 1974; Tsui & Gutek, 1984). In a meta-analysis comparing the effectiveness of female and male leaders, men and women were equally effective leaders, overall, but there were gender differences such that women and men were more effective in leadership roles that were congruent with their gender

N Women in Transformational Leadership

(Eagly, Karau, & Makhijani, 1995). Thus, women were less effective to the extent that the leader role was masculinized. For example, women were less effective than men were in military positions, but they were somewhat more effective than men were in education, government, and social service organizations, and substantially more effective than men were in middle management positions, where communal interpersonal skills are highly valued. In addition, women were less effective than men were when they supervised a higher proportion of male subordinates or when a greater proportion of male raters assessed the leaders' performance.

Another oft-cited barrier to women's advancement is the presumed gender difference in commitment to employment and motivation to lead. However, research indicates that women show the same level of identification with and commitment to paid employment roles as men do, and both women and men view their roles as workers to be secondary to their roles as parents and partners (Bielby & Bielby, 1988; Thoits, 1992). Empirical research does indicate that women are less likely than men are to promote themselves for leadership positions (Bowles & McGinn, 2005). For example, women are more likely to take on informal, as opposed to official, leadership roles, and use terms such as *facilitator* or *organizer* instead of *leader* (Andrews, 1992; Fletcher, 2001). A meta-analytic review of the research literature on leader emergence revealed that although women were less likely than men were to emerge as group leaders, they were more likely to serve as social facilitators than men were (Eagly & Karau, 1991). Another gender difference that advantages men in leadership is that men are more likely than women to ask for what they want (Babcock & Laschever, 2003). Reaching elite leadership positions is not done in a vacuum; people must negotiate with others to access the right positions, experiences, opportunities, resources, and assistance in both the professional and domestic spheres. Not only are women less likely to negotiate than men are (Small, Gelfand, Babcock, & Gettman, 2007), the negotiations needed to ascend the leadership hierarchy often are unstructured, ambiguous, and rife with gender triggers (factors that prompt gender-related behavioral responses)—exactly the type of situation that particularly disadvantages women (Bowles & McGinn, 2005).

This research must be interpreted in light of the social costs, or backlash, women experience when they promote themselves or are competent in positions of authority (Rudman & Glick, 2001). Women face significant gender biases and social disincentives when they self-promote and negotiate. Unlike men, for example, self-promoting women are seen as less socially attractive and less hirable (Rudman, 1998), and women face greater social costs for initiating negotiations than men do (Bowles, Babcock, & Lai, 2007).

 Global Female Leaders

In sum, empirical research supports small differences in leadership style and effectiveness between men and women. Women experience slight effectiveness disadvantages in masculine leader roles, whereas roles that are more feminine offer them some advantages. Additionally, women exceed men in the use of democratic or participatory styles, and they are more likely to use transformational leadership behaviors and contingent rewards, which are styles associated with contemporary notions of effective leadership. Women are no less effective at leading than men, and women are no less committed to their jobs or motivated for leadership roles than men. However, women are less likely to self-promote and negotiate than men. Furthermore, research shows a small gender difference such that women are more likely to focus on the welfare of others and ethical behavior.

Prejudice. One prominent explanation for the leadership gap revolves around gender biases stemming from stereotyped expectations that women take care and men take charge (Hoyt & Chemers, 2008). Stereotypes are cognitive shortcuts that influence the way people process information regarding groups and group members. People assign characteristics to groups, or individual members of groups, regardless of the actual variation in characteristics between the members (Hamilton, Stroessner, & Driscoll, 1994). Gender stereotypes are pervasive, well documented, and highly resistant to change (Dodge, Gilroy, & Fenzel, 1995; Heilman, 2001). Gender stereotypes both describe stereotypic beliefs about the attributes of women and men, and prescribe how men and women ought to be (Burgess & Borgida, 1999; Glick & Fiske, 1999). Men are stereotyped with agentic characteristics such as confidence, assertiveness, independence, rationality, and decisiveness, whereas women are stereotyped with communal characteristics such as concern for others, sensitivity, warmth, helpfulness, and nurturance (Deaux & Kite, 1993; Heilman, 2001).

Gender stereotypes are easily and automatically activated, and they often lead to biased judgments (Fiske, 1998; Kunda & Spencer, 2003). In addition to facing gender-based prejudice, women of color often also confront racial or ethnic prejudice (Bell & Nkomo, 2001). A vivid illustration of gender-based prejudice can be seen in the evaluation of men and women auditioning for symphony orchestras. In the 1970s and 1980s, male-dominated symphony orchestras made one simple change: All applicants were asked to audition while hidden behind a screen. This small change greatly increased the proportion of women in symphony orchestras (Goldin & Rouse, 2000). Merely seeing the applicant's sex evoked stereotype-based expectations in the judges' minds that resulted in a significant bias toward selecting men.

Military Leaders   Stereotypes

In leadership roles, gender stereotypes are particularly damaging for women because agentic, as opposed to communal, tendencies often are indispensable (Chemers & Murphy, 1995). According to role congruity theory, the agentic qualities thought necessary in the leadership role are incompatible with the predominantly communal qualities stereotypically associated with women, thus resulting in prejudice against female leaders (Eagly & Karau, 2002). Although the masculine construal of leadership has decreased somewhat over time, it remains pervasive and robust (Koenig, Eagly, Mitchell, & Ristikari, 2011). Thus, in the leadership role, women are confronted with cross-pressures: As leaders, they should be masculine and tough, but as women, they should not be "too manly." These opposing expectations for women often result in the perception that women are less qualified for elite leadership positions than men, and in harsh evaluations of effective female leaders for not being "female enough."

This prejudice against female leaders helps explain the numerous findings indicating less favorable attitudes toward female than male leaders, greater difficulty for women to attain top leadership roles, and greater difficulty for women to be viewed as effective in these roles (Eagly & Karau, 2002). The penalties for violating one's gender stereotypes are clearly illustrated in the classic 1989 Supreme Court case *Price Waterhouse v. Ann Hopkins*. Price Waterhouse told Hopkins that she would not make partner because she was too masculine, going as far as advising her to go to charm school, wear jewelry and makeup, and be less aggressive. In the end, the Court ruled that Price Waterhouse was discriminating based on gender stereotypes (Fiske, Bersoff, Borgida, Deaux, & Heilman, 1991). Gender bias was also evident in the media coverage of the 2008 U.S. presidential primaries involving Hillary Clinton. As Katie Couric noted after Clinton bowed out of contention, "One of the great lessons of that campaign is the continued and accepted role of sexism in American life, particularly the media . . . if Senator Obama had to confront the racist equivalent of an 'Iron My Shirt' poster at campaign rallies or a Hillary nutcracker sold at airports . . . the outrage would not be a footnote, it would be front page news" (Couric & Co., 2008).

Gender biases can be particularly detrimental in the decision-making processes for selecting elite leaders, given that the generally unstructured nature of those decisions allows biased decisions without accountability (Powell & Graves, 2003). Not only are the decision makers influenced by the stereotypes that disadvantage women in the leadership role, but also they may succumb to homosocial reproduction, a tendency for a group to reproduce itself in its own image (Kanter, 1977). People prefer similar others and report the most positive decisions about and evaluations of people who are most like them, biases that can clearly disadvantage women when male leaders are looking for replacements.

These stereotypic expectations not only affect others' perceptions and evaluations of female leaders, but also can directly affect the women themselves. Women who make up a very small minority of a male-dominated group are seen as tokens representing all women; they experience significant pressure as their highly visible performance is scrutinized, and they are perceived through gender-stereotyped lenses (Kanter, 1977). Women often are very aware of their gender and the accompanying stereotypes (Sekaquaptewa & Thompson, 2003). Research shows that women respond in one of two ways to the gender-based leadership stereotype: Either they demonstrate vulnerability by assimilating to the stereotype, or they react against it by engaging in stereotype-countering behaviors (Hoyt, 2010; Simon & Hoyt, 2013). Whether the threat of the gender-leader stereotype is met with vulnerability or reactance responses depends on factors such as the leader's self-efficacy, the explicitness of the stereotype, the type of task, the group sex-composition, and the power that the leader holds (Bergeron, Block, & Echtenkamp, 2006; Davies, Spencer, & Steele, 2005; Hoyt & Blascovich, 2007, 2010; Kray, Reb, Galinsky, & Thompson, 2004; Kray, Thompson, & Galinsky, 2001). Furthermore, although female leaders may demonstrate reactance to certain solitary gender stereotype threats, when such threats are combined, women are likely to demonstrate deleterious vulnerability responses (Hoyt, Johnson, Murphy, & Skinnell, 2010). In sum, substantial empirical evidence reveals that gender stereotypes can significantly alter the perception and evaluation of female leaders and directly affect women in or aspiring to leadership roles.

Navigating the Labyrinth

The number of women who successfully navigate the labyrinth is on the rise (Eagly & Carli, 2007). A confluence of factors contributes to this increase in effective female leaders (Figure 15.2). Changes in organizations are beginning to make it easier for women to reach top positions. The culture of many organizations is changing; gendered work assumptions such as the male model of work, the notion of uninterrupted full-time careers, and the separation of work and family are being challenged (Cooper & Lewis, 1999; Williams, 2010). Moreover, many organizations are valuing flexible workers and diversity in their top echelons. These organizations can augment women's career development by involving them in career development programs and formal networks, and offering work–life support. In

Stereotypes of Rhetoric

Figure 15.2   Leadership Effectiveness

Individual Level
Promoting Effective Negotiations
Use of Effective Leadership Styles

Interpersonal Level
Decreasing
Gender Stereotypes

Promoting
Leadership
Effectiveness

Societal Level
Gender Equity
in Domestic
Responsibilities

Organizational Level
Diversifying Leadership
Equity in Paternity/
Maternity Leave

addition, assigning more women to high-visibility positions and developing effective and supportive mentoring relationships for women are key strategies for reducing the leadership gap (Bell & Nkomo, 2001; Ensher & Murphy, 2005; Ragins, Townsend, & Mattis, 1998).

As Gloria Steinem famously noted, "We've begun to raise daughters more like sons . . . but few have the courage to raise our sons more like our daughters." Increasing parity in the involvement of women and men in child care and housework will go a long way in reducing the leadership gap (Eagly & Carli, 2007). In balancing work and home life, an appealing approach for women is structural role redefinition (Hall, 1972). This approach involves negotiating with both family and colleagues to renegotiate role expectations both at work and at home. For example, at home women can negotiate workload between spouses, team up with friends and family members, and, if able, hire help when necessary (Bowles & McGinn, 2005). At work, women can work for family-friendly reforms such as job-protected maternity leaves.

Beyond work–home issues, negotiations for valued positions, experiences, and resources are important social interactions on the road to top leadership positions. Thus, another approach to reducing the leadership gap is to enhance women's negotiation power and restructure negotiations to their advantage (Bowles & McGinn, 2005). For example, research has shown that

 Removing Barriers

the term *negotiation* is laden with gendered connotations, so one approach would be to reframe negotiation situations in nongendered terms such as "asking" situations.

Women who are aware of the labyrinth may circumvent barriers by starting their own ventures (Wirth, 2001). Women-owned businesses account for 40% of all privately owned businesses, employ more than 7 million people, and generate $1.3 trillion in sales (National Association of Women Business Owners Indianapolis, 2014). Women's successful foray into entrepreneurship is working to change the face of business, and by extension leadership, as we know it.

Many of the impediments women face in the leadership domain stem from the incongruity between the female gender role and the leadership role. Women face a double standard in the leadership role; they must come across as extremely competent but also as appropriately "feminine," a set of standards men are not held to (Eagly & Carli, 2003). One way women can increase their perceived warmth and their influence is by combining communal qualities such as warmth and friendliness with agentic qualities such as exceptional competence and assertiveness (Carli, 2001; Rudman & Glick, 2001). Additionally, the transformational leadership style discussed in Chapter 8 is particularly beneficial for women because it is not a markedly masculine style. This style encompasses traditionally feminine behaviors such as being considerate and supportive, and is strongly associated with leadership effectiveness. Recent research suggests that blending individualized consideration with inspirational motivation is prudent for women seeking leadership advancement (Vinkenburg, van Engen, Eagly, & Johannesen-Schmidt, 2011). The incongruity between the leadership role and the female gender role does appear to be decreasing (Eagly & Carli, 2007). Recent research indicates that women have become significantly more masculine— for example, becoming more assertive and valuing leadership and power more as job attributes, without losing their femininity (Konrad, Ritchie, Lieb, & Corrigall, 2000; Twenge, 2001). In addition, evidence suggests that the leadership role is starting to be seen as less masculine and more androgynous (Koenig et al., 2011; Schein, 2001).

In sum, we likely will see more women in elite leadership roles with (1) changes in workplace norms and developmental opportunities for women, (2) greater gender equity in domestic responsibilities, (3) greater negotiation power of women, especially regarding the work–home balance, (4) the effectiveness and predominance of women-owned businesses, and (5) changes in the incongruity between women and leadership.

Women Changing the Tone   Gender and Workgroup Performance

STRENGTHS

Understanding the research into gender and leadership can help us promote more women into the upper echelons of leadership. Doing so will fulfill the promise of equal opportunity by allowing everyone the possibility of taking on leadership roles, from the boardroom to the Senate floor. This larger and more demographically diverse pool of candidates not only makes it easier to find talented people, but it also facilitates greater levels of organizational success. Furthermore, promoting a richly diverse group of women into leadership roles will not only help make societal institutions, businesses, and governments more representative, but it can also contribute to more ethical, productive, innovative, and financially successful organizations that demonstrate higher levels of collective intelligence and are less rife with conflict (Bernardi, Bosco, & Columb, 2009; Catalyst, 2004; Forsyth, 2010; Miller & Del Carmen Triana, 2009; Nielsen & Huse, 2010; Woolley, Chabris, Pentland, Hashmi, & Malone, 2010).

A consideration of the effects of gender on leadership has important implications for a comprehensive understanding of leadership. Contemporary approaches to gender and leadership involve questions that directly affect leadership success, such as style and effectiveness differences between men and women, and the varied barriers confronting women. Gender is integral to contemporary notions of effective leadership styles that have morphed from a traditional masculine, autocratic style to the more feminine or androgynous styles of democratic and transformational leadership. Developing a more androgynous conception of leadership will enhance leadership effectiveness by giving people the opportunity to engage in the best leadership practices, and not by restricting people to those behaviors that are most appropriate for their gender.

Research on gender and leadership is productive in both dispelling myths about the gender gap and shining a light on aspects of the gender barriers that are difficult to see and therefore are often overlooked. For example, gender biases generally are no longer overt but more often take the form of subtle and implicit preconceptions and institutionalized discrimination, making them particularly potent and pernicious. These biases have a detrimental impact on the perception and evaluation of women, and they limit the range of leadership behavior deemed appropriate for women. In addition, the mere awareness of these gender biases can be detrimental to women performing in leadership roles. The changes needed to overcome these problems within organizations and society can occur only when we are aware of these often subtle and disguised prejudices.

 Non-Traditional Gender Leader Roles

 Gender in Organizations

Understanding the many components of the labyrinth will give us the tools necessary to combat this inequality from many perspectives, including individual, interpersonal, organizational, and societal approaches. In addition, this research addresses larger, more significant considerations about gender and social systems. For example, it acknowledges the profound power division between men and women, and it opens up dialogue on structural questions such as the gendered division of work in society. By acknowledging and attempting to understand issues of gender and leadership, rather than ignoring them, we can help ensure that women have equal opportunity in attaining influential leadership positions, that organizations and constituents have access to the greatest talent pool when selecting leaders, and that there is greater gender diversity in the ranks of leadership, which has been linked to organizational success.

CRITICISMS

Issues of gender and leadership can be subsumed under a more general topic of leadership and diversity. This perspective involves an understanding of the impact of various demographic characteristics on leadership, including—but not limited to—gender, race, ethnicity, and sexual orientation (Chemers & Murphy, 1995; Hoyt & Chemers, 2008). However, unlike the research examining gender and leadership, research into minority leaders is scant (Hoyt & Chemers, 2008). Although some of the issues surrounding minorities in leadership may bear similarities to those surrounding women (e.g., minorities also face negative stereotypes and resulting difficulties ascending the leadership hierarchy), the underlying dynamics and mechanisms are no doubt distinct (Gurin, 1985; Stangor, Lynch, Duan, & Glass, 1992). Leadership researchers should put a greater emphasis on understanding the role of race, ethnicity, sexual orientation, and other types of diversity, as well as important interactive effects between, for example, race and gender (Smith & Stewart, 1983), in leadership processes.

Much of the research examining gender in leadership has taken place in Western contexts; research on gender and leadership in other contexts is sparse. Because most of the findings regarding female leaders stem from the culturally defined role of women in society, many of the findings discussed in this chapter will not generalize well across cultures in which the roles of women and men differ. Therefore, we must realize the limited generalizability of the extant literature on gender and leadership, and researchers should expand their purview to address gender and leadership from a cross-cultural perspective. A final criticism concerns the dearth of essential, complementary research agendas on the domestic sphere. Research on gender and leadership focuses on decreasing the gender gap in leadership positions, thereby lessening gender segregation at work; however, the leadership gap will not be closed without a concurrent focus on closing the gender gap at home.

APPLICATION

Although the gender gap in influential leadership positions remains clearly visible, there is evidence that it is starting to close. Understanding the obstacles that make up the labyrinth and tactics to eradicate the inequality will make it easier for women to reach top positions. The labyrinth has many barriers, and the necessary changes occur at many levels, ranging from individual and interpersonal levels to organizational and societal levels. Prejudice plays an important role in the interpersonal and individual levels; the first step in dealing with these biases is to become aware of them in others and in ourselves. Women are faced with the problem of needing to bolster their leadership competence with appropriate "femaleness": Adopting behaviors such as individualized consideration and inspirational motivation is a promising approach to overcome these biased expectations. In addition, women's use of effective negotiation techniques can aid them in procuring the resources they need at work and at home to augment their leadership advancement.

Changes are also taking place at more macro-organizational and societal levels that will contribute to greater gender equality in leadership. For example, changes in organizational culture, women's career development, mentoring opportunities for women, and increased numbers of women in strategic positions will increase the presence of women in prominent leadership roles. At the societal level, structural changes regarding a more equitable distribution of child rearing and domestic duties are also contributing to the influx of women into elite positions.

CASE STUDIES

In the following section, three case studies (Cases 15.1, 15.2, and 15.3) are presented to provide practice in diagnosing and making recommendations on situations confronting female leaders in organizations. The first case is about a market analyst in a Wall Street firm, the second case is about a

 Improving Gender Equality

meeting of probation managers, and the third case is about a senior managing director at a manufacturing company. After each case, questions are provided to assist your analysis of the case. All cases were adapted from Blank and Slipp (1994).[1]

CASE 15.1

The "Glass Ceiling"

Lisa Weber never doubted that she would be a partner in her Wall Street firm. A graduate of a prestigious business school with a doctorate in economics, she had taught briefly at a major university. She was the first woman hired as a market analyst in her well-regarded firm. Within two years, she has become one of four senior portfolio managers reporting directly to a senior partner. Her clients give her the highest commendations for her outstanding performance; over the past two years, she has brought in the largest number of new accounts to the firm.

Despite the admiration of her colleagues and their seeming acceptance of her, there is a disturbing, if flattering, aspect to her job. Most of her peers and some of the partners visit her office during the day to discuss in private her opinions on market performance and financial projections. She enjoys these private sessions but is dismayed that at the weekly staff meetings the CEO, Michael Breyer, usually says something like, "OK, let's get started and bring Lisa up to date on some of the trouble spots." None of her peers or the partners mention that Lisa knows as much as they do about what's going on in the firm. She never protests this slight to her competence and knowledge of firm business, nor does she mention the almost-daily private meetings where her advice is sought. As the only woman on the executive level, she prefers to be considered a team player and one of the boys.

In the past year, one of her peers has been promoted to partner, although Lisa's performance clearly surpassed his, as measured by the success of her accounts and the amount of new business she brought to the firm. Having heard no mention of partnership for herself, she approached her boss, one of the partners, and asked about the path to a partnership. He replied, "You're doing great, Lisa, but professors do not partners make. What happens if you are a partner and you make a huge mistake? How would you take it? And what about our clients? There's never been a female partner in the 103 years of our firm."

Shortly thereafter, another woman, Pamela Tobias, was hired as a marketing analyst. Once, when the CEO saw Lisa and Pamela together, he called out to the men, "Hey, guys, two women in one room. That's scary."

During the next six months, Lisa meets several times with the CEO to make her case for a partnership on the basis of her performance. She finally realizes that there is no possibility of change in the foreseeable future and decides to leave and form her own investment firm.

SOURCE: Adapted from Blank and Slipp (1994).

Questions

1. What advancement barriers did Lisa encounter?

2. What should the firm's top executives, including Michael, have done differently to retain Lisa?

3. What type of organizational policies and opportunities might have benefited Lisa and Pamela?

4. What could the organization do to raise the gender consciousness of Michael and Lisa's male colleagues?

CASE 15.2

Lack of Inclusion and Credibility

Lori Bradley, an experienced probation officer, is meeting with Ted Stolze and Ian Bateson, two other probation officers, and their supervisor, Len Duggan, the assistant chief of probation. They are planning an orientation session for new probation officers on how to prepare investigative reports for the court.

As Lori enters the room, Ted and Ian are throwing paper clips at each other and laughing about a major play in the previous night's NFL championship game. They continue talking as she enters the room, ignoring her. When Len enters, the two men include him in their talk about the game.

After a few minutes, Len says, "OK, let's get down to business and start planning the orientation session. Any ideas?"

Lori says, "I looked again at the session prepared by Columbia County, which was described at our last meeting, and I think we should use that. It worked well for them and seems to fit our county." No one looks at

Lori or responds to her, but Ted begins making some suggestions for a different idea, and the others follow up with questions to him. After problems arise with Ted's suggestion, Ian says, "My idea would be to go for the Columbia County plan. That would work best here." Len, the assistant chief, says, "Ian, I'll go with your judgment." Ted says, "Me, too. Great idea, Ian."

Lori breaks in, "But that's what I proposed initially, and you just ignored me." Ian says, "Stop being so sensitive, Lori. We're supposed to be a team here."

SOURCE: Adapted from Blank and Slipp (1994).

Questions

1. What advancement barriers is Lori encountering?

2. What should Lori's male coworkers have done when Lori entered the room?

3. How should Len have behaved to provide a role model for Lori's male colleagues? What should Len have said after Ian made the same recommendation that Lori did?

4. What could the organization do to foster the effectiveness of all four managers?

CASE 15.3

Pregnancy as a Barrier to Job Status

Marina Soslow is a senior managing director at a manufacturing company. She has worked at the company for 10 years, gradually working her way up to a responsible position. She would like to win promotion to a top executive position and has recently finished an MBA, which supplements her master's degree in chemical engineering.

Several months ago, she found out she was pregnant. She is reluctant to tell her boss, Roy Bond, the division head, because she knows several other women who were eased out of their positions before they gave birth or shortly thereafter.

After a meeting with Roy about a new product, Marina mentions her pregnancy and says that she plans to take a three-month leave of absence after her delivery. She begins describing the plans she has carefully worked out for distributing her work. Roy cuts her short and says, "I knew this was going to happen sooner or later; it always does." He says this as if a disaster is about to occur. "There's no point in talking about this now. We'll think about it later."

Marina can tell that he's very annoyed about what he thinks is going to happen. She can see his wheels spinning and worries about the implications for her. She thinks, "Doesn't Roy know about the Family and Medical Leave Act of 1993? Legally, this company has to guarantee my job, but I know he can make it very rough for me."

SOURCE: Adapted from Blank and Slipp (1994).

Questions

1. What advancement barriers is Marina encountering?

2. What should Roy have said when Marina told him she was pregnant?

3. What could Roy do to ensure that Marina's work will be covered during her absence and that taking this time off will not hurt her advancement?

4. What type of organizational changes can be made to benefit Marina and other pregnant women in this organization?

LEADERSHIP INSTRUMENT

The Implicit Association Test (IAT) was developed by Anthony Greenwald, Mahzarin Banaji, and Brian Nosek to measure automatic associations by examining reaction times when people classify pictures or words (see Greenwald, McGhee, & Schwartz, 1998). This gender IAT was modified from a version developed by Dasgupta and Asgari (2004) to examine the gender stereotypical associations that contribute to the bias against women as leaders (Eagly & Karau, 2002).

The Gender–Leader Implicit Association Test

Instructions: This exercise begins with a practice trial. Using a pencil, classify each of the words in the middle column into one of the two categories indicated, *Flower* or *Insect,* by putting a check mark in the column to the left or the right. Please do this task as quickly as possible, taking care not to skip over any words.

Practice Trial

Flower		Insect
O	Rose	O
O	Lily	O
O	Dragonfly	O
O	Beetle	O
O	Gnat	O
O	Daffodil	O
O	Mosquito	O
O	Daisy	O
O	Roach	O
O	Tulip	O

You will now complete the two test trials; you will need a stopwatch for this portion of the test. For these test trials, the categories are Male or Female and Leader or Supporter, and the categories will be combined. If the word you read belongs to the *Male* or the *Leader* category, put a check in the left column; if it belongs to the *Female* or the *Supporter* category, put a check in the right column. You will record how long it takes you to complete this task by starting your stopwatch when you begin and stopping it after you make your final classification. Remember to work as quickly as possible, without skipping any words.

Test Trial A

Male or Leader		Female or Supporter
O	Emily	O
O	Josh	O

Male or Leader		Female or Supporter
O	Supporter	O
O	Leader	O
O	Brandon	O
O	Ambitious	O
O	Peter	O
O	Determined	O
O	Donna	O
O	Debbie	O
O	Helpful	O
O	Dynamic	O
O	Understanding	O
O	Katherine	O
O	Ian	O
O	Sympathetic	O
O	Compassionate	O
O	Jane	O
O	Andrew	O
O	Assertive	O

Time to complete Test Trial A: _____

You will do this same task a second time, but this time the combination of categories has been switched. If the word you read belongs to the *Male* or the *Supporter* category, put a check in the left column; if it belongs to the *Female* or the *Leader* category, put a check in the right column. Again, use your stopwatch to time how long it takes you to complete the task.

Test Trial B

Male or Supporter		Female or Leader
O	Supporter	O
O	Emily	O
O	Josh	O
O	Leader	O

(Continued)

(Continued)

Male or Supporter		Female or Leader
O	Ambitious	O
O	Brandon	O
O	Peter	O
O	Donna	O
O	Helpful	O
O	Determined	O
O	Dynamic	O
O	Assertive	O
O	Debbie	O
O	Katherine	O
O	Understanding	O
O	Ian	O
O	Sympathetic	O
O	Andrew	O
O	Compassionate	O
O	Jane	O

Time to complete Test Trial B: _____

Scoring

The logic behind the IAT is that the longer it takes to categorize the words when the categories have counterstereotypical pairings (i.e., *Female* and *Leader, Male* and *Supporter*) compared with stereotypical pairings, the more one automatically associates women with supportive qualities as opposed to leadership qualities.

The gender bias effect is computed by subtracting the time it took to complete Trial A (the stereotype congruent task) from the time to complete Trial B (the stereotype incongruent task). Positive scores reflect automatic associations between *Female* and *Supporter* and between *Male* and *Leader.* Many people are surprised to find out that they have a biased association favoring males and leadership, especially when it is incompatible with their stated egalitarian values. This test is designed to show people that they might hold associations that they are unaware of and to make people aware of the broad reach of these stereotypes. Please see the IAT website at Harvard University (https://implicit.harvard.edu) for more information on the IAT and a more detailed understanding of the results.

SUMMARY

Women are significantly underrepresented in major leadership positions. The barriers women encounter on their leadership journey have been dubbed the *leadership labyrinth*. Removing these barriers will help ensure equal opportunity, access to the greatest talent pool, and diversity, which have been linked to organizational success. There are a number of explanations for the leadership gender gap. One set of explanations focuses on women's lack of *human capital investment* in education, training, and work experience. There is no empirical support for the argument that women are less educated than men are or that they are more likely to quit their jobs or choose the mommy track. There is evidence that women assume significantly more domestic responsibility, which contributes to less work experience and more career interruptions. Additionally, women receive less formal training and have fewer developmental opportunities at work than men.

Another set of explanations for the gender gap focuses on *differences between women and men*. Women are no less effective at leadership, committed to their work, or motivated to attain leadership roles than men. However, women are less likely to self-promote than men are, and they are less likely to initiate negotiation, an important tool all leaders need in order to access the right opportunities and resources in both the professional and domestic spheres. Investigations into leadership style have revealed that women are somewhat more likely to use democratic and transformational styles than men are. Research looking at leadership effectiveness indicates a greater use by women of effective transformational and contingent reward behaviors.

The *prejudice* explanation for the leadership gap is strongly supported. Gender stereotypes of women as communal and men as agentic are particularly damaging to women in leadership. The incongruity between the female gender role and the leadership role leads to prejudice against female leaders, who are evaluated and perceived more negatively than their male counterparts. These biases are particularly detrimental during unstructured decision-making processes that often occur when elite leaders are selected. Gender-based leader stereotypes can threaten women eliciting either a vulnerable or a reactance response. There is evidence that this discrepancy is on the decline as the leader role becomes more androgynous and women become more agentic.

Finally, there are a number of approaches to navigating the labyrinth. Significant organizational reform will make it easier for women to reach top positions—including changes in workplace norms, changes in organizational culture, increases in career development for women, increases in effective mentoring opportunities, and women taking more strategic positions leading to higher leadership roles. Effective negotiations will help decrease the gender gap, especially negotiations regarding role expectations at work and at home. Additionally, the combination of warmth with agentic qualities and in particular the melding of individualized consideration with inspirational motivation can be effective for developing female leaders.

Sharpen your skills with SAGE edge at **edge.sagepub.com/northouse7e**

NOTE

1. Adapted from *Voices of Diversity*. Copyright 1994 by Renee Blank and Sandra Slipp. Reprinted by permission of AMACOM, a division of American Management Association International, New York, NY. All rights reserved. http://www.amanet.org.

REFERENCES

American Bar Association. (2013). *Commission on women in the profession: A current glance at women in the law 2013.* Retrieved from http://www.americanbar.org/content/dam/aba/marketing/women/current_glance_statistics_feb2013.auth checkdam.pdf

Andrews, P. H. (1992). Sex and gender differences in group communication: Impact on the facilitation process. *Small Group Research, 23,* 74–94.

Ayman, R., Korabik, K., & Morris, S. (2009). Is transformational leadership always perceived as effective? Male subordinates' devaluation of female transformational leaders. *Journal of Applied Social Psychology, 39,* 852–879.

Babcock, L., & Laschever, S. (2003). *Women don't ask: Negotiation and the gender divide.* Princeton, NJ: Princeton University Press.

Bass, B. M. (1985). Leadership: Good, better, best. *Organizational Dynamics, 13,* 26–40.

Belkin, L. (2003, October 26). The opt-out revolution. *The New York Times,* p. 42.

Belkin, L. (2008, June 15). When mom and dad share it all. *The New York Times.* Retrieved from http://www.nytimes.com/2008/06/15/magazine/15parenting-t .html?ref=jobs&pagewanted=all

Bell, E., & Nkomo, S. (2001). *Our separate ways: Black and white women and the struggle for professional identity.* Boston: Harvard Business School Press.

Bergeron, D. M., Block, C. J., & Echtenkamp, B. A. (2006). Disabling the able: Stereotype threat and women's work performance. *Human Performance, 19,* 133–158.

Bernardi, R. A., Bosco, S. M., & Columb, V. L. (2009). Does female representation on boards of directors associate with the "Most Ethical Companies" list? *Corporate Reputation Review, 12,* 270–280.

Bielby, D. D., & Bielby, W. T. (1988). She works hard for the money: Household responsibilities and the allocation of work effort. *American Journal of Sociology, 93,* 1031–1059.

Blank, R., & Slipp, S. (1994). *Voices of diversity.* New York: AMACOM.

Book, E. W. (2000). *Why the best man for the job is a woman.* New York: HarperCollins.

Bowles, H. R., Babcock, L., & Lai, L. (2007). Social incentives for gender differences in the propensity to initiate negotiations: Sometimes it does hurt to ask. *Organizational Behavior and Human Decision Processes, 103,* 84–103.

Bowles, H. R., & McGinn, K. L. (2005). Claiming authority: Negotiating challenges for women leaders. In D. M. Messick & R. M. Kramer (Eds.), *The psychology of leadership: New perspectives and research* (pp. 191–208). Mahwah, NJ: Lawrence Erlbaum.

Burgess, D., & Borgida, E. (1999). Who women are, who women should be: Descriptive and prescriptive gender stereotyping in sex discrimination. *Psychology, Public Policy, & Law, 5,* 665–692.

Burns, J. M. (1978). *Leadership.* New York: Plenum.

Carli, L. L. (2001). Gender and social influence. *Journal of Social Issues, 57,* 725–741.

Catalyst. (2004). *The bottom line: Connecting corporate performance and gender diversity.* New York: Author.

Catalyst. (2014a). *Fortune 500 CEO positions held by women.* Retrieved from http://www.catalyst.org/knowledge/fortune-500-ceo-positions-held-women

Catalyst. (2014b). *Women MBAs.* Retrieved from http://www.catalyst.org/knowledge/women-mbas

Catalyst. (2014c). *U.S. women in business.* Retrieved from http://www.catalyst.org/knowledge/us-women-business

Center for American Women and Politics. (2014a). *Women in elective office 2014.* Retrieved from http://www.cawp.rutgers.edu/fast_facts/levels_of_office/documents/elective.pdf

Center for American Women and Politics. (2014b). *Women of color in elective office 2014.* Retrieved from http://www.cawp.rutgers.edu/fast_facts/levels_of_office/documents/color.pdf

Chemers, M. M. (1997). *An integrative theory of leadership.* Mahwah, NJ: Lawrence Erlbaum.

Chemers, M. M., & Murphy, S. E. (1995). Leadership and diversity in groups and organizations. In M. M. Chemers, S. Oskamp, & M. A. Constanzo (Eds.), *Diversity in organizations: New perspectives for a changing workplace* (pp. 157–190). Thousand Oaks, CA: SAGE.

Cooper, C. L., & Lewis, S. (1999). Gender and the changing nature of work. In G. N. Powell (Ed.), *Handbook of gender and work* (pp. 37–46). Thousand Oaks, CA: SAGE.

Couric & Co. (2008). *Katie Couric's notebook: Sexism and politics.* Retrieved from http://www.cbsnews.com/blogs/2008/06/11/couricandco/entry4174429.shtml

Craig, L. (2006). Does father care mean fathers share? A comparison of how mothers and fathers in intact families spend time with children. *Gender and Society, 20,* 259–281.

Dasgupta, N., & Asgari, S. (2004). Seeing is believing: Exposure to counterstereotypic women leaders and its effect on automatic gender stereotyping. *Journal of Experimental Social Psychology, 40,* 642–658.

Davies, P. G., Spencer, S. J., & Steele, C. M. (2005). Clearing the air: Identity safety moderates the effects of stereotype threat on women's leadership aspirations. *Journal of Personality and Social Psychology, 88,* 276–287.

Deaux, K., & Kite, M. (1993). Gender stereotypes. In F. L. Denmark & M. Paludi (Eds.), *Psychology of women: A handbook of theory and issues* (pp. 107–139). Westport, CT: Greenwood.

Dobbins, G. H., & Platz, S. J. (1986). Sex differences in leadership: How real are they? *Academy of Management Review, 11,* 118–127.

Dodge, K. A., Gilroy, F. D., & Fenzel, L. M. (1995). Requisite management characteristics revisited: Two decades later. *Journal of Social Behavior and Personality, 10,* 253–264.

Eagly, A. H., & Carli, L. L. (2003). The female leadership advantage: An evaluation of the evidence. *Leadership Quarterly, 14,* 807–834.

Eagly, A. H., & Carli, L. L. (2004). Women and men as leaders. In J. Antonakis, R. J. Sternberg, & A. T. Cianciolo (Eds.), *The nature of leadership* (pp. 279–301). Thousand Oaks, CA: SAGE.

Eagly, A. H., & Carli, L. L. (2007). *Through the labyrinth: The truth about how women become leaders.* Boston: Harvard Business School Press.

Eagly, A. H., Johannesen-Schmidt, M. C., & van Engen, M. (2003). Transformational, transactional, and laissez-faire leadership styles: A meta-analysis comparing women and men. *Psychological Bulletin, 129,* 569–591.

Eagly, A. H., & Johnson, B. T. (1990). Gender and leadership style: A meta-analysis. *Psychological Bulletin, 108,* 233–256.

Eagly, A. H., & Karau, S. J. (1991). Gender and the emergence of leaders: A meta-analysis. *Journal of Personality and Social Psychology, 60,* 685–710.

Eagly, A. H., & Karau, S. J. (2002). Role congruity theory of prejudice toward female leaders. *Psychological Review, 109,* 573–598.

Eagly, A. H., Karau, S. J., & Makhijani, M. G. (1995). Gender and the effectiveness of leaders: A meta-analysis. *Psychological Bulletin, 117,* 125–145.

Eagly, A. H., Makhijani, M., & Klonsky, B. (1992). Gender and the evaluation of leaders: A meta-analysis. *Psychological Bulletin, 111,* 3–22.

Ensher, E. A., & Murphy, S. E. (2005). *Power mentoring: How successful mentors and protégés get the most out of their relationships.* San Francisco: Jossey-Bass.

Fiske, S. (1998). Stereotyping, prejudice, and discrimination. In D. T. Gilbert, S. T. Fiske, & G. Lindzey (Eds.), *The handbook of social psychology* (4th ed., Vol. 2, pp. 982–1026). Boston: McGraw-Hill.

Fiske, S., Bersoff, D. N., Borgida, E., Deaux, K., & Heilman, M. E. (1991). Social science research on trial: Use of sex stereotyping research in *Price Waterhouse v. Hopkins. American Psychologist, 46,* 1049–1060.

Fletcher, J. K. (2001). *Disappearing acts: Gender, power, and relational practice at work.* Boston: MIT Press.

Forsyth, D. R. (2010). *Group dynamics* (5th ed.). Belmont, CA: Wadsworth.

Freud, S. (1965). *New introductory lectures on psychoanalysis: Femininity.* New York: Norton.

Galinsky, E., Aumann, K., & Bond, J. (2008). *Times are changing: Gender and generation at work and at home.* Retrieved from http://familiesandwork.org/site/research/reports/Times_Are_Changing.pdf

Glick, P., & Fiske, S. T. (1999). Sexism and other "isms": Independence, status, and the ambivalent content of stereotypes. In W. B. Swann, Jr., & J. H. Langlois (Eds.), *Sexism and stereotypes in modern society: The gender science of Janet Taylor Spence* (pp. 193–221). Washington, DC: American Psychological Association.

Goldin, C., & Rouse, C. (2000). Orchestrating impartiality: The impact of "blind" auditions on female musicians. *American Economic Review, 90,* 715–741.

Greenwald, A. G., McGhee, D. E., & Schwartz, J. L. K. (1998). Measuring individual differences in implicit cognition: The implicit association test. *Journal of Personality and Social Psychology, 74,* 1464–1480.

Gurin, P. (1985). Women's gender consciousness. *Public Opinion Quarterly, 49,* 143–163.

Hall, D. T. (1972). A model of coping with role conflict: The role behavior of college-educated women. *Administrative Science Quarterly, 17,* 471–486.

Hamilton, D. L., Stroessner, S. J., & Driscoll, D. M. (1994). Social cognition and the study of stereotyping. In P. G. Devine, D. L. Hamilton, & T. M. Ostrom (Eds.), *Social cognition: Impact on social psychology* (pp. 291–321). New York: Academic Press.

Heilman, M. E. (2001). Description and prescription: How gender stereotypes prevent women's ascent up the organizational ladder. *Journal of Social Issues, 57,* 657–674.

Helgesen, S. (1990). *The female advantage: Women's ways of leadership.* New York: Doubleday.

Hengen, S., & Thomson, A. (Eds.). (2007). *Margaret Atwood: A reference guide, 1988–2005.* Lanham, MD: Scarecrow Press.

Hewlett, S. A. (2002). *Creating a life: Professional women and the quest for children.* New York: Talk Miramax.

Hoyt, C. L. (2010). Women, men, and leadership: Exploring the gender gap at the top. *Social and Personality Psychology Compass, 4,* 484–498.

Hoyt, C., & Blascovich, J. (2007). Leadership efficacy and women leaders' responses to stereotype activation. *Group Processes and Intergroup Relations, 10,* 595–616.

Hoyt, C., & Blascovich, J. (2010). The role of self-efficacy and stereotype activation on cardiovascular, behavioral and self-report responses in the leadership domain. *Leadership Quarterly, 21,* 89–103.

Hoyt, C. L., & Chemers, M. M. (2008). Social stigma and leadership: A long climb up a slippery ladder. In C. L. Hoyt, G. R. Goethals, & D. R. Forsyth (Eds.), *Leadership at the crossroads: Leadership and psychology* (Vol. 1, pp. 165–180). Westport, CT: Praeger.

Hoyt, C., Johnson, S., Murphy, S., & Skinnell, K. (2010). The impact of blatant stereotype activation and group sex-composition on female leaders. *Leadership Quarterly, 21,* 716–732.

Hymowitz, C., & Schellhardt, T. D. (1986, March 24). The glass ceiling: Why women can't seem to break the invisible barrier that blocks them from the top jobs. *The Wall Street Journal,* pp. D1, D4–D5.

Inter-Parliamentary Union. (2014). *Women in national parliaments.* Retrieved from http://www.ipu.org/wmn-e/classif.htm

Jacobson, M. B., & Effertz, J. (1974). Sex roles and leadership perceptions of the leaders and the led. *Organizational Behavior and Human Performance, 12*, 383–396.

Kanter, R. (1977). *Men and women of the corporation.* New York: Basic Books.

Knoke, D., & Ishio, Y. (1998). The gender gap in company job training. *Work and Occupations, 25*, 141–167.

Koenig, A. M., Eagly, A. H., Mitchell, A. A., & Ristikari, T. (2011). Are leader stereotypes masculine? A meta-analysis of three research paradigms. *Psychological Bulletin, 137*, 616–642.

Konrad, A. M., Ritchie, J. E., Jr., Lieb, P., & Corrigall, E. (2000). Sex differences and similarities in job attribute preferences: A meta-analysis. *Psychological Bulletin, 126*, 593–641.

Kray, L., Reb, J., Galinsky, A., & Thompson, L. (2004). Stereotype reactance at the bargaining table: The effect of stereotype activation and power on claiming and creating value. *Personality and Social Psychology Bulletin, 30*, 399–411.

Kray, L. J., Thompson, L., & Galinsky, A. (2001). Battle of the sexes: Gender stereotype confirmation and reactance in negotiations. *Journal of Personality & Social Psychology, 80*, 942–958.

Kunda, Z., & Spencer, S. J. (2003). When do stereotypes come to mind and when do they color judgment? A goal-based theory of stereotype activation and application. *Psychological Bulletin, 129*, 522–544.

Maume, D. J., Jr. (1999). Glass ceilings and glass escalators. *Work & Occupations, 26*, 483.

Miller, T., & Del Carmen Triana, M. (2009). Demographic diversity in the boardroom: Mediators of the board diversity-firm performance relationship. *Journal of Management Studies, 46*, 755–786.

Morrison, A., & Von Glinow, M. A. (1990). Women and minorities in management. *American Psychologist, 45*, 200–208.

National Association of Women Business Owners Indianapolis. (2014). *Women-owned businesses key facts.* Retrieved from http://www.nawboindy.org/pagesroot/Pages/AboutWBOKeyFacts.aspx

National Center for Education Statistics. (2011). Table 317: Bachelor's, master's, and doctor's degrees conferred by degree-granting institutions, by sex of student and discipline division: 2010–11. *Digest of Education Statistics.* Retrieved from http://nces.ed.gov/programs/digest/d12/tables/dt12_317.asp

Nielsen, S., & Huse, M. (2010). The contribution of women on boards of directors: Going beyond the surface. *Corporate Governance—An International Review, 18*, 136–148.

Nieva, V. E., & Gutek, B. A. (1981). *Women and work: A psychological perspective.* New York: Praeger.

Ohlott, P. J., Ruderman, M. N., & McCauley, C. D. (1994). Gender differences in managers' developmental job experiences. *Academy of Management Journal, 37*, 46–67.

Pailhe, A., & Solaz, A. (2006). Time with children: Do fathers and mothers replace each other when one parent is unemployed? *European Journal of Population, 24*, 211–236. doi:10.1007/s10680–007–9143–5

Powell, G. N. (1990). One more time: Do female and male managers differ? *Academy of Management Executive, 4*, 68–75.

Powell, G. N., & Graves, L. M. (2003). *Women and men in management* (3rd ed.). Thousand Oaks, CA: SAGE.

Ragins, B. R., Townsend, B., & Mattis, M. (1998). Gender gap in the executive suite: CEOs and female executives report on breaking the glass ceiling. *Academy of Management Executive, 12,* 28–42.

Rosener, J. (1995). *America's competitive secret: Utilizing women as a management strategy.* New York: Oxford University Press.

Rudman, L. A. (1998). Self-promotion as a risk factor for women: The costs and benefits of counter-stereotypical impression management. *Journal of Personality and Social Psychology, 74,* 629–645.

Rudman, L. A., & Glick, P. (2001). Prescriptive gender stereotypes and backlash toward agentic women. *Journal of Social Issues, 57,* 743–762.

Ryan, M. K., Haslam, S. A., Hersby, M. D., & Bongiorno, R. (2011). Think crisis–think female: The glass cliff and contextual variation in the think manager–think male stereotype. *Journal of Applied Psychology, 96,* 470–484.

Sandberg, S. (2013). *Lean in: Women, work, and the will to lead.* New York: Knopf.

Schein, V. E. (2001). A global look at psychological barriers to women's progress in management. *Journal of Social Issues, 57,* 675–688.

Sekaquaptewa, D., & Thompson, M. (2003). Solo status, stereotype threat, and performance expectancies: Their effects on women's performance. *Journal of Experimental Social Psychology, 39,* 68–74.

Simon, S., & Hoyt, C. L. (2013). Exploring the effect of media images on women's leadership self-perceptions and aspirations. *Group Processes & Intergroup Relations, 16,* 232–245.

Small, D. A., Gelfand, M., Babcock, L., & Gettman, H. (2007). Who goes to the bargaining table? The influence of gender and framing on the initiation of negotiation. *Journal of Personality and Social Psychology, 93,* 600–613.

Smith, A., & Stewart, A. J. (1983). Approaches to studying racism and sexism in black women's lives. *Journal of Social Issues, 39,* 1–15.

Stangor, C., Lynch, L., Duan, C., & Glass, B. (1992). Categorization of individuals on the basis of multiple social features. *Journal of Personality and Social Psychology, 62,* 207–218.

Thoits, P. A. (1992). Identity structures and psychological well-being: Gender and marital status comparisons. *Social Psychology Quarterly, 55,* 236–256.

Tsui, A. S., & Gutek, B. A. (1984). A role set analysis of gender differences in performance, affective relationship, and career success of industrial middle managers. *Academy of Management Journal, 27,* 619–635.

Twenge, J. M. (2001). Change in women's assertiveness in response to status and roles: A cross-temporal meta-analysis, 1931–1993. *Journal of Personality and Social Psychology, 81,* 133–145.

U.S. Bureau of Labor Statistics. (2013). Table 11: Employed persons by detailed occupation, sex, race, and Hispanic or Latino ethnicity. *Current Population Survey, Annual Averages: Household Data.* Retrieved from http://www.bls.gov/cps/cpsaat11.pdf

U.S. Department of Defense. (2014). *Active duty military personnel by service by rank/grade* (for April 2014). Retrieved from https://www.dmdc.osd.mil/appj/dwp/dwp_reports.jsp

van Engen, M. L., Leeden, R., van der, & Willemsen, T. M. (2001). Gender, context and leadership styles: A field study. *Journal of Occupational and Organizational Psychology, 74,* 581–598.

van Engen, M. L., & Willemsen, T. M. (2004). Sex and leadership styles: A meta-analysis of research published in the 1990s. *Psychological Reports, 94,* 3–18.

Vinkenburg, C. J., van Engen, M. L., Eagly, A. H., & Johannesen-Schmidt, M. C. (2011). An exploration of stereotypical beliefs about leadership styles: Is transformational leadership a route to women's promotion? *The Leadership Quarterly, 22,* 10–21.

Williams, C. L. (1992). The glass escalator: Hidden advantages for men in the "female" professions. *Social Problems, 39,* 253–267.

Williams, C. L. (1995). *Still a man's world: Men who do "women's work."* Berkeley: University of California Press.

Williams, J. (2010). *Reshaping the work-family debate: Why men and class matter.* Cambridge, MA: Harvard University Press.

Wirth, L. (2001). *Breaking through the glass ceiling: Women in management.* Geneva: International Labour Office.

Woolley, A. W., Chabris, C. F., Pentland, A., Hashmi, N., & Malone, T. M. (2010). Evidence for a collective intelligence factor in the performance of human groups. *Science, 330,* 686–688.

16

Culture and Leadership

DESCRIPTION

As the title suggests, this chapter is about culture *and* leadership. Like the previous chapter, this one is multifaceted and focuses on a collection of related ideas rather than on a single unified theory. Our discussion in this chapter will center on research that describes culture, its dimensions, and the effects of culture on the leadership process.

Since World War II, globalization has been advancing throughout the world. Globalization is the increased interdependence (economic, social, technical, and political) between nations. People are becoming more interconnected. There is more international trade, cultural exchange, and use of worldwide telecommunication systems. In the past 10 years, our schools, organizations, and communities have become far more global than in the past. Increased globalization has created many challenges, including the need to design effective multinational organizations, to identify and select appropriate leaders for these entities, and to manage organizations with culturally diverse employees (House & Javidan, 2004). Globalization has created a need to understand how cultural differences affect leadership performance.

Globalization has also created the need for leaders to become competent in cross-cultural awareness and practice. Adler and Bartholomew (1992) contended that global leaders need to develop five cross-cultural competencies: First, leaders need to understand business, political, and cultural environments worldwide. Second, they need to learn the perspectives, tastes, trends, and technologies of many other cultures. Third, they need to be able to work

 N Culture and Leadership ▶ Globalization

simultaneously with people from many cultures. Fourth, leaders must be able to adapt to living and communicating in other cultures. Fifth, they need to learn to relate to people from other cultures from a position of equality rather than cultural superiority (Adler & Bartholomew, 1992, p. 53). Additionally, Ting-Toomey (1999) said that global leaders need to be skilled in creating transcultural visions. They need to develop communication competencies that will enable them to articulate and implement their vision in a diverse workplace. In sum, today's leaders need to acquire a challenging set of competencies if they intend to be effective in present-day global societies.

Culture Defined

Anthropologists, sociologists, and many others have debated the meaning of the word *culture*. Because it is an abstract term, it is hard to define, and different people often define it in dissimilar ways. For our purposes, *culture* is defined as the learned beliefs, values, rules, norms, symbols, and traditions that are common to a group of people. It is these *shared* qualities of a group that make them unique. Culture is dynamic and transmitted to others. In short, culture is the way of life, customs, and script of a group of people (Gudykunst & Ting-Toomey, 1988).

Related to culture are the terms *multicultural* and *diversity*. *Multicultural* implies an approach or a system that takes more than one culture into account. It refers to the existence of multiple cultures such as African, American, Asian, European, and Middle Eastern. *Multicultural* can also refer to a set of subcultures defined by race, gender, ethnicity, sexual orientation, or age. *Diversity* refers to the existence of different cultures or ethnicities within a group or an organization.

Related Concepts

Before beginning our discussion of the various facets of culture, this section describes two concepts that are closely related to culture and leadership: *ethnocentrism* and *prejudice*. Both of these concepts can have impacts on how leaders influence others.

Ethnocentrism

As the word suggests, *ethnocentrism* is the tendency for individuals to place their own group (ethnic, racial, or cultural) at the center of their observations

 Global VS Local

 Leadership and Cultural Diversity

of others and the world. People tend to give priority and value to their own beliefs, attitudes, and values, over and above those of other groups. Ethnocentrism is the perception that one's own culture is better or more natural than the culture of others. It may include the failure to recognize the unique perspectives of others. Ethnocentrism is a universal tendency, and each of us is ethnocentric to some degree.

Ethnocentrism is like a perceptual window through which people from one culture make subjective or critical evaluations of people from another culture (Porter & Samovar, 1997). For example, some Americans think that the democratic principles of the United States are superior to the political beliefs of other cultures; they often fail to understand the complexities of other cultures. Ethnocentrism accounts for our tendency to think our own cultural values and ways of doing things are right and natural (Gudykunst & Kim, 1997).

Ethnocentrism can be a major obstacle to effective leadership because it prevents people from fully understanding or respecting the viewpoints of others. For example, if one person's culture values individual achievement, it may be difficult for that person to understand another person whose culture emphasizes collectivity (i.e., people working together as a whole). Similarly, if one person believes strongly in respecting authority, that person may find it difficult to understand someone who challenges authority or does not easily defer to authority figures. The more ethnocentric we are, the less open or tolerant we are of other people's cultural traditions or practices.

A skilled leader cannot avoid issues related to ethnocentrism. Even though she recognizes her own ethnocentrism, a leader also needs to understand—and to a degree tolerate—the ethnocentrism of others. In reality, it is a balancing act for leaders. On the one hand, they need to promote and be confident in their own ways of doing things; on the other hand, they need to be sensitive to the legitimacy of the ways of other cultures. Skilled leaders are able to negotiate the fine line between trying to overcome ethnocentrism and knowing when to remain grounded in their own cultural values.

Prejudice

Closely related to ethnocentrism is prejudice. *Prejudice* is a largely fixed attitude, belief, or emotion held by an individual about another individual or group that is based on faulty or unsubstantiated data. It refers to judgments about others based on previous decisions or experiences. Prejudice involves inflexible generalizations that are resistant to change or evidence to the contrary (Ponterotto & Pedersen, 1993). Prejudice often is thought of in the

Reducing Ethnocentrism

context of race (e.g., European American vs. African American), but it also applies in areas such as gender, age, sexual orientation, and other independent contexts. Although prejudice can be positive (e.g., thinking highly of another culture without sufficient evidence), it is usually negative.

As with ethnocentrism, we all hold prejudices to some degree. Sometimes our prejudices allow us to keep our partially fixed attitudes undisturbed and constant. Sometimes prejudice can reduce our anxiety because it gives us a familiar way to structure our observations of others. One of the main problems with prejudice is that it is self-oriented rather than other-oriented. It helps us to achieve balance for ourselves at the expense of others. Moreover, attitudes of prejudice inhibit understanding by creating a screen that filters and limits our ability to see multiple aspects and qualities of other people. Prejudice often shows itself in crude or demeaning comments that people make about others. Both ethnocentrism and prejudice interfere with our ability to understand and appreciate the human experience of others.

In addition to fighting their own prejudice, leaders face the challenge of dealing with the prejudice of followers. These prejudices can be toward the leader or the leader's culture. Furthermore, it is not uncommon for the leader to face followers who represent several culturally different groups, and these groups have their own prejudices toward each other. A skilled leader needs to find ways to negotiate with followers from various cultural backgrounds.

Dimensions of Culture

Culture has been the focus of many studies across a variety of disciplines. In the past 30 years, a substantial number of studies have focused specifically on ways to identify and classify the various *dimensions* of culture. Determining the basic dimensions or characteristics of different cultures is the first step in being able to understand the relationships between them.

Several well-known studies have addressed the question of how to characterize cultures. For example, Hall (1976) reported that a primary characteristic of cultures is the degree to which they are focused on the individual (individualistic cultures) or on the group (collectivistic cultures). Taking a different approach, Trompenaars (1994) surveyed more than 15,000 people in 47 different countries and determined that organizational cultures could be classified effectively into two dimensions: egalitarian versus hierarchical, and person versus task orientation. The egalitarian–hierarchical dimension refers to the degree to which cultures exhibit shared power as opposed to hierarchical power. Person–task orientation refers to the extent to which cultures emphasize human interaction as opposed to stressing tasks to be accomplished.

📖 Interpreting GLOBE Dimensions

Of all the research on *dimensions of culture,* perhaps the most referenced is the research of Hofstede (1980, 2001). Based on an analysis of questionnaires obtained from more than 100,000 respondents in more than 50 countries, Hofstede identified five major dimensions on which cultures differ: power distance, uncertainty avoidance, individualism–collectivism, masculinity–femininity, and long-term–short-term orientation. Hofstede's work has been the benchmark for much of the research on world cultures.

In the specific area of *culture and leadership,* the studies by House, Hanges, Javidan, Dorfman, and Gupta (2004) offer the strongest body of findings to date, as published in the 800-page *Culture, Leadership, and Organizations: The GLOBE Study of 62 Societies.* These studies are called the GLOBE studies, named for the Global Leadership and Organizational Behavior Effectiveness research program. The GLOBE studies have generated a very large number of findings on the relationship between culture and leadership.

The GLOBE research program, which was initiated by Robert House in 1991, is an ongoing program that has involved more than 160 investigators to date. The primary purpose of the project is to increase our understanding of cross-cultural interactions and the impact of culture on leadership effectiveness. GLOBE researchers have used quantitative methods to study the responses of 17,000 managers in more than 950 organizations, representing 62 different cultures throughout the world. GLOBE researchers have collected data in a variety of ways, including questionnaires, interviews, focus groups, and content analysis of printed media. The findings of the GLOBE studies will be provided in more detail throughout this chapter.

As a part of their study of culture and leadership, GLOBE researchers developed their own classification of cultural dimensions. Based on their research and the work of others (e.g., Hofstede, 1980, 2001; Kluckhohn & Strodtbeck, 1961; McClelland, 1961; Triandis, 1995), GLOBE researchers identified nine cultural dimensions: uncertainty avoidance, power distance, institutional collectivism, in-group collectivism, gender egalitarianism, assertiveness, future orientation, performance orientation, and humane orientation. In the following section, each of the dimensions is described.

Uncertainty Avoidance

This dimension refers to the extent to which a society, an organization, or a group relies on established social norms, rituals, and procedures to avoid uncertainty. Uncertainty avoidance is concerned with the way cultures use rules, structures, and laws to make things more predictable and less uncertain. For example, cultures that have a high tolerance for uncertainty, such as the

 Dimensions of Culture

 Cross-Cultural Leadership

United States, are more likely to have a thriving entrepreneurial culture, where individuals are willing to take risks and make quick business decisions. In Middle Eastern countries such as Kuwait and Egypt, taking risks and making daring decisions is not common; business deals are carefully thought through and examined before any decision can be made. As a result, business deals and negotiations take a long time, and require cultivation built on a level of trust and reliability that comes with a long-term commitment.

Power Distance

This dimension refers to the degree to which members of a group expect and agree that power should be shared unequally. Power distance is concerned with the way cultures are stratified, thus creating levels between people based on power, authority, prestige, status, wealth, and material possessions. India, which still operates under the caste system, is a good example of a country that has high power distance in that it sees power and authority as facts of life and that everyone has a "rightful place." Imagine the cultural issues that arise for an Indian software engineer who manages a department for a high-tech startup in Silicon Valley where his American subordinates, who come from a low power distance culture, openly approach and disagree with him on issues even though he is the boss.

Institutional Collectivism

This dimension describes the degree to which an organization or a society encourages institutional or societal collective action. Institutional collectivism is concerned with whether cultures identify with broader societal interests rather than with individual goals and accomplishments. North Korea is an example of a culture with high institutional collectivism. The people are ruled by a Supreme Leader who oversees the development of the country's values, which place a premium on collective efforts and nonmaterial incentives. As a result, group cohesion and loyalty is strictly required. This adherence may come partly through fear: Supreme Leader Kim Jong-il has placed the military at the center of the efforts to instill these values throughout North Korean society.

In-Group Collectivism

This dimension refers to the degree to which people express pride, loyalty, and cohesiveness in their organizations or families. In-group collectivism is concerned with the extent to which people are devoted to their organizations

 Cross-Cultural Management

or families. For example, many Middle Eastern cultures, such as Pakistan and Iran, are high in in-group collectivism. They regard family and religious affiliation above all else; there are often honor killings of family members who have done something to disgrace or defy the paternal leader of the family. Religious divisions, such as that between the Sunni and Shia Muslims in such countries as Syria and Iraq, have led to civil war.

Gender Egalitarianism

This dimension measures the degree to which an organization or a society minimizes gender role differences and promotes gender equality. Gender egalitarianism is concerned with how much societies deemphasize members' biological sex in determining the roles that members play in their homes, organizations, and communities. Sweden is considered to be one of the world's most gender-egalitarian countries, based on a firm belief that men and women should share power and influence equally. An extensive welfare system makes it easier for both sexes to balance work and family life. Contrast this with countries like Afghanistan where many girls are not allowed to go to school and are often killed for defying their families' wishes.

Assertiveness

This dimension refers to the degree to which people in a culture are determined, assertive, confrontational, and aggressive in their social relationships. Assertiveness is concerned with how much a culture or society encourages people to be forceful, aggressive, and tough, as opposed to encouraging them to be timid, submissive, and tender in social relationships. Germany is high in the assertiveness dimension. In a study on upper-level managers in Germany, Brodbeck, Frese, and Javidan (2002) found that German managers used straightforward and direct language and that conflict and confrontational debate were acceptable approaches in a work environment.

Future Orientation

This concept refers to the extent to which people engage in future-oriented behaviors such as planning, investing in the future, and delaying gratification. Future orientation emphasizes that people in a culture prepare for the future as opposed to enjoying the present and being spontaneous. Many Middle Eastern countries are "past-oriented," concerned with traditional values and ways of doing things. They tend to be conservative in management and slow to change

 Leadership and Culture

those things that are tied to the past. Americans, on the other hand, believe they can plan and control the future and idealize change for the sake of changing.

Performance Orientation

This dimension describes the extent to which an organization or a society encourages and rewards group members for improved performance and excellence. Performance orientation is concerned with whether people in a culture are rewarded for setting and meeting challenging goals. Again, the United States is very high in performance orientation. One only has to look at how the country's education department ranks schools as thriving or failing based on the results of standardized testing of students. If schools are not making the mark, there are interventions and programs to try to bring the scores up. The United States also compares its academic success with that of other countries to see where it is falling short or succeeding.

Humane Orientation

The ninth dimension refers to the degree to which a culture encourages and rewards people for being fair, altruistic, generous, caring, and kind to others. Humane orientation is concerned with how much a society or an organization emphasizes sensitivity to others, social support, and community values. Switzerland is a country that is often cited for its high humane orientation, based on the Swiss people's helpfulness to others during and after World War I and World War II. The country espouses tolerance and responsibility as its central educational goals.

GLOBE researchers used these nine cultural dimensions to analyze the attributes of the 62 different countries in the study. These cultural dimensions formed the basis for studying how the countries varied in their approach to leadership.

Clusters of World Cultures

GLOBE researchers divided the data from the 62 countries they studied into regional clusters.[1] These clusters provided a convenient way to analyze the similarities and differences between cultural groups (clusters), and to make meaningful generalizations about culture and leadership.

To create regional clusters, GLOBE researchers used prior research (e.g., Ronen & Shenkar, 1985), common language, geography, religion, and historical accounts. Based on these factors, they grouped countries into

▶ Values and Diversity

10 distinct clusters: Anglo, Germanic Europe, Latin Europe, Sub-Saharan Africa, Eastern Europe, Middle East, Confucian Asia, Southern Asia, Latin America, and Nordic Europe (Figure 16.1). These 10 regional clusters are the groupings that were used in all of the GLOBE studies.

To test whether the clusters, or groups of countries, were valid, researchers did a statistical analysis of questionnaire data collected from individuals in each of the clusters. Their results indicated that the scores of respondents *within a cluster* correlated with one another but were unrelated to the scores of respondents *in different clusters*. From these findings, they concluded that each cluster was unique. In sum, these regional clusters represented a valid and reliable way to differentiate countries of the world into 10 distinct groups.

Figure 16.1   Country Clusters According to GLOBE

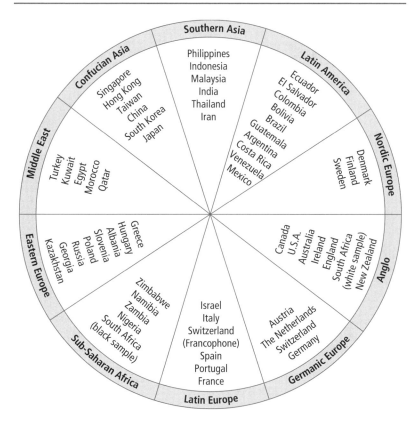

SOURCE: House, R.J., Hanges, P.J., Javidan, M., Dorfman, P. W., & Gupta, V., *Culture, Leadership, and Organizations: The GLOBE Study of 62 Societies,* copyright © 2004, Sage Publications, Inc. Reprinted with permission.

Characteristics of Clusters

In an effort to characterize the regional clusters, GLOBE researchers analyzed data from each of the regions using the dimensions of culture described earlier. Table 16.1 provides a classification of the cultural clusters in regard to how they scored on each cultural dimension. In the table, the nine cultural

Table 16.1 Cultural Clusters Classified on Cultural Dimensions

Cultural Dimension	High-Score Clusters	Low-Score Clusters
Assertiveness orientation	Eastern Europe Germanic Europe	Nordic Europe
Future orientation	Germanic Europe Nordic Europe	Eastern Europe Latin America Middle East
Gender egalitarianism	Eastern Europe Nordic Europe	Middle East
Humane orientation	Southern Asia Sub-Saharan Africa	Germanic Europe Latin Europe
In-group collectivism	Confucian Asia Eastern Europe Latin America Middle East Southern Asia	Anglo Germanic Europe Nordic Europe
Institutional collectivism	Nordic Europe Confucian Asia	Germanic Europe Latin America Latin Europe
Performance orientation	Anglo Confucian Asia Germanic Europe	Eastern Europe Latin America
Power distance	No clusters	Nordic Europe
Uncertainty avoidance	Germanic Europe Nordic Europe	Eastern Europe Latin America Middle East

SOURCE: Adapted from House, R. J., Hanges, P. J., Javidan, M., Dorfman, P. W., & Gupta, V. (Eds.), *Culture, Leadership, and Organizations: The GLOBE Study of 62 Societies,* © 2004, SAGE Publications, Inc. Reprinted with permission.

dimensions are listed in the left-hand column; the high-score and low-score regional clusters are provided in the next two columns. These are the regional clusters that were significantly higher or lower on particular dimensions than other regions. From these data, several observations can be made about the characteristics of these regional cultures.

Anglo

The Anglo cluster consists of Canada, the United States, Australia, Ireland, England, South Africa (white sample), and New Zealand. These countries or populations were *high* in performance orientation and *low* in in-group collectivism. This means it is characteristic of these countries to be competitive and results oriented, but less attached to their families or similar groups than other countries.

Confucian Asia

This cluster, which includes Singapore, Hong Kong, Taiwan, China, South Korea, and Japan, exhibited *high* scores in performance orientation, institutional collectivism, and in-group collectivism. These countries are results driven, and they encourage the group working together over individual goals. People in these countries are devoted and loyal to their families.

Eastern Europe

Included in this cluster are Greece, Hungary, Albania, Slovenia, Poland, Russia, Georgia, and Kazakhstan. These countries scored *high* on assertiveness, in-group collectivism, and gender egalitarianism. They scored *low* on performance orientation, future orientation, and uncertainty avoidance. People in this cluster tend to be forceful and supportive of their coworkers and to treat men and women equally. They are less likely to be achievement driven, to emphasize strategic planning, and to stress rules and laws as a way to maintain order.

Germanic Europe

The Germanic Europe countries, which include Austria, the Netherlands, Switzerland, and Germany, scored *high* in performance orientation, assertiveness, future orientation, and uncertainty avoidance. They were

Chinese Culture and Leadership

low in humane orientation, institutional collectivism, and in-group collectivism. These countries value competition and aggressiveness and are more results oriented than people oriented. They enjoy planning and investing in the future and using rules and laws to give them control over their environment. At the same time, these countries are more likely to be individualistic and less group oriented. They tend not to emphasize broad societal groups.

Latin America

The Latin America cluster is made up of Ecuador, El Salvador, Colombia, Bolivia, Brazil, Guatemala, Argentina, Costa Rica, Venezuela, and Mexico. People in these countries scored *high* on in-group collectivism and *low* on performance orientation, future orientation, institutional collectivism, and uncertainty avoidance. People in these countries tend to be loyal and devoted to their families and similar groups but less interested in overall institutional and societal groups.

Latin Europe

Comprising Israel, Italy, Francophone Switzerland, Spain, Portugal, and France, the Latin Europe cluster exhibited *more moderate* and *fewer high scores* on any of the cultural dimensions, but they scored *low* on humane orientation and institutional collectivism. It is characteristic of these countries to value individual autonomy and to place less value on the greater societal collective. Individuals are encouraged to watch out for themselves and to pursue individual rather than societal goals.

Middle East

This cluster is made up of Qatar, Morocco, Egypt, Kuwait, and Turkey. These countries scored *high* on in-group collectivism and *low* on future orientation, gender egalitarianism, and uncertainty avoidance. People in these countries tend to show great pride in their families and organizations. They are devoted and loyal to their own people. Furthermore, it is common for these countries to treat people of different genders in distinctly different ways. Women often are afforded less status than men, and fewer women are in positions of authority than men. In the Middle East, orderliness and consistency are not stressed, and people do not place heavy reliance on policies and procedures. There is a tendency to focus on current issues as opposed to attempting to control the future.

Nordic Europe

The Nordic Europe cluster, which includes Denmark, Finland, and Sweden, exhibited several distinctive characteristics. This cluster scored *high* on future orientation, gender egalitarianism, institutional collectivism, and uncertainty avoidance, and *low* on assertiveness, in-group collectivism, and power distance. The Nordic people place a high priority on long-term success. Women are treated with greater equality. The Nordic people identify with the broader society and far less with family groups. In Nordic Europe, rules, orderliness, and consistency are stressed. Assertiveness is downplayed in favor of modesty and tenderness, and power is shared equally among people at all levels of society. Cooperation and societal-level group identity are highly valued by the Nordic people.

Southern Asia

The Philippines, Indonesia, Malaysia, India, Thailand, and Iran form the Southern Asia cluster. These countries exhibited *high* scores on humane orientation and in-group collectivism. Southern Asia could be characterized as countries that demonstrate strong family loyalty and deep concern for their communities.

Sub-Saharan Africa

The Sub-Saharan Africa cluster consisted of Zimbabwe, Namibia, Zambia, Nigeria, and South Africa (black sample). These countries or populations expressed *high* scores on humane orientation. In Sub-Saharan Africa, people generally are very concerned for and sensitive to others. Concern for family and friends is more important than concern for self.

Leadership Behavior and Culture Clusters

The overall purpose of the GLOBE project was to determine how people from different cultures viewed leadership. In addition, researchers wanted to determine the ways in which cultural characteristics were related to culturally endorsed leadership behaviors. In short, they wanted to find out how differences in cultures were related to differences in approaches to leadership.

Global Leaders

The conceptualization of leadership used by GLOBE researchers was derived in part from the work of Lord and Maher (1991) on implicit leadership theory. According to implicit leadership theory, individuals have implicit beliefs and convictions about the attributes and beliefs that distinguish leaders from nonleaders and effective leaders from ineffective leaders. From the perspective of this theory, leadership is in the eye of the beholder (Dorfman, Hanges, & Brodbeck, 2004). Leadership refers to what people see in others when they are exhibiting leadership behaviors.

To describe how different cultures view leadership behaviors in others, GLOBE researchers identified six global leadership behaviors: charismatic/ value based, team oriented, participative, humane oriented, autonomous, and self-protective (House & Javidan, 2004). These global leadership behaviors were defined in these studies as follows:

> *Charismatic/value-based leadership* reflects the ability to inspire, to motivate, and to expect high performance from others based on strongly held core values. This kind of leadership includes being visionary, inspirational, self-sacrificing, trustworthy, decisive, and performance oriented.

> *Team-oriented leadership* emphasizes team building and a common purpose among team members. This kind of leadership includes being collaborative, integrative, diplomatic, nonmalevolent, and administratively competent.

> *Participative leadership* reflects the degree to which leaders involve others in making and implementing decisions. It includes being participative and nonautocratic.

> *Humane-oriented leadership* emphasizes being supportive, considerate, compassionate, and generous. This type of leadership includes modesty and sensitivity to other people.

> *Autonomous leadership* refers to independent and individualistic leadership, which includes being autonomous and unique.

> *Self-protective leadership* reflects behaviors that ensure the safety and security of the leader and the group. It includes leadership that is self-centered, status conscious, conflict inducing, face saving, and procedural.

These six global leadership behaviors emerged from the GLOBE research and were used to assess the different ways in which various cultural clusters viewed leadership. From this analysis, the researchers were able to identify a leadership profile for each cluster. Each profile describes the relative

 Elaine Chao

importance and desirability that different cultures ascribe to different leadership behaviors. The leadership profiles for each of the 10 culture clusters follow.

Eastern Europe Leadership Profile

For the Eastern European countries, an ideal example of a leader would be a person who was first and foremost independent while maintaining a strong interest in protecting his or her position as a leader (Figure 16.2). In addition, the leader would be moderately charismatic/value based, team oriented, and humane oriented, yet largely uninterested in involving others in the decision-making process. To sum up, this culture describes a leader as one who is highly autonomous, makes decisions independently, and is to a certain degree inspiring, team oriented, and attentive to human needs.

Figure 16.2   Culture Clusters and Desired Leadership Behaviors: Eastern Europe

EASTERN EUROPE
Autonomous Leadership
Self-Protective Leadership
Charismatic/Value-Based Leadership
Team-Oriented Leadership
Humane-Oriented Leadership
Participative Leadership

SOURCE: Adapted from House et al. (2004).

Latin America Leadership Profile

Quite different from the Eastern European countries, the Latin American countries place the most importance on charismatic/value-based, team-oriented, and self-protective leadership, and the least importance on autonomous leadership (Figure 16.3). In addition, this cluster is moderately interested in leadership that is participative and humane oriented. The profile for the Latin America cluster is of a leader who is charismatic/value based but somewhat self-serving, collaborative, and inspiring. These leaders tend to be moderately interested in people and their participation in decision making.

Figure 16.3   Culture Clusters and Desired Leadership Behaviors: Latin America

SOURCE: Adapted from House et al. (2004).

Latin Europe Leadership Profile

The Latin Europe cluster values leadership that is charismatic/value based, team oriented, participative, and self-protective (Figure 16.4). Independent leadership and the human side of leadership are downplayed in this cluster.

Figure 16.4   Culture Clusters and Desired Leadership Behaviors: Latin Europe

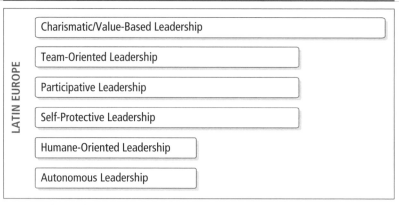

SOURCE: Adapted from House et al. (2004).

In short, the profile of the Latin Europe cluster centers on leadership that is inspiring, collaborative, participative, and self-oriented, but not highly compassionate.

Confucian Asia Leadership Profile

The leadership profile of the Confucian Asia countries describes a leader who is self-protective, team oriented, and humane oriented (Figure 16.5). Though independent and to some extent inspiring, this type of leader typically does not invite others to be involved in goal setting or decision making. In sum, the Confucian Asia profile describes a leader who works and cares about others but who uses status and position to make independent decisions without the input of others.

Figure 16.5   Culture Clusters and Desired Leadership Behaviors: Confucian Asia

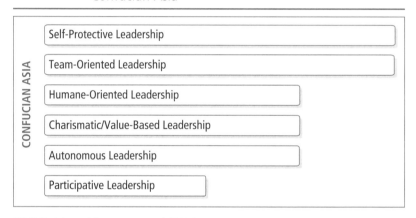

SOURCE: Adapted from House et al. (2004).

Nordic Europe Leadership Profile

An ideal example of leadership for the Nordic European countries is leadership that is highly visionary and participative, while being somewhat independent and diplomatic (Figure 16.6). For these countries, it is of less importance that their leaders be humane oriented or self-protective. Nordic Europeans prefer leaders who are inspiring, and who involve others in decision making. They do not expect their leaders to be exceedingly compassionate, nor do they expect them to be concerned with status and other self-centered attributes.

Figure 16.6 Culture Clusters and Desired Leadership Behaviors: Nordic Europe

NORDIC EUROPE

- Charismatic/Value-Based Leadership
- Participative Leadership
- Team-Oriented Leadership
- Autonomous Leadership
- Humane-Oriented Leadership
- Self-Protective Leadership

SOURCE: Adapted from House et al. (2004).

Anglo Leadership Profile

The profile of leadership for the Anglo countries emphasizes that leaders are especially charismatic/value based, participative, and sensitive to people (Figure 16.7). Stated another way, Anglo countries want leaders to be

Figure 16.7 Culture Clusters and Desired Leadership Behaviors: Anglo

ANGLO

- Charismatic/Value-Based Leadership
- Participative Leadership
- Humane-Oriented Leadership
- Team-Oriented Leadership
- Autonomous Leadership
- Self-Protective Leadership

SOURCE: Adapted from House et al. (2004).

exceedingly motivating and visionary, not autocratic, and considerate of others. Furthermore, they report that leaders should be team oriented and autonomous. The least important characteristic for Anglo countries is self-protective leadership. They believe it is ineffective if leaders are status conscious or prone to face saving.

Sub-Saharan Africa Leadership Profile

For countries in Sub-Saharan Africa, an ideal leader is modest, compassionate, and sensitive to the people (Figure 16.8). In addition, a leader should be relatively charismatic/value based, team oriented, participative, and self-protective. Leaders who act independently or act alone are viewed as less effective in these countries. In short, the Sub-Saharan Africa profile characterizes effective leadership as caring leadership. Like many other countries, these countries or populations believe leaders should be inspirational, collaborative, and not excessively self-centered. Leaders who act autonomously are seen as ineffective in Sub-Saharan Africa countries.

Figure 16.8 Culture Clusters and Desired Leadership Behaviors: Sub-Saharan Africa

SOURCE: Adapted from House et al. (2004).

Southern Asia Leadership Profile

The Southern Asia leadership profile is similar to the profile of Confucian Asia. They both place importance on self-protective, charismatic/value-based,

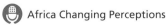 Africa Changing Perceptions

humane-oriented, and team-oriented leadership, and they both find participative leadership ineffective (Figure 16.9). Southern Asia countries differ from Confucian Asia countries in believing that charisma is an important leader attribute. The Southern Asia countries characterize effective leadership as especially collaborative, inspirational, sensitive to people's needs, and concerned with status and face saving. Furthermore, they believe leaders who tend to be autocratic are more effective than those who lead by inviting others into the decision-making process.

Figure 16.9 Culture Clusters and Desired Leadership Behaviors: Southern Asia

SOUTHERN ASIA

- Self-Protective Leadership
- Charismatic/Value-Based Leadership
- Humane-Oriented Leadership
- Team-Oriented Leadership
- Autonomous Leadership
- Participative Leadership

SOURCE: Adapted from House et al. (2004).

Germanic Europe Leadership Profile

The ideal leader in the Germanic Europe cluster has a style that is very participative while also being inspirational and independent (Figure 16.10). The ideal leader would be a unique, visionary person who is autonomous, charismatic/value based, participative, humane oriented, and team oriented, but not status conscious or concerned with face saving. In short, the Germanic European countries think effective leadership is based on participation, charisma, and autonomy but not on face saving and other self-centered attributes.

Middle East Leadership Profile

The leadership profile for the Middle Eastern countries differs significantly from the profiles of the other cultural clusters (Figure 16.11). Middle Eastern countries find self-attributes such as face saving and status are important characteristics of effective leadership. They also value being independent and familial. However, they find charismatic/value-based, team-oriented, and

Figure 16.10 Culture Clusters and Desired Leadership Behaviors: Germanic Europe

GERMANIC EUROPE	Autonomous Leadership
	Charismatic/Value-Based Leadership
	Participative Leadership
	Humane-Oriented Leadership
	Team-Oriented Leadership
	Self-Protective Leadership

SOURCE: Adapted from House et al. (2004).

Figure 16.11 Culture Clusters and Desired Leadership Behaviors: Middle East

MIDDLE EAST	Self-Protective Leadership
	Humane-Oriented Leadership
	Autonomous Leadership
	Charismatic/Value-Based Leadership
	Team-Oriented Leadership
	Participative Leadership

SOURCE: Adapted from House et al. (2004).

participative decision making less essential for effective leadership. To sum up, the Middle Eastern profile of leadership emphasizes status and face saving, and deemphasizes charismatic/value-based and team-oriented leadership.

Universally Desirable and Undesirable Leadership Attributes

One of the most interesting outcomes of the GLOBE project was the identification of a list of leadership attributes that were universally endorsed by 17,000 people in 62 countries as positive aspects of effective leadership.

Respondents in the GLOBE studies identified 22 *valued* leadership attributes (Table 16.2). These attributes were universally endorsed as characteristics that facilitate outstanding leadership.

Based on the list of endorsed attributes, a portrait can be drawn of a leader whom almost everyone would see as exceptional. That portrait is of a leader who is high in integrity, is charismatic/value based, and has interpersonal skills (Dorfman et al., 2004).

The GLOBE project also identified a list of leadership attributes that were universally viewed as *obstacles* to effective leadership (Table 16.3). These characteristics suggest that the portrait of an ineffective leader is someone who is asocial, malevolent, and self-focused. Clearly, people from all cultures find these characteristics to hinder effective leadership.

Table 16.2 Universally Desirable Leadership Attributes

Positive Leader Attributes		
Trustworthy	Just	Honest
Has foresight	Plans ahead	Encouraging
Positive	Dynamic	Motive arouser
Confidence builder	Motivational	Dependable
Intelligent	Decisive	Effective bargainer
Win–win problem solver	Communicative	Informed
Administratively skilled	Coordinative	Team builder
Excellence oriented		

SOURCE: Adapted from House, R.J., Hanges, P.J., Javidan, M., Dorfman, P. W., & Gupta, V., Culture, Leadership, and Organizations: The GLOBE Study of 62 Societies, copyright © 2004, Sage Publications, Inc. Reprinted with permission.

Table 16.3 Universally Undesirable Leadership Attributes

Negative Leader Attributes		
Loner	Asocial	Noncooperative
Irritable	Nonexplicit	Egocentric
Ruthless	Dictatorial	

STRENGTHS

Although this chapter on culture and leadership does not represent a single unified theory of leadership, it does present findings that have several strengths. First, the scope of this study is a major strength. For this study, data were collected by 170 social scientists, representing 62 countries from all regions of the world, and included responses from 17,300 managers in 951 organizations. The GLOBE project has been a massive undertaking; the findings that have emerged from this work make a powerful statement about how cultures around the world view leadership.

Second, the findings from GLOBE are valuable because they emerge from a well-developed quantitative research design. In the leadership literature, there are many qualitative studies that focus more narrowly on how people in certain countries view a small number of leadership concepts. Although these studies have contributed to our understanding of culture and leadership, they are limited in scope and generalizability. In contrast, the strength of the GLOBE project is that researchers used a quantitative design and administered standardized instruments to assess leadership and cultural dimensions in 62 countries. Thus, the results from the GLOBE studies about leadership are generalizable between cultures and within cultures around the world.

Third, the GLOBE studies provide a classification of cultural dimensions that is more expansive than the commonly used Hofstede classification system. Whereas Hofstede distinguishes between cultures based on five dimensions (power distance, uncertainty avoidance, individualism–collectivism, masculinity–femininity, and long-term–short-term orientation), the GLOBE studies identify nine cultural dimensions (uncertainty avoidance, power distance, institutional collectivism, in-group collectivism, gender egalitarianism, assertiveness, future orientation, performance orientation, and humane orientation). Although seven of the nine dimensions identified in the GLOBE studies have their origins in the dimensions identified by Hofstede, by expanding the classification system the GLOBE studies provide a broader and more elaborate way of describing dimensions of culture.

Fourth, the GLOBE studies provide useful information about what is universally accepted as good and bad leadership. Clearly, people from most cultures view good leadership as based on integrity, charisma, and interpersonal ability. Conversely, they see bad leadership emerging from leaders who are self-focused, dictatorial, and asocial. These lists of positive and negative attributes provide a useful portrait of how people around the world conceptualize leadership.

 Global Mindset

Last, the study of culture and leadership underscores the complexity of the leadership process and how it is influenced by culture. Data from the GLOBE studies highlight the need for each of us to expand our ethnocentric tendencies to view leadership from only our own perspective, and instead to "open our window" to the diverse ways in which leadership is viewed by people from different regions around the world. There are many ways to view leadership and the integration of culture; studies of leadership help us to expand and develop a richer understanding of the leadership process.

CRITICISMS

The body of research on culture and leadership also has several weaknesses. First, although the GLOBE research has resulted in a multitude of findings about perceptions of leadership in different cultures, this research does not provide a clear set of assumptions and propositions that can form a single theory about the way culture relates to leadership or influences the leadership process.

A second criticism, more narrow in scope, concerns the way researchers have labeled and defined certain cultural dimensions and leadership behaviors. For example, it is not easy to understand what *power distance* means, nor is the meaning of *self-protective leadership* clear. Because the meanings of these terms are somewhat vague, it is difficult at times to interpret or fully comprehend the findings about culture and leadership.

Another criticism concerns the way in which leadership was conceptualized in the GLOBE studies. In these studies, researchers used a conceptualization of leadership that was based on the ideas set forth by Lord and Maher (1991) in their work on implicit leadership theory. This approach frames leadership from an information-processing perspective, as the implicit beliefs and convictions that individuals have about leaders. In other words, according to this theory, leadership is the process of being perceived by others as being a leader. However, conceptualizing leadership in this way is limited: It focuses on what people perceive to be leadership and ignores a large body of research that frames leadership in terms of what leaders do (e.g., transformational leadership, path–goal theory, skills approach). Research on how people from different cultures view leadership is valuable, but there is a need for further research on how leadership functions in different cultures.

A related criticism concerns the way in which researchers in the GLOBE studies measured leadership. They selected six global leadership behaviors (i.e., charismatic/value-based, team-oriented, participative, humane-oriented, autonomous, and self-protective leadership) that were derived from an analysis of subjects' responses to hundreds of other attributes believed to be related to outstanding leadership. Each of the six global leadership behaviors was measured by a series of subscales. However, the subscales represented a very broad range of behaviors, and as a result compromised the precision and validity of the leadership measures.

Finally, the GLOBE studies provide a provocative list of universally endorsed desirable and undesirable leadership attributes. The attributes identified in the GLOBE studies are comparable to the list of traits we discussed in Chapter 2. As with the trait approach, however, it is difficult to identify a set of universal attributes in isolation from the context in which the leadership occurs. The GLOBE studies tend to isolate a set of attributes that are characteristic of effective leaders without considering the influence of the situational effects.

APPLICATION

Training programs about culture and diversity have been popular for many years. For example, in the training and development field, a wide variety of programs teach cultural sensitivity and address issues related to cultural differences. At the core of these programs, people are taught about the nuances and characteristics of different cultures, and how to be sensitive to people in other countries and cultures.

The findings in this chapter have implications for leadership training. Understanding issues about culture is useful in several ways (Bing, 2004). First, the findings about culture can help leaders understand their own cultural biases and preferences. Understanding their own preferences is the first step in understanding that people in other cultures might have different preferences.

Second, the findings help leaders to understand what it means to be a good leader. Different cultures have different ideas about what they want from their leaders. These findings help our leaders adapt their style to be more effective in different cultural settings.

Third, this chapter's findings can help global leaders communicate more effectively across cultural and geographic boundaries. By understanding cultural differences, leaders can become more empathic and accurate in their communication with others.

 Multinational Corporations

Information on culture and leadership has also been applied in very practical ways (Bing, 2004). It has been used to build culturally sensitive websites, design new employee orientation programs, conduct programs in relocation training, improve global team effectiveness, and facilitate multinational merger implementation, to name a few. These examples clearly indicate the wide range of applications for research on culture and leadership in the workplace.

CASE STUDIES

This section provides three case studies (Cases 16.1, 16.2, and 16.3) that describe leadership in various cultural contexts. The first case is about a college student who takes an internship at a Japanese-based automotive company. The second case describes how a small Midwestern bank developed a unique Islamic financing program. The final case describes how two board members from a nonprofit organization developed a capital campaign to renovate a fire station for a Hispanic community. After each of the cases, questions are provided to help you think about how cultural issues are related to the leadership process.

CASE 16.1

A Challenging Workplace

As a leader in campus organizations, Samira Tanaka, a student, often led projects and took deadlines very seriously. Her strong work ethic led to an internship offer at a Japanese automotive company.

At orientation for her internship, Samira learned that Japanese companies historically had little diversity in terms of race and gender. Women in Japan were not as prevalent in the workforce as in North America. In an effort to adapt to North American norms, Japanese subsidiaries had well-developed diversity policies. For example, Samira tracked the usage of minority-owned businesses in the company's supply base. This ensured that the company invested in local businesses that operated in traditionally economically disadvantaged areas. Investing in the local community was already an important business value in Japan, so this was a simple adaptation for Samira's company.

The company culture was a unique blend of Japanese and North American work styles. The employees in North America worked fewer hours than the employees in Japan. Around the office, it was common for employees to hear Japanese and English. However, management still had some internal conflict. Japanese advisers were perceived as focusing on the creation of consensus in teams, often leading to slow decision making. North American workers were seen as rushing into projects without enough planning. Feedback was indirect from both Japanese and North American managers.

Samira successfully completed two internship rotations and was about to graduate from college. Her new manager often asked her to follow up with other team members to complete late tasks. As she had been taught in school, she was proactive with team members about completing their work. Samira thought she was great at consistently inviting others to participate in the decision-making process. She always offered her opinion on how things could be done better, and sometimes even initiated tasks to improve processes on her own. Although she saw herself as an emerging take-charge leader, Samira always downplayed her ambitions. In school, she was often stereotyped in negative ways for being an assertive female leader, and she didn't want to be seen in that way at work.

Some of her peers at work advised her that it was important to consider working at a plant near her hometown because it would be closer to her family. However, she was not interested in following that advice. Samira thought it was more exciting to work near a large city or to take a job that involved travel. She didn't think it was appropriate to discuss with her peers her family concerns in relation to her future job needs.

Toward the end of her final internship, Samira received a performance evaluation from a senior manager. Her manager praised her as being very dependable, as planning deadlines well, and as being very competent at her tasks overall. However, he also told her she was increasingly perceived as too pushy, not a team player, and often speaking out of turn. This often irritated her peers.

Samira had never seen herself this way at work and did not understand why she was not seen as aligning with the company's core value of working with others. Good grades and campus leadership activities had gotten her this far, but this evaluation led her to question whether she could work for this company after graduation.

Samira ultimately realized that her workplace was different from the campus atmosphere she was used to. If she wanted to be an emerging leader in the workplace, she had to better adapt to her new environment.

(Continued)

(Continued)

Questions

1. What similarities and differences can you identify between North American and Japanese working styles?

2. In what way did this company reflect the characteristics of other Confucian Asia countries?

3. Why do you think Samira was not seen as a team player?

4. What universal leadership attributes did Samira exhibit?

5. What other suggestions would you have for Samira in this situation?

CASE 16.2

A Special Kind of Financing

Central Bank is a small Midwestern savings and loan institution that manages $3 billion in assets. It competes with 16 other financial institutions for customers; most of those other institutions have substantially larger holdings. To better serve its customers and attract a larger customer base, Central Bank conducted a financial-need survey of the people who lived in the area.

The survey revealed some interesting and culturally relevant information. Muslims represented a sizable minority in the community, making up about 8% of the overall population. However, a review of the bank registry revealed that few Muslims, if any, banked at Central Bank. The results of the survey were puzzling. Given the large numbers of Muslims in the community, the management wondered why there were no Muslim customers at Central Bank.

To answer this question, Central Bank invited a group of local Muslims to meet and discuss their thoughts about financing and how their ideas related to the financial services offered by the bank. The meeting was a real eye-opener for the bank management. The Muslims' ideas about banking were very different from the traditional Western beliefs about banking.

During the discussion, the management learned that the principles of Islam strongly influence the banking attitudes and behaviors of Muslims. The principles of Islamic finance were set forth in the Koran more than 14 centuries ago. For instance, Koranic law forbids paying or receiving interest. These principles stress that money is only a medium of exchange and should not be used to make more money. From the Islamic point of view, the *human element* in a business venture is more important than the money used to finance the venture. Furthermore, according to Islamic finance, the provider of capital and the user of capital should share equally in the risk of a business venture.

These ideas about finance were different from the way Central Bank thought about them. Central Bank was not accustomed to the way Muslims viewed money as a medium of exchange. Having been enlightened through these discussions, the management at Central Bank felt challenged to develop a financing program that was more in line with the attitudes and values of Islamic finance principles.

In order to attract the business of Muslim customers, Central Bank created and began offering two new types of mortgage financing, called *ijara* and *murabaha*. Ijara is a finance plan in which the bank buys a home for a customer and leases it to the customer, who pays rent plus a portion of the property purchase. Murabaha is a transaction in which the bank buys the home and sells it to the customer at an agreed-upon markup, and the customer pays for the home in installments over 15 to 30 years. Both ijara and murabaha are consistent with Islamic beliefs that prohibit Muslims from paying or receiving interest. In these two types of transactions, money is used to purchase something tangible, but money is not used to make money. Central Bank received favorable legal rulings (*fatwas*) from some of the leading Islamic legal scholars in the United States and the world to validate these types of financing.

Central Bank's Islamic finance plans have become quite popular. Although Central Bank has been successful with these plans, it has also met resistance. Some people have expressed strong disapproval of special finance programs specifically geared to the Muslim population. Others are against it because it mixes issues of faith and public finance. However, the resistance has not stopped Central Bank. Central Bank is very proud to be the only bank in the country to serve the needs of the Muslim community in this way.

Questions

1. Why do you think banks in the United States have been slow to offer financing expressly for Muslims?
2. Do you think it is fair to offer one minority group a special banking opportunity?
3. How does ethnocentrism come into play in this case?
4. How does in-group collectivism relate to Central Bank's finance plans?
5. How do you think the other banks in the community will react to Central Bank?

CASE 16.3

Whose Hispanic Center Is It?

River City is a rapidly growing city in the Midwest with a population of 200,000 people, growing at about 5% annually. It is a diverse community with a racial composition that is 65% white, 20% African American, 13% Hispanic, and 2% Native American. The Hispanic population in River City is one of the fastest growing of all segments, growing at about 10% annually.

The Hispanic community is represented by the Hispanic Center, a non-profit organization that serves the needs of the Hispanic community and broader River City community through a variety of programs and services. A board of directors and an executive director manage the Hispanic Center. Two newly appointed board members have led a transformation of the center, including renovating the physical facilities and shifting the focus of program services. The new members are Mary Davis, who has experience in neighborhood development, and José Reyna, who has experience in city government. The board of directors is made up of 15 people, 10 of whom identify themselves as Hispanic and 5 of whom identify themselves as non-Hispanic.

The Hispanic Center owned an old building that was slated for renovation so the center could have more space for offices and community programs (e.g., educational programming, cultural competence and leadership training, and legal services). The need for the building was validated by what people expressed at a series of community forums. The building was an old fire station that had been mothballed for 15 years, and the Hispanic Center bought the building from River City for $1. Although the fire station needed a lot of renovation, it was located in a perfect place, at the center of the Hispanic community. However, a complete renovation of the building was needed.

To raise funds for the renovation, the board of directors initiated a citywide capital campaign. The goal of the campaign was to raise $1.4 million, the estimated amount for a complete, first-class renovation of the building.

Along with their regular jobs, Mary and José tackled the fund-raising campaign with a full head of steam. In just 6 months, using their wide array of skills, they successfully raised $1.3 million for the project (most of which came from private foundations and corporations). With just $100,000 still to be raised, the leaders and some board members were getting excited about the possibility of the new community center. This excitement was heightened because the renovated building was going to be constructed using the latest green building techniques. These techniques were environmentally sound and incorporated healthful and highly efficient models of construction.

In order to raise the final $100,000, Mary and José proposed a new series of fund-raising initiatives that would focus on smaller donors (e.g., $10, $20, or $30 donors), primarily from the Hispanic community. To kick off a series of events, a formal event at a local hotel was proposed, with tickets costing $75 per person. Just before this event, Mary and José encountered some resistance and found out that their excitement about the renovation needed to be tempered.

During a scheduled board meeting, several members of the board expressed concern with the latest fund-raising efforts. Some board members questioned the wisdom of targeting the fund-raising to the Hispanic community, believing that Hispanic people tended to give to their churches rather than to public not-for-profit organizations. Others questioned the price of the tickets to fund-raising events that was being sought from small donors, $75. These members argued for a smaller admission fee (e.g., $20) that would allow more members of the community to attend. As the discussion proceeded, other board members expressed discontent with the fancy plans for the new green building. They argued that the renovation was becoming a special interest project and a pet project of a few ambitious visionaries.

Board members also started to question the transformation of the Hispanic Center under Mary and José's leadership. Board members expressed frustrations about the new goals of the center and about how things were proceeding. There was a sense that the request for community-based support was unreasonable and in conflict with cultural norms. In the past, the center moved slowly toward change, keeping the focus on one goal: to provide emergency services to the local community. When change came in the past, it was incremental. People were not aggressive, and they did not make trouble.

Under the leadership of Mary and José, there was a perception that the new center and programs were too grand and refined for the community they were intended to serve. The vision for the new center seemed to take things to a new sophisticated level that was not grounded in the common work or the people-oriented values of the center.

Questions

1. How would you describe the strengths and weaknesses of Mary's and José's leadership on this project?

2. Do you see any problem in targeting part of the fund-raising campaign directly toward the Hispanic community?

(Continued)

(Continued)

3. The Latin America leadership profile stresses the importance of team-oriented leadership and deemphasizes individualistic leadership. How does the leadership of Mary and José compare with the Latin America profile?

4. How do Hispanic cultural dimensions help explain the resistance some people felt and expressed toward the renovation project?

5. If you were Mary or José, how would you temper your excitement about renovating the new fire station?

LEADERSHIP INSTRUMENT

Culture and leadership are different concepts; when they are measured, they are measured in different ways using different questionnaires. Currently, there are no measures that assess culture and leadership simultaneously, nor are there measures of cultural leadership. There are questionnaires that measure culture, and as shown throughout the book, there are many measures of leadership.

Perhaps the best-known measure of culture is Hofstede's Culture in the Workplace™ questionnaire. This questionnaire measures a person's cultural preferences on four dimensions: individualism, power distance, certainty, and achievement. People can use their profiles on these dimensions to learn about themselves and to compare themselves with the profiles of people in other cultures.

The Dimensions of Culture questionnaire that follows is an abbreviated version of the original culture questionnaire used in the GLOBE studies. This questionnaire is included in the chapter for illustrative purposes only and should not be used for research. The scores you receive on the questionnaire are individual-level scores rather than societal- or organization-level scores. People who are interested in using the GLOBE scales for research should use the complete questionnaire, as referenced in House et al. (2004).

The Dimensions of Culture questionnaire will help you examine your perceptions about various characteristics of your culture. This questionnaire is not a personality measure (such as the Myers-Briggs instrument) but rather a measure of your attitudes and perceptions about culture.

Dimensions of Culture Questionnaire

Instructions: Using the following scales, circle the number that most accurately reflects your response to each of the 18 statements. There are no right or wrong answers, so provide your immediate impressions. (The items on this questionnaire are adapted from the items used in the GLOBE studies to assess the dimensions of culture, but the GLOBE studies used five items to analyze each of the cultural dimensions.)

Uncertainty Avoidance

1. In this society, orderliness and consistency are stressed, even at the expense of experimentation and innovation.

Strongly disagree   Strongly agree

       1   2   3   4   5   6   7

2. In this society, societal requirements and instructions are spelled out in detail so citizens know what they are expected to do.

Strongly disagree   Strongly agree

       1   2   3   4   5   6   7

Power Distance

1. In this society, followers are expected to:

Question their leaders   Obey their leaders
when in disagreement   without question

       1   2   3   4   5   6   7

2. In this society, power is:

Shared throughout   Concentrated at
the society   the top

       1   2   3   4   5   6   7

Institutional Collectivism

1. In this society, leaders encourage group loyalty even if individual goals suffer.

Strongly disagree   Strongly agree

       1   2   3   4   5   6   7

2. The economic system in this society is designed to maximize:

Individual interests   Collective interests

       1   2   3   4   5   6   7

In-Group Collectivism

1. In this society, children take pride in the individual accomplishments of their parents.

Strongly disagree   Strongly agree

       1   2   3   4   5   6   7

2. In this society, parents take pride in the individual accomplishments of their children.

Strongly disagree   Strongly agree

       1   2   3   4   5   6   7

Gender Egalitarianism

1. In this society, girls are encouraged more than boys to attain a higher education.

Strongly disagree   Strongly agree

       1   2   3   4   5   6   7

2. In this society, who is more likely to serve in a position of high office?

Men   Women

       1   2   3   4   5   6   7

Assertiveness

1. In this society, people are generally:

Nonassertive   Assertive

       1   2   3   4   5   6   7

2. In this society, people are generally:

Tender   Tough

       1   2   3   4   5   6   7

Future Orientation

1. In this society the accepted norm is to:

   Accept the status quo   Plan for the future

   | 1 | 2 | 3 | 4 | 5 | 6 | 7 |

2. In this society, people place more emphasis on:

   Solving current problems   Planning for the future

   | 1 | 2 | 3 | 4 | 5 | 6 | 7 |

Performance Orientation

1. In this society, students are encouraged to strive for continuously improved performance.

   Strongly disagree   Strongly agree

   | 1 | 2 | 3 | 4 | 5 | 6 | 7 |

2. In this society, people are rewarded for excellent performance.

   Strongly disagree   Strongly agree

   | 1 | 2 | 3 | 4 | 5 | 6 | 7 |

Humane Orientation

1. In this society, people are generally:

   Not at all   Very concerned
   concerned about others   about others

   | 1 | 2 | 3 | 4 | 5 | 6 | 7 |

2. In this society, people are generally:

   Not at all   Very sensitive
   sensitive to others   toward others

   | 1 | 2 | 3 | 4 | 5 | 6 | 7 |

SOURCE: Adapted from House, R. J., Hanges, P. J., Javidan, M., Dorfman, P. W., & Gupta, V. (Eds.), *Culture, Leadership, and Organizations: The GLOBE Study of 62 Societies,* © 2004, SAGE Publications.

Scoring

The Dimensions of Culture questionnaire is designed to measure your perceptions of the different dimensions of your culture. Score the questionnaire by doing the following. First, sum the two responses you gave for each of the items on each of the dimensions. Second, divide the sum of the responses by two. The result is your mean score for the dimension.

Example. If for power distance you circled 3 in response to Question 1 and 4 in response to Question 2, you would score the dimension as follows:

$$3 + 4 = 7$$

$$7 \div 2 = 3.5$$

Power distance mean score = 3.5

When you are finished scoring, you should have nine mean scores. After you have scored the questionnaire, place your mean scores for each of the dimensions in the table in "Scoring Interpretation."

Table 16.4 Cultural Dimensions and Mean Scores for Selected Cultural Clusters

GLOBE Cultural Dimensions	Mean Scores* of Selected Cultural Clusters						
	Anglo	Latin America	Middle East	Southern Asia	Latin Europe	GLOBE Overall	Your Score
Uncertainty avoidance	4.42	3.62	3.91	4.10	4.18	4.16	_____
Power distance	na	na	na	na	na	5.17	_____
Institutional collectivism	4.46	3.86	4.28	4.35	4.01	4.25	_____
In-group collectivism	4.30	5.52	5.58	5.87	4.80	5.13	_____
Gender egalitarianism	3.40	3.41	2.95	3.28	3.36	3.37	_____
Assertiveness	4.14	4.15	4.14	3.86	3.99	4.14	_____
Future orientation	4.08	3.54	3.58	3.98	3.68	3.85	_____
Performance orientation	4.37	3.85	3.90	4.33	3.94	4.10	_____
Humane orientation	4.20	4.03	4.36	4.71	3.71	4.09	_____

SOURCE: Adapted from House, R. J., Hanges, P. J., Javidan, M., Dorfman, P. W., & Gupta, V. (Eds.), *Culture Leadership, and Organizations: The GLOBE Study of 62 Societies,* © 2004, SAGE Publications, Inc. Reprinted with Permission.

*The mean scores in this table represent societal practice scores for selected cultures on each of the nine cultural dimensions. In the GLOBE studies, mean scores were derived from subjects' responses to five questions for each of the dimensions.

na = not available

Scoring Interpretation

Your scores on the Dimensions of Culture questionnaire provide data on how you see the culture in which you live and work. Table 16.4 provides information from the GLOBE project about how subjects from different cultures describe the dimensions of those cultures. The table also provides an *overall* mean for how these dimensions were viewed by people from all of the cultures.

By entering your scores in the last column in Table 16.4, you can get a better understanding of how your perception of your own culture compares to that of others. You can also compare your scores to other specific cultures (e.g., Middle East or Latin America). Do you see your culture as more or less egalitarian than others? Do you think your culture emphasizes the future more than others? Do people from other cultures stress performance less or more than your own culture? Like these questions, the table and your scores can be used to bring to the surface the ways in which your culture and the cultures of others are compatible or incompatible with each other. Understanding how your culture relates to other cultures is the first step to improved understanding between you and people from other cultures.

SUMMARY

Since World War II, there has been a dramatic increase in globalization throughout the world. Globalization has created a need for leaders with greater understanding of cultural differences and increased competencies in cross-cultural communication and practice. This chapter discusses research on culture, its dimensions, and its effects on the leadership process.

Culture is defined as the commonly shared beliefs, values, and norms of a group of people. Two factors that can inhibit cultural awareness are ethnocentrism and prejudice. Ethnocentrism is the human tendency to place one's own group at the center of one's observations of others and the world. It is problematic for leaders because it prevents them from fully understanding the world of others. Similarly, prejudice consists of judgments about others based on fixed attitudes and unsubstantiated data. Prejudice has a negative impact because it is self-oriented and inhibits leaders from seeing the many facets and qualities of others.

In the past 30 years, many studies have focused on identifying various dimensions of culture. The best known is the work of Hofstede (1980, 2001), who identified five major dimensions: power distance, uncertainty avoidance, individualism–collectivism, masculinity–femininity, and long-term–short-term orientation. Expanding on Hofstede's work, House and his colleagues (2004) delineated additional dimensions of culture, including in-group collectivism, institutional collectivism, future orientation, assertiveness, performance orientation, and humane orientation.

The GLOBE studies offer the strongest body of findings to date on culture and leadership. Using established quantitative research methods, GLOBE researchers studied how 17,000 managers from 62 different countries viewed leadership. They analyzed the similarities and differences between regional clusters of cultural groups by grouping countries into 10 distinct clusters: Anglo, Latin Europe, Nordic Europe, Germanic Europe, Eastern Europe, Latin America, the Middle East, Sub-Saharan Africa, Southern Asia, and Confucian Asia. An analysis of each of the 10 clusters revealed the particular dimensions on which each region was strong or weak and unique from other regions.

In addition, GLOBE researchers identified six global leadership behaviors that could be used to characterize how different cultural groups view leadership: charismatic/value-based, team-oriented, participative, humane-oriented, autonomous, and self-protective leadership. Based on these behaviors, researchers created leadership profiles for each of the 10 cultural clusters that delineate the relative importance and desirability different cultures ascribe to different attributes and characteristics of leadership.

One outcome of the GLOBE project was the identification of a list of leadership attributes that were universally endorsed as positive and negative attributes of leadership. From this list, it appears that the universally endorsed portrait of an exceptional leader has a high degree of integrity, charisma, and interpersonal skill. The portrait of an ineffective leader is someone who is asocial, malevolent, self-focused, and autocratic.

The scope of the GLOBE project is its main strength. The findings from this project make a major statement about how cultures around the world view leadership. Other strengths are its quantitative research design, an expanded classification of cultural dimensions, a list of universally accepted leadership attributes, and the contribution it makes to a richer understanding of the leadership process. On the negative side, the GLOBE studies do not provide findings that form a single theory about the way culture relates to leadership. Furthermore, the definitions of the core cultural dimensions are unclear, the conceptualization of leadership used in the studies is limiting, the leadership measures are not exact, and the list of universally endorsed leadership attributes does not account for the various situations in which leaders operate. Regardless of these limitations, the GLOBE studies stand out because they offer so much valuable information about the unique ways culture influences the leadership process.

Sharpen your skills with SAGE edge at **edge.sagepub.com/northouse7e**

NOTES

1. The Czech Republic was excluded from the analysis because of problems in the data.

REFERENCES

Adler, N. J., & Bartholomew, S. (1992). Managing globally competent people. *Academy of Management Executive, 6,* 52–65.

Bing, J. W. (2004). Hofstede's consequences: The impact of his work on consulting and business practices. *Academy of Management Executive, 18*(1), 80–87.

Brodbeck, F. C., Frese, M., & Javidan, M. (2002). Leadership made in Germany: Low on compassion, high on performance. *Academy of Management Executive, 16*(1), 16–29.

Dorfman, P. W., Hanges, P. J., & Brodbeck, F. C. (2004). Leadership and cultural variation: The identification of culturally endorsed leadership profiles. In R. J. House, P. J. Hanges, M. Javidan, P. W. Dorfman, V. Gupta, & Associates (Eds.), *Culture, leadership, and organizations: The GLOBE study of 62 societies* (pp. 669–722). Thousand Oaks, CA: SAGE.

Gudykunst, W. B., & Kim, Y. Y. (1997). *Communicating with strangers: An approach to intercultural communication* (3rd ed.). New York: McGraw-Hill.

Gudykunst, W. B., & Ting-Toomey, S. (1988). *Culture and interpersonal communication.* Newbury Park, CA: SAGE.

Hall, E. T. (1976). *Beyond culture.* New York: Doubleday.

Hofstede, G. (1980). *Culture's consequences: International differences in work-related values.* Beverly Hills, CA: SAGE.

Hofstede, G. (2001). *Culture's consequences: Comparing values, behaviors, institutions, and organizations across nations.* Thousand Oaks, CA: SAGE.

House, R. J., Hanges, P. J., Javidan, M., Dorfman, P. W., & Gupta, V. (Eds.). (2004). *Culture, leadership, and organizations: The GLOBE study of 62 societies.* Thousand Oaks, CA: SAGE.

House, R. J., & Javidan, M. (2004). Overview of GLOBE. In R. J. House, P. J. Hanges, M. Javidan, P. W. Dorfman, V. Gupta, & Associates (Eds.), *Culture, leadership, and organizations: The GLOBE study of 62 societies* (pp. 9–28). Thousand Oaks, CA: SAGE.

Kluckhohn, R. R., & Strodtbeck, F. L. (1961). *Variations in value orientations.* New York: HarperCollins.

Lord, R., & Maher, K. J. (1991). *Leadership and information processing: Linking perceptions and performance.* Boston: Unwin-Everyman.

McClelland, D. C. (1961). *The achieving society.* Princeton, NJ: Van Nostrand.

Ponterotto, J. G., & Pedersen, P. B. (1993). *Preventing prejudice: A guide for counselors and educators.* Newbury Park, CA: SAGE.

Porter, R. E., & Samovar, L. A. (1997). An introduction to intercultural communication. In L. A. Samovar & R. E. Porter (Eds.), *Intercultural communication: A reader* (8th ed., pp. 5–26). Belmont, CA: Wadsworth.

Ronen, S., & Shenkar, O. (1985). Clustering countries on attitudinal dimensions: A review and synthesis. *Academy of Management Review, 10*(3), 435–454.

Ting-Toomey, S. (1999). *Communicating across cultures.* New York: Guilford.

Triandis, H. C. (1995). *Individualism and collectivism.* Boulder, CO: Westview.

Trompenaars, F. (1994). *Riding the waves of culture.* New York: Irwin.

Author Index

Blake, R. R., 71, 72, 74, 75, 78, 79 (figure), 80, 81, 87
Blanchard, K., 93, 94, 95 (figure), 96, 100, 101, 229
Blanchard, K. H., 93, 94, 98, 100, 102
Blank, R., 412–415
Blascovich, J., 406
Block, C. J., 406
Block, P., 343
Boatwright, K. J., 100, 101
Bond, J., 400
Bongiorno, R., 401
Bono, J. E., 27
Book, E. W., 402
Borgida, E., 404, 405
Bosco, S. M., 409
Botero, I. C., 365
Bowers, D. G., 73
Bowie, N. E., 335, 337, 341, 342, 344
Bowles, H. R., 400, 401, 403, 407
Brazil, D. M., 100
Bresman, H., 376
Brodbeck, F. C., 433, 440, 448
Brown, M., 330
Bryman, A., 1, 7, 19, 81, 161, 164, 177, 178, 187
Bullis, R. C., 100
Burgess, D., 404
Burke, C. S., 365, 375, 384
Burns, J. M., 3, 4, 7, 11, 162, 163, 166, 177, 190, 195, 338, 339, 342, 347, 402

Caldwell, D., 376
Cameron, K. S., 208
Carew, P., 102
Carli, L. L., 399, 400, 401, 406, 407, 408
Carlson, D. S., 237, 337
Carmeli, A., 141
Cartwright, D., 73
Caruso, D. R., 27, 28
Castro, S. L., 123, 143, 147, 148
Catalyst, 398, 400, 401, 409
Center for American Women and Politics, 398

Chabris, C. F., 409
Chace, S., 277
Chan, A., 196
Chemers, M. M., 397, 404, 410
Childress, J. F., 341, 342
Chonko, L. B., 237
Chow, C., 175
Christie, A., 163, 180
Cianci, A. M., 209
Ciulla, J. B., 329, 330, 338
Cobb, A. T., 383, 384
Cogliser, C. C., 147, 148
Cohen, S. G., 363–364
Collinson, D., 1
Columb, V. L., 409
Conger, J. A., 164, 165, 179, 339
Connelly, M. S., 48, 49, 52, 53
Coons, A. E., 72
Cooper, C., 201, 208
Cooper, C. L., 406
Copeland, N., 3
Cordery, J., 376
Corrigall, E., 408
Costa, P. T., 27
Couric & Co., 405
Covey, S. R., 204, 229, 343
Craig, L., 400
Craig, S. B., 355
Crain, W. C., 331–332, 333
Crits-Christoph, P., 302
Curphey, G. J., 368
Czander, W. M., 301, 306, 308

Dalla Costa, J., 346
Dansereau, F., 138–139
Darwin, C., 297
Dasgupta, N., 415
Davenport, S. W., 365
Davies, P. G., 406
Day, D. V., 1, 140, 365
Deaux, K., 404, 405
DeBoard, R., 301, 306
DeChurch, L. A., 123
Del Carmen Triana, M., 409
De Pree, M., 229, 343
DeRue, D. S., 364, 365, 384

Subject Index

About the Author

Peter G. Northouse, PhD, is Professor Emeritus of Communication in the School of Communication at Western Michigan University. In addition to publications in professional journals, he is the author of *Introduction to Leadership: Concepts and Practice* (now in its third edition) and coauthor of *Health Communication: Strategies for Health Professionals* (now in its third edition). His scholarly and curricular interests include models of leadership, leadership assessment, ethical leadership, and leadership and group dynamics. For more than 30 years, he has taught undergraduate and graduate courses in leadership, interpersonal communication, and organizational communication on both the undergraduate and graduate levels. Currently, he is a consultant and lecturer on trends in leadership research, leadership development, and leadership education. He holds a doctorate in speech communication from the University of Denver, and master's and bachelor's degrees in communication education from Michigan State University.

About the Contributors

Alicia Cheak is a Research Associate at INSEAD Global Leadership Centre. Professionally, she has 15 years of research experience in the US and in France. Her research interests include problem solving, knowledge mapping, performance-based assessments, collaborative learning, simulation-based learning, and developing leadership instruments.

Susan E. Kogler Hill (PhD, University of Denver, 1974) is professor emeritus and former chair of the School of Communication at Cleveland State University. Her research and consulting have been in the areas of interpersonal and organizational communication. She specializes in group leadership, teamwork, empowerment, and mentoring. She is author of a text titled *Improving Interpersonal Competence*. In addition, she has written book chapters and published articles in many professional journals.

Crystal L. Hoyt completed her doctorate in social psychology at UC Santa Barbara and is an associate professor of Leadership Studies and Psychology at the University of Richmond. Her research reflects a commitment to conducting both basic and applied investigations. In her primary area of research, she explores the role of beliefs, such as self-efficacy, implicit theories, and political ideologies, in the experiences and the perceptions of women and minorities in leadership or STEM fields, or the overweight. In a more applied fashion, she examines factors, such as role models, that may or may not buffer individuals from the deleterious effects of stereotypes and discrimination. She has published nearly 50 journal articles and book chapters and she has co-edited two books.

Manfred F. R. Kets de Vries is the Distinguished Professor of Leadership Development and Organizational Change at INSEAD, France, Singapore, and Abu Dhabi. He is the author, co-author, or editor of more than 40 books, and more than 400 articles. As an educator and consultant he has worked in more than 40 countries. He is the chairman of the Kets de Vries Institute (KDVI), a leadership development consulting firm. In addition, Kets de Vries is also a psychoanalyst and a member of the International Psychoanalytic Association. He has been listed as one of the 50 most influential management thinkers of the world. He is the recipient of many awards, including two honorary doctorates.

Stefanie Simon is currently a PhD graduate student in Psychology at Tulane University and NSF Predoctoral Fellow. She earned a BA in Psychology and Leadership Studies from the University of Richmond in 2007. Her research centers on the psychology of diversity, with a focus on prejudice, discrimination, and leadership. In her work, she focuses on both the perspective of the *target* of prejudice and discrimination, as well as the perspective of the *perpetrator* of prejudice and discrimination. She is particularly interested in how leaders of diverse teams or groups can promote positive intergroup relations and reduce inequality in society.

⑨SAGE researchmethods

The essential online tool for researchers from the world's leading methods publisher

Find exactly what you are looking for, from basic explanations to advanced discussion

More content and new features added this year!

"I have never really seen anything like this product before, and I think it is really valuable."
John Creswell, University of Nebraska–Lincoln

Discover **Methods Lists**—methods readings suggested by other users

Watch video interviews with leading methodologists

Explore the **Methods Map** to discover links between methods

Search a custom-designed taxonomy with more than 1,400 qualitative, quantitative, and mixed methods terms

Uncover more than 120,000 pages of book, journal, and reference content to support your learning

Find out more at
www.sageresearchmethods.com

WITHDRAWN